MW01595040

Natural Theology

D.Q. McInerny

The Priestly Fraternity of St. Peter
South Abington Township, Pennsylvania
2020

Other Books in This Series:

A Course in Thomistic Ethics (1997; 3^d ed. 2010)
The Philosophy of Nature (1998; 3^d ed. 2014)
Metaphysics (2004; 2^d ed. 2019)
Epistemology (2007)
An Introduction to Foundational Logic (2012)
Philosophical Psychology (2016)

ISBN 978-0-9892610-3-6

Sancto Joanni Baptistae de la Salle

Patrono Omnium Magistrorum

CONTENTS

Preface

In the fifteen years since it was first published, this book would seem to have done reasonably good service in meeting the ends for which it was designed. Accordingly, I decided to leave the text, in the main, as it was originally written, which does not mean that I am not conscious of the work's limitations. Anyone who takes upon himself the task of writing books in philosophy, especially books which attempt adequately to reflect the thought of the great Saint Thomas Aquinas, feels the bite of the observation made by the poet T.S. Eliot when he wrote, "between the conception and the deed falls the shadow." A major change was made in Chapter Eight of the book, where to correct some first thoughts with second thoughts, I rewrote an entire section and added a new one. The other changes made in the text, though quite a few, are all of a minor kind.

I wish to express my comprehensive gratitude to the Priestly Fraternity of St. Peter. It was my singular privilege to be associated with that exceptional community as a teacher of philosophy for twenty-two blessed years, and I owe more to them than I could ever precisely tabulate. More specifically, and with particular regard to this book, it is with special pleasure that I express my deep gratitude, yet once again, to Nancy LaRoza, who acted as the editor, not only of this work, but of all of the volumes that make up the series in philosophy textbooks which saw its inception in 1997 with the publication of *A Course in Thomistic Ethics*. She is extraordinary. And my special thanks as well to Mary Jo Loboda, the Director of Fraternity Publications Service, for her key and indispensable contributions in making the second edition of *Natural Theology* a reality.

D. Q. McInerny
January 25, 2020
Feast of the Conversion of St. Paul

Preface to the First Edition

This volume is the fifth in a projected six volume set whose purpose is to provide a general introduction to Scholastic philosophy. I had no idea, when *A Course in Thomistic Ethics* was published in 1997, that I was embarking upon so ambitious a project, but life has a penchant for arranging things in ways we do not always anticipate. It is my hope that the final volume in the series, on epistemology, will, *Deo volente*, be published within the coming year. No more than was the case in the previous volumes, my aim here has not been originality. I simply attempted to provide the reader with a faithful, though to be sure rudimentary, account of a particular science belonging to a rich and noble philosophic tradition which, I believe, will never be dated.

I consider this work in natural theology to be an introductory text, and it was written with classroom employment very much in mind. But though an introduction, it does assume on the part of the reader some considerable background in philosophy. That reader will most benefit from the book who has at least some working familiarity with the sciences of logic, the philosophy of nature, philosophical psychological, ethics, and metaphysics. For all that, though, it is hoped that readers without such a background would nonetheless be able to gain something from the book, and it was written with those readers in mind as well.

The fifteen chapters into which the book is divided is designed to correspond with the standard fifteen week academic semester. Although I take the order with which I treat the subject matter of natural theology here to be logical, and defensible from a practical point of view, there is no reason why an instructor using the text should feel bound to following that order. Nor is there any reason why an instructor should consider that the text could not be effectively used by disregarding some of the material to be found in its pages. I have particularly in mind the rather lengthy attention I give to proofs for the existence of God that come after St. Thomas's Five Ways.

If I were to attempt to cite here all the people to whom I am indebted with regard to this book, it would turn out to be a long and tedious business. I will therefore limit myself to acknowledging, first, the gratitude I owe to my philosophy students at Our Lady of Guadalupe Seminary, from whom I am continuously learning. And warm thanks as well to my faculty colleagues, and to the administrators, at that remarkable institution. A special debt of gratitude is owed to the Rev. George G. Gabet, F.S.S.P., the North American District Superior of the Priestly Fraternity of St. Peter, as well as to the Rev. Joseph R. Howard, F.S.S.P., the District Bursar, for their generous support in sponsoring the publication of this book. Finally, my gratitude to Nancy LaRoza, Father Gabet's Administrative Assistant, is admixed with a kind of wondering awe, at the incomparable competence and efficiency with which she has brought this book into being.

D. Q. McInerny
August 20, 2005
Feast of St. Bernard

INTRODUCTION

What Is Natural Theology?

The proper place to begin in answering that question is by calling attention to the fact that natural theology is an integral part of the larger field of philosophy. As such, it can be regarded as a science within a science. How is it that a subject which bears the name theology is considered to be a part of philosophy? The explanation for that is found in the precise way our subject is described; it is *natural* theology which is the focus of our concern, in contrast to what is normally identified as sacred theology. And what is the distinction between natural theology and sacred theology?

Before we spell out that important distinction, we must first establish a settled understanding of the science of theology itself. St. Thomas Aquinas provides us with a succinct definition of theology when he tells us that it is a science whose proper subject matter is God and everything that pertains to God.[1] That definition is general enough so that it can be applied both to sacred theology and to natural theology. We are now prepared to draw the distinction between the two.

In natural theology we study God and everything that pertains to God from a purely natural point of view, meaning that we advance our study on the basis of human reason alone. In the various investigations to follow, we will not be consciously adverting to, nor relying upon, any knowledge of God that comes to us from revelation. At first glance, this approach might be seen as all too artificial, if not simply impossible to carry off successfully. But it is neither. There is nothing artificial in consciously deciding, in embarking upon a complex inquiry, not to make active use of knowledge which one actually possesses, and to do this because of the nature of the inquiry itself. And that this can be successfully done in the case of natural theology is emphatically borne out by the rich and productive history of this science. That the faith of a believing natural theologian will inevitably have some influence on how he thinks and works within the science goes without saying, but this influence need not compromise the scientific integrity of his investigations.

The believing natural theologian, in deciding not to rely on any knowledge that comes to him through faith, is not merely engaging in psychological experimentation. The principal purpose of his endeavors is to show that man can come to have knowledge of God through means other than divine revelation. Specifically, the natural theologian seeks to demonstrate that natural reason, i.e., human reason unaided by revelation, is able to attain certain knowledge that God exists, and, in addition, is able to attain knowledge of some of the aspects of the divine nature.

The approach taken by sacred theology is quite different from that taken by natural theology, in that in this case the basis and point of departure for the study of God and everything pertaining to God is divine revelation. In sacred theology we are consciously guided by all that God has explicitly revealed to us about Himself. The study of sacred theology is everywhere illumined by the light of faith. This does not mean that we do not employ human reason in the study of sacred theology, but here it is human reason that is not left to itself, sustained and governed as it is by that certain knowledge that comes to us through faith. The exercise of human reason not only figures large in sacred theology, but there is a real sense in which sacred theology, as a science, is directly dependent on human reason, as it finds its best expression in the science of philosophy. Philosophy effectively establishes sacred theology as a science, by providing it with principles, structure, and direction.[2] Given this close relation between the two sciences, there is nothing arcane nor obsolete in referring to philosophy as the handmaid of theology (*ancilla theologiae*)

The distinction between natural theology and sacred theology may be given greater accent by calling into play another distinction that Scholastic philosophy commonly applies to any science whatever. This is the distinction between a science's material object and its formal object.

The material object of a science is simply the subject matter which is the focus of its study. The formal object of a science is the peculiar point of view from which it studies its proper subject matter. In terms of what has been said thus far, it should be clear that natural theology and sacred theology cannot be distinguished in terms of material object alone, for they share, by and large, the same subject matter: God and everything that pertains to God. We must look to the formal object, then, in order to find a basis for distinguishing them. In doing so we remind ourselves that natural theology proceeds from the point of view of human reason alone, whereas sacred theology, on the other hand, proceeds from the point of view of revelation. Thus, it is their differing formal objects which clearly distinguishes them.

It was remarked just above that natural theology and sacred theology share the same subject matter, "by and large." What was the purpose of the qualification? If we look at the respective material objects of natural theology and sacred theology, we discover that natural theology's is larger in scope, and for a rather obvious reason. Faith is the principal source of sacred theology's subject matter, and we can know more about God and everything pertaining to God through the medium of faith than we could ever know through the medium of unaided human reason. So, for example, sacred theology includes among the subjects it studies mysteries of faith such as the trinitarian nature of God, the Incarnation, and the Redemption, knowledge of which human reason, left to itself, is incapable of arriving at. Such subjects, therefore, are beyond the purview of natural theology.

Natural Theology Is a Distinct Philosophical Science

What is a science? A science is (a) an organized body of knowledge, (b) founded upon and proceeding from first principles, and (c) which seeks knowledge in terms of causes. The organized body of knowledge, as currently constituted for the science of natural theology, may be said to be fairly represented, at least in its main lineaments, in the contents of this book. In the early stages of any science, its body of knowledge would of course be relatively small, but as a science becomes more firmly established over the years, and if it is a vibrant science with dedicated advocates, usually there is a steady growth in the size and quality of its body of knowledge.

The first principles are those fundamental truths that relate to the subject matter (material object) of the science. They serve as the starting points of the science, the foundational truths from which the array of subsequent truths are derived. All the later findings of a science, the secondary principles it delineates, the theories it develops, can be said to be elaborations of the basic truths contained in the first principles. The first principles of a science are its inspiring guides, and to a certain extent they influence the kinds of methods a science will adopt in its various investigations.

To say that a science seeks knowledge in terms of causes simply means that it is dedicated to a comprehensive and definitive investigation of its subject matter. If we have causal knowledge of anything we have satisfactorily answered the "Why?" question with regard to that thing. Causal knowledge is the deepest and firmest kind of knowledge, for it has to do with the very existence of a thing, revealing why it exists at all, and why it exists in the peculiar way in which it does.

Natural theology has both general first principles, and specific first principles. The general first principles of natural theology are those it shares with every other human science, the principles that govern human reasoning just as such. They are: the principle of identity; the principle of contradiction; the principle of excluded middle; the principle of sufficient reason. The specific first principles of natural theology are to be found by looking to the subordinate principle of the principle of sufficient reason, i.e., the principle of causality. The principle of causality is expressed in the following terms: every contingent existent (i.e., an existent that is not the explanation for its own being) has a cause for its existence. There are two principles that flow out of the principle of causality, and which also serve as first principles for natural theology. The first of these principles is: beginning with an effect, the human mind can conclude to the cause of that effect. The second principle is: given the intimate relation between an effect and its cause, the human mind can, even before it can determine the precise cause of a given effect, know at least something of the cause simply through the knowledge it already has of the effect. It is these first principles of natural theology that underpin the central task it sets for itself: demonstrating the existence of God.

Natural Theology Is an Integral Part of Metaphysics

Natural theology should be regarded as composing the second part of the complete course in metaphysics, the first part of which is dedicated to ontology, and which is sometimes referred to as general metaphysics. It is altogether fitting and proper, from a purely philosophical point of view, that the study of metaphysics should culminate in, have its logical finality realized in, the study of God and everything that pertains to God. This was the pattern that was established by Aristotle, the founding father of our science.

The science we now call metaphysics was not given that name by Aristotle himself, who applied to it three other names, each one of which is quite revealing. Aristotle referred to our science alternatively as First Philosophy, as Wisdom, and—of special interest to us here—Theology. Metaphysics is First Philosophy because it deals with the most fundamental of truths which apply to being just as such. For St. Thomas, a human being is deserving to be called wise who is able to see everything as related to God. Such a person, in other words, sees things as they really are. With this in mind, we can say that metaphysics is Wisdom because it is dedicated to discovering the ultimate cause, the First Cause of all being, which is of course God. Accordingly, we can then see the fittingness in calling metaphysics Theology, for it is ultimately concerned with God. Though it would doubtless come as irritating news to many a modern philosopher, philosophy, taken seriously as the love of wisdom, can have no other terminus than God Himself. The barrenness of so much modern philosophy is explained by the fact that it has abandoned its proper vocation, turning away from philosophy's natural orientation to transcendental reality, and looking for ultimate reality where ultimate reality can never be found.

The Specific Tasks of Natural Theology

The material object, or subject matter, of natural theology, as we have seen, is God and everything that pertains to God. Sacred theology, for its part, enters into engagement with its subject matter with the fullest kind of confidence, for it investigates that subject matter with the luminous guidance of the special knowledge which is provided to it by faith. The first steps taken by natural theology in its investigations, on the other hand, are, we might say, rather tentative. It initially assumes an agnostic position with regard to the central issue before it: the existence of God. As it embarks upon its study, natural theology cannot claim to have certain knowledge concerning the question of the existence of God, for it is precisely that question it is dedicated to settling. Demonstrating the existence of God is the principal task of natural theology. Once it has accomplished that task, it then devotes its energies to determining what can be known—again, on the basis of human reason alone—of the divine nature. What specific virtues or powers can the human mind properly attribute to God, in attempting better to understand His nature?

Philosophers have offered many distinct proofs for the existence of God over the course of the centuries. In surveying the sum total of those efforts, we make a basic distinction between metaphysical proofs and moral proofs for the existence of God.

A metaphysical proof is a proof in the strict sense; that is to say, it is an argument whose conclusion follows necessarily from its premises, and which is therefore compelling in its effect upon us. A moral proof, by way of contrast, is represented by an argument whose conclusion does not follow necessarily, but carries with it a greater or lesser degree of probability.

Between these two types of proofs, metaphysics devotes the larger part of its attention to metaphysical proofs. At the same time, however, we do not minimize the peculiar value of the moral proofs. The interesting thing about the moral proofs for the existence of God is the fact that, though their conclusions do not follow necessarily, experience has shown that they tend to carry greater persuasive force for more people than do the metaphysical proofs. There are two reasons for this. First, the metaphysical proofs are simply more demanding. They require, on the part of an audience, a substantial background in philosophy in general, and, in particular, a familiarity with the common modes of metaphysical reasoning. These are requirements that most people are unable to meet. Second, the moral proofs for the existence of God usually proceed from starting points with which the average person would have an immediate and easy acquaintance. They are considerably less abstract than the metaphysical proofs, and for that reason less intimidating for most people.

Once again, our attention will be concentrated on the metaphysical proofs, and, among those, primacy of place will be given to the Five Ways (*Quinque Viae*) of St. Thomas. These five arguments are to be found in the very early pages of the First Part of the famous *Summa Theologiae*.[3] Though the manner in which he stated and developed the arguments is his own, the arguments themselves, in terms of the specific focus of each, already had a long history behind them by the thirteenth century in which St. Thomas lived.

Arguments Against the Legitimacy of Natural Theology

Before we launch into the principal tasks before us, we must first call attention to two serious objections that have been directed at the very heart of our science. These objections would seem to be almost as old as the science itself.

The gist of the first objection is that any effort that is expended in attempting to prove the existence of God has to be counted as wasted effort, and that is because there is no need to prove the existence of God. The second objection also contends that trying to prove God's existence is wasted effort, but the reason given in this case is that it is impossible to prove the existence of God. St. Thomas took both of these objections seriously, and we shall do so as well.

Those who object to attempting to prove the existence of God because they think it unnecessary to do so are believers. As such, they of course subscribe to the notion that we have a certain knowledge of God's existence through faith. But they go further than that, and maintain that every human being, whether or not a believer, and simply as a child of God, has an inborn awareness of the existence of God. This being so, it stands to reason that men do not have to have proven to them what they already know.

Those who object to attempting to prove God's existence because they consider any such attempt to be futile, may be either believers or unbelievers. If they are believers, they tend to be fideists, which is to say, people who establish a strict separation between faith and reason. And they tend to denigrate the efficacy of human reason as applied to any matters having to do with faith. For the strict fideist, one believes in God, not in cooperation with reason but almost in spite of reason.

The fideist tends to keep his faith and his reason in different, and non-communicating, compartments of his life.

The application of this attitude to philosophy is shown in the sweepingly negative position its advocates take toward metaphysics in particular. Metaphysics is dismissed as effectively a bogus science, an enterprise which simply does not do what it claims to be able to do. This anti-metaphysical attitude is very much a mark of modern philosophy, the philosophy that saw its inception in the seventeenth century. The most prominent proponent of the anti-metaphysical attitude was the German philosopher, Immanuel Kant (1724–1804). Kant has proven to be immensely influential in the two centuries since his death, and we will have a closer look at some of his views in a later chapter.

St. Thomas's responses to these two general objections were thorough and detailed, and because much can be learned from their study, subsequently we will be devoting considerable attention to them.

There is yet a third objection that can be made to the central task to which natural theology commits itself. It is put forward by those who may be willing to concede that it is possible to prove the existence of God, but who wonder about what, if any, practical effects that might have. Presumably, they would argue, one goes through the trouble of constructing philosophical arguments to prove the existence of God so that those arguments can then be used to persuade atheists and agnostics of the untenableness of their positions. But, the argument continues, it very rarely is the case that those who do not believe in God are brought to believe in Him through philosophical argument. As with the first two objections, this one too will be given careful consideration in a later chapter.

Proofs Other Than St. Thomas's Five Ways

In endeavoring to fulfill the principal task of natural theology, we will, as mentioned, concentrate our attention on the five ways of St. Thomas Aquinas. But it is important that we proceed to those arguments by way of an indirect, preparatory route, for they are best understood within the larger context within which they properly belong. The first thing we need to be aware of is that there were important antecedents to St. Thomas's arguments, familiarity with which can be very beneficial. By the time the Angelic Doctor shaped his arguments, in the thirteenth century, there was already in place a distinguished tradition of metaphysics, and he was very much working within that tradition. As already mentioned, the arguments we have from St. Thomas, the Five Ways, were his formulations of arguments which, in the main, had long been in currency. In order to put St. Thomas's arguments in their proper historical context, then, we will first survey some of the outstanding arguments that preceded them.

We will begin this survey with the argument developed by Plato, to be found in Book X of the *Laws*. This argument represents, it would seem, the first systematic attempt to prove God's existence by philosophical reasoning. Next, we will move to the two arguments presented by Plato's great student, Aristotle, one in his *Physics*, the other in his *Metaphysics*. These Aristotelian arguments were going to exercise considerable influence on the thought of St. Thomas.

From the fourth century B.C. we move forward to the eleventh century A.D., and there we meet St. Anselm of Canterbury (1033–1109), who gave us, in what has come to be known as the ontological argument, one of the most challenging and controversial proofs for the existence of God ever formulated. For that reason, and also because of its intrinsic interest and its continuing influence, we will later pay concentrated attention to the ontological argument, not only in its original form, as given to us by St. Anselm, by also in the version of the argument that we owe to the seventeenth century philosopher, René Descartes (1596–1650).

Other arguments for the existence of God of major importance that have been proposed since the time of St. Thomas will also occupy our concern in the pages to follow.

The Divine Nature

Once we have completed the centrally important task of setting out and discussing the arguments intended to prove the existence of God, the focus of our study then shifts to the second major emphasis of natural theology, the determination of just what the human mind can come to know of the divine nature. In exploring this area, we shall be following along the pathways marked out for us by the thought of St. Thomas. It will be our particular concern to establish the precise quality of the knowledge the human mind is able to have of God's nature. In this context we will examine the important distinction between the negative and the positive knowledge of God, and try to come to terms with the ways this distinction operates within the thought of St. Thomas. Another issue to be treated here is what is called co-natural knowledge (i.e., innate or quasi-intuitive), and we will ask whether man's knowledge of God can be said to be knowledge of this kind.

Our consideration of the various aspects of the nature of the human mind's knowledge of God will be carried out under the guidance of an honored principle of Scholastic epistemology which states that, "Whatever is received is received according to the nature of the recipient." *(Quidquid recipitur secundum modum recipientis recipitur.)* This is a principle of epistemology, meaning that it relates to human knowledge. The basic idea behind the principle is that whatever is received, in the way of knowledge, by a knower, is necessarily qualified by the intellectual capacities of the knower. If we consider the relation between man and God, and of man's knowledge of God, we will immediately see the pertinent application of this principle. The human mind is of course finite, and its knowledge of God, an infinite being, can never be in terms of God's own infinity, but must always be in terms of the human mind's finiteness. To put it plainly, we can only know God according to the limitations of our human intellect.

In treating of the nature of our knowledge of God, much emphasis will be given to the subject of analogy. Analogical reasoning represents the only proper and productive way we can think about God, and when we speak about God we must make use of analogical language.

The Divine Essence and the Divine Operations

Traditionally, Scholastic natural theology, in dealing with the subject of man's knowledge of God, has proceeded according to a basic distinction between the divine essence, on the one hand, and the divine operations, on the other. Under the rubric of the divine essence we treat the simplicity, perfection, goodness, infinity, omnipresence, immutability, eternity, and unity of God. There are two principal subjects that are treated within the category of the divine operations: the divine intellect and the divine will. In our discussion of the divine intellect, we will be concerned with such questions as the relation between divine omniscience and the freedom of the human will. Issues to be pursued in our discussion of the divine will are the love of God, the justice of God, and the mercy of God. Finally, our discussion of God's omnipotence will lead naturally to an examination of three very important and closely related topics: divine creation, conservation, and concurrence.

CHAPTER ONE

Man's Natural Knowledge of God

Is It Necessary To Prove God's Existence?

We have already noted that the chief task that natural theology sets for itself, truly a formidable one, is to provide demonstrations for the existence of God. However, there are some who would immediately take exception to the very idea that such a task ought ever to be embarked upon. Any energy spent on such a project would be wasted, they would argue, and that is because there is no need to demonstrate that God exists. Man, simply by reason of who he is, a creature made in the image and likeness of God, is in constant possession of a firm knowledge of God's existence. It is a knowledge with which he is born, and which he can never lose. Interpreted from an epistemological point of view, such knowledge would be described as self-evident. This attitude might be called the "not-needed" objection to natural theology.

Specific Forms of the "Not-Needed" Objection

Before he presents his own trenchant arguments for the existence of God, St. Thomas deals with a variety of opposing points of view. First, he cites three specific arguments that reflect the attitude sketched above. By the way he frames the question under which he treats these arguments, it is clear that St. Thomas takes these arguments all to have the common character of regarding the knowledge of the existence of God as self-evident (*per se nota*). We will consider in turn the three arguments and St. Thomas's response to them.

We regard those things to be self-evident the knowledge of which is naturally innate to us. An example of such knowledge would be that which we have of first principles, such as the principle of contradiction. Now, St. John Damascene would seem to teach that we have just that kind of innate knowledge of the existence of God, for he writes that, "knowledge of the existence of God is naturally embodied within every human being." The existence of God, then, is self-evident to us, and there is no need for it to be demonstrated.

In responding to this argument, St. Thomas readily agrees that it can be reasonably said that all men have an in-born knowledge of God, but the quality of that knowledge leaves something to be desired. It is what might be called an oblique or indirect knowledge of God. There is, naturally embodied within every human being, a deep-set and ineradicable desire for happiness. Now, it is God alone who is able to fulfill that desire, but man is not clearly aware of that fact. So, if man has a natural, innate desire for perfect happiness, as in fact he does, he certainly knows that desire, but he does not know it precisely for what it is, i.e., as the desire for God. Man's innate knowledge of God, therefore, is a confused, obscure knowledge. It is implicit rather than explicit. He knows he desires to be happy, but he does not know that God is the source and the object of that desire. And the sad fact of the matter is, as human history amply reveals to us, men have regularly misconstrued their innate desire for happiness, thinking that it could be fulfilled by riches, or sensual pleasure, or power, or some other purely natural object.[1]

The second argument calls attention to the fact that a characteristic of what we call a self-evident truth is that, as soon as we grasp the terms in which it is expressed, we immediately see it to be true. Aristotle shows how this applies to any first principle, such as the mathematical axiom that a whole is greater than the part. As soon as we understand the meaning of "whole" and "part," without hesitancy we see the truth of the axiom. Now, there is a relation that is analogous to the one that obtains between the terms "whole" and "part," and that is the relation between the terms "God" and "exists." We can see how this is so if we reflect on just what we mean when we use the word "God." It signifies for us the idea of the greatest possible being. Now, it is obviously a greater thing to exist as an actual being in the external world, than to exist merely as an idea in someone's mind. Therefore, since the words

"God" and "exists" imply one another, as soon as the word "God" is understood, and there is present in the mind an idea corresponding to that word, we see that God must actually exist in the external world, for if He existed only as an idea in our minds He would not be the greatest possible being.

In replying to this second argument, St. Thomas begins by taking quick exception to its assumption that when we hear the word "God" we as it were automatically think in terms of "the greatest possibly being," or of "a being a greater than which cannot be conceived." Those ideas are very refined and elevated, and suggest a certain degree of metaphysical sophistication. But they are not, St. Thomas suggests, the ideas that come readily to the minds of most people when they think "God." Indeed, some men think of God in rather crude terms, regarding Him as a corporeal substance.

But let us grant that someone does understand the word "God" as referring to "a being a greater than which cannot be conceived." That would be the precise idea he has in mind. Even so, it does not follow that there exists in the world outside his mind a being that answers to that description. It is entirely possible that the only existence involved here is accidental existence; that is to say, the existence of an idea, which is a quality of the mind that is thinking that idea. One cannot argue that a thing exists as an objective fact, i.e., extra-mentally, simply because one is able to have a clear idea of that thing. An idea, however elevated and noble it might be—and the idea of God is the most elevated and noble of ideas—is, just as an idea, a purely private phenomenon. It is not in the public forum. How could my idea of God serve as the basis for an argument addressed to those who do not believe in God in the first place?[2] The position that St. Thomas is responding to here is classically embodied in what is called the ontological argument, which we alluded to in the Introduction, and to which we will give extended consideration in a later chapter.

The third argument has to do with the nature of truth. It proposes the notion that truth is self-evident. Even should we deny the truth, we are by that very act affirming it. Suppose that I should say, "There is no truth." For that statement to make any sense at all, I have to rely, in making it, on the fact that you will accept my statement, "There is no truth," as true. So, try as I might, I cannot escape the self-evident quality of truth. I must rely on what I deny. But we know that God

Himself is truth, for we read in St. John's gospel (14:6) where Christ says, "I am the way, the truth, and the life." If I can know the truth, then, because the truth is self-evident, and if God is *the* truth, it follows that the existence of God is self-evident.

The very short response that St. Thomas gives to this argument may be taken as indicative of the little weight he attached to it. The argument is using the term "truth" equivocally, referring, in one instance, to a quality of human knowledge, and, in another, to the First Truth, God Himself. While there is no contesting the fact that something that is true for us is self-evidently so, we cannot from that jump to the conclusion that *the* Truth, God Himself, is also self-evident to us.[3]

In summing up St. Thomas's response to this whole mode of argument, two points deserve emphasis. Human beings do not possess an innate, or intuitive, knowledge of the existence of God. And this means that the existence of God is not a self-evident truth for us. In terms of our natural knowledge, the truth of God's existence is one which can be arrived at only through a process of assiduous and careful reasoning.

The Existence of God Is Not a Self-Evident Truth

All of the arguments sketched above arrive, by way of different routes, at the same conclusion: human beings have an innate knowledge of the existence of God; their knowledge of God's existence is self-evident; there is no need to demonstrate the self-evident.

A key characteristic of any self-evident truth is that it is impossible to deny it without violating the principle of contradiction. If I were to attempt to deny my own existence, for example, I would obviously be taking a totally irrational position. We cannot even coherently think a thought that denies a self-evident truth. But does the statement, "God exists," express a self-evident truth? If this were the case, then to deny it would be like denying one's own existence, or one of the first principles of human reasoning. But since time immemorial people have been denying the existence of God, and although we are convinced that in doing so they are taking a most seriously erroneous position, we do not on that account suppose that the atheist who says, "God does not exist," is, in making that claim, saying something on the same level as, "I do not exist." And the reason for this is that the existence of God is not self-evident. The man who says there is no God may be foolish, but he is not, from a natural point of view, acting in a totally irrational way.

In giving closer regard to what precisely we mean by self-evident, we recognize a distinction between something, a particular truth, that is self-evident in itself (*per se nota secundum se*), and something which, besides being self-evident in itself, is also self-evident to us (*per se nota quoad nos*). A truth is self-evident in itself if the predicate term of the statement in which it is expressed is contained in the subject term, where the predicate term is giving full declaration to the very essence of what is named by the subject term. In philosophical terminology, a statement of this kind, expressing a self-evident truth, is called an analytic statement. A logical definition would be an example of an analytic statement, as with the definition of a triangle: a plane, three sided figure the sum of whose angles is equal to two right angles. The test of a true analytic statement is that the subject and the predicate terms can be exchanged, and the meaning of the statement remains exactly the same. One final note, apropos of something said just above. Before a truth can be self-evident to us, it must first be self-evident in itself, for when we recognize something as self-evident, all we are doing is clearly seeing that its truth is intrinsic to itself. Our knowing something as true does not make it true; it was true before we knew it, and will remain true after we forget it. Our knowing is simply the recognition of what is objectively the case.

Now, there are certain things that are self-evident in themselves, and immediately self-evident to us as well. These would be the kinds of truths which, as soon as we grasp the language in which they are expressed, we unhesitatingly recognize them as true. Such would be the truths contained in the first principles, as in the principle which tells that "it is impossible for something to be and not be at the same time and in the same respect" (the principle of contradiction), or in the statements of mathematical axioms, such as "the whole is greater than the part." However, there are any number of truths which, though they are self-evident in themselves, are not self-evident to us, and that is because, in the statements in which they are expressed, we simply do not see that the predicate term is contained in the subject term, and we do not see that because of a deficiency in our knowledge of the subject matter the statement is dealing with. For example, the definition of a triangle given above is self-evident in itself, for it accurately tells us what a triangle *is*, but it would not be self-evident to someone who is not familiar with geometry. It is only after one comes to learn the precise meanings of the terms used in geometry (e.g., "plane figure") that one is able to see that the predicate and the subject terms in the definition are interchangeable.

With all these considerations in mind, let us now reflect on the statement that most concerns us here: "God exists." That statement expresses a truth which is self-evident in itself; the statement, in other words, is analytic. The predicate, "exists," is contained in the subject, "God." This means that it is of the very nature of God to exist. To put it differently, the very meaning of "God" is "to be." God's existence is contained within His essence, or, more precisely, in God essence and existence are one.

But how do we know that it is of the very essence of God to exist? This is a truth that we are able to arrive at only through the exercise of reason. And that means that the statement "God exists," though self-evident in itself, as an analytic statement, is not self-evident to us because we do not immediately see that the statement's predicate is contained in its subject. This being the case, the statement, "God exists," is not self-evident to us in the way the statement, "The whole is greater than the part," would be, and therefore this is a truth that we must arrive at through the exercise of reason. If we begin with such a truth in any argument that purports to demonstrate the existence of God, we are thereby, besides appealing to knowledge that is not immediately evident to us (thus not employing the *quia* mode of argument), committing the fallacy called begging the question: that is, we are assuming to be true the very thing we have to prove to be true.

In attempting to demonstrate the existence of God, then, we must proceed from things that are most known to us, and not from things which, though self-evident in themselves, are not self-evident to us. In practical terms, this means that we must begin with effects, and from them proceed to the cause.[4]

Man's Natural Knowledge of God

We have seen how St. Thomas, in handling one of the specific objections to attempting to demonstrate God's existence, acknowledges that man does indeed have what might be called an innate knowledge of God's existence, but that knowledge is seriously imperfect. Because of its imprecision, the knowledge is not a direct and unambiguous pointer to the one true God. St. Thomas uses a rather intriguing example to illustrate the nature of the confused knowledge of God with which all of us are invested. Let us say I go to a public square to meet my brother Peter. While waiting at one end of the square I see a man coming down the walk from the opposite end. I know for certain that I am seeing a man, but, because of his distance from me, I do not know if the man I am seeing is Peter. In a comparable way, St. Thomas argues, all human beings know that they have a desire to attain that which will make them perfectly happy, but they have no clear idea what it is exactly which will fulfill this desire. It is in fact God, but they have no stable realization of that, just as I have no sure confidence that the man who is coming down the walk from the opposite end of the square is Peter. I have to wait to discover whether or not it is in fact my brother. All of us have to exercise our reason in order to discover that what lies at the bottom of the universal desire for happiness is the desire for God.

Confused, imprecise knowledge of God is, just for being such, inadequate knowledge, but it is knowledge nonetheless, and we would not want to discount it entirely for, as a matter of fact, it plays a very important role in any attempt to move toward a certain knowledge of the existence of God. It is the knowledge with which we start, and on which we attempt to build. The kind of knowledge we are addressing here can be called man's natural knowledge of God, and that is the term I will regularly make most use of. It is a natural knowledge precisely in the sense that its source is man's nature. It is not a knowledge of God whose source is supernatural. And it is natural in the sense that it is primitive; it is not the result of elaborate reasoning, but represents the point at which elaborate reasoning begins. This confused knowledge of God can also be called pre-philosophical knowledge, for, once again, it is the knowledge that comes before philosophy, just as such, commences its work.

We may speak of man's natural knowledge of God as an innate orientation toward God as man's final end. God, who is man's final end, is of course the source of man's very being. Man comes from God, and he is intended to return to God. As creatures, we cannot help but have a natural intimation, however subtle and obscure it sometimes may be, of the Creator from whom we come.

In treating of this phenomenon, Scholastic philosophy speaks of man as being naturally fit for, or capable of immediately encountering, God (*Homo capax Dei*).[5] Applying this notion to the question at hand, we say that man does not know, by nature, that God exists (i.e., he has no innate knowledge of God's existence), but he has, by nature, the ability to come to the knowledge that God exists. To better understand this important point, it might be helpful to remind ourselves of what St. Thomas says elsewhere about moral virtue and how it relates to us. Man, he argues, is not naturally virtuous, but he has a natural capacity for virtue.[6] We are not born virtuous, but we are born with the ability to become virtuous. By the same token, we are not born with the knowledge that God exists, but we are born with the ability, through the exercise of reason, to arrive at certain knowledge of His existence.

The eminent Thomistic philosopher Jacques Maritain, in his book, *Approaches to God*, develops the idea of the pre-philosophical knowledge of God in a number of interesting and informative ways. This pre-philosophical knowledge of God is naturally available to man, and it has a certain foundational quality to it for it is the kind of knowledge upon which he builds those arguments that would be successful in proving the existence of God. Maritain's central thesis is that "the knowledge of God, before being developed in logical and perfectly conceptualized demonstrations, is first and foremost a natural fruit of the intuition of existence."[7] By way of explaining what he means by an intuition of existence, he maintains that every adult human being, sooner or later over the course of his life, is struck by the simultaneous realization of two very basic self-evident truths about himself. First, that he exists; second, that he exists contingently. These twin truths, Maritain argues, lead the individual—not by way of argument but through a kind of quasi-intuitive groping—to a vague apprehension of a necessary being, that being upon which his own contingent being depends. And from that elemental apprehension, if the individual has any philosophical proclivities, he will proceed to the metaphysical proofs for the existence of God.

This analysis is helpful in that it calls attention to the fact that before we can set about formally proving the existence of God, we must have at the outset some sort of idea of what it is we are attempting to prove. This initial, working understanding of the word "God" is, perhaps we could say, what is provided to us by the vague apprehension of a necessary being that Maritain speaks of.

Exaggerated Views of Man's Natural Knowledge of God

It seems to be the case that there always has been a certain number of people, philosophers and non-philosophers alike, who were convinced that the knowledge of the existence of God was self-evident to all men. Certainly there was already a long history behind such a point of view by the time St. Thomas came on the scene in the thirteenth century, and, as we have seen, he addressed it directly in order to refute it. Unfortunately, this erroneous point of view was not put to rest as a result of St. Thomas's clear-cut response to it. Indeed, it would seem to be an error that has a persistently seductive appeal to the human mind. It is very much alive today, and not a few who identify themselves as believers earnestly subscribe to it. Especially noteworthy is the fact that some Scholastic philosophers, even some who would call themselves Thomists, have shown a weakness for this point of view, a point of view which has come to be known as ontologism.

The claim that the existence of God is self-evident often simply means, to the person making it, that the created world bears everywhere on it the marks of its Creator. And although he may, with this meaning in mind, claim the existence of God to be "self-evident"—that is, something that need not be proved by argument—there is an unstated argument lurking behind his claim. The argument, made explicit, is this: All we need do, to realize that God exists, is to look about us at the order and regularity of the created world. The explanation for that order and regularity is God. Now, we could readily agree with this, but do we have here an instance of the existence of God standing as a self-evident truth? Not really. What we have is an instance of the existence of God *being made evident* by the existence of the physical world. In other words, what is lying behind the claim is an implied argument. And it is a *quia* argument, moving from effects (the created universe) to cause (God).

But the person whom we will call an ontologist thinks along quite different lines. His general thinking runs something like this: Because man comes from God, is the creature of God, he for that very reason harbors at the deepest levels of his consciousness an intuitive knowledge of the existence of God. Man, simply because he is man, can have a "clear and distinct" idea of God, and that idea is eminently reliable; it touches upon the very essence of God. For the ontologist, we need not look outward in order to attain a sure knowledge of God, arriving at that knowledge through the exercise of reason. All we need do is look inward, and we will find, at the very center of our being, immediate assurance of God's existence.

Now, if this is true, then of course there would be no need for natural theology to demonstrate God's existence, for man would meet the reality of God merely by meeting the reality of his own being. Note well the difference between this notion and what Maritain refers to as man's pre-philosophical knowledge of God. In that kind of knowledge we have a vague intimation, a provocative suggestiveness, regarding the existence of God, but it is not certain knowledge of His existence. It is a knowledge somewhat comparable to that confused, indeterminate knowledge of God which is concealed within our desire for perfect happiness, discussed by St. Thomas.

Two observations can be made about the exaggerated view of man's knowledge of God, i.e., the view of ontologism. First, the assumption upon which the view is established—God is the source of our being—is perfectly true, but it is not a truth of which we have an intuitive grasp through natural knowledge. What is claimed by the ontologist to be natural, intuitive knowledge, is in fact knowledge which he could only have come into possession of through revelation. The kind of special knowledge that the ontologist is laying claim to, then, does not provide us with any basis on which we could build an argument to demonstrate God's existence.

The second observation. It is a basic principle of Scholastic epistemology that all of our ideas trace their origins to concrete sense images. This is demonstrated by the fact that we must in our thinking always advert back to sense images, even when dealing with the most abstract matters, matters that are most distant from the material realm. For example, when we think about circularity we must picture the image of a circle. Now, if it is true, as the ontologist maintains, that man has within himself a direct access to an idea of God that assures him of the real existence of God, he would not have to had relied on the process of abstraction in order to possess that idea, the process upon which he must necessarily depend in order to come into possession of all the rest of his ideas. He would, for this very special idea, be circumventing the process of abstraction. But because those who claim to possess such an idea of God, must, like the rest of us, advert to sense images in order to discuss the idea, it would seem that the knowledge in question here is not intuitive after all. It has its origins in sense knowledge. The ontologists, like the rest of us, gain their knowledge, on the natural level, through abstraction, that is, by beginning in the external, not the internal, world. The practical ramification of this is that, when ontologists speak of God, they cannot talk about Him as He is in Himself, but only as the mind can understand Him in comparison to created things. The Jesuit philosopher Father John McCormick expressed this point very nicely when he wrote: "If we formed our idea of God from the direct intuition of God, this idea ought to represent God as He is in Himself. Now, as a matter of fact, it does not do this, but rather represents Him under the analogy of created things."[8]

The Limitations of Man's Natural Knowledge of God

If rightly used, man's natural knowledge of God can be, as we have seen, the proximate means on which we rely when, employing natural reason alone, we set ourselves to the task of demonstrating the existence of God. This natural knowledge serves as a point of departure, then, from which we embark upon our formal and systematic investigations in natural theology. But it should also be clear to us by now that this natural knowledge of God is inadequate. In itself, it is beset by serious and insuperable limitations. The most obvious indication of these limitations is the fact pointed out by St. Thomas, that man has, time and time again down through the course of history, while relying only on his natural knowledge of God, come up with ideas of Him which were no more than fevered products of unruled imagination, and which had nothing to do with the one true God.

If it is the case that man has, without benefit of careful philosophical reasoning or divine revelation, an adequate natural understanding of God, then how do we account for the remarkable phenomenon of polytheism? Man has managed over time to fabricate a vast array of different "versions" of the divinity, some of which are bizarre to the extreme, some of which, indeed, are positively grotesque. Consider the pantheon of the ancient Greeks, the complete assembly of the various gods they believed in. Reading of the activities of the Olympian gods and goddesses, in the works of Homer, we cannot help but find their behavior anything but edifying, and scarcely divine. It is little wonder that the more perspicacious among the ancient Greek thinkers, most notably Xenophanes and Plato, condemned the prevailing accounts of divinity as blasphemous distortions of the truth.

If man, by nature, has a ready-to-hand idea of God which faithfully reflects the reality of God, what are we to make of pantheism, which obliterates the absolute otherness of God by divinizing everything, including ourselves? Pantheism, which for centuries was more or less limited to Eastern culture, where it found preeminent expression in Hinduism, would today seem to be making a vigorous come-back in the West, in good part because of the influence of the philosophy of Georg Hegel (1770–1831). Modern Western pantheism appears to be especially prevalent among intellectuals, who, having abandoned traditional religion, now seek consolation and confirmation in a religion of nature, whose central doctrinal tenet is that simply to be is to be divine.

Fideism

Many if not most of those who would argue against the need to demonstrate the existence of God are ardent believers. And many among them look askance at the whole enterprise of natural theology because of a deep-seated suspicion of reason itself, a suspicion that tells them that faith and reason do not mix well together, and the less reason intrudes itself into the realm of faith, the better it is for faith. The position being described here, especially in its more extreme forms, is called fideism. The name itself is revealing, for it is derived from the Latin *fides*, which means "faith." The committed fideist gives undue emphasis to faith, so much so in fact that what remains is not faith at all but an anemic imitation of it.

The fideist drastically short changes human intellect, and makes altogether too much of human will. The fideist is of course quite right to recognize that the assent of faith necessarily involves an act of the will, but the human will never acts, cannot act, in isolation. It is always illumined, guided, by the intellect. To say, "I believe in God," involves an act of the will, to be sure, but an act of the will can only be made in response to that which is known by the intellect. One cannot believe in a God of whom one has no knowledge.

But the most serious mis-turn taken by fideism is when it imagines that the exercise of human reason somehow constitutes a positive affront to the faith when it is applied to matters of belief. It is not that the fideist is necessarily lacking in intelligence. Sometimes he is a very intelligent fellow indeed. But he chooses to compartmentalize his life, keeping his faith separate from his philosophical cogitations. Having taken this attitude to its extreme limits, the fideist is ultimately prepared to attest, *Credo quia absurdum*, "I believe because it is absurd." One should not look for any rationality in religious belief. From the point of view of human reason, the tenets of religion make no sense, but you believe them nonetheless. One makes an act of will to spite the intellect.

It would be hard to imagine a more thoroughly un-Catholic position than that adopted by fideism. It is one of the hallmarks, and glories, of Catholic Christianity that it has from the beginning steadfastly taught the perfect compatibility between faith and reason. We would promptly concede the point that there are certain truths of the faith which transcend the powers of human reason fully to comprehend—these we call the mysteries of faith—but none of those truths go directly contrary to reason; they in no wise violate reason. In a word, they are not irrational. It should be clear that a dedicated fideist would be very reluctant to endorse the complicated employment of human reason which is required by the task of formulating cogent proofs for the existence of God.

The Case of Søren Kierkegaard

Søren Kierkegaard, the nineteenth century Danish philosopher and theologian, must be regarded as one of the more dynamic and provocative thinkers of modern times. He was born in Copenhagen in 1813, and died in the same city in 1855. Though it would not be correct to identify Kierkegaard as a fideist without qualification, he certainly had distinct fideist tendencies, tendencies no more evident than in the firmly negative stance he took toward any effort to attempt to demonstrate the existence of God. This being so, not a little can be learned, by the serious student of natural theology, by reflecting on some of the particulars in the attitude he took toward this issue.

Kierkegaard advances several reasons which he believes satisfactorily show the ineffectualness of all attempts to prove God's existence, but the reason that is of most interest to us is expressed in the following passage. "But if he [i.e., God] does exist, then it is foolishness to want to demonstrate it, since I, in the very moment the demonstration commences, would presuppose it not as doubtful but as decided, because otherwise I would not begin…."[9] The assumption which the Danish philosopher makes here, that one must accept as fact at the outset of a demonstration that what one is intending to demonstrate is already beyond doubt, is simply not true. If that were the case, then he would be quite right in contending that the demonstration is unnecessary, for why would anyone want to prove something about which there are no doubts? As Kierkegaard here describes demonstration, it is not demonstration at all, but simply begging the question and arguing in a circle, ending up precisely where one began. To admit that this in fact happens in our reasoning, perhaps more often than we would like, is not to admit that this always happens, or, what Kierkegaard seems to be suggesting, that it is the only thing that happens, as if all human reasoning were circular reasoning.

His description of demonstration, then, is quite inaccurate. In order to commence a demonstration, I do not need to believe that what I want to demonstrate cannot be doubted. Let us say that I intend to demonstrate the existence of X. In attempting to do so, I do not at all begin by supposing that X is beyond doubt. In point of fact, X *is in* doubt, and that is why I am moved to make an argument. It is just the precise existential status of X I am seeking to determine, and about which I am uncertain. I do not know if the statement, "X exists," is true or not. What is essential for me, at the commencement of the demonstration, is that I can acknowledge that the existence of X is at least a real possibility. This is to say that the statement, "X exists," does not constitute for me a contradiction in terms. I would be indeed involved in an exercise in futility if I were attempting to prove a metaphysical impossibility.

What Kierkegaard is assuming, then, apropos of the attempt to prove God's existence, is that we enter into any such attempt with a knowledge of God's existence already a permanent part of our consciousness. This is made clear when he writes: "Just to come to know that the god is the different, man needs the god and then comes to know the god is absolutely different from him."[10] The mode of argument that Kierkegaard is describing here is clearly circular. Now, he is quite aware of this, and the point he is making is that with this subject circular argument is the only type of argument that is possible. We can only come to know anything about God—in this case, that He is absolutely different from us—by having at the outset of our cogitations some sort of knowledge of God as different from us. More radically, our knowledge that God exists can be nothing more than the end point of a thinking process that began with a knowledge that God exists.

It would seem that the best explanation for Kierkegaard's attitude, which regards any effort to prove God's existence as totally unnecessary, is his conviction that the certitude of God's existence which he had through faith was so strong that it was impossible ever mentally to set that knowledge aside, and to reflect upon the subject of God's existence in purely philosophical terms, that is to say, by the light of natural reason alone. But there was something else at work in Kierkegaard's whole attitude toward this question—something perhaps more fundamental—and that was his fideist-like suspicion of human reason in general, and particularly as it relates to any issues having to do with religious belief.

St. Paul on Natural Theology

In a study of this sort, we would be remiss not to call special attention to what St. Paul has to say in the first chapter of his letter to the Romans (19–22). The pagans who indulge in ungodly and wicked behavior, he informs his readers, must be held fully accountable for their actions, and that is because they have no basis for claiming to be ignorant of "the truth of God, seeing that what may be known about God is manifest to them. For God has manifested it to them. For since the creation of the world His invisible attributes are clearly seen—his everlasting power and also his divinity—being understood through the things that are made."

This is a very telling passage, and one which should be of special interest to the student of natural theology. It would seem that St. Paul is here faulting the pagans for their bad behavior for the simple reason that they should know better. And they should know better, not because the existence of God is self-evident to them, not because they have by nature an intuitive knowledge of God, but because, solely by dint of the fact that they are human beings, rational creatures possessed of intellect, they have not only the ability, but the responsibility, to use their reason to come to an awareness of the existence of God, an awareness which would then have a direct, correcting affect on their moral lives. The pagan Romans, like all human beings, are *capax Dei*, but they are not properly responding to that fact.

They have access, through reason, to "the truth of God," because God Himself has manifested it to them. But how? Through His effects, we would say, which are everywhere visible in the natural world. God, eternally acting as First Cause, reveals Himself in "the things that are made." Once man arrives at the truth of God's existence through natural reason, he would then come to see the moral obligations he has toward God. St. Paul is calling our attention here to just that activity which is the principal concern of natural theology.

CHAPTER TWO

Can the Existence of God Be Proven?

The General Problem

Are we, as earnest students who have set for ourselves the ambitious task of proving the existence of God, embarked upon a fool's journey? Have we taken on a task which is simply impossible to fulfill? Such is the opinion which has been held by not a few philosophers over the years, and it is an opinion to which many people subscribe today. It is an opinion which we, needless to say, do not share. Nonetheless, a number of serious objections have been put forward in defense of the position that demonstrating the existence of God is impossible, and it is incumbent upon the serious student of natural theology to give these objections careful consideration.

In doing that, we will be following the lead of St. Thomas Aquinas. In the previous chapter we saw how he responded to the "not necessary" objection to proving God's existence. He next turns his attention to what we will call the "not possible" objection, an objection which, in its particulars, is quite challenging. After we have examined the specific objections dealt with by St. Thomas, we will then spend considerable time reflecting on the position of the eighteenth century philosopher, Immanuel Kant. He took a very negative view of the possibility of demonstrating God's existence, and because his influence has been so uniformly strong since his day, it behooves us to pay close attention to the arguments he put forward to substantiate his position.

"What Is Known By Faith Cannot Be Demonstrated"

The first specific objection that St. Thomas takes under consideration has to do with the fact that the existence of God is an article of faith. This particular objection would of course have application only to believers, but most especially those believers who are philosophers, and who are therefore committed to the possibility that the existence of God can indeed be demonstrated. Is the believing philosopher mistaken in this? Does the knowledge of God's existence he has through faith render null and void his attempts to prove God's existence?

The specific position this objection takes is that matters of religious belief, those things that we come to know through the virtue of faith, are, just as such, non-demonstrable. This is seen to be so because of the very nature of demonstration, whose purpose is to make apparent what initially is not apparent. But faith has to do with things which, by their very nature, are not apparent, as St. Paul makes clear when he writes: "Now faith is the substance of things to be hoped for, the evidence of things that are not seen." (Heb: 11:1) We come to know the "things that are not seen," e.g., the existence of God, through faith alone. We come to "see" the "things that are not seen," not by having them made evident to us by the force of argument, but simply by the assent of faith. And if faith is, by definition, of things not seen, it is presumptuous to suppose that human reason can make them visible, that is, demonstrate their truth through philosophical argument.

The Preambles of Faith

St. Thomas responds to this objection by making a distinction which should be recognized as one of the signal marks of his whole theology—the distinction between articles of faith, and the preambles to the articles of faith. If we think of the articles of faith as constituting the deposit of faith (*depositum fidei*), a preamble of faith would be a preparatory introduction to the deposit. A preamble of faith would be something that not only precedes and leads up to the articles of faith, but is in a certain sense a necessary antecedent to them.

Now, St. Thomas regards knowledge of the existence of God as a preamble to the articles of faith. It is properly classified as such because, although it is undeniably the case that the existence of God can be known by faith, it can also be known by natural reason, and indeed that is the very point St. Paul is making with regard to the behavior of pagans, in his epistle to the Romans, which we discussed in the previous chapter. If it were not possible that the existence of God could be known by natural reason, but could be known by faith alone, then the pagans, who are lacking in faith, could not reasonably be held blameworthy for their ungodly behavior. But St. Paul does hold them blameworthy, and that is because, simply by reason of their status as human beings, they are *capax Dei*; they have by nature what is needed to come to a knowledge of God through His created effects which are everywhere visible in the natural world. And from that knowledge they could conclude to the moral responsibility they have to be obedient to the law of God.

In his response to this objection St. Thomas makes a very important point concerning the relation between the kind of knowledge we come to have through faith, supernatural knowledge, and the natural knowledge which must necessarily precede the knowledge born of faith. The classic principle by which St. Thomas is being guided here is the idea that grace builds on nature. Grace does not transform human beings into something like angels; it makes them fully human. The specific application of that principle in this instance is to the effect that before we come to believe in God, before we reach the point where, aided by divine grace, we make the assent of faith, we must have, on the purely natural level, some sort of idea of what it is we are assenting to. More precisely, before we believe that God exists, we must know the object of our belief, must be possessed of an adequate understanding—again an understanding that comes from natural reason—of the meaning of the term "God." To put it differently, one cannot believe in God unless one is aware that there is a God to believe in.

One can come to a sure knowledge of God's existence through natural reason alone, i.e., through demonstration. But to say that this *can* be done is not to say that everyone is capable of doing it. In fact, it would seem to be the case that only a small number of people, with the requisite background in philosophy, and then with no small expenditure of concentrated effort, are able to arrive at the conviction of God's existence through the exercise of natural reason alone. As many scholars have noted, this is clearly the attitude of St. Thomas on the matter.[1] However, it is difficult not to think that St. Paul, as reflected in the passage from his epistle to the Romans alluded to more than once, takes a less rigorous attitude toward the matter. He would seem to be saying that the average adult human being has the capability of attaining a knowledge of God's existence through natural reason. Be that as it may, two points need to be emphasized here. First, there are two distinct ways of knowing of the existence of God, through natural reason, and through faith, and they may exist side by side. Second, the knowledge born of faith presupposes natural knowledge, the knowledge of the preambles of faith.[2]

"Ignorance of God's Essence Prohibits Proving His Existence"

Although St. Thomas's statement of the second objection to the possibility of proving God's existence is very brief and elliptical, it contains much, and its argument needs to be spelled out in explicit terms in order sufficiently to appreciate the peculiar value of the objection. It turns on a technical matter having to do with the nature of syllogistic reasoning, and we will need to say a few clarifying words about it here. Every categorical syllogism is composed of three terms, the major, the minor, and the middle. The peculiar function of the middle term, in the argument, is to make a logical connection between the minor term and the major term. In order to effect this connection, and thus produce a true conclusion which follows necessarily from the premises, we must know the essence, or the nature, of the entity to which the middle terms refers. So as better to see what this all means, let us consider a classical example of the categorical syllogism.

> All men are mortal.
> Socrates is a man.
> Therefore, Socrates is mortal.

The middle term in this argument, the term that appears in the two premisses but not in the conclusion, is "man." Now, this particular argument is a sound one because we enter it with a knowledge of the essence of man, and it is precisely that knowledge which allows us immediately to see the truth of the major premiss, "All men are mortal." We know immediately, not through argument, that mortality is of the very nature of this creature we call man. And that permits us to conclude that if there is any single individual who is numbered among those creature we call men, say a fellow named Socrates, then he must necessarily be marked by mortality.

Now let us consider an argument, cast in the form of a categorical syllogism, which purports to prove the existence of God. This is the kind of argument St. Thomas has in mind in articulating this particular objection.

> A being whose essence entails existence necessarily exists.
>
> But God is a being whose essence entails existence.
>
> Therefore, God necessarily exists.

The middle term in the argument is "a being whose essence entails existence." What is this if not a description of the very nature of God? But this is not knowledge which is immediately accessible to us; it must be demonstrated. True, we can have such knowledge through faith, but we can scarcely appeal to faith while attempting to prove the existence of God. The major premiss of a categorical syllogism should begin with knowledge that is self-evident and therefore common to all. That God's essence entails existence (i.e., that essence and existence are one and the same in Him) is a truth which, though self-evident in itself (*secundum se*) is not self-evident to us (*quoad nos*). In effect, then, the argument does not demonstrate that God exists, for it begins with knowledge of the nature of the being who existence is purportedly being proved. One cannot know *what* something is (its nature) before one has established *that* it is. At best, what this argument can be said to do is make explicit something about God's nature, but it does so only by moving in circular fashion.

Knowledge of God's Essence Is Not Assumed in Proving His Existence

In one of Plato's dialogues, the *Meno*, a sophistical argument is put forward that supposedly proves that the process of learning something, gaining any new knowledge, is an impossibility. The nub of the argument is this: If we consider learning as the search for knowledge, no such search ever takes place, for either we already know what we are looking for, hence no search is necessary, or, we do not know what we are looking for, hence no search is possible.[3]

Does this paradox apply to our efforts to demonstrate the existence of God? Let us first consider the notion that ignorance of what one is searching for cancels the search. Can it reasonably be said that we do not know what we are looking for as we prepare to set about proving God's existence? How, one might wonder, can we know what we are looking for until we have first found it? And if we do not know what we are looking for, it would seem that indeed we would then not even be able to begin a search. To state the problem as precisely as possible, might it not be the case that proving the existence of God is impossible because we have no idea in the first place what it is we are attempting to prove? Specifically, we have no idea to accompany the term "God."

In responding to that objection, we should take careful note of what this line of reasoning—mis-reasoning, rather—is attempting to do: establish a kind of all or nothing situation as the only real possibility as a starting point in the search for truth. We have in this ploy an excellent example of the fallacy of the false dilemma.[4] If what it claims is true, not only would it be impossible to prove the existence of God, but no demonstration of any kind, about any matter whatever, would be possible. Scientific discovery would be a pure fiction. What actually happens in the real world, in contrast to the world imagined by the argument? When we begin a research project, we do not have, it is true, a perfectly clear, fully fleshed-out idea of what we are searching for. But neither is our mind a complete blank. We always have some kind of idea, a working notion more or less elaborate, of what it is we are attempting to establish. And it is just that working notion, however vague or sketchy it might be in certain instances, which gives structure and guidance to our search. When Sherlock Holmes embarks upon an investigation to discover the culprit who committed the crime, he of course does not know at the outset the specific person whom he is after; if he did, there would be no need for an investigation. But he does know that he is after a culprit, and he does have some general ideas as to the nature of that culprit.

But might not the other part of the paradox apply to our situation here? Do we not already know the God we are looking for, and therefore no search for Him is necessary? Are we not entering into an argument that claims to prove God's existence already armed with a knowledge of God's essence, and therefore not really demonstrating anything, but only arguing in a circle? Because this is an objection we are already familiar with, we need only repeat what already has been established. If we were to build our argument upon knowledge of God that relies upon faith, we would be begging the question, assuming to be true precisely that which we are under obligation to prove to be true. Well, then, with what kind of knowledge of God are we entering into our argument? Certainly, we have to have some sort of idea of the being whose existence we want to prove, otherwise, we could not even get started. That point must be granted. We do know what we are looking for; we have an adequate working knowledge of the object of our search, even though that knowledge is not of the essence or very nature of the object of our search. Knowledge such as that will come later. First, we must establish existence, then we will see what can be determined about essence.

How could we describe the working idea of the term "God" that allows us to begin our search? What, at this stage, do we mean by that term? "God," we could say, refers to "the creator and master of all things, in whose hands is the governance of the universe."[5] Or, more simply, we could say that by "God" we mean the absolute supreme being. The idea of an absolute supreme being is not a contradiction in terms. It is possible, then, that such a being could exist. We are setting out to prove the existence of such a being.

And how, precisely, do we do that? By beginning with the effects of the cause we are attempting to establish. Those effects are represented, in their totality, by the natural world all around us, and of which we are of course a part. Again, we do not begin with the cause, i.e., God, for it is the cause which we are seeking. And we must know enough about that cause to guide us in our search. We know at least what the name "God" means, though we can say nothing at this point about His nature.[6]

"It Is Not Possible to Move from the Finite to the Infinite"

The third argument directed against the possibility of proving the existence of God begins by stating a truth with which we are in full agreement and have often repeated, i.e., in any argument attempting to prove the existence of God, one must begin with effects and from them move to the cause. The effects in this case would be created things, and the cause would of course be God the Creator. It is a basic principle of metaphysics that in order to conclude to the existence of a cause on the basis of effects, there must be a certain proportion between the effects and the cause, in the sense that the cause, somehow, must be reflected in the effects. But here, according to the objection, we run into an insuperable problem. There cannot be any proportion between created things and God, given the fact that created things are finite and God is infinite. Because of this lack of proportion between the effects and the cause in this case, the existence of God cannot be proven.

What this argument is contending, looking at it from a slightly different perspective, is essentially this: assuming the God whose existence we want to prove is an infinite being, and knowing ourselves to be very much finite beings, there is established between God and man an infinite abyss that the mind of man is incapable of bridging.

Arguments Can Be Limited Without Being Nullified

One can grant that there is not, in the strict sense, a proportion between effects and cause, and thereby admit that one is thus limited as to what can be concluded about the cause from the effects produced by the cause, without at the same time having to admit that no conclusion at all can be reached concerning the cause. If there is no proportion between effects and cause, then one surely could not come up with anything like a perfect understanding of the cause from those effects. What this means, in precise terms, and apropos of the issue immediately before us, is that we cannot, proceeding from created things, conclude to any knowledge pertaining to God's *essence*. But what we can do, and do with assurance, is argue from effects to the bare conclusion that there is, there must be, a cause. In other words, from created things, the effects, we can successfully argue to the conclusion that there exists an adequate explanation for those effects, which is their cause, and that cause is God.[7]

A Short Excursus on Demonstration

By way of providing summary responses to the various objections to the possibility of demonstrating God's existence, St. Thomas once again calls attention to that crucial passage from the first chapter of St. Paul's epistle to the Romans, where he points out that the invisible things of God can come to be understood by being perceived through the visible things of creation. What this amounts to saying is that the existence of God can be demonstrated from the existence of created things. And this is precisely what natural theology sets out to do.

What is particularly interesting about St. Thomas's response to the question whether it is possible to demonstrate God's existence is that he presents, in the main body of the article in which he deals with it, a little disquisition on the nature of demonstration. This provides us with some pertinent guidance in developing our own approach to the study of natural theology. From the outset of our discussion we have continuously been making reference to "proving" or "demonstrating" the existence of God. It would be beneficial if we were to pause at this point and make as explicit as possible what precisely we have in mind when we talk about demonstration. What does it mean, in philosophical terms, to prove or demonstrate (the two terms can be considered as roughly synonymous) something? In the most general sense, to demonstrate simply mean to make evident that which initially is not evident, to bring out into the full light of day something which had been lurking in the shadows, or perhaps even buried in complete darkness. If something is manifest and readily apparent to all, it obviously does not have to be demonstrated. It does not have to be spoken for; it can speak for itself.

The process by which anything is demonstrated is equally simple. Because the truth of that which is to be demonstrated is uncertain—it is precisely to establish its certainty that we set about our demonstration—we must begin the process with something that we know for certain to be true. The specific act that constitutes the heart of demonstration is this: to show to be true something whose truth is initially doubtful, on the basis of something whose truth is certain. So, we are making evident something (the subject of our demonstration) by moving to that something from something else that is already evident (i.e., the "evidence" that founds the demonstration). All demonstration must begin in the public forum, as it were. We must start with something whose truth is accessible to all, and which cannot be disputed, otherwise no commencement will ever be possible.

The basic move of demonstration, then, is from the known to the unknown, with the intention of making the latter known. But this can be done in two ways: we can begin with what is simply prior, without qualification, and this is what we know as *propter quid* argument; or, we can begin, not with that which is prior in itself, but which is prior according to us, and to this we give the name *quia* argument. A cause, in relation to its effect, is intrinsically prior, for the obvious reason that the cause must come first in terms of the very nature of the relation; i.e., unless the cause is in place, there can be no effect. When we are demonstrating something using *propter quid* argument, we begin with the cause whose nature we know, and we show that a particular effect follows from that cause. There are countless causes in the world of which we are quite ignorant, and which, therefore, could not form the basis of any argument we might want to make about them. However, all those causes, though unknown to us, remain intrinsically prior to the effects that they bring about, and which may be very familiar to us. There are many diseases that are known to us, but we do not know their causes. When we attempt to demonstrate something by *quia* argument, we begin, not with cause but with effects, which is to say, with that which is prior from our point of view. Under normal circumstances, it is effects that we first encounter, and that are most apparent to us. We are confronted with the hard facts of nature, then we try to figure them out, to explain them, by ferreting out their causes.

Now, every fact that we come across presents itself to us as an effect, for we immediately see that it is not the explanation for itself. We must go beyond that fact to find its explanation; we must seek its cause. It is theoretically possible, for every effect we encounter, to track down its cause. And one thing we know for certain, thanks to the principle of sufficient reason (the principle that tells us that there is a sufficient reason for everything that exists), is that everything that we can come to know by our natural powers must have a cause. Because by definition an effect depends upon a cause, if we know an effect, we may not know *what* is its cause, but we know *that* it has a cause.

How does all this apply to demonstrating the existence of God? We have a sufficiently clear idea of what we mean by the term "God" in order to be able to say that it applies to a supreme being who is the creator of all the beings we know through natural knowledge. The physical world, then, in relation to this possible being, stands as effect to cause. Now, it should be clear, in terms of everything we have established thus far, that, in attempting to show that the possible being we have in mind is also an actual being—i.e., in attempting to demonstrate the existence of God—we cannot employ *propter quid* argument, for that would mean proceeding from cause to effect, but it is precisely the cause that we do not know and whose existence we are setting out to demonstrate. The only proper approach to take, therefore, in demonstrating the existence of God, is by way of *quia* argument, that is to say, we must begin with effects, which are simply the facts of the physical universe, and then to argue from those effects to their cause. In terms of natural knowledge alone, the existence of God, as we have taken pains to point out, is not self-evident to us. What is self-evident to us is the existence of the physical world in which we live and of which we are an integral part. That is where we begin.

The General Position of Immanuel Kant

The figure of the eighteenth century Immanuel Kant looms large, and given his continuing deleterious influence, his thought falls like a long, dark shadow over the science of natural theology. There are not a few philosophers today who are quite convinced that Immanuel Kant has settled the fate of natural theology once and for all. They believe that Kant has demonstrated conclusively the utter futility of natural theology. More remarkably, perhaps, there are many Christian philosophers who share that belief.[8] This is not the place to go into a lengthy discussion of the wide and multifaceted phenomenon which is Kantian philosophy, but it is important, given the decidedly negative influence Kant has had on natural theology, that we at least directly address his supposed refutations of our science, with the purpose of showing that those refutations do not in fact accomplish what the professor from Königsberg presumed they accomplished.

Immanuel Kant thought that natural theology was impossible, and this meant for him, specifically, that he held that human reason was not capable of formulating any true demonstrations for the existence of God. By assuming this position, Kant placed himself in a tradition that had already a long history behind it before he arrived on the scene. What most importantly has to be noted about his negative attitude toward natural theology is that it is inseparable from a more comprehensive negative attitude he cherished, an attitude directed against metaphysics in general. Natural theology was futile, for Kant, because metaphysics, of which natural theology is an integral part, is impossible.

Kant rejected metaphysics, as traditionally understood, because of the peculiar metaphysical presuppositions with which he was burdened. In order to understand the central import of Kant's rejection of metaphysics, we must remind ourselves of the essential character of that most important of philosophical sciences. Metaphysics, in its investigations, moves beyond the sphere of the philosophy of nature, which focuses on material being, and gives itself over to the study of being just as such, to whatever really exists in anyway whatever. This would include non-material being. Metaphysics is dedicated to the proposition that human reason, on the basis of its real knowledge of material being, can arrive at a real knowledge of non-material being. Kant's rejection of metaphysics is founded upon his denial of the ability of human reason to make just that movement, from the material to the immaterial, which lies at the very heart of metaphysics. More precisely, Kant denies that human reason can proceed from a real knowledge of material things to a real knowledge of immaterial things, and that is because he denies that we can have real knowledge of material things in the first place. Kant's epistemology (his theory of knowledge) has effectively cut the human mind off from the world around it. The subjective order is isolated from the objective order, for, according to Kant, the human mind simply cannot know the objective order precisely as the objective order. We do not know things in themselves—i.e., we do not know their essences, or natures—we know only appearances.[9]

Kant is the quintessential idealist philosopher, which means that he puts considerably more store in ideas than in that which ideas reflect, i.e., things in the world.[10] For Scholastic philosophy, and for the perennial philosophy in general, ideas are what "connect" us with the objective order, and we fully subscribe to the basic epistemological principle that every one of our ideas has its ultimate source in the objective order, an order that we know through sense knowledge.[11] For Kant, on the other hand, the world of ideas is self-enclosed. In the final analysis, ideas are about ideas, not about things in the world,[12] and we cannot, by our ideas alone, establish anything concerning what may or may not exist in the objective order. We maintain, on the other hand, that because our ideas have their genesis in the objective order—through our ordinary experience of the world in which we live—they can lead us reliably back to that objective order. In other words, if we reason well, our ideas can tell us what really is the case in the objective order. For Kant, the most important of our ideas, rather than being derived from our experiences in the world, are antecedent to those experiences.

They cannot, therefore, provide us with any reliable information about the objective order of things.

An Antinomy of Pure Reason

Immanuel Kant was not content with simply declaring metaphysics to be an empty science; he set out to demonstrate how this was so. If it can be decided that he succeeded in that effort, then we must confess that we are but wasting our time with this business called metaphysics, particularly with the attention we give to natural theology, and more particularly with the efforts we expend in attempting to demonstrate the existence of God. Kant's principal thesis is that speculative reason, that is, reason that deals with ideas, can only tell us about ideas, and is impotent to establish anything concerning what is, or is not the case, in the objective order of things. It is important to note that this thesis, and the more elemental thesis on which it is based—that we cannot know things in themselves—are simply laid down by Kant as unquestionable truths, as if they were mathematical axioms. This points to an interesting quirk in his philosophy, or in the philosopher behind the philosophy: while never tiring of castigating those who make "dogmatic" proclamations (that is, statements that cannot be backed up by reasoned argument), Kant shows that he is himself rather adept at making dogmatic proclamations. He has a habit of simply claiming certain things to be true, as when he asserts that we are not able to know the thing in itself, and expects us to accept such claims without question or demur.[13]

While offering us nothing by way of direct proof for the thesis that speculative thought is unable to reveal anything of value about the objective order, Kant does attempt to provide what might be called indirect proof for the thesis. He does this by drawing our attention to what he identifies as the antinomy of pure reason. An antinomy is a contradiction. Kant attempts to expose the impotency of speculative reasoning by showing that any metaphysical question we pose concerning the objective order, and then systematically pursue, will yield two equally convincing, but contradictory, responses. Because the responses are contradictory, they effectively cancel one another out and this shows, to Kant's satisfaction, that no stable truth about these questions can ever be established. The general conclusion to be drawn from the exercise is that all metaphysical reasoning is futile. It cannot tell us anything worthwhile about the world in which we live.

In more specific terms, Kant's approach is as follows. He sets up four pairs of propositions reflecting very important metaphysical issues. Each pair of propositions is made up of a thesis and an antithesis, that is, of a proposition which makes a certain claim, and of another which makes a contradictory claim. The four theses and antitheses are as follows: (1) The world had a beginning in time. The world is eternal. (2) Matter is composed of elementary particles that are indivisible. Matter is infinitely divisible. (3) There is free will. There is no free will. (4) There is a necessary being. There is no necessary being. Each argument is intended to represent a metaphysical proof of either the thesis or the antithesis of each question.

Response to the Antinomies of Pure Reason

Kant's experiment can be deemed successful to the extent that it shows what he intended that it show, i.e., a situation "in which no one assertion can establish superiority over the other,"[14] a situation in which, "since the arguments on both sides are equally clear, it is impossible to decide between them."[15] But this turns out not to be the case. Of the four pairs of arguments he presents, in three of them one argument of the pair is clearly more forceful than the other, with the fourth pair being something of a toss-up. Read in the light of objective standards of logic and cogent reasoning, the argument for a created world declares its superiority over the argument for an eternal world, the argument in favor of the infinite divisibility of matter holds sway over its contradictory, and the argument for free will is stronger than that against it. But however one might judge with regard to any particular pairing of arguments, it is quite apparent that, taking them all together, they fail to make his point that it is of the very nature of metaphysical reasoning that it cannot avoid contradiction. In fact, what the arguments demonstrate, Kant's intentions to the contrary notwithstanding, is that metaphysical reasoning, far from being futile, is not only capable of arriving at different conclusions concerning a given question (this is what one would expect), but—and here is the important point—those conclusions, maintaining opposite points of view, are not of equal worth in terms of their coherence and compelling force. The competition, taken as a whole, does not end in an inconsequential draw; there are clear winners. This result is all the more remarkable because the entire experiment was under Kant's control from start to finish, and he conducted it with the idea in mind that it show just the opposite of what it ended up showing. Instead of showing that metaphysical reasoning is inherently contradictory and non-conclusive, it shows the enduring capacity of that reasoning to serve the truth. The real lesson to be learned from the experiment is that if conflicting points of view having to do with the objective order are honestly stated—and I think Kant made a sincere attempt at doing that—the truth will naturally emerge from one of those points of view and clearly declare itself.[16]

Not only do we discover in these arguments, then, a distinct imbalance that is not supposed to be there, but the entire experiment is seriously vitiated by the fact that all of the arguments, be they for thesis or antithesis, are burdened with ideas which, though they faithfully reflect Kant's larger philosophical presuppositions, can be seen to be, taken in themselves, seriously flawed, or, at the least, very much debatable. We can cite only a few of those ideas here, by way of a sampler.

While rightly rejecting the notions of absolute space and absolute time, subscribed to by Isaac Newton, which notions have the effect of conferring on space and time something like the status of independent substances, Kant errs by going to the opposite extreme, and reducing them to the status of essentially subjective entities. This is consonant with his view that space and time "are nothing but representations, and cannot exist outside our mind."[17] In contradistinction to this view, we hold that space and time have objective reality, and are not simply mental constructs that we bring to experience. We come to know space and time form our experiences, and they are as objectively real as the physical things that constitute them.

Kant claims that, in reason "there is no time sequence."[18] The untenableness of this claim can be immediately shown by adding up a column of figures, or, for that matter, engaging in any kind of reasoning process. The very nature of the reasoning process is the movement from one idea to another, such as when we move from a premiss to a conclusion in an argumentative discourse. When you move from one idea to another, you are involved in sequence, and when you are involved in sequence you are necessarily involved in time.

"Freedom," Kant contends, "is a pure transcendental idea, which contains…nothing borrowed from experience.…"[19] In fact, just the opposite is the case. Freedom is not an idea brought to experience; it is an idea that is derived from experience, specifically our experience as free creatures acting freely. For Kant, human freedom is in precisely the same category as God. Both must be accepted as postulates, and that is because neither can be either proved or disproved. We argue, with respect to human freedom, that you neither prove nor postulate that which is immediately obvious to you through your own actions.

Kant maintains that "we are entirely free to hold that any limited beings whatsoever, notwithstanding their being limited, may also be considered unconditionally necessary.…"[20] By "unconditionally necessary" here we can understand Kant as meaning absolutely necessary. But Kant's claim is tantamount to saying "A and not-A," for, by definition a limited being is a being that is not necessary, cannot be necessary. That Kant is capable of making such an incongruous claim is attributable, I believe, to his confusing absolute necessity and relative necessity. Absolute necessity applies to God alone, and allows us to describe God as a being who cannot not be. But any actually existing being can be said to exist necessarily, relatively speaking, in the sense that it necessarily exists here and now, for, if that were not so, the principle of contradiction would be violated. It necessarily exists because it could not be said both to be and not be at the same time and in the same respect.

Kant's Purported Disproofs of the Proofs for God's Existence

Immanuel Kant laid it down that there are only three basic proofs for the existence of God, and the names he gave to them are the ontological proof, the cosmological proof, and the physico-theological proof. He presents each of these proofs in turn, and then subjects them to a thorough analysis. The conclusion he draws from his analysis is that the cosmological proof and the physico-theological proofs are reducible to the ontological proof, but because the ontological proof can be shown to be non-demonstrative, neither the cosmological argument nor the physico-theological argument is demonstrative. The general conclusion of his reasoning on this issue is that there is no proof for the existence of God that is able to do what it proposes to do. In one fell swoop Kant has, to his satisfaction, demolished the very raison d'être of natural theology.

In response to Kant's argument we will begin, where he does, with the ontological argument. Now, this is an argument that we are already familiar with, and which we will be dealing with in some detail in a later chapter, so we will not enter into any in-depth discussion of it here. For now it is sufficient to say of the argument that it fails as a true demonstration because it effectively argues in a circle, assuming a kind of knowledge of God at the very outset of the argument that is not itself self-evident to natural reason. We are, then, in complete agreement with Kant on the point that the ontological argument is non-demonstrative. Kant, in fact, provides a superb analysis of the argument, in which he deftly and tellingly delineates its flaws.[21] So, it would seem that if Kant is correct in his claim that the cosmological argument and the physico-theological are reducible to the ontological argument, and if these three are the only arguments available to us, then we have no choice but to accept his more general claim that it is impossible for philosophy to prove the existence of God. As it happens, however, neither of these claims is true.

There are, in the first place, more arguments for the existence of God than the three cited by Kant, but this is a point of only peripheral interest for our purposes here. What we need to do is look at the arguments that Kant describes respectively as the cosmological argument and the physico-theological argument, and ask of those arguments two pertinent questions: (1) Do they, as presented, serve as adequate metaphysical arguments for the existence of God? (2) Do they, as presented, show themselves to be reducible, as Kant claims they are, to the ontological argument?

In order to respond to those questions we appeal, by way of seeking a reliable standard, to the classical expressions of the principal metaphysical proofs for the existence of God, which receive their clearest and most succinct articulation in the Five Ways of St. Thomas Aquinas. What Kant calls the cosmological argument is most nearly like St. Thomas's Third Way, the argument from contingent being. I say "most nearly like," for it is to be by no means confused with St. Thomas's argument. Kant states his argument as follows: "If anything exists, an absolutely necessary being must also exist. Now I, at least, exist. Therefore an absolutely necessary being exists."[22] It could be said that this fairly represents the nub of the argument from contingent being, but it is presented in so starkly elliptical a form that it comes very close to being a distortion of the argument, and a thoughtful person, responding to it, could be excused if he were not particularly impressed by it, just as presented.

But, that aside, Kant's main objection to the argument, consistent with his epistemological presuppositions, is that it fails because we cannot move from an incontestable fact of experience (the fact that we, as contingent beings, exist) to the conclusion that something which completely transcends our experience exists. We cannot do this, in effect, simply because Kant says we cannot do it, for none of the arguments he offers to back up his position are persuasive. He argues that we cannot reason from contingency to necessity and expect that in doing so we are saying anything about the real world, for contingency is but an idea, and necessity is an idea, so we are simply moving within the enclosed realm of ideas, and never succeed in breaking out of that realm into the objective order of things. But one accepts that point of view only if one has already accepted Kant's epistemological position that sees such key ideas as contingency and necessity as prior to all experience, a position which one is under no obligation whatever to adopt. Why not? Because the supposed existence of such *a priori* ideas rests entirely on a gratuitous claim on Kant's part, a claim that he never attempts to demonstrate, and for the very good reason that it cannot be demonstrated. This is no small lacuna in Kant's epistemology, for in this matter the burden of proof descends heavily upon anyone who would assert that there exist ideas that do not derive from experience which is antecedent to those ideas. Common sense and all evidence points to just the opposite conclusion: all of our ideas begin with and are dependent upon sense experience.

If, then, there is no reason to accept Kant's epistemological position, there is no reason to suppose that, in the argument he is critiquing, we are simply moving within the enclosed realm of ideas. We are, to be sure, dealing with the idea of contingency, but that is not an idea which is birthed without parentage within the virginal confines of our minds, but one which is rather derived from the objective order of things, from the way things actually are in the external world. And when we move from the idea of contingency to the idea of necessity, the latter idea too has its roots in real, extra-mental being, so we are not arguing about merely what is going on in our minds, but what is actually the case in the objective order. What Kant's analysis shows is not the failure of the argument, rightly understood, but the poverty and radical limitations of his epistemology.

Kant's physico-theological argument comes closest to the Fifth Way of St. Thomas, the argument from finality. Again, in this case, Kant's supposed refutation of the argument fails, and that is because the rationale for that refutation rests squarely on Kant's epistemology, an epistemology which, as we have already indicated, is severely wanting. It is an epistemology that has no foundation in fact. Given the erroneous epistemological presuppositions with which he approaches it, then, this argument, for Kant, deals only with ideas, and not with any world beyond ideas. But reject those epistemological presuppositions, as we do, and Kant's purported refutation of the argument collapses. [23]

Kant's contention that his cosmological argument and physico-theological argument are reducible to the ontological argument is not substantiated by him. He also contends that the physico-theological proof reduces to the cosmological proof, but his analysis of the relation between the two offers no convincing support for this contention either. There are any number of specific difficulties related to Kant's overall treatment of the proofs for the existence of God, but this is not the place to go into them.[24] But a final comment on Kant's manner of presenting the arguments is in order. If we were to take his cosmological argument and physico-theological argument as more or less representative, respectively, of the classical arguments from contingent being and from finality (St. Thomas's Third and Fifth Ways), it could hardly be said that he did either of those arguments justice. Though there is no reason to believe that there was here any ill-will on Kant's part, nonetheless, given the weak and unprepossessing way he presented the arguments, it may be suggested that we have here an instance, materially if not formally, of the straw man fallacy, the fallacy whereby an opponent's argument is debilitated by distortion and thus more easily disposed with.[25]

CHAPTER THREE

Proofs for the Existence of God
Before St. Thomas

Demonstrating God's Existence

We saw in the previous chapter that the essence of demonstration is making evident what is not initially evident, on the force of something which is already evident. The basic pattern of the kind of reasoning that takes place in demonstration can be spelled out as follows.

> (a) There is something, B, which actually exists, and
> whose existence is manifestly apparent.
> (b) Now, B could not exist unless there were A.
> (c) Therefore, we must conclude that A exists.

In the arguments that we deal with in natural theology, the letter A, in the argument above, would of course stand for God.

Anyone who constructs an argument whose purpose is to demonstrate a conclusion, must take care that the premises for that argument (i.e., what is being offered as evidence for the conclusion) must meet the following two critical criteria: (i) the premises must be true, and (ii) the claims that they are making must be subject to public verification. The data presented as evidence must be not only true, its truth must be readily obvious to all parties concerned. In addition, the one who is constructing the argument must inform his audience of all those assumption or presuppositions upon which the intelligibility of the argument depend but which may not be explicitly stated in the argument. But those who are the audience to an argument also have, for their part, serious responsibilities which they must live up to. In responding to an argument, no one should assume toward it an intellectual passive stance. An argument must be responded to actively and alertly. A demonstration is not a mere pointing. It is a rational process, and it must be carefully followed step by step if one is to be able properly to evaluate the conclusion with which it ends.

A demonstration, understood in the strict sense, is conclusive. That is to say, it is an argument whose conclusion follows necessarily from the premises, and the truth of which can therefore be held with certainty. In natural theology, our principal concern is with metaphysical arguments, arguments that are demonstrations. But an argument need not be a demonstration in the strict sense in order to have real legitimacy and to contribute to our knowledge of the world, and we will also be dealing with arguments for the existence of God that result in probable conclusions. These arguments are commonly referred to as the moral arguments, or proofs, for the existence of God, in contrast to the metaphysical proofs.

What is it, in demonstrating the existence of God, that we are attempting to make evident? It is obviously the existence of God, the fact that God *is*. It is existence, then, which is the focus of our concern. But what are we to say of God's essence, His nature? Can we assure ourselves that, once we have demonstrated God's existence, and thus know that He is, we have at the same time attained a knowledge of *what* He is? We certainly cannot say this in any unqualified way, and we need to remind ourselves of a point often repeated by St. Thomas, that we will never have in this life a knowledge of the divine essence as such. That is the kind of knowledge which is reserved for the experience of the beatific vision, which, pointedly enough, St. Thomas refers to as *visio divinae essentiae,* the vision of the divine essence. But, as we will have occasion to discuss in later chapters, establishing the fact *that* God is does provide us with the basis from which we can reason with certainty to broad conclusions about the nature of God.

In demonstration, we begin with what is evident. What, specifically, counts for that beginning point in arguments that seek to demonstrate the existence of God? We recall that the specific mode of argument we will employ is the *quia* argument, which is to say, an argument that proceeds from effects to cause. The cause whose existence we seek to prove is the First Cause, the Cause of all that exists. So, the effects in this case, considered in the most comprehensive sense, would simply be the sum total of physical reality, the material world which is all around us and of which we are an integral part. There is no denying that in this case, with these effects, we are beginning with something which is obviously true for all of us. Only those with the temerity to deny the existence of the external world would have trouble with our beginning point.

Everything that we can know of God, as philosophers, is known through His effects, through His creation. In creating the world, God has, so to speak, left His imprint upon the world; thus we refer to the *vestigia Dei*, "the footprints of God." It is by tracing those footprints that we reason to the existence of the one who left them. The philosopher Jacques Maritain writes that "what our arguments render evident for us is not God Himself, but the testimony of Him contained in His vestiges, His signs or 'mirrors' here below."[1] He continues:

> In short, what we prove when we prove the existence of God is something which infinitely surpasses us—us and our ideas and proofs. To demonstrate the existence of God is not to submit Him to our grapplings, nor to define Him, nor to take possession of Him, nor to handle anything else than ideas that are feeble indeed with regard to such an object, nor to judge anything but our own radical dependence.[2]

Maritain's words are to be taken to heart, as sober reminders of the kind of intellectual humility which is required of anyone who takes on the tasks related to the aims of natural theology. We need, on the one hand, to be fully aware of the magnitude of what we are attempting to do, and yet, on the other hand, we should be under no illusions as to the severe limitations of what we succeed in accomplishing.

As already mentioned, the central focus for us, with respect to the metaphysical proofs for the existence of God, will be the Five Ways of St. Thomas Aquinas. These arguments stand above all the rest that have been formulated over the years for their crisp pointedness and power, but by the time St. Thomas came to formulate his arguments, there was already in place a rich and varied tradition of natural theological thinking, a tradition to which his contribution stands as a kind of shining culmination. In this chapter we will look at some of the principal efforts to demonstrate God's existence that were formulated before the time of St. Thomas, beginning with that offered by Plato, next turning to those that we owe to Aristotle and St. Augustine. We will end by devoting considerable attention to the famous ontological argument, which was given its most telling expression by St. Anselm of Canterbury.

The Platonic Proof

We have reason to believe, according to the learned opinion of Professor A. E. Taylor, that the philosophic science we now call natural theology began with Plato.[3] The textual evidence for this claim is to be found in Book X of Plato's *Laws*, the lengthiest book written by the great philosopher, and the last. Like the *Republic*, which Plato wrote in his middle years, the *Laws* is principally concerned with matters pertaining to civil society. What is the ideal state, the most perfect polity? How best might men be ruled? The answers that Plato gave to those and related questions in the *Laws* differ considerably from those he gave in the *Republic*, for he had moderated many of his earlier views. Like all of his works, the *Laws* is written in dialogue form, but it differs from his other dialogues in that in this case it is not "Socrates" who shapes and guides the discussion but the "Athenian."

The immediate context within which the argument appears is created by an exchange between the Athenian and his interlocutors in which they express their concern over the fact that so many of the youth of the city are advocating views which are essentially atheistic. Specifically, the youth have adopted the position that nature, which is to say, material reality, takes precedence over soul, or spiritual reality. They argue that the most primitive reality is material, and out of that came the soul, or spiritual reality. This, to the Athenian and his companions, is to have things just backwards, for it is soul that comes first, and out of soul comes material reality, or nature. They all agree that the erroneous ideas now being entertained by the youth, if left unchecked, could prove to be seriously detrimental to the welfare of the city, and that therefore a concerted effort must be made to persuade the young people, through argument, of the truth of the existence of God. And with that decision the scene is set for the presentation of the line of reasoning which is to be used for this purpose. It is particularly interesting to note that all of the interlocutors agree that people must be brought to see the truth of the existence of God through rational argument, and accept it freely. Coercion of any kind is out of the question.

Because the basic mistake of the atheist is putting nature before soul, material reality before spiritual reality, the principal aim of the argument will be to show that in fact it is soul that precedes nature. Before there was matter, there was spirit, and matter proceeds from spirit–that is the point the argument is intended to show.

After calling upon God to help him in his endeavors, the Athenian begins the argument by directing attention to a very basic and indisputable fact, the ubiquitousness of motion. Everywhere we look there are things, material objects, and those things are constantly in motion. An elementary distinction, underlying the various ways that motion can be classified, is to be recognized between (a) a thing that is capable of moving other things but not itself, and (b) a thing that is capable of moving both itself and other things. The latter represents the most important kind of motion.

Not only is this the most important kind of motion, but it occupies a unique place in the universe, for it is "suitable for all active and passive processes and [is] accurately termed the source of change and motion in all things that exist."[4] This self-moving motion "can generate itself" and is "infinitely superior" to all else.[5] And it must be recognized as "first, in ancestry as well as in power."[6]

The Athenian gets to the heart of the argument when he invites us to consider all the multitudinous instances of motion that are taking place in the universe, where one thing produces change in another thing, and then that thing in turn produces change in yet another thing, and so on, and so on. In considering such a sequence, he asks, is there to be found an originating source of all the change that is taking place? If there is such a source, it cannot be something whose motion is explained by something outside itself. No, this initial principle "can hardly be anything except the change effected by self-generated motion."[7]

It is "self-generating motion, then [that] is the source of all motion."[8] The next step in the argument is to establish that self-generating motion and soul are one and the same thing, for "self-generating motion," according to the Athenian, is nothing else than the definition of "soul." It is soul, then, spiritual reality, which is the most ancient thing there is, and which is the generating source of all material reality. Matter thus takes second place in relation to spirit. Soul is posited as the cause of all things, and is in fact divine in nature. The governing motion of Soul, or souls (the argument makes use of both the singular and plural forms), is rational, and this means that it must be circular motion, for, the Athenian argues, circular motion is what he calls reasonable motion, whereas linear motion is unreasonable. The general conclusion reached by these various argumentative considerations is nicely summed up in the following passage.

> "A soul or souls—and perfectly virtuous souls at that—
> have been shown to be the cause of the phenomena
> [i.e., of all moving material things], and whether it is
> by their living presence in matter that they direct all
> the heavens, or by some other means, we shall insist
> that these souls are gods."[9]

And thus Plato has given us what is very likely the first systematic philosophical argument for the existence of God. That he himself was aware that he was doing something novel may be indicated by the fact that he has the Athenian say, "So it looks as if I must now argue along rather unfamiliar lines."[10] Plato established a precedent of singular importance when he based his argument on the empirical fact of motion, and his influence in that respect echoes down the ages to the present day. Perhaps the strongest point made in the argument is the idea that motion, if it is going to be explained at all, must be explained in terms of a mover which, besides accounting for the motion of everything else that moves, accounts for its own motion as well. Or, as Plato puts it, this initial mover is self-generating motion.

There is, it must be noted, a serious metaphysical problem with the idea of a self-moving mover, a problem which, as we shall see, will be later solved by Aristotle. For all that, however, Plato was quite right in seeing that in order for anything to be the originating cause of all motion, it could not itself be dependent for its motion on anything outside itself. If that were the case, then it would not be truly first, and we could not avoid the problem of infinite regress, a problem which we will take up in due season.

Plato's identifying soul, or spiritual reality, with the self-generating motion which is the source of all motion, seems reasonable enough, in that "self-generating motion" is not an altogether bad definition for soul, or spiritual being. But what is the precise nature of this being? Are we talking about souls, or Soul, about gods, or God? As the argument stands, it seems to me that it can be interpreted either way. In the summarizing passage I quoted above, Plato expresses doubts as to whether soul or souls cause the motion of things by "their living presence in matter," or by some other means. This is a rather serious question to leave hanging in the air, for if the souls exercise their influence by being present within matter, then it would seem that we would have the philosophic foundation for something like an animistic religion.

The Aristotelian Proof

The proof for the existence of God that we have from Aristotle also proceeds from an initial consideration of the ubiquity of motion. This should not surprise us, for Aristotle studied at Plato's Academy in Athens for some twenty years, and it seems reasonable to suppose that he was much influenced by both the manner and the matter of his mentor's reasoning. The most developed form of Aristotle's argument is found in Book VIII of the *Physics*, but there are important embellishments to the argument provided in Book XII of the *Metaphysics*.[11] For Aristotle, movement, or change, was not only pervasive throughout the universe, it was eternal as well. The physical world always existed, and it is forever in motion.

The two governing ideas in Aristotle's proof, ideas which will later be adopted by St. Thomas and taken as his own, are as follows: (i) everything that moves (i.e., that changes in any way whatever) is moved by another, and (ii) in any system of moving things, all of which are dependent for their movement on something other than themselves, one eventually must arrive, in order to explain all of this movement, at a mover which is *not* dependent on another.

The claim that everything that is moved is moved by another, is a fact which may not be immediately obvious to us. Indeed, it might initially strike us as not a fact at all. How about, we might ask, living beings? Do we not properly describe them as self-moving? Yes, we do, but if we consider the matter closely we come to discover that the movement of what we call self-moving beings has a revealing duality at the bottom of it; there is a distinction between the moved and the mover. Consider, for example, a human person who moves from one place to another. Quite apparently, it is the body that we see moving. But would we say that the body moves itself? No, we would say that the body is moved by the will. When Jane moves from basement to kitchen it is because Jane has decided to make that move. But how about the will? Could not we say that the will moves itself? In a way, yes, but it would not be right to assert that the will is self-moving in a completely unqualified way, for the will, very importantly, is moved by perceived goods that are external to itself and the possession of which is desired. Jane wills to move from the basement to the kitchen because there is something about being in the kitchen right now that represents a present good for her.

But the fundamental philosophical explanation for the fact that everything that moves (i.e., changes) is moved by another is found in the very important metaphysical distinction between potency and act, as it is applied to motion. Obviously, nothing could move in a particular way unless it had the capacity, or the potential, to do so. Something that is moving in a particular way here and now is said to be "in act" with respect to that movement. Now, nothing can be both in potency and in act with respect to a particular movement, for that would involve a contradiction. How so? Such a state of affairs would involve a situation where, at one and the same time, we have something that *can* move (future) and *is* moving (present). A non-moving thing could not cause its own motion, for in order to do so it would have to be both non-moving and moving at the same time.

If we accept it as fact that everything that moves is moved by another, cannot we then be content with accepting a world that is made up exclusively of such things? No, for such a world would be a world without an explanation for itself. If we have a system (for example, the actual universe) which is composed of things which move but no one of which can, of itself, provide the explanation for its movement, we have to ask: Where did the system itself come from? Whence all this movement which cannot explain itself? The idea Aristotle is developing here might be easier to grasp if we think of a series of things all of which are moved by another, that is, no one of which contains within itself the explanation for its motion. Let us say the movement of each particular moving thing is dependent on the movement of the thing immediately preceding it. Now, we might be tempted to say, in order to explain the movement of all of the moving things in the series, that there is no beginning to the series, that it is made up entirely of things moved by another, and it goes back indefinitely. That might seem to be a reasonable solution to the problem, but actually it won't do. Why not? Because we are seeking for an explanation for the movement of all these things, and if we simply claim that the series is endless we provide no explanation at all for that movement. What is the explanation, we are fully entitled to ask, for this supposedly endless series of movers? To appeal to an infinite regress is only to dodge the whole problem of coming up with an explanation by putting it off indefinitely.

We must, then, Aristotle argued, conclude to the existence of a First Mover, by which he meant a mover which is the explanation for everything that moves, but which is itself unmoving. Right here, in the fact that Aristotle's explanatory source of movement is unmoving, we see a stark contrast to Plato's explanatory source of movement, which was described as self-moving. (For Aristotle, movement or change, even if generated by the moving beings itself, would be a sign of imperfection.)We must not imagine this First Mover as being the first in a series of the kind of moving things described above; the First Mover is the explanation for the series itself, but is completely outside the series. There is, then, "only one movent [i.e., mover], the first of unmoved things, which being eternal will be the principle of motion to everything else."[12] This Prime Mover, though the cause of all physical movement, is itself immaterial, "without parts and without magnitude." [13] In the *Metaphysics*, now using the term "God" rather than "Prime Mover," Aristotle writes: "We say, therefore, that God is a living being, eternal, most good, so that life and duration continuous and eternal belong to God; for this *is* God."[14]

Given the conclusions that Aristotle arrived at through his argument, it is little wonder that St. Thomas showed great respect for the ancient Greek philosopher's mode of reasoning. It is worth remarking, however, that the God of Aristotle is not the Creator God of St. Thomas. Indeed, the very notion of creation was quite foreign to Aristotle, as it was for all of the ancient Greeks. We recall that for Aristotle the world was eternal. It was not created, because it never had a beginning. The Prime Mover of Aristotle can properly be understood as the eternal cause of an eternal world.

The Augustinian Proof

Just as the theology which was developed by St. Thomas Aquinas was heavily dependent on the thought of Aristotle, so the theology of which St. Augustine was the author was heavily dependent on the thought of Plato, especially as that thought was given expression in the philosophy known as Neoplatonism. This was a version of Platonism which was developed in the early centuries of the Christian era by the philosopher Plotinus (A.D. 205–270). Given this association, then, it is not surprising that St. Augustine's proof for the existence of God should have to it a distinctly Platonic flavor.

Though St. Augustine of course maintained that we have a sure knowledge of the existence of God through faith, he also makes clear that we can arrive at such knowledge through natural reason, albeit this knowledge, in comparison to that which comes to us through faith, is "a sure, though, as yet, very inadequate form of knowledge."[15] If one sets out to prove the existence of God, one must obviously have at the outset some sort of understanding of the term "God." St. Augustine begins his argument by asserting that we "call that reality God which has nothing superior to it."[16] The argument culminates in the conclusion that there is in fact such a reality. He gets to that conclusion through a close examination of the nature of truth, for it is precisely truth, he contends, which is the reality that has nothing superior to it. This he endeavors to show by calling attention to two principal manifestations of truth, mathematics and wisdom, which he treats very interestingly and ends by concluding that they are pretty much the same thing.

When we come upon any mathematical truth, such as the arithmetical statement that $7 + 3 = 10$, or when we contemplate the various orderly relations that exist among numbers in general, we are immediately cognizant of the fact that we are face to face with truths which, because manifestly and incontestably true, and unchanging in their truth, have to them a very special quality. There is in mathematical truth, according to St. Augustine, something of the eternal, for "seven and three are ten, not only now, but forever."[17] Number has to it a certain transcendent aspect, and therefore, by knowing number, i.e., any mathematical truth, we are led to a reality which is superior to our own mind. Truth which is superior to the human mind, a truth which provides the guidelines for the workings of the mind, cannot be a product of the mind itself. Our minds are changeable, but this truth which guides the mind is unchangeable. The fact that the human mind is able to know truth at all, but especially mathematical truth, points necessarily, then, to something which is superior to the mind, the truth by which the mind knows truth itself.

St. Augustine brings his argument, which is cast in dialogue form, to a close with this passage: "You granted that if I could prove that there was something above our minds, you would admit it was God, provided that there was nothing higher. I agreed and stated that it would be enough for me to prove this point. For if there is anything more excellent, then this is God; if not, then truth itself is God. In either case, you cannot deny that God exists, which was the question we proposed to examine in our discussion."[18]

There is much to admire in St. Augustine's argument, and at every turn it shows the workings of a wonderfully keen and probing intellect. The argument is characterized by very careful and methodical reasoning, especially noteworthy for its meticulous thoroughness. In the final analysis, however, the argument cannot be said to represent a genuine demonstration of the existence of God, and that is because it relies on a kind of knowledge which the human mind could not be expected to possess. To better see the nature of the problem here, let us recall the main thrust of the argument: mathematical knowledge, which the human mind possesses, represents transcendent and eternal truth, the kind of truth that is clearly superior to the human mind, and—this seems to be the implication—which the human mind, left to itself, would not be capable of attaining. Given the special quality of this kind of knowledge, then, we can be said to be effectively in contact with *the* transcendent, with *the* truth, which is God Himself. What the argument is maintaining, in sum, is that because mathematical truths are eternal truths (it always was and always will be the case that $7 + 3 = 10$), and because we can be in possession of such truths, we have, in that fact, a proof for the existence of God, the eternal Truth. Mathematics can lead us to God.

Mathematical knowledge, as we know from metaphysics, pertains to what we call the second level of abstraction. All mathematical concepts, though they are in themselves and just as such immaterial, have their ultimate source in the material realm, as do all our concepts, for mathematics is chiefly concerned with quantity, and quantity is the fundamental property of matter. We do not have an intuitive knowledge of number, as St. Augustine seems to have believed, but we come to know number though the knowledge of physical things in the external world that are capable of being numbered. We do not begin with the abstract concept of seven; we begin with seven concrete objects which we then count. Influenced by Plato as he was, St. Augustine looked upon number, not as following upon a knowledge of specific physical things, but as preceding them. And it therefore became part of his philosophical doctrine that our knowledge of number does not come from the senses but is somehow directly intuited, but by doing so he was assigning to natural reason a capacity it simply does not have. If, taking exception to St. Augustine's point of view, we deny that the human mind has some kind of immediate knowledge of transcendental truth, as we must, then we cannot appeal to such knowledge as a basis for proving the existence of God.

Statement of the Ontological Argument

We now turn to one of the most famous, and controversial, arguments for the existence of God, the ontological argument. It is an argument we have already been introduced to; we saw, for instance, that it figures in one of the objections St. Thomas deals with when he argues for the position that it is possible to prove the existence of God. [19] Before we get into the particulars of the argument, we must first say a few words about the significance of its name. It is called the ontological arguments because it reflects the philosophical position known as ontologism. Ontologism, generally considered, is a point of view that tends to regard existence, on the natural level, as inseparable from essence. What this means, in practical terms, is that the ontologist supposes that if he can have a clear and distinct idea of something, which would put him in contact with the essence of the thing, then, because of the way essence and existence are related to one another, he would have, with that idea, knowledge of the existence of the thing. This is a seriously defective way of looking at things, for the ontologist is supposing that essence and existence are related on the natural level, that is, within created being, in a way that suggests what can only obtain within the divine nature. In short, the ontologist is confusing the natural and supernatural orders.

As a matter of fact, there is only one being about whom one can say, indeed, must say, that essence necessarily implies existence, and that is God Himself. To be most precise about it, there is no real distinction, in God, between essence and existence; they are one. What this means is that it is the very nature of God "to be." Because of the erroneous way the ontologist sees the relation between essence and existence, he is forever exposed to the temptation of thinking that if he has a clear conceptual grasp of something (meaning, again, that he grasps the thing's essence), then he is thereby entitled to entertain the possibility that the thing in question actually exists. But this simply does not follow. Now, the idea with which the ontological argument is dealing is not just any idea, but an idea that is absolutely unique, the idea of God. Does that make a difference as far as the force of the ontological argument is concerned, giving it a legitimacy that it would not have if it were dealing with any other idea? No, as we shall attempt to make clear in what follows.

There will be three steps in our treatment of the ontological argument. First, we shall present the argument in full, according to the classic formulation of it given by St. Anselm (1033–1109), in a work of his called the *Proslogion.* Second, we shall provide a detailed explication of the argument, in order to give full exposure to its inner workings. Finally, we shall submit the argument to careful, critical scrutiny, showing that it does not in fact succeed in what it intends to do. Here, then, is the ontological argument as expressed by St. Anselm.

> And so, Lord, do thou, who dost give understanding to faith, give me, so far as thou knowest it to be profitable, to understand that thou art as we believe; and that thou art that which we believe. And, indeed, we believe that thou art a being than which nothing greater can be conceived. Or is there no such nature, since the fool hath said in his heart, there is no God? (Psalm XIV, 1). But, at any rate, this very fool, when he hears of this being of which I speak—a being than which nothing greater can be conceived—understands what he hears, and what he understands is in his understanding; although he does not understand it to exist.
>
> For, it is one thing for an object to be in the understanding, and another to understand that the object exists. When a painter first conceives of what he

will afterwards perform, he has it in his understanding, but he does not yet understand it to be, because he has not yet performed it. But after he has made the painting, he both has it in his understanding, and he understands that it exists, because he has made it.

Hence, even the fool is convinced that something exists in the understanding, at least, than which nothing greater can be conceived. For, when he hears of this, he understands it. And whatever is understood, exists in the understanding. And assuredly that, than which nothing greater can be conceived, cannot exist in the understanding alone. For, suppose it exists in the understanding alone: then it can be conceived to exist in reality; which is greater.

Therefore, if that, than which nothing greater can be conceived, exists in the understanding alone, the very being, than which nothing greater can be conceived, is one, than which a greater can be conceived. But obviously this is impossible. Hence, there is no doubt that there exists a being, than which nothing greater can be conceived, and it exists both in the understanding and in reality.[20]

Explication of the Ontological Argument

In discussing St. Augustine's argument, above, we noted that it is marked by distinct Platonic influences. Somewhat the same thing can be said of St. Anselm's argument. This is easily explained, for St. Anselm was thoroughly Augustinian in his way of thinking, and it is quite natural, therefore, that he should have adopted the Platonic propensities of his great mentor.

St. Anselm's motto was *Fides Quaerens Intellectum*, "Faith Seeking Understanding." The spirit behind that motto, which is to say, the spirit of the man whose motto it was, is clearly shown in the very first sentence of the argument, in which St. Anselm prays that he might "understand that thou art as we believe; and that thou art that which we believe." For him, it can rightly be said, the whole purpose of philosophy, of the ordered exercise of human reason, is to illuminate the faith. In this sense, then, philosophy is very properly regarded as *ancilla theologiae*, "the handmaid of theology."

One of the disputed questions that continues to revolve around this argument is, Just to what extent did St. Anselm consider the argument to be a demonstration in the strict sense? Did he have it in mind really to prove that God exists, or was the argument intended rather simply to make more explicit the nature of a God whose existence was already taken for granted? The second sentence of the argument reads: "And, indeed, *we believe* that thou art a being than which nothing greater can be conceived." (emphasis added) Now, if one begins by attesting to one's belief in God, it would seem that one is not involved in a project to prove God's existence. Faith gives sure knowledge of God's existence, hence there would be no need to prove it.

But to interpret the sentence just quoted in that way would be to read too much into it. By initially acknowledging his belief in God, St. Anselm is not thereby telling us that he is not engaging in genuine natural theology in what follows. He is, after all, doing no more than what we are doing, as believers, in this course. We freely acknowledge our belief, but we make no direct appeal to the knowledge it provides us with as we exercise our natural reason as philosophers. St. Anselm's attitude in this regard is made clear in the sentence that immediately follows the one quoted just above. The fact that, at the very outset of the argument, St. Anselm introduces "the fool who says in his heart that there is no God" would seem clearly to indicate that the argument is not directed toward believers, but toward those who deny the existence of God. I think we are justified, then, in understanding the argument as intended to serve as a bonafide demonstration.

The first key point of the argument is the observation that even the atheist must have a basic, working idea of God, otherwise his very atheism would make no sense. One cannot coherently deny something unless he has some sort of understanding of what it is he is denying. Both theist and atheist must have some shared notions of what it is they are respectively affirming or denying. So, then, the atheist is aware of what he is referring to when he uses the term "God." He might say to us: "Yes, I understand what you mean by 'God.' You mean a supreme being, the source of all being, the creator of the universe. I understand the concept perfectly well, but I maintain that there is no such being that answers to that description." To reiterate the first point: The atheist has firmly fixed in his mind an *idea* of God.

The next point St. Anselm makes in the argument is to draw a very clear distinction between purely mental existence and real, i.e., extra-mental, existence. He vividly brings home this point by using an example of an artist painter and his painting. The example holds up for our consideration the stark difference between a conceived work of art and an executed work of art. Before a painter picks up his brush and begins his artistic labors, he first forms an idea in his mind of what he wants to paint. And that may be a very precise idea. So, the artist, at this stage, understands the work of art, but he understands it as existing only in his mind. And he is also quite aware of the difference between a work of art as existing only mentally, and its existing extra-mentally, as an actually existing objective artifact, as well. As St. Anselm puts it, the artist, before executing the work, "has it in his understanding, but he does not yet understand it to be." But after he completes the painting, "he both has it in his understanding, and he understands that it exists."

Next, St. Anselm returns to the attitude of the atheist, the fool who says there is no God. Like the artist, who has a clear idea of a painting not yet in existence, the atheist has a clear idea of God whose existence he denies. St. Anselm puts the case very strongly, asserting that the atheist is *convinced* that the proper understanding of "God" is of a being "than which nothing greater can be conceived." That is his idea of God, and, as an idea, it is understood by him as existing in his own mind. Indeed, the atheist would argue, that is the only way "God" exists. There is nothing in the extra-mental world corresponding to that idea.

The subsequent step in the argument is the most critical one. St. Anselm invites us to consider the following. We have in our minds a clear understanding of the meaning of "God," an idea that conceives God as a being "than which nothing greater can be conceived." As an idea, it of course exists—mentally. But, St. Anselm argues, given the unique nature of this idea, it cannot exist only mentally. It must exist extra-mentally as well, which is to say, simply, it is an idea for which there is a corresponding entity in the extra-mental world, and that entity is God.

That is the nub of the argument. In order to be able to appreciate its force, we need first to accept St. Anselm's guiding assumption that real, i.e., extra-mental, existence is greater than mere mental existence.

This we can easily do. An actually existing painting is immeasurably superior to the mere idea of a painting. Now, the idea of God, as a being "than which nothing greater can be conceived," is a true idea, but it would not be a true idea if it were only an idea. Let us suppose that it were only an idea. By doing so, we find ourselves in a contradictory position, for if this idea of God exists only as an idea, that would mean that in fact something greater than it *could* be conceived. And what would that something be? It would be something that exists in a manner greater than the manner in which an idea exists—i.e., as an actually existing extra-mental reality. In order to avoid contradiction, then, and to have a true understanding of the idea of God as a being "than which nothing greater can be conceived," we must concede that God actually exists. It is impossible that He could exist only as an idea in our minds, for such is an inferior form of existence in relation to actual existence, and God would not be in fact the greatest of beings if He existed in an inferior way, as no more than an idea in our minds.

Criticism of the Ontological Argument

St. Anselm's argument turns on a vitally important notion that is never explicitly expressed, and that is the notion that, with respect to the divine nature, essence implies existence. St. Anselm uses the phrase "than which nothing greater can be conceived," which certainly serves as a pointed descriptive phrase as applied to God. Without falsifying the saint's intent, I think we would be justified in substituting for that phrase another, namely, "a being whose very nature it is to be."

Now, it is of course quite true that, with God, essence necessarily implies existence, for in the divine nature essence and existence are one; the very meaning of God, so to speak, is "to be." But how do we know that about the divine nature? There are two ways we can come to know this truth, through faith, or through demonstration. But if we rely on either way, the argument is vitiated. If the knowledge comes through faith, we can scarcely use it as a premiss in an argument that purports to prove the existence of God. How could we expect to convince an atheist of the existence of God if he is required to accept a premiss which would be self-evident only to a believer? The fact that essence and existence are one in God can be demonstrated, as St. Thomas shows,[21] but there is no demonstration for the fact in this argument. And because there is no demonstration here, making evident the unity of essence and existence in God, it remains non-self-evident. But that means, then, that it cannot serve as a premiss for an argument, for premisses must be self-evidently true.

But there is a much more serious difficulty involved here, if we assume, as we justifiably may, that the unity of essence and existence in God is being used as a premiss in the argument, and that is the fact that such knowledge has to do with the *nature* of God. But what is the whole intent of the argument? It is to prove the *existence* of God. In any effort to prove the existence of a being, we cannot use any knowledge pertaining to the nature of the being; that would be assuming the kind of knowledge which we could not be expected to know. First we must answer the question, *An sit*? Whether something exists? Only when we have answered that question in the affirmative can we go on to answer the question, *Quid est*? What is the nature of this being whose existence we have ascertained?

In terms of terminology we introduced earlier, what we have in the ontological argument, in effect, is a *propter quid* demonstration rather than a *quia* demonstration. A *propter quid* demonstration, we recall, is one that proceeds from cause to effect. But such a demonstration cannot properly be used here, and that is because the cause is nothing less than God Himself, whose existence we are attempting to prove.

The argument was subject to pointed criticism in St. Anselm's own day. A monk by the name of Gaunilon, from the monastery at Marmoutier, in France, argued that one could conceive of a superlative entity, such as an Isle of the Blessed, but the fact that one can entertain an idea of such an entity by no means necessitates its actual existence. St. Anselm responds to this criticism by first agreeing that we can indeed come up with all sorts of fantastic ideas which have nothing that corresponds to them in the real world. But, he effectively argues, the idea of God is like no other idea the human mind can conceive, because, in conceiving it, we must necessarily be thinking about a being, the Supreme Being, who actually exists. St. Anselm is perfectly correct in maintaining that the idea of God is like no other idea we can think, but, once again, we know that God must necessarily exist either through faith or through demonstration.

St. Thomas, although he does so in his typically respectful way, takes serious exception to the ontological argument, and does not accept it as having true demonstrative force. In his response to the argument we find in the *Summa Contra Gentiles*, he points out, among other things, that there is nothing that should lead us to believe, as St. Anselm seemingly assumes to be the case, that every atheist is going to conceive of God as a being "than which a greater cannot be conceived." Human beings have shown themselves capable of coming up with all sorts of wild ideas to which they attach the name "God." And St. Thomas reminds us that many men have conceived of God in purely material terms, as when, for example, they regard the physical world and God as one and the same thing. Such is the approach of the pantheists. If one thinks of God as a material being, as some eminent philosophers have done, then one is not thinking of God at all, for materiality implies contingency, and God is necessary being.

Furthermore, St. Thomas calls our attention to the important distinction between things that are self-evident in themselves (*per se nota secundum se*) and those things that are self-evident with respect to us (*per se nota quoad nos*). Now, the proposition "God exists" is self-evidently true—in itself, not according to us. It is self-evident in itself because in fact essence implies existence in God. It is impossible that God not be. But this is not self-evident to us. We can know "God exists" as a self-evident truth only through the knowledge supplied to us by faith, or by reason, through which we learn that, in God, essence implies existence. Looked at from a logical point of view, we say that the statement "God exists" is self-evident in itself because it is an analytic statement, one, that is, whose predicate is contained in its subject. So, once again, we are not demonstrating God's existence if we begin with the idea of God as a necessarily existing being, although this is an entirely correct idea.

St. Thomas gets to the heart of the matter in his criticism of the ontological argument when he writes as follows: "Now, from the fact that that which is indicated by the name of God is conceived by the intellect, it does not follow that God exists anywhere else except in the intellect. Hence, that than which a greater cannot be thought will likewise not have to exist anywhere else except in the intellect. From this it does not follow that there exists in reality something than which a greater cannot be thought."[22] St. Thomas's point here is very simple and straightforward, and he makes it with the emphasis characteristic of the uncompromising realist that he was. The fact that we hold in our minds an idea, an idea even of the most exalted sort—and what could be more exalted than the idea of the greatest conceivable being—does not allow us to conclude, on the basis of that idea alone, that there is, in the extra-mental world, a real existent that answers to that idea. Real being, including divine being, is not established by the *idea* of real being. Real being is established only by real being.

CHAPTER FOUR

The Metaphysical Foundations of the Proofs

Preparing for the Proofs

Many philosophers have gone to the Five Ways of St. Thomas, studied them, and come away convinced that the arguments do not do what they purport to do—prove the existence of God. The explanation for this reaction, in almost every case, is that the philosophers went to the proofs quite unprepared. To follow with proper understanding any sound metaphysical proof for the existence of God is not the easiest thing in the world to do, and St. Thomas did not hesitate to advance the opinion that it was an accomplishment which, for a variety of reasons, was beyond the reach of most people. "Only a few," he writes, "can arrive at the truth about God through philosophical reasoning, and only after a long time, and even then coming away with ideas that are admixed with many errors."[1] And it is precisely for that reason that we have been given, through the medium of faith, a certain knowledge of the existence of God.

But anyone who wants to gain an understanding of the metaphysical proofs for God's existence must come to the arguments in which those proofs are couched with the requisite preparation. This means that one must be well-versed in an important set of key principles of metaphysics. For someone lacking these principles, or having only a tenuous grasp of them, the language of the arguments will not be intelligible, with the obvious result that the ideas contained in them will not be efficiently communicated. Before we launch into our study of the Five Ways of St. Thomas, we will, in this chapter, spend some time in reviewing certain metaphysical concepts the proper understanding of which is imperative for a proper understanding of the arguments themselves. Even Scholastic philosophers, or would-be Scholastic philosophers, have been known seriously to misconstrue one or another of St. Thomas's arguments, and this because of a defective knowledge of the principles that underlie them.

The Arguments Are Existential

Each of the five arguments St. Thomas proposes are intended to prove real existence, and for that reason we say that the arguments are existential. They are not merely exercises in logical thinking, in other words. An argument is said to be existential if the propositions that compose it refer to real things in the objective order. A given proposition can be fully meaningful without being existential. For example, "Centaurs have tails"; "Hamlet lived in Denmark." A coherent argument can be made out of such propositions. Let us do so with the first statement.

> Every centaur has a tail
> Sidney is a centaur.
> Therefore, Sidney has a tail.

That is a valid argument, even though existentially it makes no sense. It makes no sense existentially because there are not, of course, in the real world, any actually existing centaurs. They can exist only as ideas in the mind.

Less bizarrely, we can construct a mathematical argument that demonstrates conclusively that an isosceles triangle, whose base angles are equal, has angles under the base that are also equal. This is incontrovertibly true, yet it need have no existential import at all. That is to say, the argument makes no claim about whether or not there are any actually existing isosceles triangles in the world. In contrast to these types of arguments, the arguments of the Five Ways are existential. They intend to show that God actually exists, not simply as an idea in the mind, but as a real being, indeed the being of beings, and existing external to the mind.

Another way of putting it is to say that the arguments are more than simply formally correct. The argument above about Sidney the centaur is formally correct; it is valid. But it is an unsound argument because its conclusion is false, and its conclusion is false because it is based on premises which are fantastic rather than real. In constructing arguments proving the existence of God, we must certainly have a care for formal correctness; that is, we must insure that our arguments follow the rules of logic. But the contents of the arguments must also be sound. The propositions that compose them must be true, and they must be rooted in the objective order.

The Analogical Status of the Conclusion

All language referring to God is analogical, meaning that it steers a middle course between two extreme modes of thought, either of which, if adopted, would burden us with an erroneous understanding of God. We say that the conclusion common to all of the arguments of St. Thomas is to be taken analogically. That conclusion is simply, "God exists." What does it mean, in more specific terms, to say that this statement is to be taken analogically? In metaphysics, we argue that all being is to be understood analogically, which is to say that there is both commonness and uncommonness to being, when looked at collectively. All being is common, on the one hand, because every single being, by reason of its status as a being, actually exists. All being is uncommon, on the other hand, because, though every being actually exists, no two beings actually exist in precisely the same way.

Let us consider more closely the conclusion at which each of the arguments of the Five Ways arrives: "God exists." The statement claims real existence for God, a real being, but the existence that is involved here is like that of no other being. God really exists, but in a manner that is absolutely unique to God Himself. The operative word in the conclusion is "exists." If we were to understand that word univocally—that would be one of the extreme modes of thinking referred to above—we would be then thinking that God exists in the same way as any other being, so that there would be no appreciable existential difference between the statement, "God exists," and the statement, "A paramecium exists." We would be erring in the extremely opposite way if we were to interpret "exists" equivocally. In doing so we would be supposing that there is no bond whatever between the being of God and that of any other being.

Someone who understands existence or being univocally would be effectively assuming a pantheistic position. If being is unqualifiedly one, then everything is God; "Nature" and "God" become synonymous terms. Such was the position taken by the philosopher Baruch Spinoza (1632–1677). On the other hand, someone who understands existence or being equivocally is committed to the notion that there is no real relation between man and God, between creatures and the Creator. There would be no commonality between statements like, "God exists" and "The governor of Minnesota exists." We could understand what it means to say that a governor exists, but the statement, "God exists," would not register with us at all, for "exists" in this case would be completely unintelligible.

Substantial Being

The arguments of the Five Ways deal with substantial being, which is to say, being that exists through itself and not through another. The whole science of metaphysics, Aristotle tells us, revolves around substantial being. Substantial being is independent being in relation to accidental being. The latter can only exists through other being, i.e., substantial being, but substantial being exists, again, through itself. A substance is an actual existent, a real being and not a fiction. You and I are substances. So is the elm tree standing outside my window, and the house finch perching on one of its branches. Anyone who is in the least bit confused about the nature of substantial being is in no position to be able to appreciate the full import of what is taking place in the arguments of the Five Ways of St. Thomas, for to be confused about the nature of substantial being is to be confused about existence itself.

There have been quite a few philosophers in modern times who have displayed just such confusion. The philosopher John Locke (1632–1704)), for example, assumed somewhat of an agnostic position toward substantial being, leaving the impression that substance was something whose existence it was necessary to accept for logical purposes, but of which we could not have any reliable knowledge. Another philosopher of roughly the same era as Locke's, David Hume (1711–1776), went a step further and simply dispensed with substantial being altogether. This was a rather brash theoretical move on his part, but of course it had no effect on reality. David Hume might regard substance as inconsequential, but Hume himself remained nonetheless firmly in place as a substance among substances.

When we conclude, in our arguments, to the existence of God, we are affirming, of God, substantial existence, though analogously so. We have an understanding of substances as subsistent being, through our knowledge of material substances. With that understanding we proceed analogously, and conclude that God is as it were the supreme substance, for He is subsistent being itself.

Contingent Being and Necessary Being

The Third Way of St. Thomas is called the argument from contingent being. In order fully to comprehend the argument we must have a firm grasp of the nature of contingent being, and how contingent being differs from necessary being. In refurbishing our memories with respect to this important distinction, let us start with necessary being, for that is very easily identified. There is only one unqualifiedly necessary being, and that is God Himself. As a necessary being, God is a being for whom it is impossible not to be. It would be a contradiction in terms of the most radical kind to say that God does not exist, for it is of the very essence of God to be. But we arrive at the existence of God as necessary being by beginning with contingent being.

If necessary being is being that cannot not be, the essence of contingent being is that it is being that *can* not be. St. Thomas often uses the expression "participated being" in referring to contingent being, which expression has the advantage of calling attention to the fact that contingent being does not exist by reason of anything intrinsic to itself. Contingent being participates in being in the sense that, in contrast to necessary being, which simply *is* being, contingent being *has* being, as a possession that comes to it from outside, and by way of gift.

We know contingent being precisely as contingent in a very direct and experiential way. First and foremost, we know ourselves as contingent being, for we know that at one time we did not exist, and we know that some day, with respect to our present mode of existence as creatures composed of body and soul, we will cease to exist. And we are contingent beings immersed in a veritable sea of contingent beings. Everywhere around us the continuing drama of generation and corruption is being played out; beings come into existence and beings go out of existence.

Necessary being has the sufficient reason for its existence within itself. We can put this truth in plain terms by saying that the explanation for God's being is God's being. Things are quite different with contingent being. The explanation for contingent being does not lie within contingent being itself, and that is why we have to look beyond contingent being in order to account for its existing at all, and in doing so we are led ultimately, inevitably, to necessary being. The dependency of contingent being on necessary being is total and continuous. Because contingent being is being whose existence is in no way imperative, there was a time when it did not exist, and that means that it had to be brought into existence. But the total dependency of contingent being on necessary being is emphasized by the fact that it must at every instant be maintained in existence by necessary being. Should the causal influence of necessary being cease, contingent being would immediately lapse into nothingness.

Potency and Act

It is to the great genius of Aristotle that we owe the illuminating analysis of change in terms of the principles of potency and act. Arguably, of St. Thomas's Five Ways, the first, the argument from motion, is the most potent, from a purely metaphysical point of view. We have already seen how both Plato and Aristotle built their arguments for the existence of God on the universal fact of motion or change. No one who is ignorant of the seminal principles of potency and act, and how they relate to motion, would be able to respond with comprehension to the metaphysical force of St. Thomas's first proof for the existence of God.

Aristotle identified the essence of motion, or of any change of whatever sort, as the actualization of a potency. If we were to consider a change of any kind, we would immediately recognize that there are certain basic elements necessarily involved in the process. There is, first and foremost, and obviously, the thing that undergoes the change; and then there is the change itself, which can be broadly described as a transition from one state to another. When we focus our attention on the thing that changes, the principle of potency comes into play.

Clearly, nothing would be able to change in a particular way unless it had the innate capacity to change in a particular way. A green apple can become a red apple because it has the capacity for that kind of qualitative change. More precisely, we say that a green apple has the potency to become a red apple, or that a green apple is in potency (*in potentia)* with respect to a red apple.

Another very basic point: every change involves a specific lack on the part of the thing that changes. A green apple can become a red apple only because its is not already a red apple. The lack of redness in a green apple is called a privation; it is that which a thing capable of change acquires after the change has taken place. We have described every change as a transition from one state to another. Let us call the first state the beginning point of the change (*terminus a quo*), and the second state the end point of the change (*terminus ad quem*). The green apple is in potency with respect to being a red apple, but it is in act (*in actu*) with respect to being a green apple, which is simply a technical way of saying that it actually is, here and now, a green apple, but it can become a red apple. After the change has taken place, and the once green apple is now a shiny red apple, the red apple is in act with respect to its being red. The potentially for becoming a red apple, which had been invested in the green apple, has now been realized.

With this vocabulary in hand, let us look at the process of change itself in order to reveal what Aristotle meant when he called it the actualization of potential. Having introduced an apple as an example of the thing that changes, we may as well stick with that. We begin at the *terminus a quo*, state one, with a green apple. The apple is now in act with respect to greenness, and in potency with respect to redness. And the privation of the green apple is redness, for that is precisely what it lacks, and toward which the change will be directed. We say the change is the actualization of a potency because what is happening in change is the realization, the bringing into actual being, of a specific capacity in a thing that has that capacity. In this case it would be a green apple, capable of becoming a red apple, actually becoming a red apple. And we could say that the change just as such is the intermediate state between the *terminus a quo* and the *terminus ad quem*, the state where the potentiality is in the process of being realized, as the apple reddens and thus gradually gains the color which it was once lacking. At the end of the change, when the *terminus ad quem* has been reached and the apple is as red as it can possibly be, then the apple is in act with respect to redness, which, once again, simply means that it actually is red.[2]

A very important thing to note about the relation between potency and act is that no one thing can be both in potency and in act at the same time and with respect to the same kind of change. An apple cannot at the same time be both potentially a red apple and actually a red apple. That would be a contradiction. But there would be no contradiction in the circumstance where a particular apple is actually a green apple and potentially a red apple. Here potency and act do not relate to the same thing at the same time.[3]

Given the central role played by the principles of potency and act in all change, it is easy to see how they then must be part of the very identity of contingent being. Contingent being is changing being, for better or worse. That is to say, it can change in ways that are perfective of the precise kind of being it is, or it can change in ways that represent departures from its proper perfection. But, whatever be the nature of the change in that respect, insofar as it is change, it involves the passage from potency to act. Because contingent being is constantly changing, it is being that is deeply marked by potency.

Quidquid Movetur Ab Alio Movetur

Quidquid movetur ab alio movetur. Whatever is moved is moved by another. Here movement is to be understood as referring to any change whatever. This principle represents one of the basic truths of metaphysics. It plays an explicit role in the first of St. Thomas's Five Ways, and it figures implicitly in the other four arguments as well. The meaning of the principle is found in the very words that express it. No thing that changes can, of itself, account for the change that it is undergoing. To locate the proximate explanation for any change, we must look to something external to the change.

This principle is not immediately self-evident. And it might at first appear to be contradicted by the behavior of living things, which we commonly identify as self-moving. However, this is not actually the case, for self-moving things, besides their having a cause of their movement external to them, can be shown also to have, within them, a distinction between mover and moved. We can better understand what lies at the heart of this principle if we see it in the light of the distinction between potency and act, recalling that it is impossible for something to be both in potency and in act at the same time and in the same respect. We saw that the essence of every change is the actualization of a potency, the movement from a state where a thing is in potency in a certain respect, to a state where it is in act in that same respect. Now, the reason why it must be so that everything that moves is moved by another, why no thing can be said to move itself, is that were it to be the case that a thing moved itself, this would mean that the thing is both in potency and in act at the same time and in the same respect, which is a contradiction.

In every change there is a distinction between the change itself and that which brings about the change, between the movement and the cause of the movement. To be actually moving is to be in act with respect to motion. Nothing can cause itself to move in the absolute sense, for that would involve its moving (being in act with respect to motion) and its not moving (being in potency with respect to motion) at the same time. Consider the case of the humble billiard ball, now tranquilly at rest upon the green surface of the billiard table. It cannot set itself in motion, but must be set in motion by something already in motion (i.e., something in act with respect to motion). If we were to suppose it could set itself in motion we would have to suppose that it is both at rest and in motion, which is of course a contradictory situation.

But let us give further consideration to the more difficult case of animate things. Are they not correctly called self-moving, and, as such, do they not give the lie to the principle that everything that moves is moved by another? If we study animate things more closely, with this principle in mind, we discover that their movement, as does all movement, reveals a distinction between mover and moved. In any ostensibly self-moving entity, we can discover, both internal and external to the entity, elements that are distinct from the movement itself and which act as the causes of the movement. Consider now the case of Dorothea, whom we observe sitting in a chair in her room, reading. We observe her put her book aside, rise from the chair, and walk across the room to the window. What we observed was this physical thing, a human body, move from one place to another. It was a body that moved, but it was moved by something other than itself. We can confidently say that what moved Dorothea's body was Dorothea's will, a faculty of her rational soul. Dorothea made a decision to get up from the chair and walk across the room. There we have an internal mover that explains the movement of her body from one place to another.[4] But we might ask, Why did Dorothea decide to get up from the chair and cross the room? The larger question is, Why do any of us make acts of the will that prompt us to action of one kind or another? We make acts of the will, even relatively inconsequential ones such as deciding to get up and cross the room to the window, because we are moved (motivated) to do so by something external to ourselves. In this case, let us say that Dorothea decided to move because she noticed that the room was getting chilly and she got up to close the window. In sum, then, when we closely analyze what we describe as self-moving things we come to discover that there is always a distinction at play between moved and mover, and thus we encounter an operative example of the principle telling us that everything that moves is moved by another.

But still we have a nagging puzzle that is not completely solved. In the case of a human person, where we can rightly say that the movement of the body is caused by the will, the rational soul, cannot we say that the will itself is self-moving? Granted, as we saw just above, the will is moved by things external to itself, but the will is not fully determined by such things, and in the final analysis it does determine itself, and this is precisely what we mean by freedom of the will. So, there would seem to be a certain sense in which it is quite correct to say that the rational soul is self-moving. Yes, but not absolutely so.

The principle that everything that moves is moved by another seeks to provide a definitive explanation for all change, for all movers and for all things that are moved. As metaphysicians, we want to know not only what accounts for the movement, but also what accounts for the movers. We seek an explanation for the being of the movement, but also, and more fundamentally, for the being of that which is moving. We want an explanation, not just for the action, but for the agent as well. The human will explains the movement of the body, but do we therefore have, in the will, the ultimate explanation for the body's movement? We clearly do not, for the will is a faculty or power of a human being, and a human being is a contingent being, a being for the explanation of whose existence we must look beyond that being. The will is a cause of human action, but not the ultimate cause, for the human person embodying that will is not the explanation for his own existence.

The Principle of Causality

A proper understanding of the Five Ways would not be possible without a proper understanding of causality, and for someone who rejects that principle the arguments presented by St. Thomas would be a closed book. This being so, for anyone enamored of the thought of a philosopher like David Hume, who effectively denied the reality of causality (this goes hand and glove with his rejection of substance), the Five Ways would carry no persuasive force. By the same token, a follower of the philosopher Immanuel Kant (1724–1804) would not be able to appreciate what the arguments are attempting to do, for such a person would deny their existential import, refusing to acknowledge that they deal with the real extra-mental world, and not merely with ideas and their interrelations. How would that be so? For Kant, causality was not a reality rooted in the objective order, and which we come to know through our experience of the objective order. Rather, causality, the *idea* of causality, was a category of the mind which, rather than being owed to experience actually preceded experience, and which was then brought to experience in order to render it intelligible. But this is to have the cart before the horse. And it is to think as an idealist philosopher.

Let us bestir our memories again, and recall what we know from general metaphysics about causality. The principle of causality may be regarded as a sub-principle of the principle of sufficient reason, which in turn is one of the four basic principles that govern the whole of human reasoning.[5] The principle of sufficient reason asserts the truth that there is a sufficient reason for everything. The principle is expressed specifically in terms of causality in the assertion that for every thing or every event there is a cause.

What is a cause? In the most general sense, a cause is simply a radical explanation, the most adequate response we can give to the question Why? Aristotle has given us a comprehensive account of causality in his four causes: material, formal, efficient, and final.[6] The cause we are most interested in here, and the one that most readily comes to mind when we think of causality, is the efficient cause. St. Thomas gives us a succinct definition of efficient cause: "A cause is that upon which a thing depends either for its very existence or for any changes it may undergo as an existent."[7] A moving billiard ball that strikes another billiard ball at rest and sets it in motion would be an example of an efficient cause (the moving billiard ball) changing the accidental status of the billiard ball it strikes, from being at rest to being in motion. The striking ball does not bring the struck ball into being, but it alters its mode of being. But the efficient causality we are most concerned with as natural theologians is that which bears upon *esse*, existence itself. The most potent kind of efficient causality is that which does not simply alter the mode of existence of a thing, but brings that thing into existence.

We know that contingent being is being that cannot account for its own existence. It is being that is utterly dependent on other being for its existence, and, as we have seen, that other being can only be necessary being. Necessary being is the efficient cause of contingent being in the most radical of ways, for it calls contingent being into existence out of nothing. But one might wonder: Could not contingent being be the efficient cause of itself, that is to say, could it not bring itself into existence? Only a moment's reflection is required to see that this would be quite impossible. Imagine the scenario. Before contingent being exists there is nothing. In order for contingent being to cause itself, it would have to precede itself, but because nothing precedes the existence of contingent being, the purported cause of something would be nothing. But from nothing you get nothing. (*Ex nihilo nihil fit.*)

Metaphysics, as we have said, is all about finding the ultimate explanations for things. The most important implication of that concern, as related to efficient causality, is the recognition that such a cause, which brings about the very existence of a thing, acts, in so doing, not once and for all at a single moment (i.e., the moment of creation), but continuously, for as long as the thing in question remains in being. To illustrate the point being addressed here, let us advert again to the example of the billiard balls. When billiard ball A (moving) strikes billiard ball B (at rest) and sets it in motion, billiard ball B can continue in motion without billiard ball A being in motion. After striking billiard ball B, billiard ball A stops, while billiard ball B proceeds across the table.

But there are other kinds of motion that can only be explained by the fact that the mover causing the motion must itself continuously remain in motion while it is causing the motion in another. So, the wagon continues to move along the sidewalk only so long as little Jimmy continues to pull it. When he stops his motion, the motion of the wagon stops. Both of these efficient causes are effecting accidental changes in things, specifically, changes from one place to another. More profoundly, and this is the kind of efficient causality with which the Five Ways are ultimately concerned, there is that cause that brings contingent being into existence. In this understanding of efficient causality, then, the existence of the effect can only be explained by the continuing action of the cause. In a passage from the *Summa Theologiae* St. Thomas provides us with a precise description of what is involved here. "Therefore, just as the becoming of a thing cannot continue when the action of the agent ceases, so neither can the 'to be' [i.e., the very existence] of a thing continue after the action has ceased, which is the cause of the effect, not only in the becoming but also in the 'to be'." [8]

Efficient causes whose continuing action is required for the very existence of a thing (*esse*) or the mode of existence of a thing (*fieri*) are commonly referred to as proper causes or existential causes. In order to accentuate the importance of this type of causality for an understanding of the Five Ways, I cite another description of it by St. Thomas, this one coming form his Commentary on Aristotle's *Physics*. "Causes operating in act [i.e., proper causes]," he writes, "exist and do not exist simultaneously with those things of which they are the causes, that is, proper causes, thus this healer exists and does not exist [precisely *as a healer*] simultaneously with him who becomes healed, and this builder exists simultaneously with that which is built." [9] For any process to continue, the agent or agents responsible for the process must be acting. The actual building process goes on only while the builders are actually building.

Imagine a chain of such causes, A, B, C, and D. The causation begins with A, and continues, through B and C, to D. Because causation begins with A, causes B and C are subordinated to it, but their subordinate relation to A is called essential, because the operation of both B and C is dependent on the simultaneous operation of A. If A should cease to exert its causative influence, both B and C would also cease to function as causes, and the final effect, D, would never come about.

The Impossibility of an Infinite Series of Causes

Figuring importantly in the first and second of St. Thomas's arguments is the principle which holds that an infinite regress is impossible. To throw some light on what the principle involves, let us consider a series of causes, A, B, C, D. A is the initiating cause. B and C are also causes, but they are called subordinate causes, or caused causes, which means that they can exercise their causal activity only because they are themselves the effects of causal activity. So, for example, in our series, C is the real cause of D, but it is able to be such only because it has been brought about by B; B, in turn, is the real cause of C, and that is because it was brought about by A. As the initiator of the series, A is a cause but not an effect; D, which ends the series, is an effect but not a cause.

We need at this point to make an important distinction, between a series of essentially subordinated causes and a series of accidentally subordinated causes. This distinction played a role in examples given above, but now is the time to call explicit attention to it. First, we remind ourselves that a subordinate cause is one that is both an effect and a cause, or, in other words, a caused cause. A series of essentially subordinated causes is one in which the initiating cause must be exercising its causal activity continuously, otherwise causal activity in the entire series will cease. Turning the crank of a hand generator (A) activates an electric motor (B) which activates a mechanism (C) which causes a little flag to wave back and forth (D). As soon as one stops turning the crank, the motor and mechanism stop, and the little flag no longer waves. A series of accidentally subordinated causes, A, B, C, D, is one in which simultaneous causal activity by all the causes in the series is not necessary. All that A, the first in the series, has to do is initiate causal activity, and its initiating action will continue down the series of subordinate causes even though it no longer acts.

Now, the question before us is this: Is it possible to have an infinite series of subordinate causes, be they related to one another essentially or accidentally? But one might wonder why such a question should even be asked. The pertinence of the question has to do with the problem of explaining the causality that is taking place in a series of causes, or in any complex network of interrelated causes, phenomena we very frequently meet with. Because of the very nature of a series of *essentially related subordinated causes*, the causal activity of none of them could be explained except by acknowledging each to be an effect, that is to say, a cause that can function as a cause only because of the operation upon it of a cause which is antecedent to it. So, for example, in our series C can cause D only because, here and now, it is being caused by B; and the same is to be said of B in relation to A, which must be, we will say, a cause which causes other causes, but which is itself uncaused. In other words, A is not an effect as well as a cause; we might call it pure cause.

But some have maintained that there is no need to posit an initiating cause which is not an effect. They claim that it is possible to have an infinite series of essentially subordinated causes. But in this claim they are quite mistaken. Remember what we are looking for here: an explanation for the causal activity of each cause in the series. We know that any individual cause is able to cause because of the causal activity antecedent to its own causal activity, and on which it totally depends. If I claim that there is an infinite series of caused causes I really do not have any explanation for the causal activity of *any* given cause in the series. The appeal to the possibility of an infinite series amounts to an abandonment of one's obligation to explain causality. It is comparable to the appeal to "chance" as an initiating cause, which is not an explanation but a flight from explanation

Imagine a supposed infinite series of caused causes. Go back along the series as far as you would want, and wherever you might choose to stop, you would be precisely where you were when you began, that is, face to face with a caused cause, a cause for whose causal activity you have no ultimate explanation. But such a situation can only be imagined; it cannot be real. This is so because, in any series of essentially subordinated causes, if there is not a first uncaused cause, there would be no subsequent causation at all.

It has commonly been held that, while it is impossible to have an infinite series of essentially subordinated causes, the same cannot be said for accidentally subordinated causes. In other words, it would not be a contradiction to suppose the possibility of an infinite series of accidentally subordinated causes. It appears, however, that such a position is not without its serious difficulties. Let us consider a series of accidentally subordinated causes, and focus our attention on a single member of that series, call it Q, that is right before us now. Q exists, and it is acting as a cause. It is able to act as a cause because it was itself caused in the peculiar way it is now causing, but, because it is related accidentally, as effect, to the cause whose effect it is, that cause need not be acting upon it right now. A good concrete example of this kind of series would be several generations of human beings in linear descent, where the causal activity in question would be human generation itself. Think of great-grandmother, grandmother, mother, daughter. The daughter exists because at one time in the past her great-grandmother exercised the causal activity which is human generation. The daughter could get married and herself now exercise that kind of causal activity, but obviously her great-grandmother, who has long since gone to her reward, would not have to be herself exercising that activity in order for her great-granddaughter to be able to exercise it. This, then, is a series of accidentally subordinated causes. The question is, would it be possible that such a series might be infinite? In other words, could there be, antecedent to the great-grandmother cited above, a series of mothers that just went on and on and had no beginning?

In attempting to answer that question, let us first consider the matter in purely abstract, i.e., specifically mathematical, terms. A series might be regarded as analogous to a geometric line, in the sense that, although it involves succession (which a line does not), it is unbroken succession. Now, it is not possible to have an infinite line. A line can be extended infinitely (i.e, indefinitely), but a line must have a beginning, at a specified point. If a line is not generated from a specific point, it has no definition as a line, which is to say, it simply does not exist.

If we suppose that an infinite series of accidentally subordinated causes is a possibility, we run into the same problem as we do in mathematics with regard to the line, that is, we suppose that it is possible to have a line that has not been generated at a specific point. Let us try to imagine a series of accidentally subordinated causes, such as, for example, linearly descended human beings, and let us go back along that series as far as we would want. We stop before a member of that series. Let us call her Martha. As a caused cause, we know that Martha had to have an antecedent, her own mother. Martha was able herself to exercise causality as a mother long after her own mother ceased causing in that way. What is to prevent us, in order to explain the very existence of Martha, now before us, from appealing, not only to the cause immediately preceding her, her mother, but to an endless series of antecedent causes? What should prevent us is the realization that by making such an appeal we have no satisfactory *ultimate* explanation for Martha, and that is because we have no explanation for the supposedly infinite series of which she is a member.

A series is a sequential progression, of things or events. There seems nothing inherently irrational in imagining such a sequential progression going on interminably into the future. But the idea of a sequential progression with no beginning is incoherent, for a succession cannot be a succession unless it has a beginning. To posit an infinite succession backward is tantamount to holding that succession proceeds from nowhere, but if the succession proceeds from nowhere, then there simply is no succession.[10]

CHAPTER FIVE

Arguments from Motion, Efficient Causality, Contingent Being

The Five Ways of St. Thomas Aquinas

We are now ready for a close examination of the Five Ways, the arguments for the existence of God as formulated by St. Thomas. This chapter will be devoted to the first three arguments; the fourth and the fifth arguments will be dealt with in the following chapter. There have been some Scholastic philosophers who have made a division within the arguments, identifying the first three as metaphysical arguments, and the fourth and the fifth as physical arguments. There would seem to be nothing particularly useful in that distinction, and I think it better, for the sake of clarity, to regard all the arguments as metaphysical arguments, for, in the most precise sense of the term, that is what they are. There is an additional practical advantage to identifying all of the arguments as metaphysical: it clearly distinguishes them from the moral arguments for the existence of God, which we will be treating in Chapter Seven of this book.

Our manner of proceeding will be as follows. First, the argument, as formulated by St. Thomas, will be stated in its entirety. The texts for each of the arguments will be those found in the First Part of the *Summa Theologiae*. Explications and commentaries will follow the statement of the arguments. The purpose of these will be to make the meaning and intent of each argument as clear as possible. The translations of the arguments, while seeking to be completely faithful to the originals, are worded in such a way so as to bring out in the most explicit fashion the conceptual heft of each sentence in St. Thomas's texts.

The First Way: The Argument from Motion, the Thomistic Text

I respond by saying that the existence of God can be proved in five ways. The first and more accessible way is based upon the fact of motion. It is a certainty, clearly confirmed by the evidence of our senses, that there are everywhere in the world things that are in motion. Now, everything that is moved is moved by another. Furthermore, nothing is moved unless it is in potency with respect to that toward which it is moved. This is to say that something moves only insofar as it is in act. The reason for this is that the motion itself, what we mean by motion, is the reduction to act of something which is in potency. Now, something cannot be reduced to act except by something which is already in act. For example, something which is in act with respect to heat, such as fire, makes a piece of wood, which is hot only potentially, actually hot when it is applied to it. And thus we say that the fire "moves" and alters the piece of wood.

It is not possible for anything to be simultaneously in potency and in act in the same way, but only in different ways. Consequently, something which is actually hot obviously cannot be potentially hot at one and the same time. However, there is no contradiction involved if something were to be actually hot and potentially cold at one and the same time. What this all means is that it is impossible that, at one and the same time, there should be something which both moves itself and is moved, or that it should be the cause of its own motion. Therefore, everything that is moved, must be moved by another.

If, then, that thing by which something is moved is itself moved, then its movement must be accounted for by yet another thing, and that other thing's movement by still something else. And so on. But you cannot proceed to infinity in this way, for in that case there would be no first mover, and without a first mover nothing at all would be in motion. That is explained by the fact that no secondary motion is possible without the motion of the first mover. So, for example, a stick held in the hand will not move unless the hand which holds it moves. It is necessary eventually to come upon something which is a first mover, i.e., something which is itself not moved by anything else. And this first mover everyone understands to be God.[1]

Explication and Commentary

The argument from motion can as well be called the argument from change, for the larger metaphysical reality which motion represents is change, change of whatever kind. Motion, specifically locomotion, the motion of a physical object from one place to another, the phenomenon on which the argument concentrates, is a particular kind of change. We are invited to reflect on this kind of change because it is readily accessible to us. We see it all around us. Change may be generally described as the transition of any particular thing from one state to another, or, more abstractly, as the actualization of the potency of any particular thing.

Take careful note of the point of departure of the argument, which clearly identifies it as a *quia* argument, that is, an argument which begins with effects and seeks to discover the cause of those effects. The cause being sought here is the ultimate cause of all things. St. Thomas begins his argument very much in the public arena, referring to observable facts manifestly apparent to all, specifically, to the ubiquitous fact of motion or change. If our senses assure us of anything, it is "that there are everywhere in the world things that are in motion." It is that motion which we are setting out to explain, not in any limited and tentative way, but in a comprehensive and definitive way. Why is there motion at all in the world? Why do things change?

After calling our attention to the ubiquitousness of motion or change, St. Thomas then cites that key metaphysical principle we discussed in the previous chapter, "everything that is moved is moved by another." (*Omne autem quod movetur, ab alio movetur.*) This could be considered as just another way of expressing the principle of causality: there is no movement or change without a cause of movement or change.

The next step St. Thomas takes in the argument is to introduce the principles of potency and act, critical principles indeed in this context, for they are what render any kind of change intelligible. It is a token of the importance he attaches to those principles, and the importance of the role they play in the argument, that a goodly portion of his text is given over to explaining them. There are two main emphases in his explanation. First, he reminds us that the essence of any change is the actualization of potency, or, to say the same thing with different words, the reduction of potency to act. What would "potency" be in reference to motion? It would simply be the capacity for a thing to be moved. And "act"? It would be the motion itself.

A key dimension of the principle that whatever is moved is moved by another has to do with how potency and act are related to one another. Something that is actually moving is said to be in act, and it is in act because the movement began in something that was in potency with respect to that act, which simply means that it had the capacity for movement in the first place. But something that was in potency in a certain respect (in this case, with respect to motion) would forever remain in potency, unless something already in act in that same respect reduced its potency to act, which is to say, put it in motion. St. Thomas uses the simple example of fire which is applied to wood to set it afire by way of illustrating this vital point. A piece of wood is flammable; it is capable of being set afire. It is in potency with respect to the act which is being on fire. But no piece of wood can, on its own, move from not being on fire to being on fire; it cannot reduce itself to act in this particular respect. In order to move from the state of simply being wood to a state of being burning wood, it needs something already in act in that respect, something which is itself on fire, to bring about the movement.

Why is it that no one thing can reduce itself to act, i.e., bring about, on its own, the movement from one state to another? It is because that would entail the thing being in two incompatible states at once: both in potency and in act at the same time and in the same respect. In terms of St. Thomas's example, this would mean that it would be necessary for the piece of wood to be burning and not burning at one and the same time.

So far, we have established that (a) at the heart of every instance of motion there is a transition from potency to act, and (b) such a transition can only be brought about by something already in act, and (c) what is already in act must be something other than the thing in potency, otherwise we would have a contradiction on our hands.

We have, then, a thing, a real existent, that is moved, changed in some specific way. Let us label that thing A. Because it cannot account for its own movement, we must seek the source of its movement in another thing, B, which is already in motion. How about B's motion? Obviously, the same principles apply to it that applied to A: unable to reduce itself to act, it had to be reduced to act by another, which we will call C. How long could a series such as this go on—a series of moved movers (i.e., moving things whose movement depends on another)? Could it go on interminably? Would it be permissible to entertain the possibility of an infinite series of moved movers? In the light of our discussion of this matter in the previous chapter, I would hope that it would be evident to all that the answer to that question must be in the negative. "But you cannot proceed to infinity in this way," St. Thomas writes, "for in that case there would be no first mover, and without a first mover nothing at all would be in motion."

What St. Thomas is referring to, clearly, is the idea that an infinite regress is impossible. But just why this should be so may not be manifestly evident, in terms of what has been said so far, and thus it is important that we be aware of precisely the kind of series we are dealing with. It is a series of essentially subordinated causes, which we met with in the previous chapter. We could be more exact about the matter and say that what we have here is a series of essentially subordinated moving things, meaning that the motion of any one member of the series is dependent on the motion of the immediately preceding member. St. Thomas does not use the term "essentially subordinated causes" in the argument, but that the series he is dealing with is of that kind is made explicit by the example of the hand moving the stick, found toward the end of the argument. He calls our attention to a stick which is in motion right now. The explanation of the stick's motion is the moving hand that is holding that stick. The motion of the stick is completely dependent on the simultaneous motion of the hand. Were the hand to cease moving, the stick would cease moving. We therefore say that the movement of the stick is essentially subordinated to (and dependent upon) the movement of the hand. Such a relation need not obtain in the case of burning wood. You could have a stick of wood, A, which is lighted on fire by a burning stick, B. But then stick B could be plunged into a bucket of water and its fire put out. Stick A, however, having been reduced to act by stick B, could continue to burn on brightly, even though stick B is no longer in act with respect to fire. In this case, we say that stick A, in the respect of its being on fire, is subordinated to stick B accidentally, not essentially.

We have, then, a series, or a complex, of moving things, all of which depend for their movement, right now, on something other than themselves. The only possible explanation for the movement of all these things (and we can imagine as many as we like) is what St. Thomas calls a "first mover." A first mover is an ultimate explanation for all motion, for all change. It is something that moves others but is itself unmoved, something that effects change but is unchanging. A first mover is that which can reduce potency to act because it is itself nothing but act, Pure Act. But what necessitates our conclusion that there must be a first mover?

Consider what we are attempting to explain: the reality of motion, of change of any kind. We have seen that nothing that moves is the explanation for its own movement. It needs something else to move it, and that moving thing in turn needs an explanation for its movement. And so on. An appeal to a supposed infinite series of such dependent movers is, we know, recalling our earlier discussion, simply evading the issue, saying in effect, "the explanation is that there is no explanation." The only explanation for all things that are moving right now is something that is moving them right now, but which is itself not moving. There must be a being that is the ultimate explanation for all change that is going on right now, the stark factualness of which is undeniable, for we cannot find, in all the myriads of changing things themselves, anything that can account for their change. And that ultimate explanation for all change is a being that is itself unchanging.

It would be to miss the rich ontological import of St. Thomas's First Way if we were to allow ourselves to become so fixated on particulars, such as burning wood and moving sticks, that we fail to see the profound truths these plain examples are meant to illuminate. This argument is in its essence about the utter dependence of all changing being on unchanging being. At its deepest level, it seeks to explain, not simply the motion of physical things, but change of whatever kind. Most significantly, the argument is, quite obviously, inviting us to reflect on (a) the phenomenon of change, but also, and perhaps even more importantly, on (b) the things that undergo that phenomenon. The argument is providing us with an account of things that change, which is to say, simply, of all contingent being, and offering us an ultimate explanation for that being.

Let us consider how this is so. As we observed, the heart of change is the transition from potency to act. Potency and act are not mere abstractions, names that serve only a logical purpose. They are real principles inherent in real things. Only real things are in potency or in act in any particular respect. There can be neither potency nor act without an existent which displays one or the other. The being "in act" which would be exemplified by movement or change is what Aristotle called "second act." He gave the name "first act" to the very act of existence of an entity, which makes its second act possible. In other words, first act is that which establishes existence; it is that which makes an actually existing simply be. Second act is the activity or behavior of any actually existing thing.[2]

Now, what we have clearly implied in the First Way is the idea that the first mover is the ultimate explanation, not only for the motion of things that move (second act), but for the very existence of those things (first act). Moving things cannot account for their own motion, much less can they account for their existence as things that are capable of motion. The first mover, then, is the ultimate explanation, not simply for a mode of being (i.e., change), but for being itself. More precisely, God is the ultimate explanation for our ability to act in this, that, or any way, but, more profoundly, He is the ultimate explanation for our very status as agents, as real beings who are subject to change. So, in the argument we move (a) from the reality of change to an explanation for change, and (b) from an explanation for change to an explanation for that which changes. The first move is explicit, the second implicit.

The relation that exists between all changing beings and God is not one to be explained in terms of accidental subordination. Our situation is not as the Deists of the eighteenth century supposed it to be. They imagined a cosmic scenario in which God set everything in motion at some moment in the dim and distant past, and then effectively stepped out of the picture, letting the fully automated universe run on more or less independently, free from the need of any further assistance on His part. According to this view, the universe, as it now stands, is an adequate explanation for itself, meaning that everything about it can be explained in purely naturalistic terms. But that is not how things stand. Literally everything that moves right now, that has its being as a thing that moves right now, moves and has its being, because, right now, the first mover, God, who is Pure Act, is "in act" with respect to all His creatures.

The Second Way: The Argument from Efficient Causality, the Thomistic Text

The second way relates to efficient causality. If we look about us we discover among things we observe a certain order of efficient causality. But what isn't found—for it would be quite impossible to find—is something which could ever be the cause of itself. Why is that? Because the thing in question would then have to be somehow prior to itself, which is absurd.

Now, it is impossible to proceed to infinity in a series of efficient causes. This is so because in every complex of ordered efficient causes, the first cause would be the cause of the intermediate cause, and the intermediate cause would be the cause of the ultimate effect. And this would be the case whether there would be only one intermediate cause or an indefinite number of them. Given this type of arrangement, then, take away the cause, and the effect is taken away. Therefore, were there not a first cause among those efficient causes, neither would there be any intermediate causes.

If we were to attempt to proceed to infinity in a complex of efficient causes, there would be no first cause. In that event there would be no ultimate effect, neither would there be any intermediate efficient causes. But this is obviously not the way things are. It is necessary, therefore, to posit a first efficient cause, a being which everyone gives the name God.[3]

Explication and Commentary

In comparing this argument with the first, one immediately notices any number of similarities between them. Some commentators have been so taken by these similarities that they have been led to conclude that the first way and second way are essentially the same argument. But this is not the case. The second way is founded upon the fact of efficient causality. We can, and should, be aware that the first argument, involving motion or change, also involves efficient causality. The "other" which is the explanation for the motion of a moving thing is the efficient cause of the thing's motion. The presence of efficient causality in the two arguments is, then, a significant similarity between them. But we should also note an important difference between the two arguments, specifically with respect to efficient causality. In the first argument the focus is on passivity, i.e., on the *moved* mover. In the second argument the focus shifts to action, the agent that causes the motion, or brings about any kind of change.

Once we have completed our tour of all five arguments, it will be clear to us how they all share certain basic commonalities. This should not strike us as strange. After all, each of the arguments is ordered to coming up with exactly the same conclusion, the truth of the existence of God. More pertinently, all of the arguments, just as arguments, are going to contain, and be guided by, either explicitly or implicitly, certain fundamental principles that govern all argumentative discourse, and among these principles perhaps the one most in play is the principle of causality. Each of the arguments, in terms of its contents, relies heavily on this principle. But from the point of view of the very structure of each argument—and again this applies to all arguments—efficient causality is always importantly at work, for the premisses of an argument can be said to cause its conclusion.

So, the second argument rests firmly upon the fact of efficient causality. This being the case, it might be well that we remind ourselves of the precise nature of an efficient cause. An efficient cause is an agent (i.e., a source of action) whose activity (a) brings a being into existence, or (b) alters an already existing being in one way or another. Some examples. Parents can be said to be the cause of their children, in the first sense. A painter painting a beige wall blue would be the cause of that peculiar transformation of the wall; the painter did not make the wall, but he altered it by changing its color.[4]

The first thing that St. Thomas does, in the early sections of the argument, is to make clear to us that he is arguing in the *quia* mode. Remember, that is the mode by which we proceed from effects to cause. "Effects," here, understood in the broadest sense, would simply mean that we are starting from the objective facts of the world in which we live. St. Thomas invites us to pay particular attention to what must be recognized as a very prominent feature of that world, the fact that efficient causality is to be found everywhere at work in it. "If we look about us we discover among things we observe a certain order of efficient causality." Notice that it is not efficient causality just in itself he wants us to consider, but the ordered context which is created by the workings of that efficient causality. When we narrow our focus we observe, let us say between any two things, that one is the efficient cause of the other, but stepping back from that very significant little scene so that we get a comprehensive view of things, we become aware that those two things, related as cause and effect, and ourselves as well, are part of a vast network of complexly interrelated efficient causes. The physical universe is a huge stage on which is being enacted the myriads of wondrous roles assumed by myriads of efficient causes.

But let us narrow our focus once again and reflect on any specific caused thing, keeping in mind the very nature of causality. What we cannot say of any such thing is that it could be the cause of itself. That would be to talk nonsense. Why? If we were to suppose that anything could be the cause of itself that would entail its having to precede itself: it would have to exist before it existed, so that it could bring itself into existence. The absurdity of such a scenario is clear enough.

We concluded our commentary on the first proof by reflecting on some of the deeper ontological implications of the argument, calling attention to the fact that it was concerned, not only with the *motion* of things, but with *the things* that move. The fundamental concern, in other words, was with existence, with offering an explanation for existence. The same holds true for the second argument. Take note of St. Thomas's wording when he cites the impossibility of anything being the cause of itself. He speaks of the impossibility of "something which could ever be the cause of itself."[5] What is clearly being referred to here is the very existence of the thing, not simply its ability to act as an efficient cause.

The next idea he turns to, the development of which occupies the greater part of the rest of the argument, is an idea with which we are now quite familiar: i.e., the impossibility of an infinite regress. The particular issue at stake in this instance is the impossibility of an infinite series of efficient causes. The reason why such a series is impossible here is much the same as it was for a series of moved movers, but it is important that we spell out the particulars, because the operative presence of the idea represents a critical phase of the argument.

As was the case in the first argument, we are dealing with a series of essentially subordinated causes. In examining such a series, if we were to pause before any particular member of it, which would be a caused cause, we would recognize that, as such, it is an entity which is able to exercise its causal influence, right now, only because it is the recipient of causal influence. In other words, it can be a cause only because it is the effect of a cause. So, we have, let us say, three entities, A, B, C, related to one another in such a way that B is the cause of C, and this is explained by the fact that it, B, is caused by A. In an arrangement of this sort, B would be properly identified as the intermediate cause.

Now, as St. Thomas tells us, we can imagine as many intermediate causes as we please, an indefinite number of them, but whether it is a matter of one or many, and remembering the fact that we are dealing here with a series of essentially subordinated efficient causes, we would have an explanation for the existence of C only if causation is taking place simultaneously all along the series. But what we need now is an explanation for the series itself. If the series, or a complex network, of efficient causes, is made up of only caused causes, then there is nothing within the series or the network which explains either. Again, it simply will not do to appeal to the possibility of an infinite series of caused causes, or an infinite network of caused causes, for that is merely to evade rather than to answer the question that concerns us. More pointedly, we would be appealing to an impossibility. Without something other than a caused cause, not only would C be without explanation, but B as well, and all caused causes.

If we were to imagine a world in which there were nothing but caused causes, we would be imagining nothing, for such a world could not exist. The only explanation for caused causes (dependent causes) is a first cause, which is to say an absolutely independent uncaused cause. This first cause exercises causative influence, but no causative influence is exercised upon it. It is the explanation for everything, but it has no need of explanation. Or perhaps we could say, it is the explanation for itself. This first cause, this uncaused cause of all things that are caused, is God.

Once again in the case of this second argument, we do not want to become so preoccupied by the specific phenomenon around which the argument is built, efficient causality, that we neglect to see the larger truth St. Thomas's exploration of that phenomenon is intended to cast light upon. One of the dangers of taking too narrow a view of the argument is that we might be led to imagine that God, as first cause, is somehow a part of the series of causes of which He is the cause. I must confess that, in all of the examples I have used thus far, speaking of series, and networks, I found it very difficult to avoid leaving the impression that the first mover or the first cause is somehow part of the series or network. This is emphatically not the case, and that has to be now stated in the clearest possible terms. To put it explicitly, God, as First Mover, is not Himself part of the universe of things to which He gives being and movement. God, as First Cause, is not to be thought of as the first of any series or network of causes, in the sense that He is Himself part of the series or network. God completely transcends everything which He brings into being and causes to act.

To recapitulate the argument. No single cause in the universe could be discovered to be exercising its causality in a purely autonomous fashion. It can cause only because it has been caused. Because all of the causes in the universe are *caused* causes, they can only be explained by a first cause, a cause which, though causing them to be, stands apart from all of them, and that is because of its absolutely unique nature as an uncaused cause, a cause which exists, indeed exists purely and simply, and yet for whose existence there is no explanation outside itself. And this uncaused cause is God. But note well, God is not simply the cause of the causing activity of all efficient causes, He is the cause of their very existence. God does not just cause causation, He causes the things that exercise causation.

Occasionally one runs across certain commentators, some of whom are philosophers, who will respond to this argument in the following manner. "You claim that God is first cause, but who or what is the cause of God?" Such a response reflects a total lack of comprehension of the very meaning of the notion of first cause. It would be like saying, "You say that one, the unit, is the generating source of all number, but what is the generating source of one?" What comes before the number one? Nothing. What comes before the first cause? Nothing. It is quite vacuous to ask for the cause of the first cause, for the first cause, by definition, is a cause which has no cause, and that is precisely why we call it "first." It is the absolute foundation and beginning of all that is. To make another comparison, to ask what is the cause of the first cause would be like asking on what principles the first principles are based. Answer: They are based on no principles, for it is with these principles that all principles begin. To ask, "Who caused God?" is to display no understanding at all of the referent of the term "God," the being who is the Supreme Being because there is nothing in any way superior or antecedent to Him.

The Third Way: The Argument from Contingent Being, the Thomistic Text

> The third way is based upon the difference which exists between possible being [i.e., contingent being] and necessary being. And it goes as follows. We find among things in the world certain existents for which it is possible that they either be or not be. This is obvious from the fact that certain things are observed to come into being as a result of generation, and then fall out of being as a result of corruption. From this it clearly follows that such beings can either exist or not exist.
>
> Now, it is impossible that beings of this sort [i.e., that come into existence and fall out of existence] should have always existed, for if it is possible for a being not to exist, then it necessarily follows that at one time it in fact did not exist. Therefore, if it were the case that all the beings that are now existing are beings that could possibly not exist, then at one time there would have been no beings at all in existence. And if this were true, then nothing at all would be in existence at this very moment. How so? Well, if

something doesn't exist, it cannot begin to exist except by something which is already in existence. Therefore, if nothing were to be in existence, it would obviously be quite impossible that anything should ever begin to exist, and thus nothing would be existing right now. But this is clearly not the situation.

From the above considerations we must conclude that not all beings that now actually exist are the kind of beings for which non-existence is a real possibility. There must be, in existence right now, beings which exist necessarily. Now, every necessary being either owes its necessity to another or it does not. And, just as it was the case that it is not possible to proceed to infinity with respect to ordered efficient causes, as has already been shown [in the previous argument], neither is it possible to proceed to infinity in a complex of necessary beings whose necessity comes from another. We must conclude, therefore, that there exists a being whose necessity belongs to itself, and is not owed to another. And this absolutely necessary being is the cause of the necessity of all other necessary beings. This being all men call God.[6]

Explication and Commentary

St. Thomas's third argument for the existence of God is particularly interesting. It is commonly referred to as the argument from contingency, or contingent being. Right at the outset of the argument, we are asked to reflect on contingent being precisely in terms of how it relates, contrastingly, to necessary being. The first order of business, for anyone harboring serious hopes of intelligently following the argument, is to insure that he has a clear understanding of just what it is we are dealing with in what we call contingent being. If you want to understand what contingent being is, St. Thomas is effectively telling us, just open your eyes and look about you. You are surrounded by contingent being. "We find among things in the world certain existents for which it is possible that they either be or not be."[7] A contingent, or possible, being is one that (a) actually exists, but (b) for which there is nothing in its nature that demands that it should exist. In other words, it could just as well not exist as exist. The proof positive of this is to be found in the fact that such beings come and go; they have no permanency in being. Consider, by way of concrete example, any organic being, such as the marigold and salvia plants blooming right now out in the front yard. Last year at this time, they did not exist; next year at this time, they will not exist. Such is the plight of contingent being. By way of an example much closer to home, consider yourself. You came into being, with generation, and one day you will fall out of being—not completely, but in terms of how you are now constituted, as a being composed of body and soul—with corruption.

A contingent being, then, is one that "can either exist or not exist." Could we imagine any kind of being other than contingent being? We could, and we can give such a being a name, and the name we give to it is necessary being. If a contingent being is a being for which non-existence is a real possibility, a necessary being is a being for which non-existence is completely out of the question. Necessary being, understood in the strict sense of the term, cannot not be; it is of the very nature of such a being to exist. Now, the fact that contingent being actually does exist, here and now, is indisputable. After all, you are here. And so are the marigolds and the salvias, and myriads of other things. The only possible explanation for the existence of contingent being—this is the conclusion toward which the argument is headed—is necessary being.

The first decisive step the argument takes in reaching that conclusion is by the assertion that, given its very nature, it is impossible that contingent being should always have existed. If there is nothing in a contingent being that demands that it should exist, then it is inescapably true that at one time it in fact did not exist. There are right now in the universe an immeasurably vast number of contingent beings, and, as far as we can see, the physical universe is composed of nothing else but contingent beings.

If we suppose that there is nothing but contingent beings in the universe, then there once was a time when there was simply nothing, no contingent beings at all. That point may not be immediately obvious, so let us consider it more carefully. If the only kind of beings there are in existence at any given point in time, no matter how vastly numerous they may be, are contingent beings, these are beings which do not carry within themselves any imperative for existing. They are so constituted by their nature that they can not-be. There had to be a previous time, then, for each and every one of them, when they did not exist. Put another way, contingent being must have a beginning, but because it is absurd to think that any being can cause itself to be, no contingent being can account for its own beginning. Now, if this is true of any individual contingent being, it is true of all of them together, for they all share the same nature. So, if this individual contingent being once did not exist, then at one time all contingent beings did not exist.

So, we imagine a situation in which there are no contingent beings actually in existence. If that were once actually the case, nothing would exist right now. Given a situation where nothing at all exists, there would never be any possibility for anything ever coming into existence, for from nothing, nothing comes. But that is obviously absurd, for we, who are ourselves contingent beings, exist, and we are surrounded on every side by contingent beings. But that is just the state of affairs that needs to be explained. How did we get here? How did all these other contingent beings get here? The only explanation for the existence of contingent beings here and now is the existence of being other than contingent being—necessary being.

The very last part of the argument might prove to be a bit confusing; in it St. Thomas speaks of necessary beings that owe their necessity to something beyond themselves. Though he does not make it explicit in the argument, St. Thomas is working here under the guidance of the distinction between relatively necessary being and absolutely necessary being, and what he is specifically referring to in this passage is relatively necessary being. There is only one absolutely necessary being, and that is God. It was angelic beings St. Thomas had in mind in speaking of necessary beings who owe their necessity to another. Following the cosmology of his mentor Aristotle, he probably was also thinking of the refined type of matter of which it was believed heavenly bodies were composed. Angels could be regarded as relatively necessary beings because, unlike human beings, who are composed of matter and form and therefore subject to decomposition, they are pure form, which is to say, entirely immaterial or spiritual. Angelic existence, in comparison to human existence, may be said to be necessary in a qualified fashion, for it is free from any possibility of losing its essential nature by decomposition. To be sure, angels, like all created beings, are composed of essence and existence, and just for this reason they cannot be regarded as necessary beings in the absolute or unqualified sense. So, when St. Thomas argues that these necessary beings (i.e., angels) owe their necessary being to another he is simply calling attention to the fact that there is only one absolutely necessary being. In the strictest understanding of the term, angels too must be counted as contingent beings, for they are beings, such as ourselves, whose essence does not entail existence. There is of course only one being whose essence entails existence, and that is God.[8]

We are considering a world composed of only contingent beings, beings that do not have to exist but which in fact do exist, and we seek an explanation for that existence. We observe that there is a vast array of intricate relations among contingent beings; that some are dependent upon others for their existence. Indeed, we witness a vast complex of dependency. In light of this, we might be tempted, by way of explaining the complex (i.e., the universe itself), to toy with the possibility of an infinity of contingent being. But as we saw in the first two arguments, that will not do.

But there is another temptation we might succumb to. Granting that the entire universe is made up of contingent beings, and granting that no single such being, by definition, can be considered to be necessary, why could we not suppose that, while there is no necessity to be found in any one of the parts of the universe (i.e., in any single contingent being), there is necessity in the sum total of the parts? If we do suppose that as a real possibility, with what does it leave us? A necessary universe made up of nothing but contingent parts. But this is an impossibility. Whence comes the necessity of the whole, when the whole is no more than the sum of its parts, and each and every one of its parts is contingent? To attempt to get necessity this way is little more than a conjuring trick, for it would be tantamount to trying to get from something what that something does not have. One can add contingent being to contingent being until Gabriel blows his horn, and the only result will be contingent being.

The conclusion of the third way, then, is inescapable. The only possible explanation for the existence of contingent being, for being that does not have imbedded within itself the rationale for its own existence, is necessary being, being that cannot not exist, being whose very nature is to exist. This is a being, in St. Thomas's words, "whose necessity belongs to itself," which may be understood as a being whose existence is totally contained within, explained by, itself. This is a being that must exist, otherwise nothing would exist. "This being all men call God."

CHAPTER SIX

The Argument from the Degrees of Being
The Argument from Finality

A Slight Shift in Emphasis

In an earlier chapter mention was made of the fact that some Scholastic philosophers have been known to make a distinction among the Five Ways of St. Thomas, calling the first three metaphysical arguments, and the fourth and the fifth physical arguments. While such a distinction, as pointed out, is not especially helpful, this is not to say that there is not an interesting difference to be noted between the first three arguments and the final two. It is best described as a difference in emphasis.

The first three arguments give explicit attention to, and are built around, a fundamental metaphysical concept or principle. The first argument, commonly referred to as the argument from motion, could just as easily be named the argument from potency to act, for motion is a species of change, and what lies at the heart of every change, as Aristotle discovered, is the reduction of potency to act. And because we know that a central truth governing the relation between potency and act is that nothing in potency (in whatever way) can reduce itself to act, we must, in seeking to explain any instance of change, go beyond that change to find the active principle (specifically, an *agens in actu* with respect to the particular change in question) that caused the change. And since no changing thing will be discovered to be both in potency and act with respect to the same kind of change (meaning that no changing thing has within itself the explanation for change), then, in order to explain the sum total of changes taking place in the universe, we must conclude to the existence of a being that, as pure act, is the explanation for all change, but which is itself unchanging. This being is the ultimate explanation for the reduction of all potency to act. And this being is God.

Now, the first argument implicitly involves efficient causality, for anything in act with respect to motion, would be the efficient cause of the motion it brings about in another thing. But in the second argument St. Thomas gives primacy of place to the principle of efficient causality, and develops around it an argument that arrives at the same type of conclusion as did the first argument. Besides the fact that it is a metaphysical impossibility for any cause to cause itself (that would entail a cause having to exist before it existed), we know from experience that every cause we encounter is a caused cause. That is, every cause is able to exercise causative influence only because it is itself the effect of causative influence. Now, if the sum total of efficient causes are caused causes, then we must necessarily conclude to the existence of a cause that is not caused, to which we give the name "first cause," and this first cause is the cause of, the ultimate explanation for, all the caused causes in the universe. And this first cause is God.

The fundamental metaphysical principle around which the third argument is built is the principle of contingency. Another name that we could give to this principle is the principle of radical dependency. A radically dependent being is one which does not contain within itself the explanation for its own existence, and that means a being that does not need to be; its non-existence is a real possibility. Now, if we were to suppose that the only kind of beings in existence were contingent beings, then we would be left without an explanation for their existence. The only thing that can explain the existence of contingent being, the existence of which is undeniable, is an absolutely necessary being, a being whose very nature is to exist, who cannot not exist. That being is God.

Because the principle of potency and act, of efficient causality, and of contingency, are as fundamental as they are to metaphysics, St. Thomas is of course going to make use of them in the fourth and fifth ways, but in these arguments he will be relying on them in more implicit fashion than was the case in the first three arguments. The shift of emphasis that we observe in the last two arguments might be described in terms of St. Thomas stepping back and taking a broader view of things. In the first three arguments our attention was focused on principles that could be seen as operative within a single being (contingency), or in the relation between, at the minimum, two beings (potency and act, efficient causality), and then we were led to see how the application of those principles bring us to a conclusion of the most momentous kind. So, in a sense we began with the particular and proceeded to the general. In the fourth and fifth arguments St. Thomas is inviting us to begin by considering being in general, for the purpose of discovering how all being is marked by degrees (fourth way), and how all being is marked by intelligence (fifth way), and then to see what conclusion is to be drawn from those large and pervasive facts about the universe in which we live.

The Fourth Way: The Argument from Degrees of Being, the Thomistic Text

The fourth way is taken from the degrees which are to be found among things. Specifically, what we find among the various existents is that a particular thing is more or less good, more or less true, more or less noble—and the same holds true with respect to other qualities. But we use the term "more" or "less" in different ways, according to how things to which we apply them approach in differing ways to that which is the maximum. So, for example, we call something hotter to the extent that it is closer to what is the hottest.

There is, therefore, something which is most true, the best, most noble, and consequently such a thing *exists* maximally, and this is because, as is pointed out in Book II of the *Metaphysics,* whatever things are maximally true are maximally in being.

Now, whatever is in this way identified as the maximum in any genus, is the cause of all of the things which belong to that genus. Thus fire, which can be regarded as the maximum with respect to heat, is the cause of all things which are hot—as was also noted in the *Metaphysics*.

Therefore, there is to be found among all things that exist, that which is the cause of their being, and of their goodness, and of any other perfection they possess. And this cause we call God. [1]

Explication and Commentary

The first thing to notice—and this should come as no surprise to us by now—is that what we are once again dealing with here is a *quia* argument. St. Thomas begins by calling our attention to a prominent feature of the things we encounter everywhere we look: they are not all the same; they do not all exist on the same level. The language we use in describing the variegated things that make up the world clearly shows that we have a natural propensity to rank them. In responding to things, we tend to think of them as good, better, or best, as regarded from one point of view or another. As St. Thomas puts it, "what we find among the various existents is that a particular thing is more or less good, more or less true, more or less noble—and the same holds true with respect to other qualities."

So, then, St. Thomas is here pointing to something quite familiar, and which would seem to reflect the way the human mind normally works. We naturally think in comparative terms, and in doing so—this is worthy of special note—our minds are faithfully responding to, and correctly registering, the way things actually stand in the natural world. That world is not simply a huge blob of homogeneous being. There are degrees of being, and this is explained by the fact that, metaphysically considered, some beings have more being than others. We will return to that very important, but by no means immediately obvious, notion later in this section.

Remaining for the moment on the level of our ordinary experience, we ask: What, in the final analysis, provides intelligibility to our comparative way of thinking and speaking? What provides the rationale for our saying, for example, that, "X_1 is better than X_2"? It is the idea of the maximum, the ultimate, the best, which is always being referred to, at least implicitly, whenever we make any comparative judgment.

Whenever I say that, "X_1 is better than X_2," I am making a claim to the effect that X_1 comes closer to the Maximum X, the ultimate in the world of X's, than does X_2. The maximum sets the standard, therefore, and provides the basis for our comparative thinking.

Two cautionary notes must be sounded at this stage of the argument. In terms of some of the examples St. Thomas uses to illustrate comparative reasoning, such as when he speaks of something being more or less noble, the impression can be left that we are concerned here only with accidental being. This is not the case. Nobility would be an accident of quality, and we know that, like any other accident, it does not exist in subsistent fashion, which is to say that it does not exist independently. The very nature of accidental being is that it exists, not through itself, but only through another, that "other" being substance. Accidental being inheres in substantial being, so that, if there is no substantial being, there is no accidental being. All this points to the fact, with respect to the quality mentioned by St. Thomas, that there can be no such thing as nobility just as such, that is, as existing extra-mentally as a real existent. There is no nobility, as an independent entity; there are only noble things, substances that possess the quality we call nobility. These elementary distinctions are important to keep in mind in order properly to understand the main thrust of this argument. What St. Thomas is focused on here is not the qualities of things, but on *the things that have qualities*. This is an argument about substantial being.

The second cautionary note I wish to sound is this: In speaking of the maximum, we are referring to a real being, and not simply to an ideal. It is quite possible, indeed I suspect that it is rather common, that in many if not most of the comparative judgments we make from day to day, the maximum to which those judgments refer is merely an ideal. It is a maximum of the mind, as it were. Let us say that you are a connoisseur of the music of Josef Haydn, and you have just come away from hearing a performance of his Symphony No. 104 in D major, the "London Symphony," and you excitedly proclaim to your friends, and to anyone who will listen, "That was the best performance of the London Symphony I have ever heard." In making that claim, the standard against which you were measuring the performance you recently heard is the maximum, what might be described as the absolutely best (meaning flawless, perfect in every way) performance of the London Symphony. Now, chances are no such performance ever existed in real life, and perhaps never will.[2] What is being appealed to is an ideal; that is what is acting as the standard in such a case. This is a perfectly legitimate way to make comparative judgments, and we are doing it all the time, our heads being full of ideal maximums which serve the very practical, and indeed necessary, service of providing us with the rationale for the countless comparative judgments we make on a daily basis, be they about sermons, or sunsets, or symphonies. But the point to be stressed in all this is that the maximum with which St. Thomas is principally concerned in his argument is by no means simply an ideal; what he has in mind is the maximum *in being*, a real existent that exists maximally. And it might be well that we remind ourselves, apropos of this point, of something that we called attention to in Chapter Four: that all of the five arguments are existential in nature. They deal with real being, not merely logical being.

Some commentators have shown themselves to be confused on just that issue, and have convinced themselves that St. Thomas, in this argument, is being guided in his reasoning by something resembling a Platonic Form. If any credence is to be given to this interpretation, then we would find ourselves in the highly problematical state of affairs where we have St. Thomas, the consummate Aristotelian, thinking like a Platonist. This serious misreading of the argument will be dealt with in some detail in the following chapter, a chapter in which various objections to the Five Ways will be reviewed.

The central existential import of the argument of the fourth way—in other words, the fact that it has to do with objective reality itself and not with subjective judgments concerning that reality—is made clear by the simple example St. Thomas uses relating to the term "hotter," as referring to something which is closer to the hottest. Heat is itself an accident of quality; as an accident, it inheres in a substance. Our focus is to be on the actual existent, the substance which is the hottest. Now, a quality such as heat can be quantified, as is reflected in the fact that we commonly refer, when we want to be as precise as possible, to degrees of heat. The hottest, a thing that is maximum with respect to the quality of heat, can be objectively determined by quantitative measurement. We may say that such a thing is maximum in being with respect to heat.

Some commentators have found somewhat troublesome this notion of the "hottest," and questioned if that could be said to refer to a real existent. In other words, are we permitted to suppose that there is an actually existing hottest thing? There are two responses that may be made to this potential difficulty. In the first place, there is nothing inherently contradictory in the idea of there existing right now in the universe an actual physical object that is hotter than any other object now existing in the universe.[3] However, whether there is or is not such an object is quite beside the point St. Thomas is attempting to make in the argument. Our attention should not be so trained on the particular quality in question, heat, that we lose sight of what we should chiefly be paying attention to, which is, *that which* is the hottest, the substantial reality. St. Thomas uses the example of the "hottest" simply to illustrate a maximum, but *the* maximum we are concerned with here, once again, is not an accidental maximum, but a substantial maximum—a maximum in being, being as understood without qualification.

The fact that St. Thomas's concentration in the argument is upon the maximum in being—a supreme being, to put it plainly—is boldly underscored by the adjectives he uses to describe that being, when he refers to it as "good" and "true." The being in question is most good, most true. The special significance of the adjectives "good" and "true" that St. Thomas uses to describe the maximum is that they name qualities that are attributes of being considered just as such. In other words, every being, simply insofar as it is being, is good; and every being, simply insofar as it is being, is true. From this we can conclude that the maximum in question is not the maximum with respect to being of this or that quality, but with respect to being just as being. Saint Thomas refers to that which "exists maximally," without qualification. And he goes on to say, after making a telling reference to Aristotle's *Metaphysics*, that "whatever things are maximally true are maximally in being." Reflecting on this in terms of comparative thinking, we can say that the more truth a thing has, the more being it has, given the fact that truth is an attribute of being just as such.

The idea that one being may be said to have more being than another, an idea central to an argument built around the theme of the degrees of being, may at first strike us as rather odd. Indeed, it may seem to be quite wrong. Could we not say that, by reason of the fundamental fact that all existents (i.e., real, extra-mental things) actually exist, that no single one of them exists any more, or less, than any of the others, however countless many things there may be in existence, and whatever their diversity? We could say that, and there would be some truth in saying it. All actual existing things have in common the fact that they represent a radical contrast to non-existence; each really *is*, and there is an infinite distance, so to speak, between being and non-being. But the principle of proper proportionality teaches us that, beginning on the level of individuals, no two things exist in precisely the same way; if they did, they would not be two things, but one. And a whole grouping of things (e.g., a biological species) has a common way of existing which is different from a common way of existing of another grouping. What is the metaphysical explanation for these differences? It is the fact that, on the most elementary level, that is, on the level of being just as such, the level of sheer existence, some beings have more being than others. And that means that any given being that can be said to have more being than any other given being is simply closer, in its substantial way of existing, to maximum being. Now, that maximum being, the being who *is* without qualification, whose nature is simply to be, is God.

Perhaps the most difficult to follow movement in the fourth way is found in the section immediately preceding the argument's conclusion. In this section St. Thomas asserts that "the maximum in any genus, is the cause of all the things that belong to that genus," and he uses the example of fire to illustrate his point. The example may prove to be more distracting than helpful, if it should lead us to interpret it in purely physical terms, thus missing the metaphysical message it is intended to convey. In order properly to catch St. Thomas's meaning here, it is of the utmost importance that we take note of the passage from Aristotle's *Metaphysics* which he cites. That citation was no casual gesture on St. Thomas's part, and he expects us to be aware of its import as we consider this section of the argument. The meaning of this section is to be found in the meaning of the cited passage from the *Metaphysics*.

With what is that passage from the *Metaphysics* concerned? It is found in the very early chapters of the work, where Aristotle is laying out the nature and purposes of what he called "first philosophy," what we know now as metaphysics. He is stressing the point that metaphysics has to do with ultimate causes. The example of fire, made use of by St. Thomas, is borrowed from Aristotle, who cites it as an example of an ultimate cause. Given a particular category of things that are marked by the quality of heat (things possessing heat to one degree or another), there is an ultimate explanation for this state of affairs, and that is fire. For Aristotle, fire would be an excellent example of maximum being; in his understanding, it is the hottest element (recall that in ancient cosmology fire was one of the four basic elements, the fundamental building blocks of all physical being), and therefore, as an ultimate, it is the cause of all heat, in whatever degree it may appear, in all things.

We may want to take exception to the example he uses because of what we see as its ineffectiveness in clearly illustrating what he intended that it illustrate, but we should nonetheless be clear as to his intention: fire was intended to represent the maximum in being. Immediately after citing the example of fire, Aristotle writes: "Therefore that is also true in the highest degree which is the cause of all subsequent things being true." [4] Now, whereas heat is a quality that can be attributed only to some beings (physical beings), truth, as we have seen, is attributed to all beings just insofar as they are beings, and thus to claim that the being which is the highest with respect to truth—which is only to say the highest being, the maximum being without qualification—is "the cause of all subsequent things being true" is to claim that the maximum being is the cause of the *being* of all subsequent things, for truth and being are one. This basic line of reasoning is confirmed by St. Thomas's commentary on this passage in the *Metaphysics*, where he writes: "Now the term *truth* is not proper to one class of beings only [e.g., beings that have the quality called heat or temperature], but is applied universally to all beings." [5]

The conclusion of the argument makes explicit the various ideas that we have been endeavoring to clarify here, ideas which are only implicitly present in the main body of the argument. "Therefore, there is to be found among all existents [i.e., real beings], that which is the cause of their being," and that is a being who is maximum with respect to being, the supreme being. "And this cause we call God."

The fourth way is the most elusive of St. Thomas's arguments for the existence of God, the hardest to grasp, and the least likely to compel ready assent. The reason for that, in my opinion, is to be found in its markedly elliptical quality. Much is left unsaid in the argument, and thus the reader must bring to it more than what is required for any of the other four—to fill in the lacunae. This is not an overly burdensome task, however, given the aid we are provided by St. Thomas himself in accomplishing it. For all its peculiar challenges, in the final analysis what we have in the fourth way is a sound and poignant argument.

I will end this commentary by attempting to provide as clear and cogent an account of the argument as I can. We look about us in the world and we see a multiplicity of being, and in comparing these beings with one another we immediately see that they are distinguishable in terms of "more" and "less"—more or less this, that, or the other thing, depending on the point of view from which we are assessing them. When we reflect on this very common and ordinary way of responding to our world, we further see that the only reason we can make such comparisons is because in doing so we are, implicitly or explicitly, making reference to a "most." To say that something is more noble, or less noble, for example, only makes sense in terms of what is most noble, the very height of nobility, or, to use St. Thomas's terminology, the maximum with respect to the noble. The maximum can be said to cause the comparative judgments we make, because such judgments would not be possible without the maximum. Now, let us think in terms of sheer existence, of being as opposed to non-being. We note, when we consider existence in this most basic of ways, that some beings can rightly be called higher beings than others. A single cell bacterium is not less an existent than is a bald eagle, but they do not exist on the same level; the bald eagle represents a higher level of being than does the bacterium. We say he has more being than the bacterium. So, there are degrees of being, understanding being in the most basic sense. Given this fact, that we can reasonably say of one thing that it is a higher being than another thing, we conclude that there must necessarily exist a being that is the highest of all beings, for it would be incoherent to claim that there are degrees of being, and yet deny the existence of a highest degree. Now, we assert that this highest is, indeed necessarily must be, the cause of all beings that are subordinate to it. How is this so? We must not, at this point, forget everything that we have learned through the first three arguments. The highest being is nothing else but Necessary Being, the Unmoved Mover, the First Cause, who, through His causality, brings every being into existence, according to the various degrees of being He has established for them.

The Fifth Way: The Argument from Finality, the Thomistic Text

The fifth way is taken from the governance of things. We see in the world any number of things which lack intelligence—for example, inanimate natural bodies—which nevertheless operate for the sake of an end. This is made obvious by the fact that these bodies operate always, or for the most part, in a uniform fashion. It is evident, therefore, that through their operations these bodies arrive at a given end, not through chance, but as if intentionally directed.

But, clearly, those things which lack intelligence could only operate as if intentionally directed toward a specific end because they were in fact directed thereto by a conscious, intelligent being—in somewhat the same manner in which an arrow is directed toward its target by an archer.

Therefore, there is an intelligent being by which inanimate natural bodies are directed to an end. And this being we call God. [6]

Explication and Commentary

This argument, the shortest of the five presented by St. Thomas, has been considered by many to be the most forceful and compelling. Even Immanuel Kant who, as we have seen, devoted considerable philosophical energy in attempting to prove that the existence of God could not be proved, was sufficiently impressed by the argument that he was willing to allow that it was not without some merits. "This proof always deserves to be mentioned with respect," he wrote. "It is the oldest, the clearest, and the most accordant with the common reason of mankind." [7]

The name most usually given to this argument, at least by Scholastic philosophers, is the argument from finality, although it is also often referred to as the argument from design. From what he says in the very first sentence of the argument, we might suppose that St. Thomas himself might call it the argument from the governance of the world. The ideas of governance and design are implied by the more basic idea of finality. Finality has to do with ends or purposes, which serve to define action, for any particular act derives its intelligibility from the end toward which it is directed and which it seeks to achieve. The final cause, we remember, is that which motivates action; it is that for the sake of which we do whatever we do, the purpose we intend to realize through our action. Finality necessarily implies intelligence, for only conscious agents, possessed of intellect, deliberately set purposes for themselves and then initiate the action that is calculated to achieve those purposes.

Governance would involve the maintenance, in orderly fashion, of a large and complex system, of one kind or another. A political system most readily comes to mind. Governance would necessarily involve finality, for the governor, in order to carry out his ordering tasks, would need continuously to establish an array of ends, on the achievement of which would depend the orderly maintenance of the system.

Design goes hand in hand with finality as well, for it would follow naturally upon finality, as effect to cause. To speak of a system as being designed is simply to say that it is intelligible by reason of its being well-ordered, and it is well-ordered, again, because ends are regularly being realized within the system. When we meet with design, then, we know that we are faced with something that can only be explained in terms of intelligence. Given how intimately they relate to each other, one could, in formulating an argument for the existence of God, choose to focus attention either on finality, or on the design that results from finality. In this fifth way, St. Thomas gives principal emphasis to finality.

The main thrust of the argument of the fifth way may be briefly expressed in the form of three basic propositions: (1) we live in a world that everywhere announces purpose (i.e., finality); (2) purpose necessarily implies intelligence; (3) the only explanation for the intelligence which is to be found in the world is an Intelligence that is the cause of the world.

We must be clear as to what lies at the heart of intelligent behavior. Intelligent behavior is simply purposeful behavior, end-oriented behavior. End-oriented behavior is behavior that gives rise to permanent patterns, which are to be found everywhere in the world, and which can also be referred to as the regularities of nature. The basis for these patterns, their cause, is the fact that things act, to use an Aristotelian phrase, "always or for the most part" in certain ways. More precisely, things regularly act for the sake of ends. It is this patterned behavior of nature that makes empirical science possible. More specifically, it is what makes scientific prediction possible.

Among the multifarious activities constantly taking place in nature, many are conducted by men, many by animals. It is easy enough to see that human beings, rational creatures, act for the sake of an end. Each of us knows this to be an indisputable fact, demonstrated time after time in our own personal experiences. We are constantly setting up for ourselves purposes to be accomplished, be they of large import or small, and then, with varying degrees of success, we go into action to accomplish them. Our very lives are given shape and sense by such incessant, end-oriented activity. When we turn our attention to animal behavior, especially that of the higher animals, it is also fairly easy to see there the pattern of purposeful behavior. The term "animal intelligence" is a familiar one; although it should not be construed as suggesting that animals are possessed of intellects, the term can serve the useful purpose of reminding us that animals regularly act for the sake of an end, that they display, in other words, intelligent behavior. But the intelligence that is reflected in animal behavior, we would argue, is not, strictly speaking, theirs.

What makes the approach that St. Thomas takes in this argument particularly interesting, and effective, is that, instead of concentrating on the more obvious instances of intelligent behavior in nature, i.e., that displayed by human beings and by animals,[8] he decides to deal with intelligence as it is manifested in inanimate things. Why is this approach so effective, given what he is attempting to accomplish in the argument? The basic assumption with which the argument begins is that intelligence is to be found *everywhere* in nature, even where perhaps we would least expect to find it, in the activity of inanimate matter. Human beings clearly have intelligence, and the higher animals have something analogous to intelligence. However, we would not be inclined to say that inanimate matter has intelligence. But if it can be shown that even inanimate matter acts intelligently, then we are forced to seek an explanation for that intelligent behavior apart from the inanimate matter itself.

Now, if we reflect seriously on inanimate things, we discover that they do indeed act intelligently, which is to say, they behave as if they were intelligent, as if they knew what they were doing, in the wonderfully consistent way they achieve ends. When certain chemical elements interact with one another, for example, the results of that interaction will be perfectly predictable. St. Thomas puts it this way: "We see in the world any number of things which lack intelligence— for example, inanimate natural bodies—which nevertheless operate for the sake of an end." To operate for the sake of an end is to act intelligently. When we speak of the intelligent behavior of inanimate things, we obviously do not mean that those things themselves possess intelligence. Clearly, they do not. But, once again, they behave as if they were intelligent, and therefore we are pressed to discover the source of the intelligence they display, if it is not to be found in them. The only conclusion to be reached is that the source of the intelligent behavior of these things, because it does not reside within them, is external to them.

Once again, when we say that inanimate nature acts consistently for the sake of an end, we are simply calling attention to the patterned regularities which are to be found everywhere in nature. And, by the way, it is just the presence of these patterned regularities which allow us to speak of "nature" at all, for what we call nature is simply the sum total of those patterned regularities; it is the grand pattern. More particularly, and as already mentioned, it is the patterned regularities that make scientific predictability possible. Empirical science can predict the future state or behavior of inanimate things precisely because, under certain conditions, those things will always act for the sake of a specific end that can be known beforehand. They are determined to the same outcome. A chemist who combines a sufficient quantity of the gas called hydrogen with the gas called oxygen, according to a set proportion between them, and then applies electricity to the mix, knows for certain that he is going to end up with the liquid called water.

If a research chemist proposes a new theory about how the inanimate world works, and if he has conducted experiments which to his satisfaction demonstrate the soundness of his theory, then those experiments should be able to be repeated by any other researcher who wants to test the theory, and those experiments should yield exactly the same results gotten by the chemist who proposed the theory. The very possibility of repeatable experiments yielding the same results underscores the reality of the patterned regularities of nature, or, to put it differently, the ubiquitous end-orientation of nature. The natural world is an eminently intelligible world. And it is intelligible because it is suffused with intelligence.

As much as hard-core materialists would want to have it otherwise, there is but a single explanation for intelligence: intelligence. The intelligent behavior of inanimate bodies cannot be explained in terms of those bodies themselves, for the simple reason that they lack intelligence. The source of the intelligent behavior of those bodies is then external to them. So much has been established. But right at this point some might be inclined to balk. Is it a fact that intelligence can only be explained by intelligence? Is finding an intelligent cause for intelligent behavior the only option open to us? Could we not simply say that the intelligent behavior we observe everywhere in nature was brought about by chance? Anyone who would be inclined to think that such an option is a real one (i.e., that it is rational), is simply ignorant of the nature of chance, and how it can be said to act as a cause. Chance, by definition, is that which does *not* happen always or for the most part. It is a departure from patterned, regular—and hence predictable— behavior. It is the exception to the rule. It would scarcely make sense, therefore, to appeal to an exception to the rule as an explanation for the rule itself. This would be like saying that the absence of order is the explanation for order. We must, therefore, conclude to the existence of an intelligence that is directing the intelligent activity of inanimate things.

"But clearly," St. Thomas writes, "those things which lack intelligence could only operate as if intentionally directed toward a specific end because they were directed thereto by a conscious intelligent agent...." And then, to illustrate this point, he uses the example of an arrow that is directed toward a target. Let us reflect for a moment on the image that example presents to us. We have an arrow that is flying through the air, and its flight is going to be terminated by its making a perfect bull's-eye. Now, we might say, that is a very intelligent thing for the arrow to do. Assuredly it is, but the intelligence in question here is not to be found in the arrow itself, but in the archer who directed the flight of the arrow. It is really the intelligence of the archer that we see manifested in the end-oriented flight of the arrow.

The formal conclusion of the argument: "Therefore, there is an intelligent being by which all intelligent bodies are directed to an end.

And this being we call God." If we confine ourselves to considering only a single instance of intelligent activity among inanimate things, or a limited set of such things, perhaps we could explain such activity by saying that it was directed by a super-human created intelligence (e.g., angelic intelligence). However, it would be putting an undo strain on the imagination to suppose that a created intelligence, no matter how great, could explain the vast array of end-oriented activity taking place in the entire universe. But, for the sake of argument, let us grant that this is a real possibility. Does that provide us with a satisfactory conclusion to the argument? It does not, for if we admit to the existence of a created intelligence, an intelligence which, by definition, is not an explanation for itself, we must then look for an adequate source of that created intelligence, and that would lead us, eventually, to a Supreme Intelligence, to God.

There are some commentators, often from the ranks of those who assume a generally skeptical view of natural theology, who take the position that all this argument proves is the existence of an intelligent being that is directing the course of the universe, but it does not prove the existence of a creator, a being who is the cause of the very existence of the universe. There are three observations that can be made in response to this position. First, anyone who is willing to concede that the argument proves the existence of a being that is directing the course of the universe hardly seems justified in saying that is "all" the argument proves. Such a conclusion is, after all, a rather formidable one, and to concede it is to concede a great deal indeed. If a being who directs the course of the universe is not God, he is most certainly god-like.

Second, the problem I cited just above, with regard to the claim that the intelligence of the universe could be explained by a created intelligence, applies to this position as well. If one is going to concede the existence of an intelligent being potent enough to direct the course of the universe, and yet balk at identifying such a being as one that is supreme in every respect (and would thus have the power to create), then one is forced to move beyond such a being in order to explain its existence. Third, and most importantly, no one who is responding to the Thomistic arguments in an appropriate way could possibly assume such a position. The fifth way is not to be taken in isolation from the four arguments that preceded it, and *on which it depends*. Saint Thomas's

Five Ways are not to be regarded as a haphazard collection, with only an incidental relation among the arguments. Together, they compose a coherent whole. St. Thomas would have been baffled by the prospect of anyone responding to the fifth argument as if the first four had never been made, and without having thoroughly assimilated their contents. What this comes down to, in specific terms, is this: the "Intelligence" that directs all inanimate bodies, whose existence is proven in the fifth way, is one and the same as the Prime Mover, as the First Cause, as Necessary Being. And what is the ultimate end toward which all created things are directed by their all-wise creator? Put another way, what is the purpose of creation? It is God Himself. God is the beginning of the world, in the sense that He is its creative source. And He is the end of the world, in the sense that its very reason for being is to be found in God.

The fifth way, as we saw, is built around the idea of finality, or of final causality. Many moderns, especially if they happen to be empirical scientists, have problems with this idea of final causality. Well, perhaps it would be more accurate to say that they simply find no need for it. It's not so much a problem for them as a nuisance. This odd point of view can be traced back very cleanly to the father of modern philosophy, René Descartes (1596–1650). Many moderns (I use that more general term because it includes philosophers as well as scientists) will cheerfully accept the reality of material cause, and of efficient cause, but final cause is dispensed with as having no real explanatory value. Now, one of the more debilitating effects of dismissing final causality is that, after doing so, one is then tempted to make the more sweeping claim that there is no finality at all to be found in nature. To say that there is no finality at all in nature is to say, to put it in plainer terms, that we live in a purposeless universe.

Aristotle would have been perfectly astonished by this point of view, for when he looked upon nature, finality, purpose, was staring him boldly in the face everywhere he turned. But the moderns don't see it, or at least they claim not to see it. It is remarkable what our theories can blind us to. The moderns who reject final causality find themselves in an anomalous position, to put it mildly. For, while their philosophy persuades them that there is no finality in nature, the science to which they are so assiduously dedicated fairly shouts it to the skies. As noted above, predictability is the very heart of empirical science, but predictability is impossible without finality. In dealing with inanimate matter, we can say with assurance how it will behave tomorrow, because of the patterned regularities it everywhere displays today. And those patterned regularities are explained by finality, the fact that all things in nature act for the sake of an end.

Another point to be made, of a very fundamental kind: those who readily accept efficient causality and yet see fit to reject final causality are vainly attempting to separate the inseperable. Final causality necessarily accompanies the operation of an efficient cause. An efficient cause acts to bring about a specific effect, which is the end, of the finality, toward which its action is ordered. An efficient cause is only intelligible, as such, in terms of its effect, which relates to it as a final cause, that for the sake of which it acts.

Chapter Seven

Objections to the Five Ways

Dissenting Opinions

In the 700 years since the Five Ways of St. Thomas have been in the public domain, they have drawn a wide variety of critical responses, ranging from mild corrective suggestions, made by generally sympathetic commentators, to wholesale rejection of the arguments on the part of those who take them to be complete failures. Considering the most intensely negative responses, those that attempt to demonstrate that the arguments are so radically flawed as to be ineffectual, it can be confidently reported that none of these attempts have proved successful. The Five Ways have come through all the attacks upon them essentially unscathed, and continue to stand as sound and compelling arguments for the existence of God. And many who have taken upon themselves the task of revealing to the world the supposed deficiencies of the reasoning of St. Thomas, have often only succeeded in exposing to public view the deficiencies of their own reasoning.

In reviewing the arguments of those who object to the Five Ways, and studying the particulars of their negative responses to them, one easily sees that the principal explanation for these responses is simply an inadequate understanding of what St. Thomas is attempting to do and how he goes about doing it. There is much missing of the point, and responding to points that are not to be found in the arguments. Certain commentators, supposing that they are up against St. Thomas, are in fact jousting with bogey-men of their own making. And what is the fundamental cause of this rather pervasive misunderstanding of St. Thomas's thought? The answer to that question will not surprise you: metaphysical deficiency. Many people come to the arguments of St. Thomas unprepared, not because they are unintelligent or short on earnestness, but because they have no grounding in metaphysics. This is especially true of modern philosophers. Would-be commentators are thus severely disadvantaged right at the outset. The language of the arguments is a foreign tongue to them. Someone who does not know Italian is not qualified to be a judge of the poetry of Dante.

This chapter consists of a survey of the various kinds of negative responses that have been made to the Five Ways, beginning with general difficulties and then proceeding to more specific criticisms. Despite the nature of its subject matter, this chapter is included in our study of natural theology for positive, not negative reasons. Of course, the best way to arrive at a sound understanding of St. Thomas's Five Ways is to confront the arguments themselves, with full intellectual engagement. Next to that, it is very helpful to read informed commentaries on the arguments. To these two approaches, a third can be added: there is much that can be learned about the arguments from those who do not take a sympathetic view of them, especially if their criticisms, though perhaps ill-informed, are nonetheless honest and intelligent.[1]

Objections Based on a General Rejection of Metaphysics

We have seen that if the Five Ways of St. Thomas are anything, they are metaphysical arguments. They begin in the physical world, and from what is discovered to be true about that world they go on to conclude to the existence of a Supreme Being who transcends the physical world and who is the explanation for that world's existence. The Five Ways are metaphysical in the specific sense that the reasoning they contain is based entirely on metaphysical principles, and, as we have repeated often in these pages, because these arguments are so thoroughly dependent on metaphysical reasoning, no one who is not schooled in that reasoning can be expected to gain what they have to offer. Ignorance of metaphysics, then, is the major obstacle to understanding the arguments. Given this to be the case, the deliberate rejection of metaphysics, the conscious repudiation of it as a legitimate mode of reasoning, would remove from anyone who takes that position the possibility of ever coming to understand the arguments. But the deliberate rejection of metaphysics is common today, and that explains, for obvious reasons, so many of the negative responses to the Five Ways.

In an earlier chapter we discussed the antagonistic position taken by Immanuel Kant against the possibility of demonstrating the existence of God, a position that was founded, you will recall, on his sweeping rejection of the possibility of metaphysics as such. Though his attempts at showing that metaphysical reasoning is ineffectual failed, Kant himself was convinced that they were successful. More significantly, Kant's many disciples, from his day to our own, were convinced that not only were their master's attacks upon metaphysics successful, but brilliantly so, and in their minds Kant had shown once and for all that metaphysics is a dead letter. A major factor, then, in the anti-metaphysical attitude that exists, even prevails, today, the attitude behind a general rejection of the Five Ways, is the influence of Immanuel Kant.

Another factor, perhaps as important, that explains the anti-metaphysical attitude, is the influence of scientism. Scientism is an exaggerated regard for empirical science, a tendency to credit empirical science with an intellectual prowess and scope which it does not have, and which is beyond its capacities ever to attain. Scientism sees empirical science as *the* single way open to man by which he will be able to gain genuine knowledge. In this view, "scientific" knowledge is the only real knowledge. It replaces all other ways to truth, such as those followed by philosophy and theology, which once may have had their limited uses, representing the best mankind could do at the time, in his still unenlightened state, but now they have to acknowledge their obsolescence and step aside, in deference to the superior way of empirical science. In its most exaggerated form, scientism makes a virtual religion out of empirical science, in the sense that empirical science is seen as now representing the sole means of salvation for mankind. It is important not to confuse scientism with empirical science; it is not empirical science, but a distorted view of it. Even so, it holds powerful sway in contemporary society, and, as perhaps one would expect, the popular media, always displaying an avid susceptibility for the *ersatz*, is much taken by it. But not a few philosophers and empirical scientists have, in one degree or another, succumbed to its seductive charms.

Two key metaphysical principles that figure prominently in the Thomistic arguments for the existence of God are, as we have seen, the principle of finality and the principle that informs us that an infinite regress is impossible. The rejection of these two principles, on the part of many empirical scientists and philosophers, represents specific aspects of the more general rejection of metaphysics spoken of above, and for that reason it would be instructive to reflect briefly on the rationale that commonly lies behind this rejection. It has become something like a standard doctrine in the philosophy of science that modern science (i.e., empirical science) has disposed of the whole notion of final causality, and for the simple reason that it has no need for it. Any number of scientific theories have been shown to be true, in the sense that they have successful practical applications in the physical world, but none of these theories contain any explicit reference to, or even peripheral concern with, the notion of final causality. Final causality simply does not seem to count as a viable factor in the actual "doing" of empirical science. Not a few scientists assume an attitude that would be reflected in a statement such as the following: "I have no concern with what the physical world might be 'for,' its putative purpose, either as a whole or in terms of its particulars. I only want to try to figure out how it works."

This is not an altogether foolish point of view. Often enough, perhaps in more cases than not, the scientist does not have to take conscious account of finality in order to achieve the practical success he is looking for. But that should not lead us precipitously to conclude that the principle of finality is somehow irrelevant, that it is not operatively in place, even though it does not have to enter into the scientist's highly limited kinds of calculations. The empirical scientist, when he is acting precisely as such, is not thinking and acting as a metaphysician. The realm of empirical science is encompassed within the realm of metaphysics, and hence governed by its principles, but the empirical scientist does not always have consciously to advert to those principles in order to do his empirical science. But, once again, that does not mean the principles are not there, and operative. It may very well be true that a scientist need not consciously think of finality as he is attempting to figure out how the world works, and he may not have to incorporate finality into his theories in any explicit fashion, but finality is as a matter of fact everywhere present in the physical world. The real existence of something does not depend on our being actively conscious of it.

We need only consider ourselves, who are very much part of the physical world, to see how that is so. In any of our many end-oriented daily actions, we do not have to explicitly formulate, in each and every instance, even to ourselves, the end toward which a particular act is directed. There is no need to do this. The act incorporates finality within itself, for it would not be a discernible act without that finality. I hope I have succeeded, in earlier pages of this work, in persuading you that empirical science is simply impossible without the abiding, ubiquitous, operative presence of final causality. But to give yet further emphasis to that important point, consider for a moment the scientist's claim that he is only interested in finding out "how things work." That is an admirable enough ambition. But, how *do* things in nature work? They work purposefully, invariably ordered in their activity toward achieving precisely specifiable ends. To know how two chemical elements work in relation to one another is to know the predictable outcome of their interactions, given the very natures of those elements. To know how a machine works is to know how it achieves the purposes for which it was designed. Those who claim that they have no use for final causality because they are exclusively occupied with discovering how the physical world works are, in that very occupation, in intimate relation with that which is supposedly of no use to them.

Just as some scientists reject final causality, others reject the notion of the impossibility of infinite regress. If those who reject finality do so because of a professed indifference toward the purpose of things, those who spurn the notion of the impossibility of infinite regress do so because they have no concern with the origin of things. We might imagine an empirical scientist saying something like the following: "You tell me that an infinite regress is impossible. That does not particularly impress me. Indeed, it leaves me quite indifferent. I do not, in my work, need to appeal to infinite regress, either to affirm it or to deny it. I can make progress in my science without it." The position expressed here is perfectly legitimate as far as it goes. But it should be noted that it represents a point of view that is content to remain, perhaps permanently, this side of metaphysics. It is certainly reasonable to suppose that a scientist could do productive work within his particular field without bothering to inquire into the origins of the things he is dealing with. An ichthyologist, for example, may come to have command of a great deal of knowledge of various species of fish, without harboring any interest in how those species may have come to be what they are in the first place. And, more fundamentally, he may never entertain any serious philosophical thoughts about the origin of life itself. By doing so, however, he would remain within the rather narrow, but relatively comfortable, confines of empirical science. The working empirical scientist might put aside any consideration of the impossibility of infinite regress simply because it is of no practical use to him. That is fair enough. He may evince no interest in how the things he is dealing with originally came to be, but what he cannot do is deny that the things he is dealing with at one time did in fact originally come to be. By not thinking about the origins of things he is simply not thinking as a philosopher. It is of the very essence of philosophy to think about the origins of things, which is to say, to think about first causes, and that is why a philosopher could never be content with the attitude assumed by our ichthyologist. And because philosophy is dedicated to the task of discovering first causes, it gives the utmost attention to the notion that an infinite regress is impossible. To assent to the possibility of an infinite regress, as we have said more than once, is effectively to abandon philosophy.[2]

Another explanation for the general rejection of the Five Ways is to be found in the dominance of the naturalistic and materialistic world-views adhered to by so many of today's influential intellectuals, very much including philosophers and scientists. Naturalism is that philosophic position that holds that "Nature" is all in all, that there is only one order of things, one sphere of reality, and that is the natural order. There is no supernatural order. Naturalism and materialism are indistinguishable, for the "Nature" that supposedly constitutes all that actually exists, is the physical or material world. So, what the naturalistic philosopher is telling us is that there is only a single reality and that is material reality. Spiritual reality, for him, is pure fiction. Naturalism is not necessarily to be linked with either scientism or the anti-metaphysical attitude spoken of above, although not a few of those with a weakness for scientism would also be inclined to accept a naturalistic world-view, and the same could be said of those who harbor an entrenched prejudice against metaphysics. It would stand to reason that a thoroughgoing naturalist would have no truck with the Five Ways of St. Thomas. Indeed, he would be completely blind to their meaning. The naturalist position begins with the assumption that metaphysical reasoning is vacuous.

Because of the stunning practical success of the empirical sciences over the past 350 years or so, a success which has its concrete expression in the wonders of modern technology, empirical science, or at least its more enthusiast advocates, has too often succumbed to something like an overweening pride on account of its accomplishments, and it was this which in great part led to the genesis of the phenomenon called scientism. In recent times science has adopted a more modest attitude, and most scientists today show an intellectual humility which was not always to be found among their predecessors, particularly not among the scientists of the nineteenth century. For all that, however, there are many scientists today who continue to show little regard for philosophy, and are more than a little reluctant to admit the subordinate position that empirical science holds in relation to philosophy. Scientific knowledge, although it unquestionably qualifies as genuine knowledge, is not, as the fervid proponent of scientism would have us believe, the only real knowledge. And it very definitely is not foundational knowledge. The reason why this is so, in more cases than not, is because the scientist mistakes his science for philosophy, which is to say, he erroneously believes that its scope is greater than in fact it is. But there is an opposite kind of mistake to be made, when the philosopher, become too bedazzled by the practical successes of empirical science, begins to think that science can in fact do what only philosophy can do.

Objection: The Five Ways Are Based on a Flawed Cosmology

Another general objection that is leveled against the Five Ways is that they cannot be relied upon as sound arguments because they are based upon a cosmology, a philosophy of nature, which is now obsolete. The physical science of the thirteenth century, around which St. Thomas built his arguments, was entirely deficient, as has been demonstrated by modern science, and therefore the arguments themselves cannot be regarded as trustworthy. In a word, the arguments are unstable because the science on which they were based was unstable.

A good part of medieval physical science took its inspiration from the works of Aristotle, particularly the *Physics* and *On the Heavens*, and Aristotle did hold views about the nature of the physical world that have been shown to be erroneous. For example, Aristotle believed that there were two basic types of matter, sublunary or earthly matter, and celestial matter, of which the heavenly bodies were composed, which was considered by him to be a more refined, superior kind of matter. And it is evident that St. Thomas adopted this and other Aristotelian theories about the physical universe, that we now know to be wrong.

Before addressing the central point of this objection, it would be appropriate to comment on the status of medieval physical science in general. The people of English-speaking Western countries continue to labor under the serious handicap of having been subjected, by several generations of less than scrupulous historians, to a considerable degree of misinformation about the Middle Ages in general and about medieval physical science in particular. These historians, having swallowed the great fiction fabricated by the Renaissance, portrayed the Middle Ages as a retrogressive era, an embarrassing halt in mankind's otherwise steadily progressive march toward full enlightenment. Thanks to the impressive research done by historians such as Etienne Gilson, Pierre Duhem, and Fr. Stanley Jaki, just to name three among many eminent scholars, the educated world now knows better. It will no longer do to consider the word "medieval" as roughly synonymous with "benighted" or "backward." To be sure, the science of the thirteenth century was not the science of the twenty-first century, nor would anyone who is aware of the developmental nature of science expect it to be. But for what it was, it was quite impressive, and cannot be dismissed as the bumbling work of people who were the blind slaves to an oppressive authoritarianism. More and more historians now recognize that the physical science of the Middle Ages was the *sine qua non* pre-condition of the scientific revolution that occurred in the seventeenth century.

And as for Aristotle, yes, he was wrong about some things, but the wonder is the so many things he was so right about, things of the deepest significance. Aristotle was one of the great geniuses of all time, and there is something verging on the comical in the spectacle of certain moderns passing supercilious judgment on his work, chiding him for his mistakes, as if oblivious of the fact that so much of what they know today is directly depended on the knowledge developed by the man from Stagira. If they would only look down at their feet they would see that they stand perched on the shoulders of a giant, and those shoulders belong to Aristotle.

But now to the particular objection, that the Five Ways are based on a flawed cosmology, and are therefore themselves flawed. The premise is false, and therefore the conclusion does not follow. To be sure, there are any number of questionable, not to say egregiously erroneous, tenets to be found in medieval cosmology, but not a single one of them is to be found in the Five Ways, much less as exercising anything like significant governing influence over their mode of reasoning. All of the foundational ideas of the arguments are metaphysical principles, which are as sound today as they were in the thirteenth century, and as they were in the time of Aristotle, and that is because they relate to, and reflect, the very nature of the world in which we live. I have in mind, of course, principles such as potency and act, efficient causality, final causality, contingent being.

Rejection of the *Quidquid Movetur* Principle

As we have seen, the metaphysical principle, *quidquid movetur ab alio movetur*, "whatever is moved is moved by another," plays an explicitly important role in the argument of the first way, but it is implicitly at work in the four other arguments as well. The rudimentary idea that is being pointed to by this principle is the radical dependency of all created being, of every existing thing that we can come to know through our sense experience. More particularly, and as applied to physical being, the principle tells us that any change of position of a physical object (i.e., locomotion) is always to be accounted for by an object other than the one whose position is changing. And the deeper metaphysical description for that state of affairs, we know, is that an object which is in potency, and not in act, in a certain respect cannot reduce itself to act. Concretely, no physical object in a state of rest can transfer itself from that state to a state of motion.

Some have called into question the legitimacy of this principle, claiming that it is nullified by a principle of classical physics, the principle of inertia. The principle of inertia, also known as the first law of motion, can be stated as follows: "A body remains at rest, or, if already in motion, remains in uniform motion with constant speed in a straight line, unless it is acted upon by an unbalanced external force."[3] If we were to carefully reflect on this principle, we would see that there is no conflict between it and the *quidquid movetur* principle. The two are completely compatible.

The first thing to be noted about the law of inertia is that it makes no mention of how a body that remains in uniform motion with constant speed in a straight line got to be in that state in the first place. Now, if this principle had been formulated by Aristotle, who believed in an eternal world, we might want to say that there is no need to wonder about how a moving body got to be in motion, for perhaps it was in motion from all eternity. But this principle was formulated by Isaac Newton, who believed that the world was created, had a beginning in time, and therefore we must conclude that objects now in motion were at one time set in motion, albeit simultaneously with their very creation. However, we do not need to go outside the principle in order to conclude that whatever is in motion needs an explanation for its being in that state, for the principle itself provides us warrant for reaching that conclusion. In the latter part of the statement of the principle we are told that any change in the uniform motion of a body will be brought about by an *external force*. In other words, *any* change of state of a physical body, from rest to motion, from motion to rest, an alteration in the direction or rate of motion, is to be explained by something other than the body to which the change is being attributed. The "force" here would be that of another body, or bodies. Once again, there is nothing in the principle of inertia that militates against the principle that whatever is moved is moved by another. To the contrary, the former confirms the latter.

Albert Einstein saw empirical confirmation of the principle of inertia in the fixed stars.[4] That represents a rather authoritative endorsement of the principle. But could we rightly say that the principle just as such is empirically verifiable? In fact, the law would seem to be unconfirmable in any direct manner. The law suggests that if a physical body is in uniform motion it will remain in uniform motion forever, unless interfered with by another body. (This is assuming that the only knowledge we have is that provided to us by this law.) The only observer that could verify this law, assuming an Aristotelian eternal universe, would be an eternal observer. We must say, then, that the law, just as stated, applies to no actually existing physical system within the realm of our experience, and the physicist Isaac Asimov is quite correct in noting: "The Newtonian principle of inertia therefore holds exactly in an imaginary ideal world in which no interfering forces exist: no friction, no air resistance."[5] In the real world of physical bodies, the motion of any given body owes its motion to other moving bodies, and no motion of any given body goes unmolested by the motion of other moving bodies (i.e., any external forces). When we say that everything that moves is moved by another, we do not have to interpret the "other" in concrete terms, as if it referred to a single, specifically identifiable body. It could of course be that, but the "other" can refer as well to any physical condition external to a body and which acts upon the body, such as, for example, a magnetic field, or gravity.

Objection: The Theory of Relativity Destroys the Assumptions on Which the Five Ways Are Based

This objection could be seriously made only by someone who has not taken the time to acquaint himself with the theory of relativity. Albert Einstein, the father of relativity theory, took an attitude toward certain basic metaphysical principles, such as the *quidquid movetur* principle[6] and the principle of efficient causality, that figure so prominently in the Five Ways, which reveals many similarities between his thought and the thought of St. Thomas. In his book, *Relativity: The Special and General Theory*, Einstein makes use of a simple example, much like the kinds of simple examples employed by St. Thomas, which can serve as an excellent illustration of the *quidquid movetur* principle, as well as the principle of efficient causality.[7] We will recall from an earlier discussion that either one of these principles always implies the other.

So central was motion, and the causes of motion, to Einstein's whole way of viewing the physical universe, that these phenomena served for him as the foundations for his two theories, and led to his eventual rejection of the Newtonian notions of space and time. For Isaac Newton (1642–1727) space and time were considered to be quite distinct from the physical bodies, and their motion, with which they were related, and indeed they had been given by him the status of independent entities, as if each were separate substances.[8] In rejecting Newton's ideas of space and time, Einstein was in effect returning to an essentially Aristotelian–Thomistic understanding of them. He described space, for example, as "motion relative to a practically rigid body of reference."[9] What this means is that space should be considered as constituted by bodies and their motion. Einstein's understanding of time is also essentially Aristotelian–Thomistic, for its foundation is in the world of moving physical objects, welling up, as it were, out of that world.[10] For Einstein, space and time were inconceivable without physical bodies in motion. That is a very Aristotelian way of looking at things.

In sum, relativity theory, whatever may be its future, cannot, as it stands today and as it is commonly interpreted, be rightly thought of as antipathetic to the basic lines of reasoning that govern the arguments of the Five Ways. In general, the manner in which relativity theory regards the nature of the physical universe is quite compatible with the manner in which those arguments regard the physical universe. And, as indicated by the above comments, Einstein himself tended to be very much an Aristotelian in the way he looked at the world; he was in his heart of hearts a philosophical realist.[11]

Objection: Quantum Theory Destroys the Assumptions on Which the Five Ways Are Based

Quantum theory, or quantum mechanics, is that sub-field of physics that focuses its investigations on elementary particles, matter as it manifests itself at the sub-atomic level. Do the antics of matter in this exotic realm of particle physics force us to scrap conventional ways of regarding the world in which we live, and draw up entirely new schemata in an attempt to explain that world? Specifically, must venerable principles such as that of efficient causality now be called into question, at least in terms of its having universal applicability? The answer to both questions is No. The physicist Werner Heisenberg, one of the pioneer researchers in the field of quantum theory, and the man who gave us "the principle of indeterminancy," after explaining, in his book, *Physics and Philosophy*, that, as far as he is concerned, matter and energy are the same thing, goes on to ask, What is the most salient property of the matter/energy entity? "Energy," he reponds, "is in fact

that which moves; it may be called the primary cause of change...." [12]
That description would fit nicely with the Aristotelian-Thomistic notion
concerning one of the foundational features of physical reality. Also,
note the implied reference to the *quidquid movetur* principle in the
statement.

We gave considerable stress to the importance which the concept
of substance plays in the Five Ways. Dr. Heisenberg, in a later chapter
than that from which the above quotation is taken, writes the following:
"If one would want to express our modern experience in the language
of older philosophers, one could consider mass *and* energy as two
different forms of the same 'substance' and thereby keep the idea of
substance indestructible." [13] No one who is open to keeping the idea
of substance indestructible can be said to be interpreting the physical
universe in ways that run radically counter to the general spirit of the
Five Ways. All in all, there is nothing in the account of quantum theory
provided by Heisenberg which shows that it is, in the main, antithetical
to the general ideas respecting the physical universe which are to be
found in the Five Ways.

But how about the notion of efficient causality? Does not the
principle of indeterminancy imply that causal relations, at a certain very
primitive, micro-level of physical reality, do not hold, as they would hold
on the macro-level of physical reality? The principle of indeterminancy
tells us, specifically, that we cannot simultaneously measure both the
velocity and the position of a particle. If we determine its velocity,
we can say nothing of its position; if we determine its position, we
must surrender any knowledge of its velocity. The significance of this
state of affairs is that it has a decidedly adverse affect on our ability
to make predictions about the future state of any given particle. Now,
predictability, the very core of empirical science, is based squarely
on the cause/effect relation. Are we not then forced to conclude that,
because predictability is not possible at this level, efficient causality
itself is not operative?

This line of reasoning would seem to be considerably too hasty.
What is the precise nature of the problem? It is our inability to come
up with exact measurements of certain phenomena, and because of
that we in turn lose our ability to make exact predictions, and therefore
have to be content with statistical estimates. We end by concluding that
because *we* cannot register clear cause/effect relations, they are not there

to be registered. But, as the physicist Father Stanley Jaki has pointed out, we are making an unjustified shift here from the epistemological to the ontological realm. We are transferring the limitations in our knowledge to what we suppose to be the limitations in the way things actually stand in the real world. Again, and specifically in terms of efficient causality, because we cannot precisely determine it, we say that it is not operative. "It is a non-sequitur," Father Jaki writes, "to claim that if an interaction cannot be measured exactly, it cannot take place exactly." This, he explains, constitutes an illegitimate "jump from the operational to the ontological domain." [14]

The Objections of Anthony Kenny

We will complete this chapter by considering some more specific objections to the Five Ways as presented by three philosophers, one British, Anthony Kenny, and two American, Mortimer Adler and George H. Smith. Anthony Kenny, who was Master of Balliol College, Oxford, wrote an entire book on the Five Ways of St. Thomas, in which he took a rather jaundiced view of them. In the Introduction to this work he makes his attitude toward them crystal clear when he announces that the arguments that follow will be intended to show that "the Five Ways fail." [15] I cannot, in this short section, hope to make an adequate response to the arguments that Dr. Kenny develops in his book; to do that would require a book in itself, one at least as long as Dr. Kenny's, and very likely longer. What I will do here is concentrate on a single chapter of the book, the chapter given over to his treatment of the fourth way.

In our own discussion of the fourth way, in the previous chapter, we made mention of the fact that some commentators take the view that what we have in this argument is the revelation of a decidedly Platonic mode of reasoning. Specifically, the claim is made that St. Thomas's "maximum" is to be interpreted as comparable to a Platonic Idea or Form. Dr. Kenny is very much of this school. He begins his critique by straightforwardly stating his assumption that the argument represents a Platonic way of thinking, and he informs us that he is not alone in making this assumption. "All agree," he writes, "that it is the way [i.e., the fourth way] in which, for better or worse, St. Thomas comes closest to Platonism." [16] There is no citation accompanying this claim, and one would give worlds to know to whom the "all" refers. But, putting that aside, there is no question but that Dr. Kenny is convinced that he has caught out St. Thomas in the act of trafficking in Platonic ontological thought. Now, Dr. Kenny has every right to make the assumption he does, and in fact it is a common and respectable way of proceeding in argumentation to state one's assumptions at the beginning of the discourse. But then the whole purpose of the argument which follows is to show that your assumptions are founded. Dr. Kenny does not do this. He begins with an assumption, and ends with an assumption. One of the more remarkable things about this chapter of some twenty-five pages, ostensibly dedicated to a close scrutiny of the fourth way, is that it says relatively little about the fourth way. There is much talking around St. Thomas's argument, but the argument itself is seldom addressed directly. A goodly part of the chapter is taken up with a discussion of Platonic ontology, and with the treatment of various logical questions, whose bearing on the fourth way is not always abundantly clear. Dr. Kenny does spend some time treating larger aspects of St. Thomas's thought, most notably, his ideas relating to essence and existence, and he has some interesting things to say on this matter, but the applications he wants to make of his interpretation of St. Thomas's understanding of essence and existence, which he opposes to that of Professor Henry Geach, are highly questionable.

But, once again, the central disabling fact about Dr. Kenny's whole argument is that it makes an assertion, a very bold assertion indeed, which is never supported. His assumption remains an assumption. However, that assumption grows over the course of the argument, receives considerable embellishment along the way, and, by argument's end, takes a form that is recklessly extreme. St. Thomas had formulated a phrase, since become famous, which he intended to describe, insofar as human language can ever do so, the nature of God: *Ipsum Esse Subsistens*, "Subsistent Being Itself." The phrase represents an attempt to convey the sublime idea that with God there is no real distinction between essence, His nature, and existence. What this means, put in plain terms, is that it is the very nature of God to exist. God, in other words, is the Necessary Being. It is hard to imagine any three word phrase that could be more successful than this one in fulfilling the lofty aim for which it was intended. It is a masterpiece of succinctness and precision. What is

Dr. Kenny's response to the phrase? He informs us that it "turns out to be the Platonic Idea of a predicate which is at best uninformative and at worst unintelligible." Just previous to making that assertion, he had declared that the conclusion of the fourth way was Platonic, for St. Thomas's "God" is but "the Platonic idea of Being."[17]

Those, then, are the assumptions with which Dr. Kenny's argument ends, the specifications, as it were, of the general assumption with which the argument began. As I said, he does not give us any real substantiation for those assumptions. He does not demonstrate them to be true. Morever, given what he has himself committed himself to in his argument, he is unable to offer any demonstration for them. As I mentioned, Dr. Kenny spends much time in his argument discussing Platonic ontology, paying specific attention to Plato's understanding of the Ideas, which figure so prominently in his philosophy. In summing up this discussion, he observes, quite correctly, that it is no easy matter to determine precisely what Plato meant by Idea. What exactly did he believe the ontological status of an Idea to be? What is the exact existential relation between an Idea and a thing in the physical world which, somehow, reflects that Idea? These and like questions have taxed the wits of eminent Platonic scholars for centuries, and no definitive responses have been given to them. And it is unlikely that, what with the lack of clarity to be found in the Platonic texts themselves concerning these matters, that definitive responses will ever be given. As Dr. Kenny points out, Plato himself raises some of the most poignant criticisms that have been directed against the whole theory of Ideas. The upshot of all this is that we simply cannot say with any kind of certainty what Plato meant by a Platonic Idea. If this is true, what is the basis of Dr. Kenny's assurance in claiming that St. Thomas's "God" is simply the Platonic Idea of being? Let us put aside the question whether that assertion is true or false. The more basic question is, What possible meaning could such an assertion have? If Plato himself was, by every indication, unsure of what he meant by the Ideas, if the rest of us, including Dr. Kenny, are equally unsure, what clear cognitive content is being conveyed by saying that something is a Platonic Idea? It is like saying that something is an "I-do-not-know-what."

It is hard to imagine that Dr. Kenny, given his background, was unfamiliar with the metaphysics that one must bring to St. Thomas's arguments in order properly to appreciate them and correctly to interpret them. But if he once knew and was committed to that metaphysics, he decided to abandon it, and he became a dedicated proponent of analytic philosophy. Indeed, his book on the Five Ways could pass as a textbook exercise in analytic philosophy. This is a philosophy which pays more attention to the language we use to talk about things than to things themselves, and which, very significantly, is marked by a deep anti-metaphysical bias. It is, at bottom, a system rooted in philosophical idealism. Analytic philosophy saw its inception in the early years of the twentieth century, and eventually became the dominant intellectual force in British academe, so much so that it might well have been called the national philosophy of Britain.

In the end, one must say that it is Dr. Kenny's claim, "the Five Ways fail," that fails, in the prosaic sense that he simply does not demonstrate it to be the case. His book leaves the integrity of the Five Ways entirely intact. But there is an oddity that he should have written the book at all, given the admission he makes on the very first page of the work. "I shall not try to prove or disprove the existence of God," he writes; "I should like to do one or the other, but I cannot do either." [18] He confesses to not being able either to prove or disprove the existence of God. Presumably, because he is the scholar he is, he assiduously plied himself to these tasks and was unsuccessful at them. Now, because Dr. Kenny cannot prove the existence of God, that does not mean that it cannot be done, nor does he suggest as much. But would one who admits his inability to prove the existence of God be the best judge in determining whether others succeed or fail in attempting to do so? If I have known nothing but failure in pursuing a certain project, how would I know what counts for success in it? And at what point might "I cannot do it" become "It cannot be done"?

The Objections of Mortimer Adler

No more than with Anthony Kenny, the philosopher Mortimer Adler could not be accused of an ignorance of metaphysics. One of the foremost American philosophers of the twentieth century, Adler was perhaps best known as a dedicated student, and enthusiastic expositor, of the thought of Aristotle and of St. Thomas Aquinas. He was a prolific writer, and can be taken, all in all, as an eminently reliable philosophic guide. But for all his admiration for, even devotion to, St. Thomas, he took pointed exception to the Five Ways, considering them to be in the main ineffectual.[19] His objections to the arguments center around a single notion, the notion of contingent being. As we well know, the argument of the third way is built around that concept, but Dr. Adler's concern is not limited to that argument alone, for, as he rightly says, the notion of contingent being is to be found operative, albeit implicitly, in the other four arguments as well. So, he takes the notion of contingent being to have a bearing on all of the arguments. If there is a problem with that notion, which he believes to be the case, then we have a problem which applies to the Five Ways as such.

Dr. Adler makes a distinction between radical contingency and superficial contingency. A radically contingent being is one that depends on another being for its very existence (*esse*); a superficially contingent being is one that depends on another being only for a peculiar mode of being (*fieri*). This is a distinction which we would readily recognize and accept. Now, the contingency that St. Thomas definitely has in mind in his arguments is radical contingency. Dr. Adler acknowledges this, but claims that St. Thomas is mistaken. He argues that although it is most certainly the case that the world is populated with contingent beings, those beings are superficially contingent beings, not radically contingent beings. In other words, the contingent beings we know are not dependent upon another being for their very existence, but for their existing in this or that way, for example, as hot or cold, or as moving, or as knowing geometry. Furthermore, there is no need to appeal to anything other than superficially contingent being to explain the changes that take place in that type of being, for clearly one superficially contingent being can have causal influence on another superficially contingent being. Now, if the only kind of contingent being that exists is superficially contingent being, you cannot use that type of being as the basis for arguing for the existence of a necessary being, because, once again, superficially contingent being is sufficiently explained by superficially contingent being. You do not have to go outside the realm of superficially contingent being in order to explain it.

With that account, it should be clear that the success of Dr. Adler's argument rests entirely on the soundness of the premiss which asserts that the only kind of contingent being is superficially contingent being. As it happens, this premise is false. What is the rationale behind his making the mistaken claim that the only kind of contingent being is superficially contingent being? It has to do with his failure to appreciate the significance of substantial change, a poignant example of which would be the death of a living organism. In developing his argument, Dr. Adler himself uses the example of a living organism. He contends that a living organism is not a radically contingent being, because when it dies it does not really cease to exist. A being could only be considered to be radically contingent, he argues, if, absent the being on which the contingent being is supposedly radically dependent, the contingent being would be annihilated. But no annihilation occurs with the death of a living organism for, after death, the matter with which the organism was once composed remains.

Let us consider that scenario more closely, and think in terms of a specific living organism, a chipmunk. The chipmunk, Dr. Adler would claim, is not a radically dependent being, for when it dies there is no annihilation. But in fact there is annihilation, the annihilation of a chipmunk. After death, there is no chipmunk. Granted, there remains the matter of which the chipmunk was once composed, but that is not *its* matter (as Dr. Adler would maintain). All secondary matter is informed matter, otherwise it would not exist. While the chipmunk lives, the matter of which it is composed is informed by its animal soul or life principle (the substantial form of the chipmunk). When the chipmunk dies, the matter of which it was once composed takes on several new forms (e.g., the substantial forms of chemical elements). There is nothing of the chipmunk in that matter. The chipmunk, therefore, like all other substances, be they animate or inanimate, are radically contingent beings, because they can really cease to be the substances they are, and their continuance in being, as substances, represents a dependency on nothing else but a necessary being, God.

The Objections of George H. Smith

In 1974 the California philosopher George H. Smith published a highly polemical book bearing the rather arresting title, *Atheism: The*

Case Against God. In it, among other tasks he sets for himself, he subjects various proofs for the existence of God to a rather stern and uncompromising critique, his purpose being to show that these proofs are of no avail. Now, it is scarcely surprising that a professed, indeed zealously militant, atheist such as Mr. Smith would take exception to any attempt to prove the existence of God. Given his presuppositions, how could he interpret such an attempt as anything but an exercise in futility? After all, if you begin with the assumption that there is no God, proofs for the alleged existence of a non-existent being would have to be dismissed *prima facie* as complete nonsense. And Mr. Smith endeavors to show that is precisely what such proofs are. There would seem to have been no doubt in his own mind that he succeeded in that endeavor. On that pivotal point we would beg to disagree

Mr. Smith does not attack the Five Ways as such. You will not find in his book any of St. Thomas's arguments presented as St. Thomas presented them, and quoted in full. Indeed, it is an open question whether Mr. Smith had direct access to the Thomistic texts. All of the arguments that Mr. Smith attacks are, for the most part, as formulated in his own words. Now, there is nothing at all wrong in formulating another's argument in your own words, just so long as your formulation fairly reflects the original. But what we run into here is the same kind of problem we found when we were dealing with Immanuel Kant. As was the case with Kant, so too with Mr. Smith, the arguments as presented do less than full justice to the originals, and in some cases they amount to little more than caricatures of the originals. Without in any way questioning the integrity of Mr. Smith's subjective intentions—he may sincerely have thought that he was presenting the arguments in their strongest forms—what we have, objectively, is the operative presence of the straw man fallacy. A knowledgeable theist, one who is well versed in the Five Ways, as well as being familiar with other classical arguments for the existence of God, would not be especially impressed by Mr. Smith's various offensives. He might say: "Well, you may have nicely devastated *those* arguments, but they are not arguments that I would be prepared to recognize and call my own."

More pointedly, Mr. Smith is capable of getting very specific, and critically important, things entirely wrong. I will cite but two items, from the many we have to choose from. Speaking of what he calls the first cause argument (which we may take to be remotely, very remotely, related to the second way), he writes: "According to this version of the first-cause argument, we must posit a *temporal* first cause, i.e., a first cause in *time*."[20] (emphasis his) First, one would dearly want to know where he got the "version" of the argument he presents to us. Second, and to the point, the assertion he makes here, emphases and all, is simply false. Not only is it false, it is silly, and shows a radical misunderstanding of the whole thrust of the argument. One does not *posit* a first cause, in or out of time. The point of the argument is to prove the existence of a first cause. To posit such a cause would be to commit the fallacy of begging the question, assuming to be true what you are obliged to prove to be true.

In dealing with the argument from contingent being, or, rather, his version of the argument, Mr. Smith makes the categorical statement: "Everything exists necessarily."[21] This is true in the qualified sense that no actually existing being can both be and not be at one and the same time, for that would clearly involve a contradiction. (We may call this relative necessity.) But in the strict sense of necessity (absolute necessity), it is not true that everything exists necessarily, for if that were the case, it would be impossible for anything that actually exists ever not to exist. And the all too familiar phenomenon of things passing away would be no part of our experience. In the course of his discussion of this argument Mr. Smith uses an example that not only shows a fundamental confusion in his understanding of the difference between contingency and necessity, but it lands him in a rather flagrant inconsistency, if not outright contradiction. He writes: "So, for example, we might say that a building exists contingently, meaning that, if certain men had decided to act differently, the building would never have been constructed."[22] To say that an actually existing building exists contingently because those who built it might have decided not to build it, is simply to say that the building itself, which actually exists, need not necessarily exist, and this is to assent to the Scholastic philosopher's understanding of contingency, which he has presumably rejected by his claim that everything exists necessarily. One cannot simultaneously claim that something exists necessarily, in the sense Mr. Smith apparently wants us to understand it, and also claim that it exists contingently, in any way whatsoever, for necessary existence and contingent existence are mutually exclusive.

Mr. Smith's book is replete with bold categorical declarations for which he offers no substantiation of any kind, the expectation presumably being that the reader will accept what he says simply on the weight of his having said it. He expatiates with great assurance on what theists think about this, that, or the other thing, as if he were gifted with some sort of preternatural insight into the minds of men. And the book abounds in non sequiturs, such as the following: "To say that god [sic] caused the universe to exist is to argue that man can never comprehend the existence of the universe."[23] But it would be an endless task to continue to point out the difficulties that attend this book. I mentioned in the previous section that it would take a book longer than Dr. Kenny's adequately to respond to its arguments. To do justice to Mr. Smith's book would require a response that would make up at least a couple of volumes. But should those volumes ever be written, just what affect, one might ask, would they have on a naturalistic thinker like Mr. Smith?

A metaphysician, responding in detail to a naturalist's arguments, could only respond as a metaphysician, and that would make him a virtual non-person as far as the naturalist is concerned. In other words, the metaphysician would be reasoning in ways, and speaking a language, the very legitimacy of which the naturalist refuses to acknowledge. The naturalist lives in a closed, and hermetically sealed, system. For him, nature is all; beyond that, there is simply nothing, other than the fantasies of benighted theists. Nature is the naturalist's Procrustean Bed, and everything must be either stretched out, or cut down to size, in order to fit its dimension, otherwise it simply cannot be taken as real. Either you meet the naturalist on his own terms, which means you forfeit the game before it even begins, or no meeting will be scheduled. Intellectual atheists like to pride themselves on the fact that they are men of quintessential rationality, and they would regard theism and irrationality as pretty much synonymous terms. But what one discovers, however—and it takes no great labor to make this discovery—is that the "reason" of the intellectual atheists tends to be of a very narrow and desiccated kind. He wants severely to limit the scope of reason, and in this respect his views often coincide with those of the advocate of scientism, who maintains that the only "real" reason is that which is exercised within the ambit of empirical science. But human reason is a large and capacious faculty, and it will not put up with artificially imposed limits. Reason most certainly manifests itself in empirical science. But it does so in art, as well. And in religion. We live in a much larger, and more wondrous, universe than the naturalist imagines, than his naturalism *allows* him to imagine. The fervent devotee of reason is sometimes just the one who sells reason radically short.

Chapter Eight

Proofs for the Existence of God
After St. Thomas

The Tradition Continues

The Five Ways of St. Thomas, taken together, represent the single most telling effort to demonstrate the existence of God. The principal task of natural theology could be said to have reached its peak accomplishment in those arguments, peculiarly brilliant for their pointed succinctness and cogency. But efforts to demonstrate the existence of God did not cease with St. Thomas Aquinas. Of course, St. Thomas's own arguments had a continuing influence in the centuries following his death, carried along as they were within the tradition of Scholastic, specifically Thomistic, philosophy, and often given new life and impetus by sensitive and knowledgeable commentators and explicators. But other philosophers, some who could be identified as being only marginally within the Scholastic tradition, some clearly outside that tradition, tried their hands at demonstrating the existence of God. They met with mixed success in these efforts. This is said not to disparage those efforts, for the motivations behind them were often quite commendable, but simply to underscore the fact that, when one compares the various attempts to demonstrate God's existence which followed those of St. Thomas, the superiority of the Five Ways becomes all the more evident.

This chapter will consist of a brief survey of some of the proofs for God's existence that have been proposed since the thirteenth century. We will begin our survey in the seventeenth century, with the proofs of René Descartes. We will then move on to the eighteenth century, and consider the proofs offered by G. W. Leibniz and William Paley. Our survey will end in the twentieth century, as we treat of the proofs formulated respectively by C. S. Lewis, Jacques Maritain, and Mortimer Adler. In acquainting ourselves with these six proofs, we will encounter a variety of approaches and emphases, and that will be to our benefit, for it will serve to broaden and enrich our understanding of the multiple ways in which natural theology has gone about its principal task.

The Proof of René Descartes

René Descartes is commonly considered to be the father of modern philosophy.[1] Descartes had convinced himself that all the philosophy that had preceded him was open to very serious questioning, if not outright rejection. He felt that he had to begin the business of philosophizing all over again, this time getting it right. This ambitious project entailed razing the decrepit structure which represented traditional philosophy, and building an entirely new, and decidedly improved, edifice upon the ruins of the old. The process of effectively erasing the philosophical past, to which Descartes dedicated himself, was given concrete form in his method of systematic and thoroughgoing doubt. He set about doubting the truth of everything that he had once taken to be true, one thing after another, until he was eventually arrested in his descent into free-falling skepticism at the point where he realized that there was one thing the truth of which it was impossible for him to doubt, and that was his own existence. He even made a little argument to prove this, the satisfying conclusion of which was that he existed. From that point he began the positive part of his project, constructing the new philosophical system within which, he was convinced, were reestablished, and on much firmer ground, all the truths which he had once methodologically doubted. Every key tenet of his new system was to take the form of a clear and distinct idea, which meant, an idea the truth of which it would not be possible to doubt, such as the idea of his own existence. But while caught up in the demanding effort of reconstituting philosophy, Descartes came to realize that the certainty of some very important ideas, such as the real existence of a world external to his own mind, or even a seemingly incontestably true mathematical idea like $3 + 2 = 5$, were not immune from being doubted. The only way the truth of such ideas could be guaranteed, Descartes reasoned, was by their being sponsored, as it were, by an all-powerful and benevolent God, a God who would provide Descartes with the psychological assurance that what appeared to be true to him was in fact true. So, in the end he became convinced that the existence of God was an absolutely crucial condition for the integrity and stability of his brand-new philosophy.[2] He therefore set about proving the existence of God. The proofs that he devised constitute an essential part of his whole philosophy. So important are they in fact that, if they fail, then—by the weight he himself attached to them—his philosophy can be said to fail.

Descartes formulates two demonstrations for God's existence, and they both figure prominently in one of his most important works, *Meditations on First Philosophy*. This work is composed of six distinct parts, or meditations. One of the proofs is found in Meditation V, and we will only refer to it in passing here, for it is essentially the ontological argument, with which we are already quite familiar. It should be said, however, that the ontological argument, in the skilled and articulate expression given it by Descartes, carries with it considerable force, and I think it safe to say that many who are not especially persuaded by the argument as presented by St. Anselm would be likely to react more favorably to Descartes' version of the argument. The particular Cartesian proof we will be concerned with here is found in Meditation III. It is a very interesting argument, but in the end it is, as I shall endeavor to show, no more than a variation of a theme, the theme being the ontological argument. But first we must present the argument.

The argument begins with Descartes stating one of the central tenets of his philosophy: "all things I perceive very clearly and very distinctly are true."[3] Now, of the various, indeed countless, ideas that Descartes is capable of thinking, some are more qualified to be considered clear and distinct ideas than are others, and that is because, as he says, they contain "more objective reality...participate in a higher degree of being or perfection."[4] Moreover, these ideas, rather than having their sources outside himself (which would, for Descartes, seriously count against their reliability) seem to well up from his very being. They are, in other words, innate ideas. Among these select ideas is the idea of God. Descartes is going to use the fact that he has a clear and distinct idea of God as the foundational supporting datum for the conclusion that God exists, not simply as an idea in his mind, but actually, as an extra-mental reality.

What kind of idea, precisely, is this idea of God? What are the specific contents of the idea? It is an idea, among other things, of a supreme being, a being that is, most significantly, infinite. Now, it will not do, Descartes argues, to say that an idea of an infinite being, even though that idea be harbored within a finite mind, could have originated in that mind, for if that were true you would have a circumstance where the finite gives rise to the infinite. And that is impossible. To show the impossibility of such a circumstance he cites, quite aptly, the metaphysical principle which informs us that the perfection of the effect cannot exceed the perfection of the cause. All this leads Descartes to the conclusion that if he has in his mind an idea whose source cannot be his own mind, then someone else must be responsible for his having that idea. And that allows him, initially, to form the consoling conviction that he is not alone in the world.

Concerning any other idea that he might entertain (the idea of an angel, for example), there is nothing to argue against its being simply the combination of ideas that do have their origins in his own mind, but he is not able to say this about the idea of God. This idea is unique, and after reviewing once again the various specific contents of this idea, he is brought to the point where he can assert: "hence, from what has been already said, we must conclude that God necessarily exists."[5] So commanding, so central, so elemental is this idea of God, of infinite being, that it actually precedes, Descartes tells us, the idea of finite being; indeed, he has the idea of God before he has the idea of himself.[6] There can be no idea more clear or more distinct—therefore more true—than the idea of God.

Descartes goes on to reflect on the nature of his own being, which stands in stark contrast to the being represented by his idea of God. He sees himself as a radically contingent being, a being who cannot account for his own existence. From this he concludes that he owes his existence to God. And reflection on his own contingency, on himself as someone who "exists potentially only,"[7] serves but to reinforce his principal conclusion, that God exists, for no being that exists only potentially could ever be the source of an idea of a being that is actually infinite, i.e., God Himself. As he brings his argument to a close, he makes explicit the point that his idea of God is an innate idea, not derived from his experience of the world, and in that respect his idea of God is comparable to his idea of himself.[8] Let us listen as Descartes sums up his argument. "And the whole strength of the argument which I have made use of to prove the existence of God consists in this, that I recognize that it is not possible that my nature should be what it is, and indeed that I should have in myself the idea of a God, if God did not veritably exist—a God, I say, whose idea is in me...."[9]

Response to Descartes' Proof

The first thing we should notice about this argument is that it most definitely is not a *quia* argument. Descartes does not begin, as does St. Thomas, with things in the world. He begins with things in the mind, ideas. This puts the argument at the greatest sort of disadvantage right at the outset. Why? Because it does not begin with facts to which all have access. The facts on which he builds his argument are purely mental facts, ideas, *his* ideas, and therefore they are facts to which he alone is privy. If the basic premises on which an argument rests are ideas, and nothing more, then, strictly speaking, the only one who could be expected to be persuaded by the conclusions reached by such an argument would be the person who is entertaining those ideas.

When Descartes describes the specific contents of his idea of God, he lists familiar attributes such as infinity, eternity, immutability, omniscience, and omnipotence. Now, those qualities would not strike any believer as being strange, for we learned them as children in our catechism lessons. Descartes himself, very much a believer, would of course have become acquainted with those attributes as part of his own Catholic upbringing. So what Descartes is doing here is appealing to knowledge which was gained by him, to put it in general terms, by his experience in the external world. But Descartes would have us believe that his idea of God, with all its rich contents, is an innate idea, an idea, that is, not derived from experience. But this claim, that his idea of God is an innate idea, must be counted as empty. It can carry no weight in argument. Any claim that asserts the existence of innate ideas is empty because it can be neither proved nor disproved. However, it should be quickly added that all of our experiences emphatically support the view that every one of our ideas has its ultimate source in the external world. This being so, one does not feel a pressing need to prove what one takes to be obvious. The burden of proof on this question falls squarely and heavily on the shoulders of those who insist upon the existence of innate ideas. Descartes, for good reason, does not even attempt to prove his claim that there are innate ideas. He simply states it as a fact. It is precisely that claim that he wants us to advert to and rely on as the substantiation for another of his claims: that his idea of God's infinity is not a negative idea. This means that he denies that we arrive at the idea of the infinite by beginning with the idea of the finite, and then remove from that idea (process of negation) everything that pertains to finitude. But this is precisely how Descartes, and everyone else, must arrive at the idea of the infinite, by starting with the idea of the finite. Our idea of the infinite, then, is in fact a negative idea. His tactic here is an offense to logic, for he is attempting to support one unproven claim by appealing to another: his idea of God's infinity is not negative, because it is innate. Descartes exacerbates the situation by claiming that his idea of the infinite is not only innate, but that it actually precedes his idea of the finite. This is to turn the epistemological world upside down.

But let us consider again the specific contents of Descartes' idea of God—every item in which, by the way, is quite correct—but now looked at from the point of view of faith. We have no argument with the contents of Descartes's idea of God, but the point to be emphasized here is that it is *his* idea of God, and an idea that is clearly derived from his own faith. Furthermore, it must be kept in mind that it is his idea of God which is the foundation for his whole argument. This being the case, what is to prevent someone else from rejecting the argument simply on the basis of the fact of their having an idea of God which is entirely different from Descartes' idea? People can entertain widely disparate ideas, and yet to all those ideas they will attach the same name, "God." And human history is replete with examples of people who have nurtured ideas of "God" that are positively ungodly. You may recall that this was one of the points raised by St. Thomas when objecting to that mode of arguing for the existence of God which begins with the idea of God.

Descartes' argument is not without its fetching qualities, and it is quite obvious that there was behind it a mind of no mean proportions. But, as I mentioned earlier, it comes down to being a variation on a theme, i.e., the ontological argument. It cannot be considered to be demonstrative in the strict sense because it does not begin where true demonstration of this sort must always begin—in the public arena, with effects that are apparent to all. And to that must be added the salient note, by way of pointing to the fatal flaw in the proof, that one cannot conclude to real existence from merely mental existence. No idea, no matter how singular an idea it might be, and just as an idea, can serve as evidence for real, extra-mental existence.

The Proof of Gottfried Wilhelm Leibniz

G. W. Leibniz (1646–1716) was one of the most learned men of his age, and he was a seriously religious man as well. He developed a rather elaborate philosophy over the course of his life, a philosophy not without its serious difficulties, but our concern here is with his thought as it was concentrated on various issues which relate directly to natural theology, and so long as he operated within that sphere he can be considered to be, by and large, a trustworthy mentor. Leibniz has given us a rather abstract proof for the existence of God in a work called the *Monadology*, and another is to be found in his *Theodicy*. It is the second proof, more accessible, and I think considerably more compelling, that we will be focusing our attention on here. The title *Theodicy*, which means "the justice of God," was a neologism apparently made up by Leibniz himself. The *Theodicy* was the only book-length work he published during his lifetime, although he was a prolific writer and to this day many of his writings remain unpublished. A principal purpose of the *Theodicy* was to show that, not only is there no opposition between faith and reason, but that reason is to be seen as in every way an aid to faith. As he put it, his intention in the book was "to place reason at the service of faith [rather] than in opposition to it." [10] Much of the book is taken up with responding to various other writers, the Frenchman Pierre Bayle in particular, who, Leibniz thought, had gotten many things quite wrong concerning the nature of God and how He relates to the world He created. The *Theodicy* is hefty with tight and detailed reasoning; Leibniz is remarkably thorough in the many issues he deals with, and the erudition of the man is evident on every page. What Leibniz attempts to show throughout the book, often in the process of responding to views he takes to be erroneous, is that there is no contradiction between the various attributes of God, rightly understood, and the actual events that take place in the world about us. Specifically, he argues that there is no contradiction between the omniscience of God and the experience we have of ourselves as truly free creatures. And he argues that there is no contradiction between the goodness of God and the evil we experience in the world, be it moral evil or physical evil. In all, it is a very impressive work, magisterial in its way.[11]

Though to the best of my knowledge there is not to be found in Leibniz's works any explicit or elaborated form of the ontological argument, this is an argument for which, given certain propensities in his general philosophy, he would have had a weakness.[12] But the argument with which we will be occupied, found in the *Theodicy*, has no direct connection with the ontological argument. It is most similar to St. Thomas's fifth way, and indeed it can be rightly identified as Leibniz's version of the argument from finality. The argument is not compactly stated in any one place in the book, but its various elements are scattered throughout its pages. Indeed, some of the more important presuppositions of the argument are to be located, and stated in more explicit terms, in other of his works. So, what I have done is gather together from various places all the essential elements of the argument, and that is what I present below.

We have noted in the earlier pages of this book that one of the hallmarks of modernist philosophical thinking is a marked tendency to do away with final causality. Leibniz, who lived just at the time when modern philosophy was being birthed, was aware of this bias against final causality that was being nurtured, and he opposed it.[13] As a necessary entailment of one of the key tenets of his philosophy, i.e., that the universe is knit together by God in a pre-established harmony, Leibniz saw that the "realms of efficient causes and that of final causes are parallel to each other."[14] Now, efficient causality is a specific expression of the more basic principle of sufficient reason. The importance of that principle cannot be exaggerated, for, "Were it not for this great principle we could never prove the existence of God."[15] Well, how does one go about doing this?

Clearly, for Leibniz, we must do so by employing *quia* argument, proceeding from effect to cause. This approach leads directly to the argument from finality. One begins by giving attentive regard to nature, and by doing so one comes to see that it is everywhere deeply marked by order and intelligence. On the basis of that evidence one concludes to the existence of a governing intelligence, God. "These admirable laws are wonderful evidence of an intelligent and free being, as opposed to the system of absolute and brute necessity...." [16] What we find in Leibniz's *Theodicy*, then, is an argument for the existence of God that, though not so neatly and compactly expressed, bears any number of resemblances to St. Thomas's fifth way. While Leibniz's proof is not without certain minor difficulties—difficulties that often result from ambiguous language—it can be pronounced as being, taking it all in all, a successful, even a forceful, argument.

The Proof of William Paley

William Paley (1743–1805) was an Anglican clergyman who, after serving ten years as a lecturer in Christ's College, Cambridge University, his alma mater, spent the remainder of his life occupying the various pastoral positions in his church, ending up as the archdeacon at Lincoln cathedral. While faithfully fulfilling his professional duties, and raising a family of eight children, he at the same time maintained the role of an assiduous scholar. His main interests, as one would expect, were in theology. One of his most important books, the one for which he is best known, published in 1802, and the work we are interested in here, is entitled, fittingly enough, *Natural Theology*.

Many people are familiar with the anecdote which appears in the early pages of the work and sets the tone for what follows. Paley asks us to imagine someone who is walking across an open field. Along the way he notices something glittering in the grass. He stoops down and picks it up. It is a watch. Now a watch, as Paley describes it, is an intricate contrivance, a complex little machine. The last thing the person who found the watch would think, if he were thinking at all clearly, is that this watch just fell out of the sky, or that it grew up out of the ground, or that it was no more than the end product of a succession of purely chance natural events that took place over the course of time. No, the watch is clearly a little machine designed for a very specific purpose, to tell time, and because it was so designed there was necessarily a designer behind it, an intelligent efficient cause who accounts for the watch's existence. The heart of the argument of *Natural Theology*, stressed throughout the work, is that wherever you find design you have an intelligent designer to explain that design. You simply cannot have design without a designer.

In the early stages of the argument, Paley responds to those who might try to escape the conclusion that design demands a designer by appealing to the possibility of infinite regress. Paley asks us to imagine that the watch that is found is a rather extraordinary one in that it is capable of generating other watches, and that watch by yet another watch, and so on. Could we not suppose that this sequence stretches back into the past ad infinitum? One could, but nothing would be gained "by running the difficulty further back, i.e., by supposing the watch before us to have been produced by another watch, that one from a former one and so on indefinitely. Our going back ever so far brings us no nearer to the least degree of satisfaction upon the subject. Contrivance is still unaccounted for. We still want a contriver." [17] Earlier Paley had given a succinct summary statement of the argument around which the book is built: "There cannot be a design without a designer; contrivance without a contriver; order, without choice; arrangement, without anything capable of arranging; subserviency and relation to a purpose, without that which could intend a purpose; means suitable to an end, and exercising their office in executing that end, without the end ever having been contemplated, or the means accommodated to it." [18] And what do we find everywhere in the world? Design, contrivance, order, arrangement, subservience and relation to a purpose, means suited to an end. The conclusion to be drawn from this is inescapable: "The marks of *design* are too strong to be gotten over. Design must have a designer. That designer must have been a person. That person is God." [19]

Paley provides an abundance of examples of design and contrivance. There is no doubt that he is arguing from effects to cause. After providing many examples from human anatomy, he moves on to make a sweeping tour of the whole of the natural world. The purpose of all of his examples is to show that whatever "contrivance" he deals with was clearly designed to achieve a specific end, so he clearly has finality in mind. "I take my stand on human anatomy," [20] he asserts, and that is the subject to which he gives most attention. As for astronomy, "My opinion of astronomy has always been, that it is *not* the best medium through which to prove the agency of an intelligent Creator." [21] The emphasis he gives to human anatomy is explained by his conviction that there is in the human body a veritable symphony of design. The description he gives of the human eye is especially detailed and complete, his intention here being to make the point that it would be impossible ever to regard so wondrously contrived and intricate an organ to be the result of blind chance. The human eye was designed for the purpose of seeing.[22]

One of the most striking features of Paley's book is the continuing emphasis he gives to what he calls mechanism. He argues that mechanism, or contrivance, is inseparable from design. He would challenge any naturalist philosopher to give a coherent account of mechanism, the ubiquitous presence of which in nature he would have to acknowledge, without including in his account the notion of design. The only way we can understand a machine is to have some minimal sense of what it does, what it is for, its purpose. And as soon as you introduce the idea of purpose, you must necessarily admit that there had to be an intelligence that intended the purpose, and designed the machine so that it might achieve the purpose.

There are those who maintain that there is no need to appeal to an Intelligent Designer to explain the design we see in the world, for that can be adequately explained simply by recognizing it as the effects of the workings of the laws of nature. To this objection Paley warmly responds that "it is a perversion of language to assign any law as the efficient operative cause of anything. A law presupposes an agent, for it is only the mode according to which an agent proceeds, it implies a power, for it is the order according to which that power acts. Without this agent, without this power, which are both distinct from itself, the 'law' does nothing—is nothing." Another way of stating the point he is making here is to say that the laws of nature merely describe the way the physical world works, they do not *make* it work as it does. He continues: "What has been said concerning 'law' holds true of *mechanism*. Mechanism is not itself power. Mechanism without power can do nothing."[23] If the naturalist is prepared to acknowledge that there is order in the universe—and it would be difficult to imagine him not doing so—then, for Paley, by that very acknowledgment he must admit to an intelligent being who orders. "Order itself is only the adaption of means to an end: a principle of order, therefore, can only signify the mind and intention which so adapts them."[24]

The naturalist might then offer chance as the explanation for the design and order we see in the universe. Paley regards the appeal to chance as a non-explanation posing as an explanation. "I desire no greater certainty in reasoning than that by which chance is excluded from the present disposition of the natural world. Universal experience is against it."[25] Paley does not deny real chance occurrences. His point is that human reason cannot accept chance as a reasonable explanation for the order that is to be found in nature. Paley would seem to have foreseen some of the arguments which were eventually to play key roles in orthodox Darwinian theory. For example, he attacks the notion that some of the intricate natural mechanism that he describes in his book could have arrived at their present flawlessly functioning state as the result of the accumulation of countless minute changes that took place over eons of time. He rightly argues that there are insuperable difficulties attached to that line of reasoning. Having just described the exacting operations of the epiglottis, he writes: "There is no pretending that the action of the parts may have gradually formed the epiglottis: I do not mean in the same individual, but in a succession of generations. Not only the action of the parts has no such tendency, but the animal could not live, nor consequently the parts act, either without it, or with it in a half-formed state. The species was not to wait for the gradual formation or expansion of a part which was, from the first, necessary to the life of the individual." [26]

Response to William Paley's Proof

Paley's *Natural Theology* is in many respects a very impressive work. It is remarkable for the wealth of detailed and intrinsically interesting information it provides the reader. He amasses an abundance of evidence in support of his central thesis that design necessarily implies a designer, that the intelligibility of design points to intelligence. Paley argues that neither law nor mere mechanism are adequate explanations for the design and order to be found in nature, and that is because neither can act as causes. Laws need a law-maker behind them, and mechanism is inert if there is no power that accounts for its mechanical action. The implication is that God is the Law-Maker, and He is the Power that moves the myriads of the world's "contrivances" of whatever kind. Paley clearly has finality in mind as he develops his ideas, and thus it might appear that his argument is very much like St. Thomas's Fifth Way. However, this is not ambiguously the case.

The key point that St. Thomas makes in his Fifth Way is that finality is something which is intrinsic to nature. Every agent, every created being in its action, acts for the sake of achieving a given end (*omne agens agit propter finem*), and that implies that agency necessarily involves finality. The effect brought about by the efficient cause, the end toward which it is directed, its purpose, is a final cause. Finality, then, end-orientation, is something intrinsic to nature.

The emphasis in Paley's argument has the effect of regarding the finality to be found in the things of nature as something which is not intrinsic to them, but as having been bestowed upon them by an extrinsic source. The time-telling finality of a watch is not intrinsic to the assemblage of material parts that make up that particular contrivance, but is granted them by the watchmaker; the actions of various parts of the watch are not naturally ordered to the telling of time. Paley clearly intends to prove the existence of an "intelligent Creator," but it is just on that critical point that his argument is less than successful. He gives a plenitude of telling examples of design. There is no gainsaying the fact that design and the order coterminous with it are everywhere in evidence in nature, and that design calls for a designer, but the designer, or contriver, need not be God the Creator. Some commentators have aptly observed that the explanatory source of all the purposeful activity to be found in nature that Paley presents in his argument could reasonably be attributed to something like a Grand Architect of the universe, a Cosmic Contriver as it were, certainly an impressive being, but not necessarily the Creator of heaven and earth. If Paley's argument does not entirely miss the metaphysical heart of the matter—that finality is intrinsic to nature, the result of God's creative act—its presence in the argument is only implicit, and that seriously qualifies its success, given what he intended that it prove.

The Proof of C. S. Lewis

The English literary scholar C. S. Lewis (1898–1963) has offered us, in his book, *Miracles: A Preliminary Study*, a sketchy but nonetheless provocative proof for the existence of God. It can be described very briefly, and in doing so I will make liberal use of Professor Lewis's own words. Lewis argues that: "A man's Rational thinking is *just so much* of his share in eternal Reason as the state of his brain allows to become operative." [27] He goes on to assert that, "one's own thinking cannot be merely a natural event, and that therefore something other than nature exists." [28] He sums up the above observations with the following: "I have advanced reasons for believing that a supernatural element is present in every rational man. The presence of rationality in the world is therefore a Miracle by the definition given in Chapter 2." [29] The definition of miracle to which he refers is: "an interference with Nature by a supernatural power." [30] Though not explicitly stated, the conclusion that is to be drawn from his discourse is that God exists, a conclusion that is made clear enough by a later observation: "God pierces her [i.e., Nature] wherever there is a human mind." [31] In the syllogism which follows—which is of my own, not Lewis's, devising—I think I have succeeded in capturing the essence of his argument.

Miracles are proof of God's existence.

Human reasoning is a miracle.

Therefore, human reasoning is a proof of God's existence.

It should be readily apparent that the weakness of the argument, indeed a seriously debilitating one, is to be found in the minor premiss of the above syllogism. The specific notion that lies behind the premiss is Lewis's assumption that human reasoning is a supernatural phenomenon. There is nothing to support such an assumption, however. Human reason is completely natural, and, in fact, bears all the earmarks of a fallen nature. If human reasoning were not a natural process, then—among other difficulties that could be cited—the whole enterprise of natural theology would find itself in a rather awkward position, for in this science we claim that we can, through the exercise of *natural* reason, reach the supernatural. But if human reason is supernatural to begin with, we would, simply by exercising it, already be in the realm of the supernatural. In summary response to Lewis's argument, we can say that an appeal to human reasoning offers us no foundation upon which we can conclude to the existence of God.

The Proof of Jacques Maritain

One of the most prominent Thomistic philosophers of the twentieth century, Jacques Maritain (1882–1973) has presented what he identifies as a new argument for the existence of God, suggestively entitled, A Sixth Way. It appears as Chapter III of his book, *Approaches To God.*

The argument, by Maritain's own admission, is a subtle one. "It may, indeed," he writes, "appear too subtle, and for a long time I regarded it as belonging to the domain of research hypotheses."[32]

However, he eventually came to regard it as a genuine demonstration. He explains that the proof has nothing of the simplicity of the arguments proposed by St. Thomas. This is clearly the case. Maritain begins the argument by drawing a distinction between pre-philosophical knowledge and philosophical knowledge. It is only when we are working within the realm of philosophical knowledge that demonstration in the strict sense is possible, so it is obviously with philosophical knowledge that the argument is going to be concerned. But not exclusively so. And it begins with pre-philosophical knowledge, for, Maritain argues, such knowledge is the natural antecedent to philosophical knowledge; it lays the groundwork for philosophical knowledge. Pre-philosophical knowledge consists in intuitive experience, which is necessarily highly personal. In the argument, it is Maritain's own intuitive experiences he makes reference to.

He describes such an experience. He is engaged in very intense, completely absorbing thinking. Suddenly, his thought is interrupted with the startling reflection—actually, it is more like a conviction—that he could never have been born; it seems to him an impossibility that he should ever have had a beginning. This would be the intuition. What provoked it? The sense that this process in which he is involved, thinking, has something timeless about it, and so he too, the thinker, must have something timeless about himself. He finds it difficult to believe that there ever was a time when he was not, somehow, caught up in thought. But, no sooner does that intuition visit itself upon him than he sees its absurdity, for he knows that in fact he had a beginning. Like the rest of men, he was born of woman. So, at this stage of the argument he is left with a contradiction on his hands: he has this vague, intuitive sense that he had no beginning, and yet he *knows* he had a beginning. He must resolve this contradiction.

The next stage of the argument takes place on the philosophical level, where Maritain attempts to demonstrate that there is something to the vague, intuitive sense that he had no beginning. The ultimate conclusion to which the argument is leading is that God exists. Maritain argues that it could be said that he did not have a beginning, that he always existed. He did not of course always exist actually, in terms of his own proper essence, but as it were virtually, as an idea in the divine intellect. He explains, "that the creature which is now I, and which thinks, existed before itself eternally in God—not in exercising in Him the act of thinking, but as thought by Him." [33] The pre-philosophic intuition of not having a beginning—an intuition, recall, that burst forth from a bout of intense thinking, and was apparently caused by that thinking—is not without something like a basis in fact, then, for the person who has such an intuition is as it were recalling its non-proper-essence pre-existence in God. What such an intuition does, therefore, is point to the existence of God. Point to, not prove.

In order to make his argument a demonstration, and not simply a suggestion, Maritain appeals to the process of thinking as evidence for the existence of God. And on that point his argument has a striking similarity to that proposed by C. S. Lewis. The main thrust of Maritain's reasoning is as follows. Thinking, the exercise of human reason, is essentially supra-temporal. "Thought as such is not in time," he writes. "The distinction between the *spiritual* and the *temporal* appears here in the primary sense." [34] The suggestion being made is that thinking puts us in the realm of the spiritual, the supernatural. Thinking, then, in the argument, becomes the verifying experience of our having no beginning, of our once having existed in a supra-temporal order, and that is so because thinking itself is a supra-temporal experience. And what else is that supra-temporal order but the realm of the supernatural, the realm of God. So, what we have here, then, is a demonstration for the existence of God.

Response to Jacques Maritain's Proof

It would be difficult to decide just where to place this proof, in terms of our familiar distinction between *propter quid* and *quia* argument. In order for the argument to qualify as a genuine demonstration for the existence of God, it would have to be a *quia* argument. That, in turn, implies two things: (1) the argument begins with effects; (2) the objective factualness of those effects must be accessible to all. It is the second point especially that poses pressing difficulties for this argument. Just how public, how accessible to all, is the intuition with which the argument begins, and which plays a critically important role in its later development? Is the intuition Maritain describes a common experience? How many people would regard it, and it seems not without justice, as rather odd? Be that as it may, the larger problem is that the pre-philosophical experiences with which the argument begins, regarded as intuitional in nature, are as such (whatever their specific contents) necessarily and unavoidably subjective, and therefore they are experiences which could not be accessible to all. And therefore they cannot serve as a reliable point of departure for what is intended to be a genuine philosophical demonstration. If we consider more closely the basic structure of Maritain's argument, its central premiss is recognized as being the contention that thinking is essentially supra-temporal. In the hope of clarifying matters, I will, as I did with Lewis's argument, set what I take to be the essence of Maritain's argument in syllogistic form.

> Direct experience of the supra-temporal is proof of God's existence.
> Thinking is direct experience of the supra-temporal.
> Therefore, thinking is proof of God's existence.

As was the case with Lewis's argument, so too here, the problem is with the minor premiss of the syllogism. The contention that human thought is supra-temporal is ambiguous at best, and its ambiguity is brought out by Maritain's own attempts to explain the meaning of the contention. We quoted him above as saying, "Thought as such is not in time." And yet just a few lines above that statement we read: "The operations of the human intellect are in time, and, indeed, subject to time...." [35] What else could the operations of the human intellect be but thought, the activity of thinking? If the operations of the intellect are in time, thought is in time. And it does not do much to clarify matters when Maritain goes on to explain that the operations of the human intellect are in time only extrinsically. [36] The difficulty here is that the claim that human thinking is supra-temporal, upon which the whole argument rests, does not admit of any clear, straightforward interpretation. It does not, therefore, have the strength to sustain the weight that is placed upon it.

This is an intriguing argument in many respects, but in the final analysis we have to say that it does not convey very much compelling force. It is altogether too subjective in orientation, and therefore lacks that public character which, as we have said repeatedly, is critical to the kind of demonstration with which natural theology is principally concerned.

The Argument of Mortimer Adler

We are already acquainted with Mortimer Adler (1902–2001), having discussed, in the previous chapter, his objections to the Five Ways. Although Dr. Adler was of the strong opinion that St. Thomas's arguments were not demonstrative, he was not closed to the possibility that there could be a certain qualified legitimacy to attempts to prove the existence of God. He believed that one could make a strong case for God's existence, but it would seem that he ruled out the possibility of demonstration in the strict sense. We could never have the same kind of certitude about the existence of God, in terms of natural reason alone, that we could have about, say, the truth of the conclusion of a valid mathematical proof. Dr. Adler himself offered an argument for the existence of God, and we will end this chapter by considering that argument. It appears in the same book which contains his critique of St. Thomas's Five Ways, *How To Think About God.*

At the core of Dr. Adler's conviction that the Five Ways of St. Thomas fail to demonstrate the existence of God is the distinction he makes between superficial contingency and radical contingency. A thing is radically contingent, for Adler, if the only alternative to its being is its non-being. A thing is superficially contingent, on the other hand, if the alternative to its present state of being is being under another form. Adler's notion of superficial contingency is, as we have shown, seriously defective, and the way he applies it creates major metaphysical problems. What Adler calls radical contingency could well be identified as contingency, pure and simple. Dr. Adler rightly recognizes that what he names radical contingency is what St. Thomas is dealing with in his arguments. But he goes on to contend that St. Thomas was misadvised in this respect because, for Dr. Adler, everything existing in the universe is superficially contingent only.

Adler recognizes that one needs radical contingency to attempt to prove the existence of God, for the simple reason that superficially contingent being is effectively self-explanatory. In other words, in order to account for the existence of superficially contingent being, all you need do is appeal to other superficially contingent being. [37]

Convinced that the need for a radically contingent being is not going to be met by any individual being existing in the universe, he asks if we could not gain radical contingency by considering all of those beings together. His reasoning is as follows: while each thing in the universe is only superficially contingent, the universe itself, the sum total of those things, is radically contingent. That is the key point on which his argument turns. He calls his argument "a truly cosmological argument" because it deals with the cosmos itself. It takes into account the entire universe, not the parts but the whole.

In attempting to argue for the existence of God by focusing our attention on the universe, it is important, Dr. Adler emphasizes, that we operate under the assumption that we are dealing with an eternal universe, one that had no beginning in time, and which will never end. The importance of making this assumption is that if we were to assume the opposite, that the universe had a beginning in time, then we would be committing the logical fallacy of begging the question. That is to say, we would be taking to be true at the outset of our argument the very thing we are supposed to be proving—the existence of God. [38] But is the universe in fact radically contingent? That is the key question. In attempting to answer that question in the affirmative, we would not be justified in concluding that the universe is radically contingent by appealing to all the things that make up the universe, for all those things are superficially contingent, and we could add up a countless number of superficially contingent things and we would nonetheless end up with a sum total that remains superficially contingent. But even if we were to assume that all of the things in the universe were radically contingent, we could not on that basis conclude that the universe as a whole is radically contingent. Were we to do so, Dr. Adler maintains, we would be committing the logical fallacy of composition, which is to suppose that what is true of the parts is necessarily true of the whole as well. [39]

Dr. Adler decides that the best approach to take in order to arrive at a reasonable degree of certitude that the universe is radically contingent is to consider it in terms of its being a possible universe. A possible universe is a universe that does not have to exist. It could very well not be. Furthermore, if left to itself, it could lapse into nothingness. But what could be cited as evidence that this universe is a possible universe? Adler offers two items for our consideration. The first is the conjecture that this is not the only universe that could exist. Any number of other universes, perhaps an infinite number, are also possible. The second and weightier item is what he cites as the fact of the present universe's disorder and disarray, its being ridden by chance occurrences. [40] Ours is a fragile universe, which is to say, a radically contingent universe. As such, it needs a necessary being, God, to keep it in existence. We can thus conclude that God exists. Recall that all along we have been assuming the universe that we are dealing with is eternal. That would mean that God, also of course eternal, would be conserving the universe in existence from all eternity. But, Adler argues, once we have established God as the conserver of the universe, we then have a basis for arguing that the universe began in time, and that therefore God is the creator of the universe. The point I mentioned earlier, that Dr. Adler did not consider his argument to be a proof in the strict sense, he makes abundantly clear in bringing the argument to a close. "The conclusion that God exists has not been proved or demonstrated. Nothing that has been said should result in conviction or certitude." [41] What Dr. Adler believes he has done, in the end, is provide us with "reasonable grounds for affirming God's existence." [42]

Response to Mortimer Adler's Argument

The key assumption on which Dr. Adler's argument rests, that the universe is radically contingent, is one that is not to be contested. But because he takes that to be an assumption, he commits himself to the obligation of having to convince his readers that the assumption is a sound one, one that can be shown to be true beyond a reasonable doubt. It is an open question whether Dr. Adler does provide the evidence for a radically contingent universe that his argument requires . If he does not, the failure is explained by the fact that he was looking in the wrong place for it. What is most disadvantageous for the whole argument is his conviction that the universe is composed only of superficially contingent things, which is to say, of things which are not really contingent, at least not according to the common understanding of the term. If one is not prepared to recognize real (i.e., radical) contingency in the things of this world—the fact that things really do, as the things they are, come into being and pass out of being—then one is forced, as was Dr. Adler, to seek that contingency in large abstractions pertaining to the universe as a whole. He had all the contingency he needed in concrete particulars, but, strangely, it was not evident to him.

There is something that can be said in favor of Dr. Adler's assuming, at the outset of his argument, the universe to be eternal, but the assumption is not without its perils. Once one admits the possibility of an eternal universe, that is, once one concedes that *this* universe, the physical world in which we live, can reasonably be regarded as having no beginning and no end—eternal in the strict sense of the word—then one is hard pressed to come up with sturdy responses to typical retorts of the materialist and of the pantheist. The materialist will say, "If the universe is eternal, what need is there for a God to explain it?" The pantheist will say, "If the universe is eternal, the universe is God."

There are other things that can be said in response to Dr. Adler's argument, but my including them here would prolong a chapter already sufficiently long. For those who want to go more deeply into various matters, I refer you to the notes for this chapter, which contain additional commentary on the argument. I will end with these reflections. Dr. Adler's argument has a real attractiveness to it, and it is not without compelling qualities. But one wonders if Dr. Adler's own tentativeness toward what he has done here does not in a way rub off on the reader, and leave him less receptive to the possible force of the argument than he otherwise would be. Another thought: Does Dr. Adler's clear assertion that he has not offered a demonstration of the existence of God suggest that in fact he believed that no such demonstration was possible, that the best we could do was provide "reasonable grounds" for God's existence? And if that was indeed the case, did that belief antecedently affect his approach to the Five Ways of St. Thomas?

CHAPTER NINE

The Moral Arguments for
the Existence of God

The Difference Between Metaphysical Proofs and Moral Proofs

The metaphysical proofs for the existence of God are proofs or demonstrations in the strict sense. A demonstration, strictly understood, is an argument whose conclusion follows necessarily from its premises. Given the truth of the premises, given the validity of the argument's structure, the conclusion is clearly and unarguably true. Its truth cannot be denied. A moral proof, on the other hand, is not demonstrative in the sense just described. Here the conclusion does not follow necessarily from the premises. The conclusion is probable, and the degree of its probability will naturally vary with the strength and compelling quality of the premises that support it. Though "moral proof" is a commonly used term, "moral argument" would more accurately describe what we will be dealing with in this chapter, and that will be our term of choice. A moral argument seeks to persuade, but it does not demonstrate in the strict sense.

Between the two, the metaphysical arguments and the moral arguments, the former have more intrinsic worth than the latter, just as arguments, but to say this is not to denigrate the special value of the moral arguments. In more cases than not, and considered from the point of view of practical effectiveness, the moral arguments, for most people, tend to have more compelling force than do the metaphysical arguments. The reasons for this are clear. Having yourself encountered several metaphysical arguments, you are now better able to appreciate that it takes considerable effort to reach the point where the arguments can be adequately understood. In short, a significant background in metaphysics is required in order to be able to do justice to them, and the fact is that not many people have the time, the talent, or the energy to acquire that background.

The conclusion of a moral argument is the same as that of a metaphysical argument—"God exists"—but because it is a probable and not a necessary conclusion, the degree of its probability will, once again, depend in good measure on the persuasive impact of the entire argument. This means that presentation—the wording of the argument, the way it is delivered—plays an important role. The more rhetorical skill that is brought to an argument, the more persuasive it is likely to be.

There is no exact number of moral arguments for the existence of God, and that there should ever be anything like a complete set of such arguments is quite improbable. The number of possible arguments could be said to be limited only by the limitations of the human imagination. There are, however, a half dozen or so arguments that are most frequently made use of, and these compose the major portion of the sampling that is provided in this chapter. There are no firmly fixed names for the moral arguments, but the names I employ here are fairly common, and, in any event, they serve the useful purpose of describing the main theme of each argument with fair accuracy. In this chapter we will present eight moral arguments for the existence of God. They are: The Argument from Conscience; the Argument from the Universal Desire for Happiness; the Argument from Universal Belief; the Argument from Moral Goodness; the Argument from the Universal Desire for Justice; the Argument from Beauty; the Argument from the Universal Desire for Immortality; and, the Argument from Laughter.

The Argument from Conscience

One of the most famous versions of this argument has been given to us by John Henry Cardinal Newman, in his book, *An Essay in Aid of A Grammar of Assent,* in a section of that volume entitled, "Belief in One God." In the early pages of that section Cardinal Newman explains, "what I am directly aiming at, is how we gain an image of God and give a real assent to the proposition that He exists." [1] He sets about achieving that aim by calling our attention to the plain and obvious fact of human conscience. Human conscience, one could assume, is a reality that no one would be prepared to deny. But just what is the nature of human conscience? More precisely, what does it give rise to within us? What are its natural products, so to speak? First of all, and most basically, it is from conscience that we get our sense of right and wrong. We could call that our moral sense. Very closely allied with the sense of the distinction between right and wrong, there is an added sense of obligation, by which we feel duty bound to do what is right and to avoid what is wrong. So, then, there are these two aspects of conscience: the simple recognition of the reality of right and wrong, and then the practical response to that recognition.

Cardinal Newman, in going on to describe conscience as, "not a rule of right conduct but a sanction of right conduct," [2] is making a very important point about the nature of conscience, and in doing so emphasizing something which, unfortunately, many people today get quite wrong. There is a prevalent contemporary understanding of conscience, which has its source in an individualistic mind-set, that claims that it is the function of conscience to *establish* moral standards, not simply to recognize them and abide by them. In other words, it is up to each person to decide what constitutes right and wrong. This radically erroneous view has the effect of opening the door to the chaos of moral relativism. Cardinal Newman stresses just the opposite point of view, the correct point of view: conscience is not the source of right and wrong, but that by which its objective reality is acknowledged.

But what happens when we go against the knowledge we have of right and wrong, when, specifically, we fail to do what is right, or we willingly do what is wrong? What happens is that we feel guilty. And we feel guilty because we have the clear conviction that we have offended someone to whom we feel responsible. That someone is God. Cardinal Newman spells out the main thrust of his argument in the following terms. "If, as is the case, we feel responsibility , are ashamed, are frightened, at transgressing the voice of conscience, this implies that there is One to whom we are responsible, before whom we are ashamed, whose claims upon us we fear." [3] In other words, what we find in the activity of our conscience is evidence for the existence of God. Conscience, Cardinal Newman argues, has the effect of impressing upon us "the picture of a Supreme Governor, a

Judge, holy, just, powerful, all-seeing, retributive...."[4] Thus, what we have in conscience is "a connecting principle between the creature and his Creator."[5]

Notice where the special emphasis in this argument lies. The activity of our conscience, for Cardinal Newman, does not provide us with simply a *concept* of God, but with an *image* of Him. It is our imagination that is most immediately affected here, and our emotions. We have a "picture" of God, and as a result of that picture a number of feelings are stirred up in us: responsibility, shame, fear. God is not merely an abstraction for us, but a real person, the quintessence of person, and, as such, He evokes an emotional response in us.

With Cardinal Newman's guiding thoughts in mind, I offer the following summary of the argument from conscience. Human conscience, a reality which no one would deny, provides us with a vivid and abiding sense of right and wrong, of right and wrong not as something that we invent, but as objective realities. And we recognize right and wrong, not simply as interesting facts that we can choose to attach importance to, or choose to ignore, but as making direct and pressing demands upon us. As soon as we recognize right and wrong for what they are, we concomitantly realize that we have a solemn responsibility to do what is right and avoid what is wrong. And if we fail to live up to our responsibility in this regard, we feel guilty about it. Why? Because we know that, just as right and wrong are themselves objective realities, so too there is an objective foundation for our sense of obligation toward them. In other words, that sense of obligation is not directed toward ourselves, but toward Someone beyond ourselves. It is important that we realize that a sense of obligation is always rooted, ultimately, in persons. All of us, whatever our state in life, are bound by an array of rules and laws. In the most immediate sense, our obligation is toward the rule, to keep the rule. But if we reflect on the matter a moment, we see that in the final analysis our sense of obligation is directed ultimately toward the person who is the source of the rule. Because the basic rules for right moral conduct—as found in the natural law, for example—must have a personal source, we conclude that their source is God. And it is ultimately toward Him, and not toward the rules just as rules, that we feel a sense of obligation.

Our sense of right and wrong is most basic in that it is rooted in our very being, but though rooted in our being it points to something that transcends our being, indeed, to *Someone* who transcends our being supremely. Conscience, and the sense of right and wrong it incorporates, points directly, and emphatically, to God. Cardinal Newman puts it even more strongly when he says that conscience is what connects us to God. To state the matter in the simplest terms: I feel an obligation to do right and avoid wrong because I know that there is a Supreme Good, God, whom I am bound to honor and obey. And I feel guilty when I do wrong, not simply because I have failed myself, but because I have offended God. Conscience and all that it implies—a sense of right and wrong, a sense of obligation, a sense of guilt—stands as evidence for the existence of God.

There are two objections that might be leveled against this argument, one having its source in naturalistic psychology, the other emanating from a superficial cultural anthropology. Freudian psychology would have us believe that conscience—what it labels the superego—is nothing more than the internalization, a psychological assimilation, of various external sources of authority in a person's life: first and foremost parental authority, but beyond that, an array of other authorities which are part of the larger social environment in which any individual finds himself—police, professors, princes, palm-readers, pop-stars, whatever they might be. According to this view, then, conscience is not to be interpreted as pointing to something beyond the natural; it can be fully explained in purely naturalistic terms. This being so, guilt, which the Freudians would readily acknowledge to be a real psychological phenomenon, is also to be seen as something which can be explained without referring to anything beyond nature. Freud himself explains that, "our moral sense of guilt is the expression of the tension between the ego and the superego." [6] Guilt is a purely subjective problem, in other words, a psychological problem, which, with the right kind of therapy, can be happily resolved.

Analysis such as this, which presents itself as authentically scientific, is thin and superficial, and displays a decidedly short-sighted understanding of human nature and of human experience. No one who has ever felt a profound and oppressive sense of guilt for a real and serious wrong he has committed could ever be led to believe that the guilt weighing him down can be explained in purely mechanistic terms, as no more than a condition in which two parts of the psyche are at odds with one another. Rectify the internal tension, and a "cure" will ensue. What we have here is an attempt to remove guilt from the moral realm and turn it into a purely medical problem. But it is to trivialize guilt to regard it as no more than a disease. It is better compared to physical pain, the symptom of a disease. This is not to deny that in some cases a sense of guilt can be aberrational, just as can a sense of righteousness, but that happens when our feelings of guilt have no foundation in objective reality. In more cases than not, however, we *feel* guilty for the simple reason that we *are* guilty. And we are guilty because we have offended against objective standards of right and wrong, standards which though of course composing part of the natural order, have their ultimate source in that which transcends the natural order. The authority we ultimately feel subject to, and obligated toward, is not simply internalized natural authority; it is an authority which gives meaning to all natural authority, and to which all natural authority is subject.

Another possible objection to the argument comes from the early research findings of cultural anthropology, at the time when that was still a fledgling science, research findings which turned out to be rather seriously garbled. The force of the argument from conscience is in good part founded upon the assumption that there is a distinctly universal quality to human conscience. That is, the basic sense of right and wrong, the first product of conscience, is something that is shared by all men. What we have in that sense, then, is a rudimentary moral standard which is common to the human race as such.

But then, in the decades of the first half of the twentieth century, some cultural anthropologists proposed that, in fact, there are no universal standards for human morality, a doctrine which was usually promoted under the banner of what was called cultural relativism. What we find, their argument went, when we study the various cultures of the world, is that there is, from the point of view of morality, great diversity among them. So that, for example, where Culture A might consider Behavior X to be altogether heinous, Culture B will have no moral problems at all with Behavior X, and, indeed, may actually endorse and promote it. The sense of right and wrong, then, can vary radically from society to society, and from this we are to conclude that there is no moral code that could be called universal in any meaningful sense. Importantly, the varying notions of right and wrong have their sources in the societies themselves. This being so, they are to be explained by criteria to be found entirely within the natural order, and not by appealing to anything that transcends that order.

That assessment turned out to be somewhat hasty, however. It was, in fact, a rush to judgment, based on too little evidence, or on evidence that was egregiously misinterpreted. In some instances the misinterpretations were due to a cultural myopia on the part of the interpreters; in others, it was the result of ideological presuppositions on their part, which distorted their perspective. What was found was not what was actually there, but what the researchers wanted to find. The "science" turned out to be not very scientific. As time passed, however, cultural anthropology matured as a discipline, and the account it now gives of things is quite different. The picture has been discovered to be in a sense more complex, and in a sense more simple. Today there would seem to be something like unanimity among the professionals that there are what can rightly be described as "moral universals," that is, a set of basic moral truths, of "rights" and "wrongs," upon which all human beings agree, running right across the cultural spectrum. All peoples are in agreement when it comes to certain fundamental principles governing human morality. Of course, we did not really need a consensus of cultural anthropologists to assure us of this. This is just another case of social science catching up with common wisdom. If there were not in the world a basic shared sense of what constitutes right and wrong, an institution such as the United Nations, whatever its faults, would not even be possible, and a document like the International Declaration of Rights could never have been written, much less officially subscribed to by all the countries of the globe.

The Argument from the Universal Desire for Happiness

There is no man in his right mind who does not want to be happy. If there is any one desire that is unquestionably universal, it is the desire for happiness. All peoples in all ages give the better part of their time and energy striving to attain those things which they are convinced are necessary for their happiness. But this happiness that all men seek has shown itself to be an exasperatingly elusive thing. Aristotle noted centuries ago that all men agree that they want to be happy, but there is no agreement among them in what they consider happiness to be, in what they believe they have to achieve in order to be happy.

During the course of their lives human beings chase after a wide variety of things—riches, sensual pleasure, fame, power, respect, just to name a few of the general categories—in either the hope or the conviction that, once the things are attained, happiness will follow. But it never happens. There may be success in attaining this, that, or the other thing which was supposed to bring happiness with it, and in the immediate aftermath of that attainment there may be a period of relative satisfaction and contentment, but then, sooner or later, but more often than not sooner, the great guarantor of happiness begins to lose its luster and becomes tarnished. And then the chase begins all over again. The pursuit of happiness becomes incessant, and increasingly more frustrating, for it seems as if we are panting after a diaphanous phantom that is ever receding in front of us. Is man's universal desire for happiness fated to be forever frustrated, then, because it can never be fully satisfied? If that is the case, then human beings, reputedly rational creatures, do not display a great deal of rationality in this particular matter, for rarely does the frustration ever lead to the conviction that it is time to give up the futile chase. Time after time we attain something that we think is going to make us happy, and time after time we are disappointed, and yet we continue the pursuit, telling ourselves that the next thing, what we are pursuing right now, *that* will finally do the trick. What is it that fuels this relentless pursuit, in the face of so much failure?

A more pointed question: Just why is it that we are so continuously frustrated in our pursuit of happiness? Could it possibly be that we are pursuing the wrong things? In that possibility we put our finger on the source of the problem. There is nothing at all in the nature of things that dictates that man's universal desire for happiness is designed to be frustrated. Just the opposite is true. We were made to be truly happy, but only by attaining that for which we were truly made. There are any number of things that we come to possess over the course of our lives that are genuinely good things, and we acknowledge them to be such, but we also know that, good as they are, there are limitations to their goodness. What lies at the bottom of the universal desire for happiness is the more basic desire to be completely fulfilled, perfected, in our nature as human beings. It is the good that perfects us, that fulfills us as human beings, but if that good is anything less than the ultimate good, Goodness itself, God, then there will always be a lack in our lives, a radical lack, that cuts to the very core of our beings. There is a sense in which our desire to be happy is infinite in its dimensions, infinite in its longing. That is why, though grateful for limited goods, we ever look beyond them, for something more. That is why our desire for happiness can only be satisfied by the infinite.

Our hearts are made for God alone, St. Augustine tells us, and they will not rest until they rest in God. Our restlessness is a sign of our yearning for God. For St. Thomas, man's universal desire for happiness, properly understood, is no more than a desire to be perfectly and permanently united with Him who is the very source of our being. What we have in that desire, then, is clear evidence for the existence of God, for it is unthinkable that a desire so deep, so ineradicable, should be implanted in us only to be frustrated. The desire for happiness is part and parcel of our very nature, a nature created by God, who, in giving us the desire for happiness, has left within us the indelible mark of His creative action.

The Argument from Universal Belief

There have always been atheists in the world, and doubtless there always will be, but there never has been an atheistic society, and I think we can say with confidence that there never will be one. All men of all times have been essentially religious, that is to say, they have believed in the existence of a supernatural realm, a plane of reality which stands above and is superior to the natural world. There is a considerable degree of variety to be discovered in the religious beliefs of man, both over the course of the centuries and at the present time. One of the most prominent features of that variety is the distinction between monotheism and polytheism. That distinction would seem to call into question, or at least diminish some of the poignancy of, what we call a universal belief in the supernatural. The first thing to be said on that score is that one should not put so much emphasis on the difference between monotheism and polytheism that one loses sight of the very large factor which they have in common. They both acknowledge a supernatural realm. In sum, there is a universal religious sense, founded in a shared belief in the supernatural, that has continuously manifested itself among human beings down through the ages, although that religious sense has manifested itself in many different ways.

Another point that has to be made with respect to the distinction between monotheism and polytheism, besides the fact that it should not be exaggerated, is that one must be careful not to mistake what seem to be polytheistic societies for what in fact are not such. It has happened more than once that societies which were initially thought to be polytheistic turned out to be, upon closer examination, monotheistic. The polytheism was a veneer, as it were, under which was to be found a belief in a single, all-high God, to whom all the lesser deities were subordinate.

Nonetheless, polytheism was and is a fact, and it remains problematic for any notion of universal belief in the supernatural which would have the requisite coherence for what we intend for it here—to serve as evidence for the existence of God. There is the added problem that not only have human beings had the unfortunate tendency to believe in a multiplicity of gods, many of the gods they chose to believe in were decidedly ungodly. These are problems for our argument, but not insuperable ones, and to put them in proper perspective it would be helpful if we recall what is the case with respect to the universal desire for happiness. Human beings continuously get the nature of true happiness wrong, pursuing all sorts of things which will in fact not contribute to their true happiness. They chase after the wrong things, but the basic meaningfulness of the chase itself remains, for there is in fact an object which is adequate to their desire. Man's many falsifications of happiness does not mean there is no true happiness, and, in fact, all those falsifications indirectly attest to the existence of true happiness. By the same token, the fact that human beings have so often gotten it wrong about the one true God, by supposing that there could be many deities, or in fabricating deities that are more hellish than heavenly, does not mean that there is not in fact one true God. It only means, once again, that man's knowledge of Him has often been imperfect, and sometimes even grossly so.

But there is another problem that has to be faced. I said above that there never has been any atheistic societies. Is that true? What are we to say of all those Communist governments in Eastern Europe and in the Far East that were such a grim part of the international landscape for the better part of the twentieth century? They were officially atheistic, were they not? They were, but there is a large difference between an officially imposed state atheism and a truly atheistic society. The first is totally artificial. When I contended that there never has been an atheistic society I was referring to what we might call a natural atheistic society. A natural atheistic society is one in which atheism wells up spontaneously, and is accepted by the populace as offering a true account of the way things really are; it is not forced upon them as part of a political ideology. To repeat the point, with qualification, there have been no actual examples of a *natural* atheistic society. What was commonly the case in those countries where atheism was state sponsored and state enforced—Poland is a good example of this—is that there was a very large discrepancy between the beliefs of the rulers and the beliefs of the people. A small godless elite lorded it over the godly masses. There was something particularly ironic about atheistic Communism, as many scholars have pointed out, and that is the fact that, while investing so much of its energy in suppressing religion, it became a kind of religion itself. Communism ended up imitating what it most detested. Man's irrepressible religious instinct had the final say.

What are we to make of modern secular culture, however? Could not that rightly be called atheistic? Two comments can be made on that subject. Secularism, though a very grave problem, is not to be equated with atheism. There is, to be sure, much practical atheism abroad in the land today. A practical atheist is someone who lives his life as if there were no God. If we were to compare the way the practical atheist acts with the way a professed atheist acts, we would detect no noticeable difference in their behavior. But, very likely, the practical atheist, if asked, would earnestly assure us that he believes in God. The belief is there but it is not manifested in his conduct. It is a faith without works, and therefore dead.

The second thing to be said about secularism is that, like Communism, it can be turned into a kind of religion, and therefore what we often find in secularism, at least in some of its manifestations, is a back-handed acknowledgment of true religion. What is at work here, then, is essentially the same principle discussed just above, where false gods indirectly attest to the true God. And, actually, there is something almost inevitable in the process by which secularism is transformed into an *ersatz* religion. Try as he might, man cannot suppress the deep need he has for the transcendent. If he consciously rejects the one true God, he will unconsciously establish false gods to take the place of what he has rejected, gods which he will make the objects of his fervent, even sacrificial devotion. For the Communist, it is the Party, or the Future. For the modern secularist it can be any number of things—sex, the environment, justice and peace, scientism, rights, a financial portfolio, "choice," freedom, security—the list is endless, for false gods are beyond counting.

What, then, is the nub of the argument we are presenting here, the argument from universal belief? It is this: man's universal belief in the supernatural can be offered as evidence for the existence of God. Man's belief in the supernatural points to the reality of the supernatural. When we consider the remarkable strength and consistency of this belief as it has manifested itself throughout the entire course of human history, when we consider its emphatic universality, can we seriously suppose it to be possible that virtually all men of all time have been dead wrong on so critically important a matter? Can we suppose that the universal belief in the supernatural is no more than a grand delusion—indeed, if a delusion, this would have to count as the grandest of all delusions— when it has displayed such vigorous and astonishing endurance? Could human beings be reasonably considered to be so monumentally stupid on this issue, when they have shown themselves to be so impressively clever on so many others?

Strictly speaking, we would have to confess, that in fact human beings *could* be wrong on this matter—after all, the belief itself does not *prove* that there is a God—but once again we must ask ourselves: How *likely* is it that man should be wrong here? Which seems to be the more reasonable supposition, that the universal belief in the supernatural strongly suggests that there is something to support that belief, or that such a belief has no basis in reality whatsoever? Certainly there would be something reckless in brushing aside man's universal belief in the supernatural as if it were not worth any consideration by serious minds. That would be poor science. What we have here is not just evidence, but overwhelming evidence, and it must be evidence of something. Those who would deny that it could serve as evidence for the existence of the supernatural are under obligation to come up with a better suggestion, and it simply will not do to dismiss it as a delusion. Besides being irresponsible, that is positively insulting to human intelligence. But if one is going to insist that all we have here is no more than a delusion, let us pause and consider more closely the precise nature of the phenomenon we are dealing with. This is not just a routine, run–of–the–mill delusion; this is the deepest and most tenaciously persistent delusion the human race has ever been burdened with. This is an altogether remarkable delusion; it is a perfectly astonishing delusion. In fact, I think we can say that, as delusions go, it is absolutely unique. How to explain such a delusion? Where does it come from?

The intellectual atheist, who prides himself on being an eminently rational soul, loves to score theism for being the very quintessence of irrationality. For him, the person who believes in God is a person suffering from serious self-deception, someone who, by his theism, is effectively betraying his nature as a rational being. From the Olympian heights of his pristine rationality, the intellectual atheist looks down pityingly upon the poor benighted believers in God, who do not know enough to know better. While he is bathed in light, they grope about in stygian darkness. Now, that is a rather precarious attitude the intellectual atheist chooses to assume, especially when one pauses to consider some of the intellectual giants down through the ages who have believed in God—Socrates, Plato, Aristotle, St. Catherine of Alexandria, St. Augustine, Boethius, St. Thomas Aquinas, Dante, Chaucer, St. Teresa of Avila, Shakespeare, Galileo, Kepler, Isaac Newton, Louis Pasteur, Alexander Solzhenitsyn, just to cite a very, very short list. Does the intellectual atheist actually think that his intellect towers above theirs, that he sees farther, penetrates more deeply into the nature of things, than did they? If he does, he would be well advised to stop and think again.

The Argument from Moral Goodness

Many atheists have used the existence of evil in the world, physical evil in particular, as evidence that supposedly proves either that God does not exist, or, if there is a God, that He cannot be a God of goodness. It would be foolhardy to deny that there is evil in the world, and no thoughtful believer would take so cavalier an attitude toward evil as to pretend that its presence cannot be very disturbing, and that sometimes it can be a severe test of one's faith. But as a matter of cold, logical fact, the existence of evil in the world proves neither (a) that there is no God nor (b) that God is lacking in goodness. To better see how this is so, I will put in the form of a conditional syllogism one of the standard atheistical arguments against the existence of God.

If evil exists, then God does not exist.

But evil in fact exists.

Therefore, God does not exist.

In conditional argument, the truth of the conclusion depends entirely on the fact that the major premiss (the first statement in the argument above) is true, and the truth of the statement implies that there is a necessary connection between the statement's antecedent (its first part) and its consequent (the second part). With that in mind, what are we to make of the major premiss of the argument? While the coexistence of evil and God can be said to be problematical (especially for finite minds who try to reconcile the two), there is nothing inherently contradictory in this state of affairs. Thus the major premiss is false. The conclusion, therefore, does not follow.

Evil can affect us deeply; it can, at times, when its presence is especially prominent and persistent, fairly sweep us off our feet. It has a way of establishing itself as the commanding center of our attention. And because of the peculiarly perverting effect it has on our imaginations, it can on occasion come close to persuading us that it is the dominant factor in the world. But is that really the truth of the matter? Is evil king? The philosopher Gottfried Leibniz, whom we met in the previous chapter, boldly and unabashedly contends that it is not. And he is right. Leibniz asks us to stop and consider the matter closely, give it our full attention, look at the actual facts of the matter. If we do so we will discover that, in purely quantitative terms, there is more good in the world than there is evil. [7]

Calm reflection will reveal to us that evil—let us think in terms of physical evil—comes as an interruption to the general smooth flowing of the good. It is the exception, not the rule. And it is precisely because it is a departure from the norm that it is upsetting, even shocking. It is something that we are not used to, something which, because of its very nature, we do not want to get used to. An earthquake can be a terrible occurrence, but earthquakes that wreak serious harm are rare.

The argument with which we are concerned, the argument from goodness, is not an invitation to stick our heads in the sand and pretend that there is no evil in the world, but to put that evil in its proper perspective. That is the negative part of the argument. The positive part is an invitation to give principal consideration to what deserves principal consideration—the goodness that is to be found everywhere in the world, but most especially the moral goodness, the goodness of men. The argument cites that moral goodness as evidence for the existence of God. If we are amazed at times, made wondrous by the existence of evil, we should be all the more amazed, made all the more wondrous, at the existence of moral goodness. There is something truly amazing, not simply in the existence of moral goodness, but in the fact that it is so pervasive. One does not have to go out of the way to discover it. We are surrounded by it. There are millions upon millions of truly good people in the world. Just stop and consider your own life, and how many such people you have known, or have known of. We are all acquainted with, may even be in daily contact with, people whose lives are characterized by a singular selflessness. They invariably think of others before they think of themselves. They regularly go out of their way to help others in whatever way they can, and they seem to have a sixth sense that tells them when others are in need of help. They do not simply react to the needs of others, they anticipate them. And there is a marvelous consistency in their charity. It is not a sometime thing, but seems to be part of their very nature. These people have a way of transforming the atmosphere around them. It is good to be near them.

But then think of all those people in the world whose goodness takes on truly extraordinary proportions. These are the people whose lives are thoroughly self-sacrificial. They are willing to diminish themselves so that they might more fully live for others and better serve them. They show no concern for their own comfort or ease. They are indifferent to material things, and sometimes make do without what most of us would consider to be the basic necessities of life. They work incessantly, and yet they seem tireless, and there is always the element of joy. Their lives fairly radiate joy. The cynics of the world, those who are so hardened that they find it difficult to accept the reality of true goodness, would tells us that these extraordinarily good people have serious psychological problems. Among other things, they suffer from low self-esteem. But the cynics' reaction is too foolish for comment. We all know that truly good people are the sanest people in the world.

But here is one of the most interesting points to be made about the people whom we have been describing, and the most salient point as far as our argument is concerned: if you were to ask these people why they act as they do, why they live the kinds of lives they live, the overwhelming majority would tell you that they do so for the sake of God. With but rare exceptions, consistently altruistic people, people whose lives are luminescent with genuine charity, and especially people who lead self-sacrificing lives, are not motivated by purely natural ends, and certainly do not act in order to achieve some kind of egocentric self-fulfillment. The truly good people in the world are invariably people who believe in God, and not only do they believe in God, they profess great love for Him. And that love explains their lives. Yes, they love their fellow man, but that is the natural outcome of their love of God, whom they love above all else. And some of them would tell you that if they did not believe in God, if they did not love Him, they would not live as they live.

Well, then, are all these truly good people of the world to be taken seriously when they cite their belief in God as *the* motivating factor in their lives? Or are we glibly to conclude that all we have here is just another case of profound self-deception? That would be quite irresponsible on our part. We have every reason to take these people at their word. And therefore the moral goodness they display should prove to be very instructive for us. What we have, in fact, in the presence of moral goodness in the world, is evidence for the existence of God. The only way moral goodness can be adequately accounted for is by acknowledging the inspiring source behind it. Because moral goodness is real, God is real.

The Argument from the Universal Desire for Justice

The virtue of justice tells us that all human beings, simply by reason of their unique status as persons, should always receive what is properly due to them, from those in authority, from their peers, and from those who are subordinate to them. But we know that this is not always how it goes. In fact, some might be prepared to argue, perhaps altogether too cynically, that true justice is a very rare commodity in this vale of tears. Justice demands that when injustice is done to people, that injustice should be promptly redressed. But it has to be admitted that many people are the victims of severe injustice, and no action is ever taken to remedy the wrong that has been done to them.

When we survey the contemporary scene, casting our eye across the various countries and cultures of the world, the picture we see is not a particularly pleasant one. There are large discrepancies in the manner in which human beings live their lives. Some people find themselves in very comfortable, even luxurious circumstances. They are surrounded by all the latest mechanical and technological conveniences, they have abundant leisure time, they have access to the best medical services available, they live in large nicely furnished houses, they garb themselves in expensive if not attractive clothes, if they do not always eat the best food they seem to be always eating, they have more money than they are able to spend in a lifetime. In sum, these are people who "have everything."

In dramatic contrast to these people and the circumstances in which they find themselves, there is another segment of humanity, by far and away the larger segment. Here we find people who live in anything but comfortable circumstances, and luxury is but a word for them. Indeed, they live in dire want. These are the "have nots" of the world. They are fortunate if they can manage to scrape together just the bare necessities of life. Leisure is unknown to them, for in more cases than not they have to spend all their time and energy merely keeping body and soul together. They must labor incessantly to acquire the minimum in food, clothing, and shelter. In the worst possible cases, their lives compare unfavorably with the lives of animals that are kept in zoos.

Now, in reflecting on the great contrast that exists between the rich and poor of the world, one might be tempted to think that perhaps the material circumstances in which people find themselves are just the material circumstances they deserve. In other words, the rich of the world are rich because of their moral superiority, and the poor of the world are poor because of their moral inferiority. But one has only to express such a thought to see how wrong it is. That kind of analysis simply will not do. To be sure, there are rich people who are morally good, but we could reasonably conjecture that many of them are quite immoral, and while there are poor people who are morally bad people (contrary to what some sentimentalist might think, poverty does not go hand in hand with virtue), there are many poor people who live morally upright, even exemplary, lives.

But if we consider the human condition from perspectives other than that of the radically uneven distribution of material goods, we readily recognize that there are many other ways as well in which things seem to be seriously out of joint. Why is it that a beautiful and talented and virtuous young girl, a girl who was full of promise and seemed destined to make a real difference for good in the world, has her young life suddenly snatched from her in an auto accident? It just doesn't seem right. Why is it that so many people in this world seem to "get away with murder," while other people, innocent people, are constantly being preyed upon and victimized? Many people have to suffer the severest kind of injustices, and nothing is ever done about it. In certain cases, as soon as the damage is done, there is no remedy for it, for the damage is irreparable. I have in mind all those innocent people who have had their most precious possession wrested from them—their lives. Consider the countless millions of babies who have been aborted the world over in recent decades. What could be more unjust than that? Nothing. What did they do to suffer the definitive violation of their most basic right, the right to life, just as they were beginning to exercise it? Nothing.

In sum, when we look around this world of ours, we see that there is much injustice in it, there is much in it that "just ain't fair." There are many things that are severely bent out of shape, and no action is taken, perhaps no action will ever be taken, to straighten them out. Must these injustices go unresponded to forever? We say, No, that cannot be. Paradoxical though it may seem, the injustice in the world can be put forward as evidence for the existence of God, for injustice demands redress, and if it does not receive it here, it will receive it hereafter. We assert, then, that there is a God, an all-just God, and He will surely remedy the injustices suffered by His people. In the final analysis, we can be assured that justice will be done.

The Argument from Beauty

What is it about beauty that so deeply affects us? It is impossible to put it into words, and yet who has not felt the overwhelming power of beauty at some time or another in his life? Beauty is powerful, but its power is of a peaceful, gentle kind. It is not oppressive. Beauty has the capacity to arrest us, literally to stop us in our tracks. It interrupts and offers restful contrast to our overly-busy, distracted daily lives. Without ever being rude, it insists upon our attention. "Stop, look at me!" beauty seems to say. And we stop and we look, and a great nameless calm comes over us. Who can look into the deep black eyes of an innocent child and not be stunned into something like a contemplative swoon? Who can stand on the deck of a ship sailing the waters of the South Pacific and look up into the cloudless night sky which is almost white with stars and not be struck speechless with awe? Who can view the Grand Canyon, the Alps, Minnehaha Falls in early spring, and not fall into a silent, reverent reverie? Who has not stood dumbstruck before a stunning sunset spread spectacularly across the Western sky, trying vainly to register and assimilate the fleeting patterns and delicacies of color that no painter could ever duplicate, no camera could ever capture? Who can experience such things, beautiful things, and not be moved to the very depths of his soul?

When we attempt to be philosophical about the experience of beauty, when we subject it to careful analysis in order to explain what it is about beautiful things that they should affect us in the way they do, we come up with notions like order, like the harmonious relation among parts, and while these ideas have some limited usefulness in helping us to better understand beauty, in the end we have to admit that they are really quite inadequate in providing us with a fully satisfactory account of what is happening to us when we experience it, in telling us what is the essential message beauty is communicating to us. And that is because what is being communicated to us in the experience of beauty is the sense of the ineffable, of that which cannot be expressed in words. God is The Ineffable, He who cannot be expressed in words. Therefore we can confidently say that beauty is one of the surest signs we have of the existence of God. The ineffableness of beauty announces the ineffableness of God. Beauty is the signature of God, which He has written across His creation.

The Argument from the Universal Desire for Immortality

An integral part of the universal belief in the supernatural is a belief in an afterlife. The two go hand in hand. The most obvious evidence we have of the universal belief in an afterlife is the solemnly respectful way human beings have always treated their dead. The tomb, wherever it may be found, stands as a monument to immortality. No one wants to die. We tolerate death, because we have no choice in the matter, but we never really accept it. We can never fully reconcile ourselves to it. There seems to be something radically wrong about the whole business.

Oh, to be sure, we will usually go along with the received wisdom that assures us that death is, of course, a perfectly natural thing, it happens to everybody, and therefore any mature, healthy-minded human being should be fully accepting of something as perfectly natural as death. That is what we would say for public consumption, to show how thoroughly modern we are. But in our heart of hearts we have great difficulty in buying into that eminently reasonable way of looking at things. How can it be natural to cease to live, when all one's deepest urgings and longings are pressing in just the opposite direction? We want to go on living, and on, and on. The committed naturalist tries to make the best of a very difficult matter. If death is so natural, we ask, and if we are supposedly an integral part of nature, what is it in us that makes us fight it so? The naturalist will answer, it is simply the instinct for survival? But why do we want to survive, not just for another day, a couple of weeks, a few more years, but—if we are really honest with ourselves—forever? If the human race were to be polled on the question tomorrow, it is very likely that 100% would unhesitantly avow that, if they were given a choice, they would prefer, thank you, to avoid death, permanently; they would have no serious objections to living forever.

Man does have, always has had, a deep, unquenchable longing for immortality. Is this an aberration? Could it be interpreted as simply the manifestation of a kind of collective infantilism with which the human race as a whole is afflicted? Is it just a case of universal arrested development? Human beings refuse to grow up and face the harsh facts of life, the harshest of which is death? At first blush that might sound like an acceptable description of the situation. But it cannot stand up under close scrutiny. No, that explanation won't do, especially when there is a much better one available.

It is not for nothing that man's longing for immortality is so integral a part of his consciousness. Even without the benefit of revealed religion, man, relying on natural reason alone, indicates that he knows more than he knows when he reverently buries his dead, in the calm conviction that they are not really dead. Man's universal desire for immortality points to the fact that man is immortal. The desire, therefore, can be taken as evidence for God's existence. The desire for immortality is man's natural response to the kind of creature that, by nature, he truly is, the kind of creature God created him to be.

The Argument from Laughter

It might seem rather odd to offer laughter, or, more precisely, man's sense of humor, as the basis for an argument for the existence of God, and I must confess that this particular argument is seldom found on any of the standard lists of the moral arguments. But I do think that it is suggestive enough to warrant inclusion in this chapter. What lies at the bottom of a human being's sense of humor? What makes us laugh? There seems to be agreement among those who have given serious thought to the matter that the key to humor is incongruity. It is our perception of incongruity—the awareness that we are confronting a circumstance that represents an abrupt and therefore surprising departure from how we expected things were going to be—that causes us to laugh. A circus clown reaches into his pocket seemingly to get a handkerchief, and pulls out a bed sheet. An incongruous situation is one in which things are put together oddly, in a strange and unusual manner. That tends to tickle us.

One of the more telling things about laughter is that it is always a sign of great mental alertness. We are very much aware of the things we laugh at. We pay strict attention to them. Now, because incongruity lies at the bottom of our sense of humor, we could just as well call a sense of humor a sense of incongruity. We are noticing that things are at sixes and sevens, that there is disorder in the situation we are laughing at, and by acknowledging that disorder we are acknowledging, albeit indirectly, the order without which the disorder would not even be possible. The order in question here is a universal order. By acknowledging the order, in turn, we are at the same time acknowledging the One Who Orders. In a funny sort of way, then, whenever we laugh we are attesting—once again, indirectly, and as it were unconsciously—to the existence of God. Life is not a tragedy, but a comedy, and a divine comedy at that.

CHAPTER TEN

Man's Knowledge of God

Knowing *That* and Knowing *What*

We are now at that stage of our course where we will shift our focus from the first to the second principal concern of natural theology. Having studied the various ways in which the demonstration of God's existence can be attempted, with primacy of place having been given to the Five Ways of St. Thomas Aquinas, we now turn to the question of the kind of knowledge we are capable of having of the essence, or nature, of that being whose existence has been demonstrated.

The key question that has thus far been commanding our attention is, *An sit?* Does God exist or not? Having answered that question in the affirmative, we need now to go on to consider what we are capable of knowing concerning the nature of that being whose existence is no longer a matter of doubt. It might be helpful at this point if we remind ourselves of the very real practical differences that obtain between knowing *that* something exists, and just *what* it is that is doing the existing. Because we know that every created thing is composed of essence (what it is) and existence (that it is), we can also, if we have succeeded in establishing the fact of real existence, and simply by having done so, have at least some rudimentary knowledge of its essence, at the least as a material "something" of this or that kind. But in most cases I will have to be content, initially, with my knowledge of essence being quite minimal. To give more substance to my knowledge, I must investigate further. For example, let us imagine that I am out on the Western plains. As I look across the landscape, baking under the

August sun, I espy something in the far distance. I know for sure that I am seeing *something* off there in the haze, but I can give it no more precise identification than that. What exactly is it—a small building, a buffalo, a bush? I need to make use of my binoculars in order to satisfy my curiosity on that score.

In God, essence and existence are one. That fact certainly does not imply that knowledge of the existence of God brings with it knowledge of His essence, in any kind of unqualified way. But does the fact that we know that God exists carry with it any reputable knowledge at all of God's essence? St, Thomas maintains that it does, and in his commentary on Boethius's *De Trinitate* we read: "Concerning no thing is it possible to know that it is, without having some kind of knowledge of what it is, either a perfect knowledge or a confused kind of knowledge."[1] The kind of knowledge we can have of God's "whatness" would be a confused kind. But the basic point to be emphasized is that knowledge of *that* brings at least some degree of knowledge of *what*. Again, the knowledge we have of God's nature that follows from our knowledge of His existence would be far from perfect, but it would be real knowledge nonetheless. Perfect knowledge of God would be knowledge of His essence without qualification, and, as St. Thomas never tires of reminding us, such knowledge will always be lacking in this life. Perfect knowledge of God's essence, that is, knowledge of Him as He is in Himself, is the kind of knowledge which will accompany the Beatific Vision.[2]

The Negative Knowledge of God

It goes without saying that man's knowledge of God is limited knowledge, limited by the finiteness of our intellects. By way of giving further qualification to our limited knowledge of God, we say that it is essentially negative knowledge, by which we mean that all of our knowledge of God is initiated by and founded upon our making a series of clarifying declarations as to what God is not, in one particular respect or another. So, for example, when we speak of the infinity of God we are saying first and fundamentally that God has nothing of the finite about Him; there are no limitations whatsoever to His being. And thus we may say that our approach to the knowledge of God is by way of the *via negativa,* through negation, a process by which we separate off from God, as it were, everything that cannot belong to Him because it partakes of finitude in one way or another. St. Thomas provides us with a precise summary of the issues that are at stake here. He writes: "Wisdom does not consist merely in knowing that God exists, but in approaching a knowledge of what He is, but this is not something we are able to do in this life except insofar as we know what God is not." [3] The way of negation, then, is going to prove to be for us the most basic way of coming to a knowledge of God through natural reason alone.

When we refer to our knowledge of God as fundamentally negative, we do not mean to imply by this that the knowledge is without content— if that were the case it would not qualify as knowledge at all—nor that it is unproductive. Consider for a moment the real value that negative knowledge can have for us in our daily lives. The point that is being stressed here is that, in dealing with negative knowledge, we are not dealing with something that is all that exotic. We exercise this knowledge whenever, for example, we advance toward the positive identification of something, let us call it X, by a process of elimination. Suppose that we are at the stage of our investigations where we do not as yet have any positive knowledge of what X is, but because of our general familiarity with the large context in which we know that X is to be found, we can, one by one, preclude various things that we know for certain X cannot be. If all goes well, this negative process will eventually yield positive consequences, for by eliminating unlikely possibilities for X we are effectively clearing the path that leads to X, and thereby increasing the possibility of its eventually being positively identified. An approach such as this is regularly used by medical researchers, as they attempt to isolate the cause of a disease, and by all the detectives of the world, as they track down the villain who murdered the butler. St. Thomas, in the continuation of the quotation cited just above, calls attention to the most signal benefit that follows from employing the process of negation. "For he who knows a thing as distinct from all other things," he writes, "approaches a knowledge of what that thing is." [4] If I am able to say confidently that X is not A, nor B, nor C, I am getting closer to a positive knowledge of X.

It would be well at this point that we remind ourselves that the knowledge we are discussing here, under the general rubric of man's knowledge of God, is the kind of knowledge that properly pertains to our science of natural theology. In other words, it is natural knowledge, the kind of knowledge that we are able to attain through the exercise of natural reason alone. We are obviously in no position, as philosophers, to deny those kinds of knowledge of God that someone can come to possess by means other than the exercise of natural reason. Needless to say, much of our knowledge of God, and indeed the most reliable knowledge of God, comes to us through revelation. But there is also that knowledge of God which can come to a person through the direct action of divine grace. This infused knowledge is of an especially privileged sort, and implies a distinct intervention, within the natural realm, of the supernatural.

What the Five Ways Reveal About the Divine Nature

The principal purpose of the arguments of the Five Ways was of course to demonstrate *that* God is, and not explicitly to say anything about God's essence or nature.[5] Even so, in the very process of showing that God exists, they succeed in revealing something of His nature. And this could not really be otherwise, if we recall St. Thomas's observation that at least a minimum knowledge of a thing's nature accompanies our knowledge of its existence. A brief review of the Five Ways will show us how this is the case with regard to the nature of God. In the first way, we learn of a God who is immutable, unchanging, and that implies a being that is completely devoid of potency. But such a being must be a perfect being, lacking nothing, for the presence of potency in a being always indicates that there is something lacking in that being. The second way provides us with the significant knowledge of God as First Cause, the originating source of all that exists; this implies an omnipotent being. Also, because God, as First Cause, is an uncaused cause, that means that the explanation for His existence is to be found entirely within Himself. This is turn points at least indirectly at the great truth that, with God, essence and existence are one and the same. In the third way we come to understand God as a necessary being, and this also suggests the unity of essence and existence in God, that He is a being whose very nature is to exist.

The fourth way makes known to us a God who is the ultimate, the *ne plus ultra* in being, the Supreme Being. As such, God is absolutely unique, for there cannot be more than one supreme being. The fourth way also instructs us, concerning the nature of God, that He is the being to whom all other beings are subordinate, and upon whom they are absolutely dependent. Finally, through the fifth way we are made explicitly aware of the fact that God is an intelligent being. As such, He is not a being who possesses intelligence, as is the case with us, but He simply *is* intelligence. Intelligence is one with His very essence. God is Supreme Intelligence, to whom everything that is intelligible must ultimately be referred.

God Is Infinitely Intelligible in Himself

The being who is Supreme Intelligence is supremely intelligible, which is to say, supremely knowable. But we have to modify that statement by adding the very important qualifying phrase, "in Himself." What does it mean to say that God is supremely intelligible? The answer to the question has to do with the very nature of the being of God. Intelligibility is intimately associated with being itself. In order that any knowledge at all be possible, there must be an object of the knowledge. that which is known, a being, or some aspect or another of being. Being is the proper object of the human intellect, St. Thomas tells us. But we also know that not all beings are the same, and although it may be a rather clumsy way of speaking, we say, in order to get at the most significant differentiating factor among beings, that some beings have more being than others. They have more "contents," as it were; there is more there to be known. An eagle has more being than a flea, and is therefore more intelligible. Now, all created being, from the highest angel down to the lowliest flea, relate to being as possessor to possessed. Creatures *have* being, and, indeed, they have it as a gift. But God does not have being; it is not something He possesses. God is pure being, or Pure Act (*Actus Purus*). Or yet again, we can simply say, God is, in that it is of God's nature to exist, something which we might express, reverently, in an equation: God = "to be." In light of all this, then, we can see that, if being is related to intelligibility, and if God is the Supreme Being, then God is supremely intelligible. He is supremely knowable.

But supremely knowable to whom? To God alone. And this leads us to the important distinction, regarding the objects of knowledge, between those that are intelligible in themselves (*secundum se*) and those that are intelligible to us (*quoad nos*). It has to be noted, first of all, that a thing must be intelligible in itself, intrinsically intelligible, before it can be known to us, for to identify something as intelligible in itself is simply to say that it can be known. A thing must have the possibility of being known before it can actually be known. But something can obviously be knowable in itself, but not known to us. In almost every case, a situation of that sort is explained by a deficiency in our knowledge, not simply the deficiency that we call ignorance, but a deficiency in our intellectual capacities, our very ability to know. We do not have to advert to the supernatural level to find things that are intelligible in themselves but not to us, for there are any number of things in the natural realm, in the world all around us, that are intelligible in themselves but that we do not understand. They make perfectly good sense, so to speak, but we do not grasp that "sense." This distinction between intrinsic intelligibility and intelligibility from our point of view is one that is quite familiar to us from our ordinary experience.

In this case, however, we are giving special application to the distinction, so that it spans, so to speak, the natural and the supernatural realms. We speak of God, who is intelligible *secundum se*, but whose intelligibility is completely beyond the human mind to grasp, and, we might add, permanently so. On the natural level there are any number of things which are unintelligible to us but not permanently so, for we can turn our attention to them, study them, and after a time come to understand them. But because God's intelligibility is infinite, and the human mind is finite, our understanding of the being of God will forever be limited. Once again, only God knows God as He is in Himself.

Man's Knowledge of God Is Limited by Man's Nature

Another important principle of Scholastic epistemology needs to be called to our attention within the context of this discussion, and that is the principle which tells us that whatever knowledge we come to possess as human beings , we possess precisely, and only, as human beings.[6] That might sound like little more than a truism. To be sure, it is a truism, but, like all truisms, it is true, and in some cases truisms express truths that are as profound as they are plain. This is such a case. In order to understand all that the principle is attempting to communicate to us, we must begin by reminding ourselves of the elementary fact that the human mind is finite. It is not simply limited, but radically limited, in its capacities. The most obvious instance of this fact is to be found in the quantitative limitations of the human mind, putting bounds to the amount of things it can know. We cannot know all there is to know. More significantly, the mind is limited qualitatively as well, meaning that our knowledge of any one thing is never going to be exhaustive, and it will never be perfect knowledge of the thing. There will always be a weakness, an insufficiency in our knowledge of anything, and this is an unavoidable consequence of the weakness and insufficiency of our minds. We could put that in more formal terms by saying that whatever is known by human beings can be known only as framed within the ontological limitations of our human nature. What this all comes down to, as far as our specific interests here are concerned—and to put it now in the simplest terms—is that man can know God only as man. But is not that obvious? Yes, it is, but man has an unfortunate tendency to forget what is obvious, especially in this matter, and to think that he knows God in ways that far exceed his natural capacities. Of course, any such "knowledge" must necessarily be seriously distorted, and the "God" about which man is inclined to speak so boldly is often no more than a figment of the human imagination. Man, who is very susceptible to intellectual pride, must constantly remind himself that he can only know God humanly, never divinely.

One of the specific limitations of man's knowledge of God, or, for that matter, of his knowledge of any immaterial entity, has to do with the fact that all of our knowledge comes to us through the senses.[7] But not only does all our knowledge begin with sense knowledge, it can never, no matter how elevated above sense knowledge it may become through increased abstraction, completely cut its ties with the sense knowledge in which it is anchored. All of our ideas have their immediate source in the phantasm, or sense image. A sense image, by its very nature, is an image of something in the material order. But what happens when we conceive thoughts of things which, though having real being external to our minds, are completely immaterial, such as angels, and more importantly for our discussion here, God Himself? How can we have a sense image of that which cannot be sensed? And if it is true that all of our thought is grounded in sense knowledge, how are we to explain our ability to entertain ideas of purely immaterial entities?

In order to be able to think about immaterial things we must in effect supply them with a sense image. Given the way the human mind is constituted, there is no alternative to that process. (Be advised that we are talking here about the *natural* workings of the human mind.) Because of this state of affairs, there are bound to be some distortions in our ideas about purely spiritual beings. For example, when we attempt to think about angelic being, we cannot help but "picture" an angel, i.e., create a sense image of the angel. In doing this we are picturing something which in the strict sense, because it is the kind of being it is, cannot be pictured. And the same thing is true when we think about God. We call to mind these psychological particulars pertaining to our mode of knowing simply to underscore a specific limiting factor in our knowledge of God. [8]

Ontologism, Agnosticism, Modernism

Over the course of history there have evolved three major errors with regard to our natural knowledge of God, more particularly, regarding the source of our natural knowledge of God. Because of the deleterious influence these errors have had, and continue to have, on natural theology, it is important that we be aware of them. The names given to these errors are: ontologism, agnosticism, and modernism.

Ontologism is that position—it could be called at once a philosophical and a theological position—which holds that man is so constituted naturally that he is able to have a direct, intuitive knowledge of the very essence of God. It should be obvious to you by now that this is a position that we could by no means subscribe to. The name borne by this position might suggest that it has some necessary connection with the ontological argument. There may be a connection between the two, but it is not a necessary one. As we would recall, the ontological argument assumes a knowledge of God which is not self-evidently true, and it is just this that disqualifies the argument as a genuine demonstration. But some who sincerely make use of the ontological argument, regarding it as a bonafide proof, depend upon revelation for the privileged knowledge of God on which the argument turns, even though they do not explicitly acknowledge in the argument the source of this knowledge. This would seem to have been the case with St. Anselm. However, if an ontologist were to employ the ontological argument, he would explicitly cite the source of his privileged knowledge of God, and it would not be revelation. It would be his own being. And this brings us to the heart of the position of ontologism. In citing revelation as a source of knowledge about God, we are of course citing a supernatural source. The ontologist argues that we have a *natural* source of the knowledge of God's essence. It does not come from revelation, but wells up, as an intuition, out of the center of our beings. The ontologist does not deny the reality of revelation, nor its efficacy; he simply asserts that we have another, and much more immediate, source for a privileged knowledge of God.

Now, if it were true that we all have, simply by reason of our shared human nature, an intuitive knowledge of God, then a case could be made for the legitimacy of the ontological argument. On the other hand, if we did possess such intuitive knowledge of God, one could then ask if any argument at all would be needed concerning the matter of God's existence. What would have to be proved? Presumably, an intuitive knowledge, of anything at all, would have to rank among the most certain kinds of knowledge we would be capable of possessing. So, if all of us are gifted, as the ontologists claim, with an intuitive knowledge of God, a knowledge not only of His existence but of His essence as well, then it would seem that no one would have to persuade anyone of anything concerning these most important of matters. In such a setting, any attempt to demonstrate the existence of God would be like attempting to demonstrate the principle of contradiction. There is no need to demonstrate the self-evident.

Agnosticism is the position that maintains that it is impossible to have any kind of reputable, reliable knowledge of God. This position, then, would be directly opposite to that taken by ontologism. And both the ontologist and the agnostic would take vigorous exception to the position that is being expounded in this book. The ontologist would disagree with us because, whereas we assert that no immediate knowledge of God's essence is to be attained through our natural faculties alone, he would say, to the contrary, that such knowledge is quite possible and even fully natural. The agnostic would take us to task for defending the position that a human being can, through the exercise of natural reason, arrive at a certain knowledge of God's existence, as well as, beyond that, a degree of knowledge pertaining to the attributes of God. No, the agnostic would insist, not even that is possible.

Modernism is the point of view that claims that we can have a direct knowledge of God, and in that respect the modernist would be in agreement with the ontologist. The difference between the two positions might be accurately described in this way: the dominant orientation of ontologism is toward the intellectual, whereas the dominant orientation of modernism is toward the affective. More precisely, they would differ as to the source of the privileged knowledge of God they claim. For the ontologist, that source is intuition—an immediate insight into the truth of things, including things of the highest import. For the modernist, that source is the affective response to our experiences. The ontologist "sees" God; the modernist "feels" Him. The modernist approach has managed to garner a considerable amount of popular support over the years, and of these three erroneous attitudes regarding our knowledge of God, modernism stands today as the most influential. Doubtless the soundest explanation for this is to be found in the fact that we live in an age in which human feelings have come to be regarded as a virtually infallible source of truth. And thus it is that many people are blown about helplessly, riding upon the unpredictable winds of whimsy.

The Quality of Our Knowledge of God

To repeat an important Thomistic point: In this life we will never have anything like an unqualified knowledge of God's essence, of God as He is in Himself. We have already cited some specific ways in which our knowledge of God is limited. We want now to examine in more detail the quality of our knowledge of God. We have stressed the point that what knowledge we do have of God is essentially negative in its foundations. But, remember, negative knowledge is not negligible knowledge. Obscure and imperfect though our knowledge of God may be, we are nonetheless capable, as St. Thomas instructs us, through the process of negation, of attaining a knowledge of God which is truly *proper* to Him. By that is meant that the knowledge pertains indeed to the one true God, and to no other being. However limited it may be, it is knowledge of God and of God alone. St. Thomas explains this important point clearly in a pertinent passage from the *Summa Contra Gentiles*. "And thus, proceeding in order, by such negations God will be distinguished from all that He is not. Finally, there will then be a proper consideration of God's substance when He will be known as distinct from all things. Yet, this knowledge will not be perfect, since it will not tell us what God is in Himself."[9] We might say that the most important positive result to come from this whole negative approach to God is the sure knowledge that He is utterly unlike any other being; He is unique in the strictest sense of the term.

How then do we continue to proceed in deepening our knowledge of God through the means of natural reason alone? In our efforts to demonstrate the existence of God, we relied exclusively on the *quia* argument, proceeding from effects to cause. We shall not depart from that eminently reliable procedure. The principal way we come to know God in this world is through His creation. But to lend greater structure and system to the manner in which we go about doing this, we turn to St. Thomas for some helpful guidance. He lays out three ways to be followed in coming to a greater knowledge of God through natural reason: the way of causality, the way of negation or remotion, and the way of transcendence.

To illustrate what is involved in following the way of causality, let us consider a particular attribute of God, His goodness. We would all agree that God is good, that goodness is of the very being of God, and that it would be irrational not to think of God as all good. But how do we arrive at knowledge of this sort? Certainly we can know such truths about God through revelation, but we are concerned here with knowledge of God that is attained through natural reason alone. Following the mode of *quia* argument, we start with the world. What we quickly discover about the world in which we live is that it is everywhere deeply marked by goodness. There are good things in the world, and there are good people in the world. Sooner or later, after the pervasiveness of goodness sinks into our consciousness, we begin to wonder about the source of all this goodness. Where did it come from? How is it to be explained? We are convinced that it must have a cause. Goodness does not just happen. In pursuing this line of reasoning, and having already established by argument that God is the cause of the world and all things in it, we reach the conclusion that if the creatures that God has created are good, then it must necessarily be that the Creator is good, for from where else would the goodness of the creatures come, if not from the being who created them? In sum, then, what we do by following the way of causality is to argue to the goodness of God (cause) from the goodness that we find in His creation (effects).

What is involved in the way of negation or remotion? In order to explain this approach to a knowledge of God, we will continue to consider the attribute of God's goodness. The goodness that we come to know as a result of our experience in the world, though it can tell us that God is necessarily good, can give us no adequate idea of what the goodness of God is actually like. In the first place, we need to realize that all the goodness that we can know through our experience exists accidentally, not substantially. In other words, we do not know goodness as a "something," but rather as a quality of a something—e.g., a good person, a good book, a good cup of tea. This circumstance serves to call our attention to the vast difference between the goodness of God and the goodness of any other being. In God, there is no distinction between substantial being and accidental being, as there is in creatures. This means that goodness, for Him, is constitutive of His very being.

In order to gain greater clarity and precision about the goodness of God, we engage in a conscious process by which we separate every understanding that we might have of the nature of goodness (e.g., that it is an accident of quality) from goodness as it exists in God. This is the same process of negation, or remotion, which we discussed earlier. In consequence of engaging in this process, we come to see that whereas in creatures goodness is something that is possessed, in God goodness is one with His very being. We possess goodness; God is goodness. Furthermore, by removing from our idea of God's goodness every understanding of goodness that we gain through our ordinary experiences in the world, we conclude that the goodness of God must be unlimited. If we reflect on the matter, we see that goodness in creatures is necessarily limited, and that is because the very beings of creatures are limited. But because God is unlimited being, and because goodness is one with His being, then His goodness too is unlimited.

The way of transcendence involves a mode of thinking whereby we elevate everything we properly attribute to God to the superlative plane. The operative idea here is to make explicit our understanding that any particular perfection that we might attribute to God, such as goodness, exceeds, or transcends, whatever knowledge of that perfection that we have gained from our ordinary experiences. To say that God's goodness is transcendent means that his goodness exceeds, and indeed exceeds infinitely, any other goodness that we know, or could ever come to know, or even could ever imagine.

A very useful summary of these three ways of attaining knowledge of God through the exercise of natural reason is provided by St. Thomas himself, in the example he uses to illustrate them. In his example the attribute of God he considers is the divine wisdom.

> There is a threefold application of terms to God. First, affirmatively: for instance, I can say that God *is wise,* since there is in Him a likeness to the wisdom that derives from Him. But since that wisdom is not in God as we understand it and name it, we can truly deny this wisdom of God, and say: God *is not wise.* Again, since wisdom is not denied of God as though He were lacking in wisdom, but because in Him it transcends wisdom as we know it and name it, we must say that God *is super-wise.* Accordingly, Dionysius explains perfectly by these three ways of ascribing wisdom to God, how these expressions are to be applied to God.[10]

The Names of God

We give many names to God, and the process that lies behind our doing so is the same as that which lies behind our giving names to anything whatever. The process is an inextricable part of the way our intellect naturally operates. A name, or a word, is attached to a concept, and the concept, or idea, points to a thing that exists in the world. St. Thomas provides a brief, concise description of the essentials of this pattern. "Words are the signs of concepts," he writes, "and concepts are the likenesses of things. And thus it is clear that words signify things through the concepts of the intellect. Therefore, according to the way a thing can be known to us, so it can be named by us."[11] The fact that we are able to apply any names at all to God—what we call the attributes of God could count as "names" of God—no matter how qualified those names may be, shows that we have real knowledge of God, severely limited though it is.

But the very fact that we have to give so many names to God provides emphatic evidence of the inadequacy of our knowledge of

God, for, after all, He is perfectly simple. Yet, the way we proceed in this matter is the way we have to proceed. We are but obeying the natural restrictions that attend human knowing. Our limited intellect cannot grasp the reality of God in a single concept. The names we apply to God—e.g., goodness, wisdom—do not signify the very essence of God, for the simple reason that we do not know that essence.

In reflecting on the various names we apply to God, we have to ask ourselves what is the quality of those names with respect to the classical manner in which terms are distinguished, i.e., as univocal, equivocal, and analogous. Our specific concern is this: Are the terms we apply to God univocal, or equivocal, or analogous? Remembering your logic and metaphysics, you will immediately see that the question can only be answered by precluding the possibility that anything we say of God could ever rightly be said of Him either univocally or equivocally. We thus immediately eliminate those two possibilities.

Let us stir up our memories so that we can see the justification for this. Once again, we will consider the goodness of God. If we were to apply the term "goodness" to God in exactly the same way—in other words, univocally—as we apply it to creatures, two things would necessarily follow. First, and most seriously, it would mean that there is no ontological difference between God and any other being in the universe. And thinking of things in that way would open the door to pantheism. Second, it would suggest that we know the essence of God, for we are able to apply a term univocally only to those things whose essences we know. But, as we have repeated often, we do not know the essence of God.

With like confidence we can reject the notion that when we apply names to God we do so equivocally. Consider an example of an equivocal word in English, "secretary." We call that an equivocal term because, though one word, it can signify two quite distinct, essentially different, things: a clerical worker, and a large bird of prey indigenous to southern Africa. Now, if a word like "goodness" were considered to be equivocal, that is, if it were to bear two radically different meanings, and then if it were to be applied both to God and to creatures, there would be a complete break-down in coherent communication. Any hope that we might have entertained to the effect that a stable knowledge of God could be reached through natural reason would be dashed. Indeed, knowledge of God would be quite impossible, for we literally would have no sure idea what we meant when we called God "good," or when we spoke of His "goodness."

The Names of God Are Analogous

If a univocal term is one that has a single, steady meaning, if an equivocal term is one that can have at least two quite different meanings, what we have, then, in those two kinds of terms, is an accent on sameness (in the case of univocal terms) and an accent on difference (in the case of equivocal terms). An analogous term is one that combines both accents, connoting both sameness and difference at the same time, as recognized as existing in whatever things to which we may apply the term. Now, if we are using language correctly, every term we apply to God, every name we give to Him, is done analogously. Or, to put it more precisely, the terms themselves are analogous. So, for example, when we say that, "God is good," there are two very important messages being communicated in that statement. We are saying, first, that there is a note of sameness between the goodness of God and that of every other thing that we call good. Second, we are saying, in the very same breath, that there is a difference, indeed the most profound of differences, between the goodness of God and the goodness of every other thing we know. We are asserting at once that the goodness of God is both like and unlike all other goodness.

If the goodness of God was completely unlike all other goodness (that we know through direct experience) then, as noted above, we would not really have any clear idea what we were talking about when we called God good. If the goodness of God was completely like all other goodness, we would, in calling God good, be putting Him on the same level as His creatures.

The most important analogous term in our philosophical vocabulary is "being." Everything that actually exists is a being. And we say that God is a being. But God is a being as is no other being, so obviously when we say that, "God exists," and, "a man exists," we are not meaning, we cannot be meaning, precisely the same thing. On the other hand, neither can we say that the two statements, "God exists," and, "a man exists," have no shared meaning whatever between them. If that were so, there would be an unbridgeable chasm between God and man. But there is no such chasm. We might say that there is an infinite distance between God and man, but that distance has been traversed, by God. The relation between man and God is of the most intimate kind, for it is a relation founded upon absolute dependence, of the creature upon the Creator.

There is another, more abstruse, way we can think analogously about the relation between man and God, and that is by reflecting on what we may refer to, for want of better words, as the relation between the mode of being of man and the mode of being of God. In doing so we have chiefly in mind what is called the analogy of proper proportionality. Every created being, we know, is minimally composed of essence and existence. The distinction between the two, and how they relate to one another, are real. In other words, they do not refer to a merely logical distinction or relation. Now, in God, although we may refer, because of the limitations and imperfection of our knowledge, to His essence and His existence, the distinction in this case is logical, not real, which is to say that the distinction exists only in our minds, as a help to our understanding, but not in God Himself. There is no real distinction in God between essence and existence; they are one. To be God means "to be."

Despite the vast, indeed infinite, difference between the being of creatures and the being of God with respect to essence and existence, we can nonetheless grope our way toward an understanding of a poignant point of comparison with respect to the two, and we will attempt to give it adequate expression in the following terms. In creatures—specifically in man, let us say—essence relates to existence as potency relates to act, while in God there is no relation between essence and existence, for the two are one. In man, act, or existence, is given to him, whereas God is act, indeed Pure Act, *Actus Purus*. So, there is a comparison, or analogy, to be recognized here between man and God, a comparison having to do with essence and existence: in man, we have a relation between the two; in God, we have identity.[12]

Ego Sum Qui Sum

Of all of the names that we could use to refer to God, certainly none could be superior to the name that God has given to Himself. We read in the third chapter of the Book of Exodus that when Moses asked God for His name, the response he was given, in the Latin of the Vulgate Bible, was *Ego Sum Qui Sum,* which can be literally translated as "I am who am." It could also be rendered as, "I am the one who is." One English translation of the pertinent passage reads as follows: "And God said to Moses. I am the God who IS; thou shalt tell the Israelites, THE GOD WHO IS has sent me to you." [13] And in the Challoner-Rheims translation we read: "This is what you shall tell the Israelites: I AM sent me to you." All of these renderings give sufficient emphasis to the fact that existence is of the very nature of God, that, to put it negatively, it would be impossible for God not to be. (This is a point that is completely lost on the atheist.) And of course this is what we mean when we refer to God as a necessary being. Exploring the implications of this awesome name further, we are able to cite why it should be considered the best, in the sense of being the most revealing, name of God.

The name clearly and emphatically, even dramatically, indicates that in God essence and existence are one. The essence, or form, of every other being tells us that a being *has* existence. But God does not have existence; it is not something with which He has been invested, as is the case with us. With creatures, existence is as it were something which is added to their essence, or quiddity. But there can be no such composition in God. Existence, be-ing, is the very identity of God. He is existence.

Note that God does not reveal Himself as existing in any particular way. He does not say, "I am this," or, "I am that." He says simply, and most significantly, "I am." In grammatical terms, He is not predicating anything of Himself, as if to accentuate the truth that He is the one to whom nothing by way of a perfection can be said of His being which would not simply reiterate His being, and that is because He is all in all. The "I am" tells us that there is in God not the slightest suggestion of any limitation. He is absolutely unlimited, determined in no way whatsoever.

And take special note of the tense of the statement—the present tense. God is eternal, or as St. Thomas puts it, simply and tellingly, God is eternity. We are totally immersed in time, and cannot imagine any other mode of existing than being in the constant flow of successive events, the one-thing-after-another which is the very essence of time. This makes it difficult for us to think about eternity, for it is no part of our experience. But we form concepts about it which give us at least some inkling of the nature of God, who, following the thought of

St. Thomas, is better conceived as being, not "in" eternity, but simply as being one and the same with eternity. We say that there is no past or future in God. For Him, everything is now, an eternal now, and a now that is infinitely full. God is not He who was, or He who will be, but He who *is*.[14]

As rational creatures, as creatures who have an unquenchable passion to know, we cannot help but think and talk about God, no matter how feeble our thoughts, no matter how shallow and wayward our words. Despite all our best efforts to be as conscientious and careful as possible in crafting our language when we attempt to address the reality of God, it inevitably falls short of the lofty ends we intend for it. His ways are not our ways. And we can only speak of Him in terms of our ways. But this is nothing to be despondent about. It simply reminds us of the practical realities we must face with respect to our nature, of who we are, and what we are and are not capable of. And this reminder, far from being a cause of discouragement, should engender in us that peculiar kind of incentive to know which is the natural accompaniment of genuine intellectual humility. We will end this chapter by quoting some pertinent words from St. Thomas.

> Whatever knowledge our intellect can have of God fails adequately to represent Him: and so the nature of God always remains hidden from us. This, then, is the best knowledge we can have of God in this life: that He is above any thought we can have concerning Him.[15]

Chapter Eleven

The Attributes of God

In the Footsteps of St. Thomas

In the first part of his magisterial *Summa Theologiae,* after having presented his famous five proofs for the existence of God, St. Thomas then goes on to provide us with a careful, systematic account of the attributes of God, eight of them in all. They are: the simplicity of God; the perfection of God; the goodness of God; the infinity of God; the ubiquity of God; the immutability of God; the eternity of God; the unity of God. That is the order in which he deals with the attributes, and we shall be following the same order here. But we shall also, in this chapter, be following his thought in a particularly detailed way as he explores this important subject. The reason for this is simply the fact that it would be hard to find a more thorough and penetrating treatment of the attributes of God than can be found in St. Thomas.

The Simplicity of God

The complexity of a thing relates to the number of parts it contains, so the more parts it has, the more complex it is, and, accordingly, a thing is more simple to the degree that it contains less parts. Any thing would be perfectly simple if it contained no parts at all. When we speak of the simplicity of God we refer to the fact that He is without composition of any kind. There are no "parts" in God, even if that term were to be understood as referring to purely spiritual entities. There are no real distinctions in God, other than those that pertain to the Blessed Trinity.

But that is a subject which is beyond our province here, belonging as it does to the domain of sacred theology. However, we can assert at least this much without reservation, that there is no contradiction between the simplicity of God and the Trinitarian nature of God.

But do we not have, in the several attributes of God that we are considering in this chapter, what would appear to be instances of the existence of "parts" in God, and concomitantly, of real distinctions as well? Appearances aside, this is in fact not the case. Certainly we are dealing with distinctions here, but they are logical distinctions, whose source is the human mind. Constructing these logical, or purely mental, distinctions is something which, given the limitations of our minds, we need to do in order better to understand things. And this is the way we must proceed even as we attempt to understand the nature of God, while relying, in doing so, principally on the resources of natural reason alone. What we are able to accomplish is governed by the limitations of the human intellect. We see now through a glass, darkly, St. Paul tells us,[1] and we have to think many thoughts and say many words in order to achieve what feeble knowledge is possible for us concerning the nature of the ineffable God.

Because a material body necessarily implies parts, the first thing St. Thomas does, in arguing for the simplicity of God, is to show that God cannot be a body. He gives three reasons to support this conclusion. First, every body moves, for movement is an inseparable feature of corporeal being. But everything that moves, as we know, is moved by another. It is this principle which figures so prominently in the argument of the first way, where God was shown to be the unmoved mover. Well, if it is the case that all bodies move, and if God is the unmoved mover, then God is not a body. And if God is not a body, then He has no parts (for all bodies are composed of parts). Therefore He is simple.

The second reason St. Thomas gives to show that God is not a body has to do with the fact that the movement of every body necessarily entails the presence of potency in that body, for movement or change, in terms of its essence, is simply the actualization of potency, or the transition from potency to act. But a deeper analysis of the nature of potency reveals that it always involves a lack or a privation, for a thing can only be said to be in potency with respect to something else because it is deprived of that something else. With these considerations in mind, we clearly see that it cannot be the case that there should be any potency in God, for He lacks nothing at all. But if there is no potency in God, that means He is not a body, and not being a body He has no parts, and therefore He is simple.

Thirdly, St. Thomas argues that because of the inherent limitations of corporeal being—e.g., in terms of its having parts, and being marked by potency—no body can ever be considered to be the "maximum" with respects to being itself. But, as we have learned in the fourth way, the "maximum" in being is precisely what God is. Therefore, God cannot be a body.

St. Thomas offers a different approach to understanding the simplicity of God by considering the two key principles of matter and form. Every material being is composed of matter and form. We have already established the fact that God is not a body, from which it would then naturally follow that there is no distinction in Him between matter and form. There is the additional consideration that, if we were to suppose that there were matter in God, that would introduce the principle of potency, and we have already seen that there can be no potency in God. So, God is not in any way composed. He is simple. If we want to think of God at all in terms of form, we should regard Him as being the purest form. The divine form, St. Thomas notes, "is not subject to reception in any matter, but it subsists in itself."[2]

All immaterial created beings, though of course not composed in the sense that they bear within themselves the distinction of matter and form, are nonetheless not without composition. They are composed in that most fundamental of ways which is common to all created beings, material or immaterial, in that there is a real distinction within them of essence and existence. But, as we have had occasion to point out more than once in earlier pages of this book, in God essence and existence are one and the same. This is a pivotal truth to which we will be giving continuing attention as we proceed. The fact that essence and existence are one in God accentuates in an especially emphatic way His simplicity. God is simple because He is His own nature.

This great truth about the nature of God, that in Him essence and existence are one, is known to us through revelation, for, as we have seen, this was the central meaning of "I Am Who Am," the name by which God identified Himself to Moses. St. Thomas, in the course of his discussion of the simplicity of God, shows that it is possible, through the exercise of natural reason alone and without benefit of revelation, to arrive at the truth that there is unity of essence and existence in God. He does this through employing a form of argument called *reductio ad absurdum*. The argument begins by assuming to be true just the opposite of what you want to prove to be true. So, if you are intending to prove that "A" is true, you begin by assuming that "not-A" is true. Then you ask, what would follow if we assume "not-A" to be true? If you can show that only contradiction would follow from such an assumption, then that can stand as proof that the opposite of "not-A" is true. So, the truth of "A" is proved by showing the falsity of its contradiction. In this particular case, and following the pattern of argument just described, St. Thomas begins by assuming that in God essence and existence are *not* the same. What would follow if we assume this to be true? He argues that three contradictions would follow form such an assumption.

The first thing that would follow if we were to assume that essence and existence are not one in God is that He would then have a cause. How is that? As we reminded ourselves just above, every created being is composed fundamentally of essence and existence. That is what it means to be a created being. Existence, or *esse*, is something the creature "has"; it is a possession. This means that the creature was caused to be, for if existence is a possession and not part of a being's very nature, then it has to be given to the being. This is simply to say that the being is a created being, for creation, from the point of view of the creature, is the gift of being. Now, if essence and existence were not in fact one in God, we would have to conclude that God was caused to be. But that is an absurd conclusion, for as we have seen in the second way, God is the First Cause, which means that, not only is He the cause of all things, He Himself is uncaused.

The second thing that would follow if essence and existence were not one in God is that there would then be passive potency in God. This is so because, as we learn in metaphysics, essence relates to existence as potency to act. Obviously, then, if essence were a principle really distinct from existence in God, His being would be marked by potency, and that would mean that He would be lacking in some way or another, and would therefore be imperfect. But that makes no sense. Clearly, then, it is necessary that in God essence and existence must be one.

The third thing that would follow if essence and existence were not one in God is that He would then have to be regarded as a participated being. In other words, He would be like ourselves, as "having" being instead of simply be-ing being. It cannot be said of ourselves that we simply *are*, i.e., that the fact of our existence constitutes a declaration of our very nature. Our nature is something quite distinct from the fact that we exist. Now, if we were to say the same thing of God, He simply would not be God. As St. Thomas pointedly puts it, if God were a participated being (i.e., a being for whom existence is a possession), "He would then not be the First Being, but that would be an absurdity." [3]

To sum up, what St. Thomas has done in this argument is to cite three consequences that would necessarily follow if we assume it to be true that there is no unity of essence and existence in God, and then to show that all of these consequences end in absurdity. If, then, we end up in absurdity by making such an assumption, that proves the contradiction of the assumption to be true. Therefore, in God, essence and existence are one. And in this argument we have powerful reinforcement of the truth that God is simple.

Before I go on to consider further arguments of St. Thomas pertaining to the simplicity of God, I want to consider briefly a possible implication of the demonstration that we have just reviewed. You may recall that in discussing the ontological argument for proving the existence of God we saw that the key problem in the argument was that it assumed a knowledge of God's nature which would seem to have come from a source other than natural reason, namely, revelation. And that assumption amounted to begging the question (assuming what needs to be proved), for how can you know the nature of the being whose existence you are endeavoring to prove? Specifically, that knowledge of God—though this is never stated explicitly in the argument—is the knowledge of the unity of essence and existence in Him. We can identify this as privileged knowledge because it is not gained through natural reason. But now, in the argument just reviewed, St. Thomas has shown us that the knowledge of the unity of essence and existence in God, though indeed known to us through revelation, can also be arrived at through the exercise of natural reason. Given this to be the case, does not that then legitimize the ontological argument?

It does not. To see how this is so, the first thing to do is simply note where St. Thomas's argument appears in the *Summa Theologiae*. It comes after the presentation of the Five Ways. The logic of this placement is evident. A demonstration of the unity of essence and existence in God has obviously to do with His nature. But no demonstration concerning the nature of any being could carry any weight if the very existence of that being were in doubt. So, the first order of business is to demonstrate the existence of a being, then, that task accomplished, one goes on to treat the nature of that being. With this is mind, we can see that the fact that the unity of essence and existence in God can be demonstrated by natural reason affords no help in rescuing the ontological argument, for that argument is attempting to prove the existence of God, and one cannot employ any knowledge of God's nature, however it might be obtained, in an argument whose purpose is to prove His existence. To do so is effectively to employ the impermissible *propter quid* mode of argument.

The next step St. Thomas takes in his treatment of the simplicity of God is to argue that God does not belong to any genus. What does that have to do, one might ask, with God's simplicity? The first thing which needs to be said is that, if any being belongs to a genus, this implies there is complexity in the being, and this in itself rules out the possibility that God could be in a genus. A genus is simply a large class of things, such as, for example, the genus "animal." It is made up of smaller classes called species. From metaphysics we learn that a genus relates to any one of its species as potency to act. Given that fact, it immediately becomes obvious that God cannot be in a genus, for there cannot be any potency in God, given the fact that potency necessarily implies imperfection.

Another thing that metaphysics teaches us about the relation between genus and species is that genus stands to species as essence to existence. A genus tells us what a thing is (i.e., it reveals the thing's quiddity), but says nothing about its existence. Consider the genus "animal" again. We know what an animal is, and are therefore able to make a list of its essential characteristics, but there is no existing thing called "animal." There are only specific kinds of animals—cats, dogs, gorillas, gophers, etc. Existence comes with species. Because there is this split between essence and existence in the relation between genus and species, this precludes the possibility of God belonging to a genus, for that would entail His essence being distinct from His existence, which we already know cannot be the case. In sum, showing that God cannot be in a genus is another specific way of demonstrating His simplicity.

St. Thomas attaches an interesting addendum to the above arguments, in which he makes two salient points: (a) God cannot be defined; (b) in dealing with either the existence or nature of God, it is impermissible to use *propter quid* argument. God cannot be defined because, as we know from logic, the very heart of a definition is the genus and the species of that which is being defined. But because God is not in a genus, nor, *a fortiori*, in a species, He cannot be defined. Secondly, no *propter quid* argument can be made about God because in that mode of argument we proceed from cause to effect, but in order to argue in that fashion one must know the essence of the cause one is dealing with. But to know God's essence would be to have, in effect, a definition of God, but, as we have just seen, a definition of God is impossible. The only mode of argument open to us in this case, then, as we have stressed often enough, is *quia* argument.

St. Thomas argues for the simplicity of God from the fact that there are no accidents in God. Accidents necessarily imply composition, i.e., the basic composition of the substance and the accidents. Accidents can be, in any given substance, many in number, and by their very nature they owe their existence to substance. But we have already established that there can be no composition in God. This forbids the possibility of there being any accidents in God, a fact which provides us with one more proof of His simplicity.

St. Thomas ends his treatment of the subject of God's simplicity by summing up the basic points he has established in his various arguments. We can confidently conclude that there is no composition in God because all composed being must have causes (i.e., to "compose" them), and God, as First Cause, is the uncaused cause. Furthermore, composition implies the distinction between potency and act, and that definitely rules out there being any composition in God, for it is impossible that there be any passive potency in Him. "Therefore," St. Thomas writes, "since God is perfect form, or, better, existence itself, in no way can He be composed." [4] And that means that He is perfectly simple.

The Perfection of God

Generally speaking, when we say that God is perfect, the principal idea we intend to convey is that there is nothing whatever lacking in

Him. He is the fullness of being, or, as St. Thomas expresses it, existence itself. And, as soon as we say that a being is perfect, we are saying at the same time that the being is good. A being, a real existent, is such because, as we say, it is in act (*in actu*), to one degree or another. In the argument of the second way we learned that God is the First Cause of all being, of all that is in act. Now, for God to be the cause of all that is in act, He must of course Himself be in act, but supremely so. He must be maximally in being, for, as St. Thomas explains, "to be the first principle of being for others it is necessary to be maximally in act, and, as such, the most perfect being." [5] So, we assert that God is Pure Act (*Actus Purus*). To be pure act is simply to be perfect without qualification.

As we look about us in the world we are greeted with examples of perfections on every side. Think of a perfect rose, or a perfect day, or a perfect musical performance. These perfections are nothing else but the effects of God's creative activity. We thus see in them the reflections, however faint, of God's own perfection. And because God is the source of all perfections we see in the world, those perfections must necessarily be found in Him, but in a preeminent degree, without any qualification. All perfection comes from Him who is the most perfect.

Perfections can be nothing else than the perfections of actually existing beings. Knowing that God exists maximally, we know that He is the supreme being. "Thus," St. Thomas writes, "since God is subsistent being itself, it is not possible that any perfection relating to being be lacking in Him." [6] If existence just as such denotes perfection, and if God is the ultimate in existence, then God is the ultimate in perfection.

The perfection we see in creatures, the effects of God's creative action, are wonderfully diverse. The perfection of a flower is not the perfection of an insect. And yet all that diversity can be said to come together in the most intensely concentrated form in its source—God. All those countless perfections are to be found in the perfect unity and simplicity of the being of God. St. Thomas gives precise expression to this point: "And thus, all those perfections which in themselves are diverse and even opposed to one another, preexist in God in perfect unity, without the least detriment to His simplicity." [7]

The Book of Genesis instructs us that God made man in His image and likeness. And Our Lord enjoins us to be perfect as our heavenly Father is perfect. What these startling texts suggest to us is that there is a real similarity between man and God. What is the nature of that similarity? We must first take careful note of its direction: it is man who is similar to God; God is not similar to man. Man is similar to God in the most fundamental way possible, metaphysically speaking; that is, simply in terms of being. "And in this way," St. Thomas writes, "those things which are from God, are similar to Him simply as beings, and thus related to the first and universal principle of all being." [8] God, the source of all being, has made man similar to Himself by bringing him into the realm of being. Because this is so, we can learn something of the perfection of God by the perfections of this creature who was created in the image and likeness of God. And this is why we study the lives of the saints, and try to imitate their actions.

The Goodness of God

In discussing the goodness of God, St. Thomas begins by reminding us of the metaphysical principle that being and goodness are convertible. This is to say that every being, simply insofar as it is a being, is good. We thus identify goodness as one of the transcendental attributes of being. If everything is good simply by reason of the fact that it exists, and if everything that exists owes its being to God because He is the First Cause, then God, as the cause of all that is good, is an all-good cause. We know that whatever is to be found in effects is necessarily to be found in the cause of those effects, and in this case the good which is in the effects (i.e., the whole of created being) is to be found preeminently in the cause. We could say, then, by way of summary, that because all goodness comes from God, He is to be called, not simply good, but the supreme good.

God is the final cause of creatures simply because He is the supreme good, and therefore the ultimate explanation for the inextinguishable yearning for the good which is to be found in every creature. If all creation is ordered toward the supreme good, who is God, to what good may we say God is ordered? To none other than the supreme good who is Himself. The only appropriate finality for an infinite being is infinite being. He who is the fullness of all being, and therefore of all goodness, can have no end other than the divine essence itself, because God is good through His very essence.

We noted above that man can rightly be considered to be similar to God by reason of the fact that he possesses being as the result of God's creative activity. In a certain sense, the creature bears some resemblance to the Creator. Given the intimate association between being and goodness (i.e., in that goodness is a transcendental attribute of being), this similarity of man to God would also obtain with respect to goodness. So, we can say that men are good as God is good. But careful qualifications have to be made here. Men are not good as God is good in the sense that they share in the divine essence, but rather in the sense that they were created by one who is all-good. To suppose that man is good as God is good because man somehow shares in the divine essence would be to flirt with pantheism.

The Infinity of God

Because infinity is a negative term, designating that which has no limits, we speak of God as being infinite in the sense that He is in no way limited. God is without any bounds. The infinity of God is best expressed by the powerful phrase, "Subsistent Being Itself" (*Ipsum Esse Subsistens*). In an analogous sense, we correctly refer to any substantial being as subsistent, meaning that it exists independently, through itself (*per se*), and not in another. It is accidental, or dependent, being that exists, that can only exist, in another, that "other" being of course a substance. But in the strictest usage of the term, "subsistent" can be applied without qualification only to God, and that is why we refer to Him as Subsistent Being Itself. God subsists absolutely. To subsist absolutely simply means "to be" in the fullest and completely unqualified sense. Such absolutely subsistent being, the being of God, cannot be subject to any curtailments or limitations whatever. Qualified subsistent being, the kind of being possessed by ourselves, is, as noted, being "through itself" (*per se*), but in order to stress the absolute uniqueness of the divine subsistence, we say that God's being is "of Himself" (*a se*), from which we get the English term "aseity," as applied to God. God's being is of Himself in the sense that He and He alone is the explanation for His being. One does not go outside of God to seek an explanation for the being of God.

One of the more common confusions that enters into discussions of the infinity of God is to think of His infinity as if it were the same as mathematical infinity. Though the name is the same, the concepts which they represent are entirely different. Infinity, as understood literally, can apply to God and God alone. When mathematicians use the term infinity, when referring, for example, to an infinite series of integers, they are referring to a series that can be extended indefinitely, that has no end to it. Comparably, when the metaphysician speaks of primary matter as being infinite, he means that it is entirely undetermined and is therefore receptive to an indefinite number of substantial forms. In both of these usages, then, "infinite" can properly be considered to be synonymous with "indefinite." Neither the mathematician nor the metaphysician is referring to the actual infinite, for if that were the case it would not be subject to any alternation. [9]

The only actually existing infinite is the being of God. The infinity of God has nothing to do with quantity, as is the case with the mathematical infinite, nor does it have anything to do with potentiality, as in the metaphysician's usage of the term. God is infinite in the sense that He is utterly complete. No addition to His being is in any way possible. The infinity of God should not be imagined as a kind of divine "extension" that goes on, and on, and on, but as sublime stasis, the most vibrant and most intense fullness of being. God is without limits because He is Himself the inexhaustible source of all the riches of being.

The Ubiquity of God

The ubiquity, or ubiquitousness, or omnipresence, of God refers to the fact that God is everywhere. This is a truth that we learned as children, but we must take care that we do not now understand it in the way children often do. To be everywhere could be said to mean the same thing as to be in every place, but misinterpreting the latter phrase could cause problems. We know from the philosophy of nature that the only kind of being that can be in a place in the literal sense is a material being, a being that is essentially characterized by extension. But God is not a material body, He has no extension. Are we to conclude from this that God cannot be everywhere, because He cannot be in a place as a physical object can be in a place? Obviously not. We need to understand just what it means to say that God is everywhere.

In exploring the question of the ubiquity of God, St. Thomas begins by asking if it is appropriate to speak of God as being in all things. He responds affirmatively to the question, but while making an important qualification. We can say that God is in all things in that He is the Creator of all things. But we need to be precise about the peculiar import of the preposition "in." God is not in His creation in the same way that parts are in a whole, or as accidents are in a substance. Rather, God is to be said to be in His creation "as an agent is present in that upon which he exercises his agency." [10] To cite an example of this kind of presence, on the purely natural level, we could say that the writer George Bernanos is "in" his novel, *The Diary of a Country Priest*. But an example such as that offers only a very dim analogy of the way that God is present in all things. He is present in them *operatively*, as the source of their existence, and—this is the kind of relation that is never found on the purely natural level—as the explanation for their continuation in existence from moment to moment. As St. Thomas explains, "wherever something is operating, *there* it is. But God is operating continuously in all things." [11] If that were not the case, they could not remain in existence. So, the very existence of things all around us announces the presence of God. In light of this awesome truth, St. Thomas observes that, not only is God in all things, but He is so in the most intimate of ways, as sustaining their very being.

In order to arrive at the most exact sense of how it is that God is present in His creation, it would be helpful to think of the relation between the human body and soul. Although it is common practice to speak of the soul as being in the body, it is actually more correct to say, according to St. Thomas, that the body is in the soul, for the soul, as the animating principle of the body, contains within its vivifying embrace every part and particle of the body. In a comparable way, St. Thomas notes, "God is in all things as containing them." [12] God has the whole world in His hands. While it could be said that God is removed from all things, in the sense that He is infinitely above His creation because of the surpassing excellence of His nature, nevertheless, for all that, it is equally right to say that He is intimate to all things by the immediate way He exercises His power in sustaining them in existence. Regarded from this point of view, God is not at all distant from His creation. He is, as spiritual writers are wont to remind us, closer to us than we are to ourselves.

God is everywhere, then, "for He is in all things, as one giving to each existence, power and operation." [13] As we noted above, God, not being a body, cannot be thought of as being "in place" as we normally understand that phrase. But God can rightly be considered to be "everyplace" in the sense that there is no actual physical place that does not feel the effects of His operative power. And how is that so, specifically? By reason of the fact that God gives existence to all the physical things that occupy places. St. Thomas returns to the relation between body and soul, and asks how we are to interpret the statement, often made, that the soul is in every part of the body. The statement cannot be taken in the literal sense, for the soul is purely immaterial, and therefore it has no extension. Having no extension, it cannot be said to be everywhere in the body in the sense that it is spread out spatially. That which is spiritual cannot be spread out. What, then, do we mean when we say that the soul is in every part of the body, for the assertion is certainly meaningful, and its meaning is important. We mean that, as mentioned above, the spiritual soul exercises its vitalizing power throughout the entire body, and—here is the point St. Thomas wants to emphasize by bringing up the issue—it does so in a manner that is analogous to the way in which God, who is pure spirit, exercises His conserving power throughout the whole of creation. We cannot say that there is part of the soul in "this" part of the body and another part of the soul in "that" part of the body, for the soul has no parts. The soul is, in its simple, unified totality, by reason of its essence, "in" all parts of the body as animating all parts of the body. The effects of its spiritual power is felt in all parts of the body. "Therefore," St. Thomas concludes, "just as the soul is, in its totality, in every part of the body, so God, in His totality, is in each and every thing that exists." [14] As the soul is to the body, God is to the whole of creation. But, now looking at the situation principally with the relation between body and soul in mind, and applying a point about that relation he had made earlier, St. Thomas observes further that, "it is more the case that things are in God, than that God is in things." [15] The whole of creation is encompassed within the divine embrace.

Using an observation of St. Gregory the Great as his point of departure, St. Thomas considers what it means to say, as did St. Gregory, that God is everywhere "by essence, by presence, and by power." To say that God is everywhere by essence (*per essentiam*) means that he is present to all things by reason of being the cause of their being. To say that God is everywhere by presence (*per presentiam*) means that everything is constantly under God's providential surveillance. Nothing ever happens to any thing, anywhere, at any time, that is outside the knowledge of God. "All things," St. Thomas writes, "are laid bare and fully exposed to His eyes." [16] Finally, to say that God is everywhere by power (*per potentiam*) means that all things in the heavens and on earth are subject to His governing hand. So, just as a king can be said to be everywhere in his kingdom by reason of the universal jurisdiction he has over the realm, so God is everywhere in the universe because the universe is His domain by reason of its owing its very existence to His creative generosity.

As with all the attributes, we can say that ubiquity is truly proper to God, meaning that it pertains to Him and to Him alone. This is so, St. Thomas explains, "because no matter how many 'places' one might imagine, God must be present in each one of them, not in a partial way, but in terms of His entire self." [17] God and God alone can be everywhere in the various ways that have been discussed in this section. Although it might not have been immediately evident in what has been said, the negative knowledge which we spoke of earlier has been quietly at work in the treatment of God's ubiquity. But what is especially negative in the claim that God is everywhere? It is to be found in the fact that in making that undeniably positive claim, we are implicitly putting aside any understanding of "being somewhere" that we derive from our ordinary experience. From this point of view, God's ubiquity means that His presence is in no way confined or limited, as is the case in the common understanding of presence, for to be "in place," as the phrase is normally taken, implies being confined for the present to a particular place.

The Immutability of God

When we say that God is immutable we mean that He is utterly unchanging in every aspect of His being. A mutable God would in fact not be God at all, for mutability, or change, necessarily implies privation, and privation means imperfection. If you imagine a changing God, you are imaging a being who has not attained perfection, for the only reason for him to change would be to become more perfect. But if, on the other hand, you imagine a supposedly all-perfect God who nonetheless changes, the only possible way he could change in this case would be to become less perfect, for the all-perfect obviously cannot increase in perfection.

But our imaginations can betray us in other ways with respect to the immutability of God. We must not suppose that His immutability implies a cold and rigid lifelessness. Nothing could be farther from the truth. In our experience, unmoving things are non-living things. But God's immutability bespeaks the very quintessence of dynamic activity. God acts, He *is* act, but He does not change. In an attempt to better grasp what to us is an impenetrable mystery, we might attempt to explain things by saying that God does not change because He does not need to change. He who is the fullness of being has fulfillment, so to speak, entirely within Himself.

St. Thomas offers a three-faceted argument to demonstrate the immutability of God. All change, we know, involves the principle of potency, which is simply the capacity to change. But God, as we have already established, is Pure Act, in that, in Him, essence and existence are one. Obviously, pure act excludes potency. Therefore, because there is no potency in God, He cannot change in any way.

A second elementary fact we know about the nature of change is that, for it to take place, there has be a subject of change, that which changes. The subject of change maintains its identity throughout the course of the change. So, in the case of accidental change, it is the substance that remains stable from the beginning to the end of the change. This points to the fact that only things that are composed are capable of change, and, in this case, it is the composition of substance and accident that is prominent. It is just this link between composition and change that highlights the impossibility of change ever taking place in God, for, in that He is utterly simple, He is in no way composed. Therefore, He is immutable.

Yet a third important element in the phenomenon of change is the principle of privation. Unless there is a termination for the change, some very precise way in which the subject of change can be changed, then no change is possible. It would make no sense to say that a thing changes if, before the change, it was not in a state of privation with respect to that into which it eventually changes. And the removal of that privation is that toward which the whole dynamic of the change is directed. Because there is no privation in God, for He lacks nothing, it is impossible that He could change in any way. Therefore, God is immutable.

Immutability is proper to God in that He alone in unchanging. It is the very mark of their creatureliness that created beings should change, especially if they should be composed of matter. But even purely spiritual creatures, such as angels, undergo change, for example, in the fact that their knowledge of the divine essence is ever increasing. When we grow in knowledge we are actualizing a potency, perfecting ourselves intellectually. But in God, the all-perfect, there is no potency, and His immutability is, as seen from our perspective, the logical accompaniment of His perfection.

The Eternity of God

St. Thomas develops his reflections on the eternity of God within the framework of a famous definition of eternity which has come down to us from the philosopher Boethius (c. 480–c. 526 A.D.). The definition is as follows: "Eternity is the everlasting, totally simultaneous, and perfect possession of life."[18] St. Thomas approves of this definition, and doubtless that is the reason he gives it a central place in his discussion of the eternity of God.

Perhaps the most common misunderstanding we succumb to in thinking about eternity is to imagine it as endless time. But if this is a common misunderstanding, it is also an excusable one, for we are creatures who are thoroughly immersed in time, and as a matter of fact we cannot approach any sound understanding of eternity except by beginning with concepts that pertain exclusively to time. Time is a complex phenomenon. Eternity, on the other hand, is simple. This being the case, St. Thomas offers us useful counsel when he writes that, "in arriving at an understanding of simple things, we can do so only through composition, so with respect specifically to our understanding of eternity, we must come to it through our notion of time."[19] In doing so we have to shed certain time-related notions which, if retained, would actually impede our understanding of eternity, which is accomplished through the process of negation. We start with the complex notion of time—as involving, for example, motion, the numbering of motion, the notions of before and after and now—and we subtract from it these and all other features that pertain to it just as time. The elementary idea that we carry with us, as we move from time to eternity, is the idea of duration. Both time and eternity are modes of duration.

Motion is the very essence of time, a fact we are reminded of by St. Thomas when he quotes Aristotle's classic definition of time as, "the numbering of motion in terms of before and after." [20] But there is no motion in eternity, which means that there is nothing to be numbered or measured. And that being the case, there is nothing in eternity which could be called before or after. The most important thing to understand about eternity, St. Thomas tells us, is that it is completely outside all motion, all change. A critical feature of motion is that it must have a beginning and an end, and succession in between. But none of this is to be found in eternity. It is specifically the lack of succession in eternity (which lack of succession removes the before and the after) which Boethius so nicely captures in his phrase "totally simultaneous" (*tota simul*). Things are not extended sequentially, as they are in time—one thing after another—but everything is at once, encompassed within a permanent now. The word *tota*, totally or completely, underscores the point that this "now" is inexhaustibly rich; nothing that is good is absent from it.

The "perfect" of Boethius's definition, modifying "possession," indicates that the now of eternity is entirely different from that of time. We have duration in both cases, but the duration of time is the duration of succession; the duration of eternity is the duration of permanency. The temporal "now" is that which separates and distinguishes the before and the after. This is not to be interpreted as meaning that time is a composition of many "now's." This is no more true than that a geometric line is composed of many points. We might think of the temporal "now" as a moving separator, allowing us to distinguish between before and after. St. Thomas uses a vivid image in describing the temporal "now" as a "flowing now." And he proposes this as a stark contrast to the "now" of eternity, which is an "unmoving now" (*nunc stans*). [21]

From everything that we have said thus far about the nature of eternity, it should be clear to us just how it is that God is eternal. But let us make the matter as explicit as possible. Motion is essentially related to time; without motion, there is no time. But God is immutable.

Therefore, God and time are completely separate from one another, and this is simply to say that God is eternal. We have an inclination to say, in casual speech, that God is "in" eternity. But to be as precise as possible we should say, with St. Thomas, that "eternity is nothing else but God Himself."[22]

God is eternal, then, because He is immutable. Another way we can look at the eternity of God is from the point of view of the fact that God has no beginning. The "totally simultaneous" aspect of eternity, as we have seen, excludes the principles of before and after, which are integral to time. This radically differentiates time and eternity. And, St. Thomas adds, if we are right in describing time as the measure of motion, we are equally right in describing eternity as the measure of permanence. As to that common misunderstanding of eternity, which regards it as endless time, we can respond to it by saying that if it were true that eternity were no more than endless time, that would have to mean that we had a time that had no beginning and that will have no end, but because it is time it would necessarily involve succession, one thing after another. But, as we have seen, succession and eternity are completely incompatible, for the duration of eternity is not constant motion, but pure permanence. Therefore, it is contradictory to think of eternity as endless time.

St. Thomas ends his treatment of the eternity of God by discussing a phenomenon known in Latin as the *aevum*, which is usually translated into English as "aeviternity." Aeviternity is neither eternity nor time, but is a type of duration which is between the two. The concept was introduced in order to explain the mode of existence of immaterial creatures, specifically angels. If we were to describe these three kinds of duration, eternity, time, and aeviternity, in terms of their accidental rather than their essential characters, we would say the following. Eternity has neither a beginning nor an end; time has both a beginning and an end; aeviternity has a beginning but no end. But in order to describe them in terms of their essential differences, we must refer to the three modes of existence with which they are associated, which is to say, respectively, the existence of God, the existence of man and other corporeal beings, and the existence of angels.

Eternity is duration that is associated—more precisely, is one and the same with—the unqualifiedly perfect permanency of being which is that of God and God alone. Time is duration which is associated with existence that involves change, particularly that type of substantial change which is generation and corruption. Aeviternity is duration that is associated with existence which is permanent with respect to being as such, but which nonetheless experiences change as an accompaniment to being. What this means, more precisely, is that the angels (to whom this mode of existence pertains) cannot be said to change as we understand it, for, being purely spiritual beings, they do not experience the motion of matter. But angels can be said to change in that, as St. Thomas points out, they experience "changeableness with regard to choice, and also changeableness with regard to knowledge, with regard to affections, and with regard to place, in their own manner." [23]

The Unity of God

Unity, metaphysics teaches us, is one of the transcendental attributes of being. Being, insofar as it is being, is unified. But if God is the supreme being, is simply "being" in the fullest, most profound, completely unqualified and unlimited sense, then God must be perfect unity, perfectly one. The simplicity of God, discussed at the beginning of this chapter, thoroughly corroborates the unity of God, for, as St. Thomas notes, "that which is simple, is undivided both with respect to act and potency." [24] A being is one because it is undivided, and if there is not the remotest possibility for division in that being—which is obviously the case with God—then that being is perfect unity. A composed being can be one, and indeed must be one, i.e., unified, otherwise it would not even be identifiable as *a* being. But the unity of any composed being pales in comparison to the perfect unity of God, which, we may say, is founded upon the perfect simplicity of God.

God is one in that He is perfect unity. But He is also one in the sense that He is unique, which is simply to say that there is only one God. The oneness or unity of God, again, follows necessarily from His simplicity. Furthermore, and as implied in what we mean when we say that God is His very nature (i.e., essence and existence are one in Him), we assert that the notion that there could be many Gods is self-contradictory. The reasoning behind that assertion is as follows. For creatures such as ourselves, it cannot be said of any one of us that we are our nature. Let us consider the case of Marcus. He is a human being, and thus he has a human nature. But that human nature is not his and his alone; it is shared by many others. Therefore, there is no contradiction in there being many beings when their nature does not belong to any one of them exclusively, but which is shared by all of them. But with God it is quite different. Because He is His nature, that nature (divine nature) is exclusive to Him, and cannot be shared by many. It is impossible, therefore, that there can be many Gods. St. Thomas expresses this truth in an interesting way when he says that it is the same to say "God" and "this God." We can see what he means by that if we reflect on how we speak about man. If I say "man" and "this man" I am not saying the same thing. In the first instance I am referring to man in general, humankind; in the second instance I am referring to a particular individual, let us say, Marcus, mentioned above. In other words, with us human beings, our nature can be distinguished from the many individuals who share that nature, and it can be spoken of in abstract terms. But because God is His nature, to say "God"—let us say, as referring to the divine nature—is to say the same thing as "this God," for there is only one being who *is* that nature. St. Thomas brings the argument to a close with the succinct statement, "it is impossible to have a multitude of Gods." [25]

St. Thomas presents a second argument supporting the fact that there can be only one God, an argument which is based upon the infinite perfections of God. God encompasses within Himself all the perfections of being. Now, let us suppose that there were two Gods, that is, two beings concerning both of which we want to claim that they encompass all the perfections of being. Now, because they are two, they necessarily must differ in *some* way, for if they did not they would be completely indistinguishable, and therefore would be one, not two. There are only two possible ways in which they could differ. (1) One of them would have a privation (i.e., lack something that the other possesses), in which case it could not be said to encompass all the perfections of being, and therefore it could not be God. (2) One of them would have a perfection which the other does not have, in which case the other could not be said to encompass all the perfections of being, and therefore the other could not be God. The conclusion: it is impossible to have a multitude of Gods.

The third argument that St. Thomas proposes to prove that there is but one God has to do with the unity of the universe. That the universe is one, a unified whole, a cosmos, is reflected in the very name we give it, uni-verse—"turned into one." But the universe is a unified whole that is made up of a vast multitude of diverse things. It is a one that is composed of many. But how could this immense collection of multifarious things be brought together in this marvelously integrated and harmonious whole? How is such diversity transformed into such unity? It certainly could not have been done by the diversity itself, for from diversity you get only more diversity, until, eventually, unless some unifying force intervenes, there is a descent into complete chaos. Nor could it have come from more than a single unifying force. There is only one possible explanation for the wondrous unity of the universe—which is simply to say, for the very existence of the universe—and that is perfect unity itself: God. The unity of the universe is a testament to the unity of God. There can be only one God, otherwise there would be chaos, not cosmos.

CHAPTER TWELVE

The Divine Intellect

The Divine Operations

Having now completed our survey of the attributes of God, which pertain to the divine essence, we will, beginning with this chapter, turn our attention to what are known as the divine operations. There are two dimensions or aspects of the divine operations, the internal and the external. The internal operations are those which pertain to God Himself; the external operations are those which, though having their source in God, manifest their effects in what is external to God. What is external to God can be generally described as His creation. Another way the distinction between God's internal and external operations may be described is to refer to the first as having to do with immanent action, and the second as having to do with transitive action. Immanent action is action which begins and terminates with the agent who is the source of the action. An example of immanent action, in human beings, would be thought or emotion, or, on the purely physiological level, digestion. We say that immanent action is perfective of the agent which is its source, meaning that the end of the action is the agent itself. Transitive action, on the other hand, is action which begins in the agent that is the source of the action, but terminates in an object that is external to the agent. And we say of transitive action that it is perfective of the object it affects, because the end of the action is realized in that object. A soccer player kicking a ball down the field would be giving us an example of transitive action: the action originates in the player, and terminates in the moving ball.

When we speak of God's external operations as being transitive, we are using that term somewhat loosely. The common way of expressing the matter is to say that God's external operations represent virtual, not real, transitive action. By calling it virtual transitive action we mean that it is comparable to real transitive action in terms of the effects its produces. But it cannot be real transitive action, for that would involve a passage from potency to act, and, as we know quite well, there can be no potency in God.

Guided by this distinction between God's internal operations and His external operations, we will first give our attention to the internal operations, which are manifested by the divine intellect and the divine will. After that we will turn to the external operations. These can be said to be summed up in what we refer to as the omnipotence of God. Consideration of God's omnipotence leads directly to the subject of creation and conservation, and those subjects, in turn, naturally point to the large and commanding subject of divine providence. Finally, consideration of divine providence inevitably invites discussion of the existence of evil, and with that discussion we will bring the book to a close.

Divine Knowledge

Is God capable of knowing anything? Is there such a thing as divine knowledge? Those might seem to be recklessly impertinent questions, if not simply downright silly ones. But, as we proceed here, you will come to see their relevance to our discussion. Before we can determine whether or not God is capable of knowing, whether or not there is in fact divine knowledge, we must begin by asking the more basic question—very basic indeed—What do we mean by knowledge? What does it mean, operationally, to know? When we respond to those questions, by refreshing our memories concerning some elementary matters regarding human knowledge, then it will become clear to us that the questions with which we began this section were considerable more than rhetorical tricks by which to arrest the reader's attention.

The fact is, everything that we know about knowing comes, naturally enough, from our own human experience of knowing. Given that fact, we would quickly encounter serious problems if we were to suppose that God's mode of knowing is pretty much like the human mode of knowing, and that therefore divine knowledge is comparable to human knowledge.

The basic mechanism of human knowledge, the process by which we come to know things, is the conformity of the human mind to the object of its knowledge. A relation, a relation of the most intimate kind, is established between the knower and the known, between the knowing subject and the object of his knowledge. And it all begins with our senses, with the knowledge which is derived from sense experience. More than once in the earlier pages of this book we have taken sharp exception to those philosophers, such as René Descartes and Immanuel Kant, who maintain that we human beings are in possession of innate ideas, ideas which are not the result of experiences we have in this world, but with which we enter the world. These innate ideas, they argue, do not follow upon sense experience, but precede it. They are the ready-made mental tools that enable us to deal effectively with the world. We reject the idea that there are innate ideas, not only because the assertion that there are such cannot be demonstrated, but, more tellingly, because the idea goes against what our immediate, everyday experiences tells us is the case. We appeal to and abide by that central principle of Scholastic epistemology, that "nothing is in the intellect which is not first in the senses." All the knowledge that we come to possess through the use of our natural intellectual powers is rooted in sense experience, which means that its ultimate source is extra-mental entities: real things in the real world.

How does it all happen? Our knowledge begins, again, with things in the world. They are real things, meaning that they are in act, and as such they activate our senses, which are completely passive with respect to them. An eye that is perfectly healthy, organically, cannot see unless light stimulates it to see, nor can the physiologically flawless ear hear unless sound stimulates it to hear. As the result of this external stimulation there are formed in the mind internal sensible species, or images, of the object in the external world which is the source of the stimulation, first the sensible species called the percept, then the completed sensible species to which we give the name phantasm. The phantasm can be said to provide us with a complete picture of the particular, concrete thing that is the object of sense knowledge, but only as an existing thing. At this stage, the mind knows that it is dealing with something, but it does not know *what* it is dealing with.

It does not know the quiddity of the thing, the form that makes it the peculiar thing it is. So the mind, focusing on the phantasm, with the power of what is known as the agent intellect, divests the phantasm of everything that is material and singular, and abstracts from it the basic nature of the thing. (This action underscores a very important aspect of human knowledge, or knowledge of whatever kind, and that is that its contents are immaterial. The abstraction which is a crucial part of our knowledge is a process of de-materialization. Because the human mind is purely immaterial, everything that it comes to know in the form of ideas must also be rendered immaterial.) The abstracting action of the agent intellect results in an image of the thing, called an intelligible species, and from this image the mind conceives an idea. The idea, or "mental word" as St. Thomas likes to call it, is a sign, or a representation, of the substantial form of the object in the world, so that we have effectively a marriage of forms, the form of the thing, and the form which is the mind (the rational soul is the substantial form of a human being). It can be truly said, then, that when we human beings know, we become what we know. If the idea of the thing is a faithful representation of the thing as it is in itself, then the mind is properly conformed to the thing, and knows truly. So we say that the human mind is measured by the things it knows, meaning that the things in the world, not the mind, constitute the standard for truth. Things dictate, the mind dutifully records. The mind is shaped by reality; it does not shape reality.

Even with that very rough sketch of what is involved in the process of human knowing, it should be readily apparent to us that we would encounter grave difficulties in attempting to interpret divine knowledge in terms of human knowledge, and those who would be inclined to do so are those who would be apt to ask, quite seriously, Does God know anything? Is there such a thing as divine knowledge? But let us spell out some of those difficulties. The first and most obvious would relate to all the various kinds of change, of motion, which necessarily takes place in the process of human knowing. That would clearly rule out knowledge of this kind taking place in God, for God is immutable. Secondly, and to make explicit a point that is implied in the first, wherever there is change there is potency, and there is privation. Neither of these can have any place in God, and so here too we have an additional reason why divine knowledge can be nothing like human knowledge. Third, human knowledge, which finds its home in the human mind, is very much dependent on things that are external to the human mind; the human mind must defer to things, so to speak, must wait until it is activated by them. Indeed, we can say that the human mind is subservient to things in that, as we noted, the human mind comes to know truly when it conforms itself to that which it knows. Obviously, there can be no dependency, no subserviency, in divine knowledge. Fourth, in what we have called the percept, the phantasm, the agent intellect, the intelligible species (and several more things could be named), we clearly have, in human knowing, any number of real distinctions. But God, as we know, is perfectly simple. Thus we have another reason why divine knowledge must be completely different from human knowledge. Fifth, the species that figure so importantly in human knowledge, first the sensible species, then the intelligible species, constitute a composition within the human mind, for the mind is quite distinct from the species. But God, being utterly simple, would admit of no such composition. Finally—though this is not an exhaustive list of the problems which would ensue if one were to imagine divine knowledge to be like human knowledge—there is the fact that the human mind, in order to know material things, must, through abstraction, de-materialize them. But God is pure spirit; there is no matter at all associated with His being. Therefore, divine knowledge could not be like human knowledge in this respect either.

To sum up and make as explicit as possible the salient points of the foregoing, we say first of all that divine knowledge is totally different from human knowledge. What this means, in more specific terms, is that there is no composition involved in divine knowledge, no change, and therefore no potency and no privation, and there is no dependency whatever, in divine knowledge, on anything other than God Himself.

In a positive vein, we can say of divine knowledge that it is without comparison in terms of its excellence and perfection. Human knowledge, as we saw, necessarily involves abstraction, the process of de-materialization. Everything that the mind knows must be raised up to the mind's spiritual or immaterial level. We can thus equate knowledge, or more precisely intelligibility or knowableness, with immateriality. And the quality of our knowledge depends on the degree to which we can raise things to the level of the immaterial. The more remote they are from the material, the more knowable they are. We can do this with no small success because of our powers of abstraction, but because we are not pure spirits, we are always somewhat impeded, by our materiality, as to the degree and quality of the knowledge we are able to achieve. Our minds abstract the form of the thing known, so that we are able to grasp its quiddity or nature, but we can never completely break ties, in our knowledge, with the material. So, for example, we must, in order to have knowledge of individuals, constantly revert back to the phantasm, which is a sensible species and directly representative of a concrete, material object.

At the other, sublime extreme, there is God Himself, who is of course an immaterial being, and maximally so. He is pure spirit, and the purest of spirits. Consequently, His knowledge can have no imperfection, no limitation, attached to it. "Since God is supreme with respect to immateriality," St. Thomas writes, "it follows that He is supreme with respect to knowledge." [1] Because there is no potentiality in God, His knowledge is immediate and perfect, and not the least bit obscure. As Pure Act (*Actus Purus*), He is Pure Knowledge (*Scientia Pura*).

The Proper Object of Divine Knowledge

Unlike what the philosopher Immanuel Kant would have us believe, we human beings are really capable of knowing the nature of the things we encounter in the world, what Kant referred to as the things in themselves. We know not only phenomena (i.e., accidental forms), but the substantial forms in which the accidental forms inhere. But we do not know things with a direct, intuitive knowledge. We know things through the media of species, images formed by the mind, sensible species for sense knowledge, intelligible species for intellectual knowledge, or knowledge in the full sense. St. Thomas stresses the point that it is not the concept or the idea which is the proper object of the mind, but the thing which the idea represents. The idea is the means by which, so to speak, we get to the thing. Thus, the proper object of the human mind is being, not the accidental being which is our ideas, but the substantial being which exists external to and independent of the mind.

In dramatic contrast to the human mode of knowing, the divine intellect does not know by indirection. It has no need of media through which things come to be known. If, as St. Thomas rightly asserts, the proper object of the human intellect is being, we may say the same of the divine intellect, but with a very important qualification. The proper object of the divine intellect is being, yes, but what being? It can only be being that could prove to be an adequate object for such an intellect, which is to say, Subsistent Being Itself—infinite being for an infinite intellect. What all this amounts to is that what God knows first and finally is Himself, the divine essence, and He knows all other things in that essence. Once again, we human beings know through the medium of an intelligible species. There can be no species in the divine intellect which are in any way different from the divine intellect itself, so if we want to say that God knows through a species, that species is none other than the divine essence. This means that, in God, knowledge, the act of knowing, and the object of knowledge, are in every respect the same. It is as if God looks into Himself, and there finds, within His very essence, all that is to be known. The logic of this, which we will draw out in more explicit terms presently, is founded upon the fact that God is, after all, the source of all that can be known.

Something is intelligible, knowable, precisely to the extent that it is in act (*in actu*), which is to say, precisely to the extent that it simply *is*. Something which is only in potency to being is not yet really "something," and its potential for being has to be reduced to act before we can have knowledge of it as a real existent. We have already said that God, the divine essence, is the proper object of God's knowledge. In an earlier discussion in this book we learned that God, although He is certainly not to us the most intelligible of beings, He is so to Himself. God's being is intrinsically the most intelligible of beings. The metaphysical explanation for this fact is that God is pure act. If something is intelligible to the extent that it is in act, then it follows necessarily that the being who is pure act is the most intelligible, is, we may say, intelligibility itself.

We say that God not only knows Himself, He comprehends Himself. To comprehend something means to know it totally and without any qualification. Needless to say, we do not now have, nor will we ever have, a comprehensive knowledge of the divine essence, for that would involve the impossibility of the finite encompassing the infinite. It is not unusual to hear it said that people have comprehensive knowledge of natural objects, but such language is not be taken literally. The human mind is not capable of a comprehensive knowledge of anything at all; only the divine intellect can have such knowledge. God has comprehensive knowledge of Himself because there is no distinction between the knowledge and the object of the knowledge, as is the case with us. God knows Himself comprehensively because He is His comprehensive knowledge.

We commonly refer to "knowing oneself." What is involved in this rather familiar experience? (I call it a familiar experience in that we all often engage in the effort of trying to know ourselves. To what degree we succeed in this effort is a separate question.) If we were to reflect on the experience, we would discover that in it a kind of dichotomization takes place. That is to say, it is as if two "I's" come into being, not ontologically, of course, but psychologically. There is the "I" who is doing the knowing, and there is the "I" who is being known. We spoke above of God knowing Himself, of the divine essence being the proper object of the divine intellect. Should that suggest to us that a dichotomization, somewhat comparable to what takes place in us when we strive to know ourselves, also takes place in God when He knows Himself? It should not. The perfect, absolute simplicity and unity of God can never in the least bit be impaired or compromised. When considered in relation to the divine knowledge, the divine simplicity and unity are in fact given greater emphasis by the recognition that the divine knowledge and the divine essence are the same. Subject and object, so to speak, are identical. We have repeated often the elementary truth that God is His nature, or, as it is often expressed, God is His "to be." To that we can now add that God is His "to know." With us there is always a marked difference between who we are and what we know. There is no such difference in God. We say that we know ourselves, but to the extent that we succeed in doing so, it is always by way of indirection. We know ourselves through the means of the ideas we have of ourselves. But God knows Himself by knowing Himself, as St. Thomas puts it. [2]

If God's knowledge were not His very substance, there would then be something (i.e., the object of His knowledge) which would be in act with respect to the divine essence. And this would imply in turn that the divine essence would be in potency with respect to that object, and in that sense divine knowledge would then be like human knowledge. But that analysis results in egregious contradiction, for there can be no potency in God. So, it cannot be otherwise than that God's knowledge and His essence are one.

We said above that God knows Himself first and finally, and that He knows all things in Himself. That second point has now to be brought out more clearly. God knows all things because, as First Cause, He is their source. Surely, God must know, and know perfectly, what He Himself has brought into being. Let us tend to the words of St. Thomas as he explains the precise nature of this aspect of God's knowledge. "God sees all things as they are in themselves," he writes, "but He sees them, not in themselves, but in Himself, in the sense that the likeness of things are contained in the divine essence, as being from the divine essence." [3] God sees things most truly and perfectly as they are in themselves by seeing them as they existed from all eternity in the divine mind. What are all the things that exist external to God's being but the effects of His creative action? Given this to be the case, they are most perfectly known in the perfect cause that brought them into being.

Some philosophers in times past have maintained that God does not know things outside Himself, or if He does He does not know them as individuals, but only in a general way, as members of a genus or species. In other words, according to this opinion, God would know "animal" (animality), but He would not know this or that animal. He would know "man" (humanity), but He would not know George or Georgette. We can immediately see the erroneousness of this point of view, not to say its ridiculousness, for it attributes gross imperfection to an all-perfect being. If human beings are capable of knowing individuals, are we to suppose that God does not? St. Thomas exposes this point of view for what it is worth, and he sums up his treatment of it with this pointed observation: "Everything preexists in God, not only with respect to that which is common to all creatures [i.e., knowledge of creatures in relation to what genus or species they belong to], but also with respect to how creatures are distinguished one from another." [4] And later in the same article he writes: "Thus it is obvious that God knows all things according to what is unique to each." [5]

God's Knowledge Is Not Discursive

Human knowledge is discursive. We do not know things as the result of a single, smooth intuitive leap. We have to reason our way to the truth gradually, step by step, and not unseldom the journey is long and laborious. We begin with a known truth, then we attempt to see what truth, or truths, are to be derived from that initial truth. That is the way of discursive thinking, or reasoning. We cannot do without it. But it plays no part in divine knowledge.

In terms of what we have learned thus far about the divine nature, we perhaps can see how this is so. In the first place, the simplicity of the divine essence would preclude the kind of successive movement that is inevitably involved in the discursive process. And there would necessarily come into play, if it were the case that the divine intellect depended on discursive thought, the peculiar kind of causality which is integral to reasoning. When we are exposed to a sound argument and are impressed by the strength of its premises, we then accept its conclusion. Indeed, if it is a deductive argument whose conclusion follows necessarily from the premises, we have no choice, unless we are going to abandon reason, but to accept the conclusion. In such a case we say that the premises of the argument cause the truth of the conclusion, so that there is a cause/effect relation established between premises and conclusion. Now, in that type of situation we have at least two instances of composition. There is, most obviously, the composition of premises and conclusion, and then there is the composition of potency and act, for wherever you have causality at work you have change, and wherever you have change there is necessarily the distinction between potency and act to be acknowledged. Given the composition that is involved, it is evident that, because God is perfectly simple, the divine knowledge cannot have anything to do with discursive thought.

If there is no discursive thought in the divine knowledge—which is simply to say that God has no need of the process of reasoning—are we then to conclude that God's knowledge depends upon intuition? Intuitive knowledge stands in contrast to knowledge that is derived from discursive thought in that it involves no inferential move; there is no methodical proceeding from one idea to another. Intuitive knowledge, we could say, involves but a simple intellectual glance.[6] Angels have intuitive knowledge. May we say, then, that God knows in the same way as do angels? No. The angel, it is true, has only to cast his regard on an object to have knowledge of it, but we need to recall what we have already established concerning divine knowledge and its unity with the divine essence. God does not cast his regard on anything in order to know it in the most perfect way. He simply regards Himself. Once again, God sees everything in Himself, encompassing all that exists at once, in a single, penetrating eternal glance.

God's Knowledge Is Causative

There is no immediate effect in the external world following upon human knowledge. A more precise way of putting this is to say that human knowledge, just as such, does not function as an efficient cause. In order for efficient causality to take place the agent who possesses a certain kind of knowledge must bring his will to bear upon that knowledge, and by executing his will a definite effect is then brought about. However, that much being said, we need to recognize that human knowledge just as such can exercise a causality of sorts, to which we give the name of exemplary causality.

We can get a better idea of what is involved here if we consider the case of a human artist and how he goes about producing a work of art. It all begins with an idea in his mind, an idea that envisions the work of art that he intends to produce. That idea would constitute the exemplary cause. It is knowledge which establishes the end which the artist intends to achieve, and then guides his hand throughout the productive process until he eventually realizes his intention (the idea with which he began the process), and presents to the world the completed work. Now, although we can easily recognize that knowledge is essential to this whole process, it is not enough; the knowledge must be acted upon by the will in order to bring about the effect which is the completed work of art. But the will does not necessarily follow up on the exemplary cause and bring it to fruition. An artist may formulate in his mind a very elaborate idea of a particular work that he wishes to produce, but for one reason or another he never gets around to realizing that idea. His will is never applied to his knowledge.

With God, knowledge is causative in a way which may be said to be roughly comparable to how human knowledge is causative, but there are several important distinctions between the two that must be cited. First of all, there is an infinite difference between the quality of divine knowledge and that of human knowledge. Divine knowledge is absolutely perfect, without flaw or limitation of any kind. Human knowledge, on the other hand, is radically limited. And the limitation of human knowledge goes a long way toward explaining those rather common situations where the things we intend to produce often turn out to be considerably less than what we expected, and wanted, them to be. This may be accounted for by incompetent execution, where an essentially good idea is not brought to fruition because of efficient causality that is not up to the task. More often than not, however, it would seem that it is the idea, the exemplary cause, which is lacking, so that the ultimate explanation for the failure could be said to be deficient knowledge on the part of the producer. Divine knowledge is the ultimate source of being, for it is the exemplary cause of what takes on real existence external to the being of God. But in order for the effect to take place the divine intellect must be conjoined to the divine will. What happens on the human level is similar to this only faintly, for whereas with us there can be tensions and conflicts between intellect and will, this can never be the case with God. As has been noted, we can plan to produce a work of art but never execute that plan. But because in God there is perfect consonance between intellect and will—they are in fact one with the divine essence—such a failure to effect what has the form of an exemplary cause in the divine mind is inconceivable. And of course in God there can be nothing of the composition, the change, the temporal element, which are part and parcel of human making. So, then, when God knows something as actually existing, i.e., as a being external to the being of God, the divine knowledge accounts for the existence of that being. "It is therefore obvious," St. Thomas writes, "that God causes things to be through the intellect, since His 'to be' is His 'to know.' And thus it is necessary that His knowledge is the cause of the existence of things, insofar as it is conjoined with the divine will." [7] And we can add, simply to emphasize a point, that if God's knowledge is of a thing as actually existing, then the divine will is inevitably conjoined with the divine intellect.

The Scope of Divine Knowledge

God knows all actually existing things, past, present, and future, but He does not know them in the past, present, and future. Rather, He knows all actual existents in the permanent now of His eternity. But from our time-bound perspective, we are permitted to say that God also knows things that do not exist, that is, things in our past and our future that do not have actual being in our present. And thus St. Thomas observes: "Whatever it is possible for creatures to change, or to think, or to say, and whatever it is possible to make, all this God knows. And for that reason we say that He has knowledge of things that do not exist." [8] Relying on the language of metaphysics, we assert that all those things which, from our perspective, have a potentiality that will be realized in the future, such potentiality is known by God as already realized. But what are we to say of those things whose potentiality will never be realized? Does God know that as well? He does. God knows not only all things that have actually existed, and all things that will ever actually exist, He also knows all those things that can possibly exist but which in fact will never actually exist.

Evil, we know, recalling St. Augustine's famous definition, is not something, but the absence of something. More precisely, it is the absence of something in a thing which should be present, given the nature of the thing. But with this understanding of evil, could we not then say that God does not know evil, for if evil, in itself, is nothing, a mere absence, there would then be nothing to know? Is there a real object to be known with respect to evil? It would be false to claim that God does not know evil, and that is because there is indeed an object to be known with respect to evil, which is just that object that is suffering some lack or privation. Those who would claim that this understanding of evil, as essentially a privation, effectively makes evil unreal, fail to grasp what the theory is intending to convey. Once again, evil is as real as the thing that is suffering a privation. The reality of evil is fixed and founded in that actually existing thing which is lacking something that is proper to its nature. A missing limb (an instance of ontological evil) is as real as the animal that is missing that limb. The evil of injustice (the absence of justice) is as real as the unjust man.

Now, all actually existing things, insofar as they exist, are good. That is what we mean when we assert that goodness is a transcendental attribute of being. God created all things as good, but in creating them He knew that some things, especially material things, would be susceptible to suffering privations of various kinds. In other words, He knew that they would be subject to evil. What God knows, then, in knowing evil, are those things that are subject to evil. "It is altogether appropriate," St. Thomas writes, "that whoever knows anything perfectly [and of course this would describe the knowledge of God and of God alone] knows everything that could possibly happen to the thing. And there are certain things, good in themselves, that can be affected in such a way that they are corrupted by evil."[9]

Thus, with respect to moral evil, God created man as entirely good, but He created man with a free will. It is of the very nature of free will that it can be abused, for a creature would not be truly free if he were necessitated always and only to choose the real good. God knew, then, in creating man with a free will, that man would be susceptible to evil. There was susceptibility, but no inevitability, in this matter. If it were inevitable that man should abuse his free will, then on that account too he could not be regarded as truly free.

Some philosophers have questioned the possibility that God could know the infinite, for is not the infinite that which never comes to an end, such as is the case with the mathematical infinite, where, for example, we have a series of integers that can be extended indefinitely? This seeming puzzle is quickly solved if we remember that what God knows first and finally, the proper object of His knowledge, is Himself, an infinite being. God knows the infinite, then, simply by reason of His knowing His own infinitely rich and inexhaustible being. There is nothing whatever "outside" God that escapes His knowledge. As for the knowledge of an indefinite series of numbers, it might be argued that God knows it for precisely what it is, a series of numbers to which other numbers can always be added. A further reflection on that subject: a series of numbers is not extended by its adding numbers to itself; numbers are added to the series by conscious agents who make free choices in doing so. It might be suggested, then, that God knows indefinite series of numbers as He knows future contingents, a matter to be discussed in the following section.

The Knowledge of God and Free Will

One of the most taxing of problems for philosophers and theologians with respect to the divine intellect has revolved around the question of whether God knows future contingents. A future contingent is something that may or may not happen in the future, depending on the action of a free agent. Another way of describing future contingents, then, is simply to call them free acts in the future. It is a future contingent whether or not you will take a walk tomorrow afternoon. It may happen, or it may not happen; it is contingent upon the action of your free will. God knows all things, past, present, and future. We say that He has foreknowledge of what is going to happen tomorrow afternoon. That term, foreknowledge, as applied to God, is somewhat of a misnomer, to the extent that it suggests that God is somehow looking ahead into the future, as we do. But we must remind ourselves that God is eternal; there is no before or after for Him, no past or future. God sees everything in the total simultaneity of His eternal now. When we speak of God's foreknowledge, then, we refer to the fact that He sees, in His eternal now, what is future for us. In other words, God knows now whether or not you are going to take a walk tomorrow afternoon. He knows precisely how you are going to exercise your free will. But does that not mean that your action, whatever it might be, is not truly free? If God already knows what you are going to do tomorrow, then it would seem that you really do not have any choice in the matter, any truly free choice, that is. The knowledge of God determines the way you will actually choose. You may think that you are acting freely, but you are simply playing out a script that has been written from all eternity. Such, then, is the nub of the problem.

Though much controversy has swirled around this problem in recent centuries—that is, since the time of St. Thomas—we need not detain ourselves by getting into the particulars of the controversy here. The solution to the problem can actually be stated quite simply, as follows: God's knowledge of future free acts does not in any way diminish, much less negate, the freedom of those acts, and that is because He knows them *precisely as free acts*. We can get a dim glimmering of how this is so by reflecting on the completely natural knowledge of future contingents that we ourselves are capable of having. Let us say that you know someone very well, a sister; we will call her Cecilia. Your knowledge of Cecilia and her ways is so thorough that you are able to predict, with a very high degree of accuracy, how she is going to respond to certain situations. You have done it often. Let us take a particular type of situation, S, and Cecilia's typical response to such a situation, R. Now, you happen to know that tomorrow afternoon Cecilia is going to find herself in situation S. With this knowledge, you confidently predict that Cecilia is going to respond to S with R. And let us say that things turn out exactly as you predicted they would.

Does that mean that your knowing beforehand how Cecilia was going to react in any way made her react in the way she did? Clearly, it did not. Cecilia freely responded to S in the way she did, and her action was not the least bit less free because you had foreknowledge of it. This analogy is far from perfect, for, among other things that could be said about it, God's knowledge of future contingents, unlike any such knowledge we might claim, is perfect and infallible. Your knowledge of Cecilia's future free action would be in the line of educated guess-work: prediction based upon past experiences. But the analogy nonetheless might at least suggest to us how it is that God's knowledge of future free acts does not affect their character as truly free.

Let us consider this matter in terms of potency and act. God knows all that is in act, and all that is in potency to act. A human being, a free agent, is in potency in relation to any number of future free acts. God knows exactly how any given potential is going to be realized in any given case. But that does not mean that His knowledge determines the actualization in one way or another. What God has determined, if we want to speak in those terms, is that the act be truly free, i.e., that the proximate and direct cause of the act be the agent himself. In such a case, then, what happens is that a potentially free act is actualized as none other than a free act. God knows it as actualized, in one way or another, as a free act.

The Divine Ideas

The Jesuit philosopher Father Henri Renard calls our attention to an interesting fact about St. Thomas's vocabulary, in pointing out how the Universal Doctor used the word "idea."[10] We normally employ that term to designate a "being of reason," a product of the human mind which is precisely identified as an expressed intelligible species that is brought forth by the possible intellect. When St. Thomas refers to this intelligible species, his common practice is to use terms like "concept," or "notion," or "mental word" (*conceptus, notio, verbum mentis*). But the term "idea" (*idea*) he tends to reserve for the purpose of referring to the ideas in the divine intellect, the exemplary causes, or models as it were, which are the originating sources of all existing things.[11]

There is some suggestion of Platonic influence in this Thomistic usage, albeit indirect. For Plato, an Idea (or Form) was an eternal spiritual substance that served as the real reality behind all those things in the material world which are related to it as so many shadowy imitations. St. Augustine, who was not unfamiliar with Platonic philosophy, did not accept the doctrine that the Ideas existed as independent substances. Rather, he argued, they were better understood as being part of the divine substance, ideas in the mind of God. St. Thomas accepted this Augustinian interpretation, and indeed states quite explicitly that, "it is necessary to place the ideas in the divine intellect." [12]

The ideas in the mind of God are to be regarded as the exemplary causes of all the things that exist. They are, to speak loosely, the specifications of the divine intellect with respect to individual things. To better understand the basic principles involved here, let us think again of human artistry. Before Fra Angelico painted his *Annunciation*, he conceived it in his mind; that is where the painting began. And then, as he gradually brought this work of art into full being, he was guided in his work by the model for the painting which he retained in his mind. Now, of course, there is nothing like the complexity—the fits and starts and hesitancies and backtracking, which are common to human artistry—to be found in the divine creative act. But the point of comparison between the two would lie in the intellectual source of what comes to be, immediately in the case of God's creation, in successive stages in the case of human artistry.

There are many exemplary ideas in the divine intellect, corresponding to all the things that actually come to be. But, if this is true, do we not have a contradiction on our hands, with regard to the simplicity of God? How can we speak of there being "many" things in God, who is, as we know, perfectly simple? Let us recall that we are concerned here with divine knowledge, with regard to which we have already established that God knows all things by knowing Himself, in the perfect unity and simplicity of the divine essence. Now, when we human beings know many things, it is only, and necessarily, through the media of many intelligible species, or ideas. We know many through many, as it were. But God knows many through one, His divine essence. There are not many species in God, but His very essence may be considered to be a single species, in which He knows all things. In his typically lucid way, St. Thomas explains: "But it is not at all contrary to the simplicity of the divine intellect that He knows many things. On the other hand, it would be contrary to God's simplicity if His intellect were to be formed by many species."[13] That, however, we know not to be the case. To repeat, then, God knows many things in the absolute unity of the divine essence.

God and Truth

This section could just as appropriately be entitled, "God Is Truth," for it is only because God exists that truth exists. The essential character of truth is that it is a relation, more precisely, a relation of conformity between a mind and something other than the mind. The direction of that conformity, so to speak, in the case of human knowledge, is from the mind to the thing that is known. As was noted at the beginning of this chapter, the human mind knows truly by being measured by the object of its knowledge. The mind adjusts itself to the thing, as it were, until there is a perfect fit between the two. The human mind knows truly if the idea that it has conceived as representing the object of knowledge is in conformity with that object, meaning that the mental representation of the object (i.e., the idea) faithfully reflects the object. It is reality, then, things external to the human mind, that serve as the foundation, that represent the final standard, for what we call logical truth. So, then, in sum, we know truth by conforming our minds to things. Those things, as being in act (i.e., as really existing), are what reduce the potency of our minds to act.

God knows, and God knows with perfect truth, but that cannot mean that the divine intellect is conforming itself to anything other than the divine intellect, for, as we have seen, the proper object of God's knowledge is God Himself. And we also saw that the divine knowledge is causative, for, as perfectly conjoined with the divine will, it creates. What is known by God is brought into being by His very knowledge. Whereas for man the standard of truth is external to himself, and he conforms his mind to that standard, with God, His divine knowledge creates the standards, in that His knowledge evokes existence, brings things into being. Human knowledge is measured, but divine knowledge measures, and indeed is the measure of all things.

God can be said simply to *be* the truth in two respects. First, He is the truth because His knowledge consists in the perfect conformity of the divine intellect with the divine essence. Again, His "to be" is His "to know." God is perfectly at one with Himself. Second, God is the truth because He, as the creative source of all things, makes all truth possible, for He creates the human mind, and He creates the things to which the human mind conforms itself in order to know the truth. "It therefore follows," St. Thomas sums up, "that not only is truth founded in God [as the source of all being],but He is the supreme and the first truth." [14] We human beings succumb to falsity when we get things wrong, when the ideas we have conceived in our minds do not faithfully reflect what they are intended to represent. But because God is truth itself, there is no deeper nor more fatal falsity into which we can fall than to reject Him who, as the truth, is the source of all truth.

God, Knowledge, Life

The best and most immediately obvious proof for the presence of what we call life is self-motion. There are any number of other things involved, but this could count as the most basic. Living things are things that move themselves. We detect life by observing a certain operation, movement. But life itself is not an operation. It is what accounts for operation. Things are not alive because they move; they move because they are alive. Put another way, we can say that life is not something attached to live things, as if it were an accident. Life is of the very substance of live things; it is what they *are*.

Well, then, all live things are identified as such because they are self-moving. Now, everything that moves, that changes in any way, does so for a purpose, and that purpose is to attain a definite end.[15] Plants represent the lowest form of life, and that is because, though they indeed act for the sake of an end (i.e., they nourish themselves, and grow, so that they might produce fruit and by that reproduce), they have no knowledge of the ends toward which their activity is ordered. Animals represent a higher form of life because with them knowledge enters into the picture, specifically, sense knowledge. An animal can be quite conscious of the ends it pursues by its actions (e.g., the fox chasing the rabbit), but the animal does not consciously choose those ends. They are established as part of its nature in the form of instincts. When we reach that level of life represented by human beings, we find here the presence of knowledge of an altogether different kind; we could call it knowledge in the fullest sense, the knowledge of a rational creature. And it is precisely the possession of this rational knowledge by human beings that establishes them on the highest level of physical life. Human beings are obviously conscious of the ends they pursue, but, what is more, they consciously choose those ends. And yet, for all that, there is a significant limitation to our knowledge in this regard, for, though it is true that we can choose this or that particular good, we do not choose the good just as such. That is, we will invariably pursue what we perceive to be good; we cannot do otherwise. We are naturally ordered toward the good, for that is how God created us to be.

But now let us consider the knowledge of God. As we have seen, there are no limitations whatever to that knowledge. It is perfect and comprehensive knowledge, because it is knowledge of the divine essence itself. Given the fact that, as just noted, the greater and the less limited the knowledge, the greater and the less limited the life, we may conclude that God is maximally alive, for His knowledge ("to know," *intelligere*) is one with His being ("to be," *esse*). This fact gives added poignancy to what Our Lord says of Himself, "I am the way, the truth, and *the life*." [16] St. Thomas offers a succinct summary statement of the salient truths involved here: "But that being whose nature is one and the same with its knowledge, and whose nature is not in the least bit determined by anything external to itself, such a being achieves the highest grade of life. But that being is none other than God Himself. Therefore, in God we find the maximum expression of life." [17]

CHAPTER THIRTEEN

The Divine Will

The Nature of Will

In this chapter we will continue our investigations into what are commonly referred to as the internal operations of the divine nature. Having considered various aspects of one of those operations, the divine intellect, we will now give our attention to the second of those internal operations, the divine will.

In order better to prepare ourselves for this discussion, it would be helpful if we were first to review some of the general characteristics of will. What is the nature and function of will? Of course, the responses we give to that question will be based on the knowledge we have of will which is derived from our immediate experiences. We are creatures possessed of a will, and we are quite familiar with its functions. So, our point of departure in this discussion will be human will. But because our principal concern is the divine will, we shall eventually be making application of our human-based knowledge of will to the divine will. In doing so we shall obviously have to make any number of adjustments, in moving from the natural to the supernatural plane, as we had to do when treating the divine intellect. We shall discover that there are some aspects of human will which can be applied to the divine will, analogously as always, and some which have no application at all. Nonetheless, there are any number of fruitful comparisons that can be made between human will and the divine will, and we shall attempt to derive as much benefit from those as we can. That such comparisons are available should not surprise us, for our human nature is, after all, the effect of the divine causality, and indeed in a very special way, for we have been created in the image and likeness of God, the essential meaning of which, according to St. Augustine, is that we were created with intellect and will. The human will, then, can be considered to be a dim reflection of the divine will.

The human will, along with the human intellect, constitute the two principal faculties, or powers, of the rational soul. The intellect is the knowing faculty; the will is the appetitive faculty, which is to say that it is the faculty which is directed outward from the subject, drawn toward things other than the subject. As we saw, being—actually existing things—is the proper object of the human intellect, but specifically under the aspect of intelligibility, or knowableness, or , by extension, truth. Being is also the proper object of the human will, but under a different aspect, the aspect of the lovable, or, simply, the good, for the good is what the will naturally loves. In sum, we can say that the intellect is *for* truth, in that truth is its end; the will is *for* the good, in that the good is its end.

When the human intellect knows being, through the process of abstraction, it assimilates it to itself, and so becomes what it knows. That is the most intimate kind of union imaginable. The human will also seeks union with that which it loves, but this is union of a different kind, not a union of assimilation but of association. The will loves, is drawn toward, a thing because it perceives it as good. It is the good which is the "motivator" of the action of the will.

The will is known in Scholastic parlance as the intellectual appetite. It is called that because it always works in union with the intellect. The will is naturally ordered toward the good, but it cannot of itself identify the good. For that it needs the assistance of the intellect. The intellect illumines the will, informs it of the presence of the good. It is impossible simply to will. There always has to be an object of the act of willing, the "something" that is willed, and that must be a known something. The will, blind in itself, needs the eyes of the intellect to lead it to the good. Whenever we will something, then, it is always in terms of our total identity as rational creatures. We always will something knowingly, conscious of the fact that we are pursuing the good. But the will, the intellectual appetite, is not the only appetite which we possess. We have a whole set of sense appetites—the passions, or basic emotions—which are also ordered toward the good, but the good in this case is the concupiscible, or material good. The appetite for food would be an example of a sense appetite. The sense appetites, in their initial movements, are not under the illuminating guidance and direction of the intellect, and for this reason we call them non-rational appetites.

We have said that the human will is naturally ordered toward the good. It is so ordered in a very general and comprehensive way. In this general ordering toward the good there is necessitation, in that we human beings cannot do otherwise than to want the good. Let us put this basic and important truth of human psychology in a different way. How would we best describe a state in which we were completely fulfilled, in the sense that we had in our possession all the goods we could possibly desire? That would be a state of happiness. To say that we cannot do otherwise than to want the good is to say the same thing as that we have a deep-set and ineradicable desire for happiness. Human beings cannot not want to be happy, without, that is, going against their very nature. We always want the good, and we always pursue the good, but—note this—it is the good *as perceived* by us. Unfortunately—and perhaps this could be identified as the chief cause of tragedy in human life—our perceptions in this matter are often quite wrong. So we must recognize an important distinction between a real good and an apparent, or false, good. A real good is one which is genuinely perfective of the subject who comes to possess it. An apparent good, on the other hand, is one whose possession will not only fail to be perfective of the subject, but will prove to be positively harmful to the subject.

When we examine closely the operation of the will we discover that it involves some interesting complexity. There are several distinct movements or acts in the operation. To begin with, and with reference to the end, there is the most basic movement of the will, simple volition, which may be described as the elementary awareness of the good on the part of the subject, and a turning toward that good. Closely following upon that basic movement there is the act of intention, by which the good is not simply recognized but desired. The act of intention indicates a definite commitment to the good on the part of the subject.

Then come several acts of the will that are related to the means that are to be employed in order to attain the intended end, the first of which is called consent. Consent is a general, non-particularized commitment to take whatever means are necessary in order to attain the end. It signals that the subject's attitude toward the good is significantly more than one of vague, vacillating wishing. The subject is serious about attaining the good. Then comes the act called counsel, or deliberation, the act by which the subject ponders the various possible means that can be taken in order to attain the end, with the idea in mind of deciding which is the best among them. After counsel comes the act of choice, by which specific means to attain the end are selected. When we speak of freedom of the will it is particularly this act of choice we have in mind. Once the specific means have been determined, it is time for the internal acts of the will to manifest themselves in external action. That is effected by the next act, command, which is simply the will giving the order that the selected means be followed. The final act of the will is called use, and it is the execution of the command to follow the specified means. External action then takes place and, if all goes well, the subject actually comes into the possession of the intended good. Capping all these acts of the will is an experience which St. Thomas calls fruition (*fruitio*), which is the subject's enjoyment of the possessed good.

Perhaps one of the most important features of the human will, and one which, it would seem, needs special emphasis in the times in which we live, is the fact that the will is truly and fully free in its action. What do we mean, positively, when we say that the will is free? We mean simply that the will is the originating source of its own action. Putting it in negative terms, the assertion that the will is free means that it is not determined or necessitated by anything external to itself. Nor, for that matter, is it even determined internally. The will, as we saw, must be shown the good by the intellect. The information thus supplied to the will by the intellect is critically important for the will, for without it volitional action is impossible, but it does not carry with it imperative force. The will is under no necessity to follow the guidance offered to it by the intellect. It can choose explicitly to reject that guidance, or simply ignore it. The intellect can point out a particular good to the will, then, and the will can refuse to form any intention regarding it. This is a state of affairs with which we are all familiar through our own experiences. I have in mind the kind of situation in which we have clear knowledge of a right action that should be done (the intellect has supplied us with correct information in this regard), but we do not act upon that knowledge (the will refuses the guidance of the intellect).

The Will of God

In light of that sketchy summary of the nature and function of the human will, the first thing that we need to say about the divine will is that, unlike the human will, it is not a faculty. A faculty, to repeat, is simply a power, and as such it is distinct from the subject that possesses the power. This is manifestly the case with respect to human will, and we are all quite conscious of the fact that "I" and "my will" are not the same thing. If they were one and the same, then we would never experience those trying internal conflicts where the "I" and the will seem to be quite at odds with one another, such as in those situations where we berate ourselves for not doing what we know to be the right thing to do. There may be firmness of purpose, but it is accompanied by weakness of will. So, with respect to the human will, we do not say that it is the same thing as the person. But this is precisely what we do say of the divine will. God is His will. Thus, we have here the same truth that obtains with respect to the divine intellect. The divine intellect, as we saw, is one and the same with the divine essence. In like manner, the divine will is also one and the same with the divine essence.

Why, we might ask, if it is true that the divine intellect and the divine will are one and the same with the divine essence, do we even bother to make a distinction between them? In response to that we say, first of all, that this distinction, although it is not real with respect to the divine essence, is scarcely an arbitrary and idle one on our part. We make it because it signals a difference in the effects of God's action upon us, as we experience them in our lives. And the distinction is therefore an efficacious means by which we strive better to understand, on the basis of natural reason alone, the nature of God. The source of the divine action is of course absolutely one and simple; but the effects of that action, as experienced by us, are diverse. Specifically, we apprehend the divine action as manifesting itself in distinct ways: God as knowing, God as willing.

As is his habit when he digs into a serious subject, St. Thomas begins his treatment of the divine will by asking a very basic question, and in this case a somewhat disarming one. It is: Does God have a will? His answer to the question is of course in the affirmative, but the reason he asks such a question is that it provides him with the opportunity to make some very rudimentary clarifications concerning the nature of the divine will. The reasoning St. Thomas uses in arguing for the reality of the divine will gives special emphasis to the following principle: it is in the very nature of things that intellect is always accompanied by will. Wherever there is knowledge, there is an accompanying power to act on that knowledge. But God, as we have already established, has an intellect. Therefore, God has a will. And then, to put things in more precise terms, and by way of calling our attention to the fact that what is true of the divine intellect is also true of the divine will, St. Thomas writes that, "just as God's 'to know' is His 'to be,' so His 'to will' is also His 'to be'." [1] With respect to the divine intellect, the divine will, and the divine essence, there is perfect unity.

As we saw above, one of the ways we distinguish between human intellect and human will is in terms of their finality, the ends toward which they are ordered: the end of intellect is truth; the end of will is the good. From the previous chapter we will recall that the human intellect is in possession of the truth when its thought is consonant with, conforms to, what actually is the case in the external world. In dramatic contrast to this, the divine intellect establishes what is the case in the external world. The general object of the human will is any good, real or apparent, which is other than the willing subject. God wills, and God cannot will other than what is truly good, but that does not imply that what happens on the supernatural level is like what obtains on the human level, where there is a distinction between will and object of the will, and where the object is external to the willing subject. We will goods external to ourselves because we see those goods, rightly or wrongly, as perfective of ourselves. But God, who is all-perfect, could not will anything that might be called perfective of Himself, for there is no such thing. An all-perfect being cannot be perfected. A vessel that is full to the brim cannot receive another drop. The proper object of the divine will, then, could only be God Himself, for He is goodness Himself, the Supreme Goodness (*Bonum Supremum*). "The object of the divine will," St. Thomas writes, "is His own goodness, which is nothing else than His very essence." [2] The only fitting object of God's will is His own essence, because it is the only object that is adequate to that will.

God's Will Embraces All Good

In our discussion of the divine intellect, we saw that God knows all things, knows them perfectly, as they are in themselves, but—and here is the important point—He knows them simply by knowing Himself, for He is the source of all things. In a comparable way, God wills the good of all things—which means that He wills them to be—but He does so simply by willing Himself. (To say that God wills Himself is the same thing as saying that God loves himself.) Goodness, we say, is diffusive, meaning that it is of the very nature of goodness to overflow itself, to spread out, to share itself with others. This is preeminently so when it comes to the divine goodness, but even on the human level we can find examples of the naturally diffusive quality of goodness. There are very few human beings, even among the most insular and selfish, who do not feel the urge, at least on occasion, to have others participate with them in a good they are enjoying. A shared good somehow seems better than one kept entirely to oneself. But, for all that, given the fact that we are creatures for whom selflessness does not come easily, the goods that we possess are too often dammed up by egoism and do not flow out toward others. So, the diffusion of the good which is witnessed on the human level is of mixed quality.

The goodness of God is, we might say, unrestrainedly diffusive. God, who is the source of all goodness, the Supreme Good, freely wills to share His goodness in the most generous way. And He "wills" all creatures in the sense that He desires that they all be ordered toward their proper end, which is Himself. God is the Supreme Good for us in the critically important sense that He is the ultimate end of all that we do, whether we are conscious of that fact or not. He is the source of our being, in that we were made by Him: He is the purpose of our being, in that we were made for Him.

The Divine Freedom

The human will can be said to be necessitated, in the sense indicated earlier, that we cannot help but want the good, we cannot help but pursue happiness. It is simply part of our nature. There have been some philosophers, such as Baruch Spinoza (1632–1677), who have maintained the position that the will of God is necessitated. According to these thinkers, God cannot will other than how He in fact wills. For example, God had no choice but to create; He could not have done otherwise. And He was compelled by necessity to create just the universe He did create, and no other. This is, needless to say, an egregiously erroneous position. To suppose that God is necessitated is to suppose that there is some constraining power outside, and superior to, God Himself, to which He is subject. But if that were true, God would not be God.

In discussing the question of the divine freedom, St. Thomas first reminds his readers that there are two basic types of necessity. There is absolute necessity, and there is the necessity of supposition. Absolute necessity is in play where the very essence of something demands that it be precisely what it is and nothing else than what it is. So, for example, it is absolutely necessary, given its very essence, that a triangle be a plane, three-sided figure whose internal angles equal two right angles. If that were not the case, a triangle would not be a triangle. Necessity of supposition describes a situation in which a particular thing is in fact in a given state, though the nature of the thing does not dictate that it must be in that state; but because the thing is in fact in that state right now, it is necessarily in that state, for, if it were not, the principle of contradiction would be violated. For example, Patrice, as it happens, is right now sitting at her desk. There is no absolute necessity in her sitting at her desk right now, for, without ceasing to be Patrice, she could be standing up, or she could be doing laps in the swimming pool. But so long as Patrice is sitting down right now she is necessarily sitting down, for it would be a contradiction if she were sitting down right now and not sitting down right now.

Is God in any way necessitated? He is, but not in the way Baruch Spinoza thinks He is. What we mean, when we say that God is necessitated, is simply that He must be true to His own nature; we do not mean that He is constrained to act in one way and one way only. Specifically, we say that God is necessitated to will His own goodness. It would constitute a supreme contradiction were He not to do so. The proper end of will is the good. God is the Supreme Good. He must, therefore, will His own goodness first and finally. Apropos of this point, St. Thomas remarks that God is necessitated to will His own goodness in a way that human beings are necessitated to want to be happy. We would be betraying our very natures if we were to want not to be happy. So too, God would be, so to speak, betraying His nature were He not to love His own goodness. Let us repeat an important point, for the terminology we use here could be misunderstood: to speak of God being necessitated is not in the least to suggest that God is somehow coerced by some force that is external to Himself. The necessity is, so to speak, entirely within, welling up from the fathomless depths of the divine essence. God is necessitated in the sense that He is simply consistent with Himself. This is, we may say, a dimension of His perfect unity. He does not go counter to the dictates of His own nature.

However, there is no necessity whatever when God wills things other than Himself. When He exercises His will in that way, the effects are existing beings. In this respect, His will is creative, and it is absolutely free. There was no necessitation in God's willing to create the universe, or in His willing to create this particular universe. All things that He wills to create He wills freely. God can will to act, or not to act, and, having willed to act, He can will to act in this or that fashion. We human beings have the same kinds of freedom of the will: the freedom of exercise, and the freedom of specification. But we are mutable creatures; God is immutable. We can and do alter our acts of will; we can choose something today, and negate that choice tomorrow. This is impossible with God. Once God has willed something, He never, so to speak, goes back on His will. Thus, God has willed to create human beings as immortal. Our status as immortal creatures cannot change, for God cannot repudiate His own will act, an act that emerges from perfect wisdom. And, of course, for God to alter His will, for Him to "change His mind" as it were, would directly contradict His simplicity and immutability.

God's Will Is Causative

We saw in the previous chapter that the divine knowledge is causative; it brings things into existence. The divine will, like the divine intellect, is one and the same with the divine essence. We can assert with equal assurance, then, that the divine will is also causative, for creation is the effect of the unified action of the perfectly unified divine nature. The divine intellect and the divine will work together in perfect harmony.

If there is no necessity in God's causative activity—it is absolutely free—what might we say is the explanation for that activity? What "motivates" it? It is simply God's infinite perfection. God's causative activity, the effect of which is the created world, is the free out-flowing of His infinite perfection. Goodness, as we have said, is naturally diffusive; a supreme goodness would be infinitely so. Another way we could describe God's creative causality is to call it an act of pure generosity. The whole of creation is a gift. The nature of a gift is such that it is given freely. There is no element of obligation on the part of the giver, and there is no element of deservedness on the part of the recipient.

God is eternal. From our time-constrained point of view, we are led to speak of the effects of God's causative action, i.e., what He actually chooses to create, as preexisting in the divine essence. Because goodness is a transcendental attribute of being, everything that exists, precisely as existing, is good. It is simply good to be. Now, in terms of what preexists in the divine intellect, may we say that when God brings those ideas or exemplars into actual being, He does so because He sees them as good? In other words, does He bring them into existence because they are good? No, that would be to have it just backwards. God's creative action does not cause something that is good to be; rather, it causes something to be, and with that it becomes good. Put another way, because goodness is part and parcel of being, it follows upon being, so to speak, and does not precede it. Something is good because God wills it *to be*. It gains goodness with being. We exist for no other reason than that God is good, St. Thomas argued. God's goodness is the foundation for His willing everything that exists.

"In no way," St. Thomas firmly states, "does the will of God have a cause."[3] The reason for this is that any reference to a cause of God's will would be an appeal to something external to God. The human will can be said to be caused in several ways, one of which would be with respect to the good to which the will aspires. Specifically, the good, the end, serves as a final cause which stimulates the efficient causality of the will. With God, however, the good is not something which acts as a cause of the divine will, either internally or externally. But did we not say that God wills His own goodness, as the only appropriate object of His will, and on that account would not it be proper to interpret His own goodness as a cause of His will? It is true that God wills His own goodness, but that provides us with no warrant for concluding that His goodness causes His will. To speak of causality within the divine essence would go counter to the divine simplicity, and introduce all the other complications that are attendant upon causality. We must remind ourselves that God's will and the divine essence, which is the Supreme Good, are perfectly one; there is no dichotomy here, no distinction between cause and effect within the Godhead. There is no causative action that explains the fact that God wills His own goodness, for to say that He loves His own goodness simply means that He is perfectly one with Himself.

As I mentioned just above, causal activity in human willing is exemplified in the peculiar role played by the end, acting as the final cause. That relation gives rise to the distinction between the end and the means that are taken to achieve it. With that distinction in mind, we can say that the end is the cause of our willing the means. There is no operative distinction between ends and means within the action of the divine will, and thus no question of one causing the other. When God wills there is but a single act in which end and means are willed simultaneously. Therefore, we cannot speak of the will of God having a cause other than itself. But what would be entailed by the supposition that willing the end and willing the means are not the same thing in God? If we were to suppose that, composition would enter the picture—i.e., first willing the end, then willing the means—and with composition the divine simplicity would be negated. So, once again, we say that God's willing a certain end includes, in that selfsame act, His willing the means that are necessary to achieve that end.

God's Will Is Always Done

It is impossible that the divine will should ever be frustrated. Indeed, it is a matter of the strictest necessity that the divine will should always be fulfilled. In arguing this point, St. Thomas builds his case on the metaphysical principle that the quality of any effect is a reflection of the quality which is to be found in the cause. If, therefore, we have an effect which is deficient in one way or another, this is to be explained by a deficiency in the cause. This describes a situation with which we are all quite familiar, through the many particular causes we confront in our day to day experience. But in contrast to the countless particular causes operative in the world, commonly giving rise to less than perfect effects because they themselves are less than perfect, there is the universal cause of all things, the First Cause, God Himself. There is no deficiency whatever in this cause. And therefore there can be no deficiency in the effects which issue forth from it. We will all sorts of things that do not yield the results intended. Our wills are often frustrated. But whatever God wills is infallibly fulfilled.

At first hearing, those assertions do not seem to ring true. How about the existence of evil in the world, most especially moral evil, sin? Would not the presence of sin in the world contradict the assertion that the will of God is always fulfilled? Surely God does not will that sin should exist, and yet sin does exist. Though it might seem to us otherwise, God's will is in fact not frustrated by the presence of sin in the world. To state the case in the starkest terms: God's will is absolutely sovereign; it is the ultimate explanation for everything, and absolutely nothing can countervail it. In dealing with the specific instance of moral evil, or sin, St. Thomas begins with the general observation that what would seem to be thwarting God's will, looking at things from one perspective, is seen to be not thwarting His will at all, as viewed from a different, more comprehensive perspective. So, then, if we look at things from a narrow perspective which focuses our attention on the sinner, it would seem that God's will is being frustrated, for the sinner, by his sin, is certainly not fulfilling the divine will. But if we view things from a larger perspective, which leads us to consider the justice of God, then we see that His will is perfectly fulfilled by the fact that no sin goes unpunished, and punishment is the manifestation of God's justice. So, in sum, in terms of this or that individual act, it would seem that the will of God is being frustrated, but if we place that act in the larger context, the big picture in which even the crooked lines contribute to the total coherent composition, then we see that the will of God is perfectly fulfilled. All things work together unto good, even sin, but, to be sure, in a way that is beyond our capacity to understand in any precise, particularized sense.

Another way of looking at the matter is to keep in mind that the principal cause of sin is always the sinner, the free agent who chooses to abuse his freedom by turning away from God. Now, God never wills the sin, but we can say without sentimentality that He always wills the sinner. That is to say, He always wills nothing but the good of the sinner, a good He established by creating the sinner. And He created the sinner precisely as a free agent. That, we might say, is the most signal effect of God's creative action: bringing into being a rational creature whose will is truly free. When the sinner sins, there is no question but that by doing so God's will is not being fulfilled. But what makes it possible for the sinner to sin at all? Only the fact that he is truly a free agent. By the sheer exercise of his freedom, then, in a larger sense the will of God is being fulfilled, for, by exercising his freedom, even though he is abusing that freedom by sinning, he is acting according to his proper nature, the nature God gave him in creating him. The will of God is definitely not being fulfilled by the sin itself, but it is being filled by the fact that a creature is acting according to his proper nature, not in sinning, but in acting as a free agent. If he were not acting as a free agent, there would not even be the possibility of sin.

God is eternal. At the very moment God created the sinner, He knew every detail of the man's life that was going to devolve over time, and He knew that sin was going to be part of that life. God did not will the sin—that would be impossible, for it would mean that God willed that He should be repudiated by one of His creatures—but He willed the whole in which the sin takes place, the comprehensive whole that is God's providential plan for the human race. Sin is a part of the whole, but its being such is not going to frustrate what God wills for the whole. Looked at from the perspective of the whole, it is sin that is going to be frustrated, for in spite of itself, according to God's will for the whole, sin contributes to the final good of the whole.

God's Will Is Unchanging

We made mention above that the will of God is unchanging. In this fact we have of course a dramatic contrast to what obtains with respect to the human will. The human will is famous for its fickleness. If we recall how human will is related to intellect, the rather commonplace occurrence of our undoing an act of will we made previously is easily explained. Because intellect is antecedent to will, in that it enlightens and guides the will, a change of will is accounted for by an antecedent change of mind. But what occurs with fair frequency with us can never occur with God, for if we were to claim that it were possible that God could will something, and then subsequently will something contrary to the first act of will, we would immediate have two major contradictions to contend with, one having to do with God's immutability, the other having to do with His eternity. An immutable God cannot change, with respect to will or with respect to anything else; and an eternal God allows for no sequence: first one act, "subsequently" another.

If change of will in human beings is explained by change of mind, because will is dependent upon intellect, we have in that state of affairs a clue that offers us an indirect explanation for why the divine will is unchanging. Because the divine intellect and the divine will are one and the same, and because the divine intellect is unchanging, it must then be the case that the divine will is also unchanging. "It was made evident earlier," St. Thomas writes, "that the divine knowledge, as one with the divine essence, is utterly unchanging. It must be the case, then, that the divine will is also utterly unchanging." [4]

It is extremely difficult for us to imagine how it could be that God undergoes no change whatever in His acts of will, especially when we think of one particular act which has inestimable consequences for each and every one of us: the act whereby God brings the rational soul into existence. If there is a single fact about the created world that stands out with the boldest kind of prominence, it is the fact of change. And yet He who is the cause of that ever-changing world is Himself unchanging. This is a great puzzle and mystery for us, but, as St. Thomas observes, there is no contradiction in this circumstance, puzzling and mysterious though it be, for it is quite possible to have someone who, by a single, permanent unchanging act of the will, wills into being things which are themselves changing. [5] That "someone" he is referring to is of course God. The immutable can give rise to the mutable.

The Divine Will and Human Freedom

In our treatment of the divine knowledge we had to deal with the problem that arises from the fact that God has knowledge of future free acts. Does not His foreknowledge effectively remove the freedom from the purportedly free act? We saw that in fact it does not. We confront a similar problem with respect to the divine will. And the solution to it is much the same as the solution to the problem respecting the divine intellect. God's will is causative of being, as we have already ascertained. Metaphysics makes a distinction, with regard to being, between what is called first act and second act. First act is foundational, for it is the very act of be-ing itself, the act that establishes a thing in existence. Second act refers to the sum total of the actions that are performed by an actually existing being. It is first act that accounts for the very existence of Simon. Simon's throwing a football would be an example of second act. Behind that physical act there is a mental act of the will. God is the cause of both first act and second act in every human being. He is obviously the cause of the existence of someone like Simon, but He is also the enabling cause of every act of the will Simon makes, as well as all his other acts.

It is the fact that God is the cause of second act that poses a problem. If it is true that God is the cause of Simon's acts of will—in the sense that he could not make such acts, nor any other, without God's sustaining power—how can we say that Simon is really a free agent, for would it not be the case that God, in enabling Simon to make an act of the will, is determining him to act in a particular way? Simon's supposed freedom, then, would be but a delusion.

Let us begin our response to the problem by underscoring the fact that there are two things in this circumstance which are incontestably true, and because this is so they do not contradict one another. The first is that Simon cannot make acts of will without the enabling power of God. The second is that Simon is perfectly free in making his acts of will. God's causality, relating to free acts of the will, does not in any way override or cancel out their freedom, and that is because God enables those acts *precisely as free*. In other words, it is God's sustaining and supporting power that causes Simon to act freely, but it does not cause him to act in this or that way.

God wills certain things to act in ways that are completely necessitated—for example the whole material universe that is governed by the laws of nature—but He also wills things to act in ways that are completely free: rational creatures whom He has endowed with free will. God's causative activity capacitates the free will to act; it does not determine it to act in any specific way. To put it in different terms, the power of God enables the will to choose, but it leaves the actual choosing entirely up to the free agent. Consider this analogy which, though quite imperfect, might serve to clarify the matter a little. The electric power that comes into a home enables a vacuum cleaner in that home to operate. But the electric power does not determine that the vacuum cleaner be operated to clean the living room rather than the dining room. That is left up to the operators to decide. If God willed that the whole of His creation should act out of necessity, St. Thomas observes in matter of fact fashion, that would mean that there would be no free will. But in point of fact, "God wills that certain things should come about by necessity, and certain other things as the result of free action, and thus is established an order among things which brings a fitting completion to the universe." [6] There is an additional consideration. If one is going to contend that God's causative influence on second act determines the human will in its specific choices, then one could not escape the conclusion that God is the direct cause of sin.

God Is Not the Cause of Evil

God never directly wills evil. Evil has yet to be given a better definition than that provided by St. Augustine, when he identified it as the privation of good (*privatio boni*). We must take note of the important distinction between ontological evil and moral evil. Of the two, moral evil is by far the more serious, for it represents a conscious, deliberate turning away from God on the part of a rational creature.

Ontological evil is a deficiency in a thing that is accounted for by a lack, in the thing, of something which is proper to its nature; something is missing (with respect to the physical make-up of the thing) that should be there. This lack impedes the proper functioning of the thing. An animal missing a limb, or its having a malfunctioning organ, would be examples of ontological evil. Any disease is an ontological evil. What are we to say of "natural disasters"? There is nothing intrinsically disordered in large environmental disturbances such as floods, earthquakes, tornadoes, hurricanes, and the like, but they can be classified as instances of ontological evil, in an extended sense, to the degree that they bring harm to man and to lower forms of life. God does not will ontological evil directly, but only indirectly, as part of a larger order which He has brought into being, and which He wills directly and without qualification. God, in willing the physical order of nature, wills what is inevitable to physical nature, and that is corruption. It is of the very nature of material things to undergo corruption, to lose their proper physical integrity and eventually cease to be. But if we were to focus on corruption with a kind a monomaniacal intensity, to the point where we see the part and not the whole to which it belongs, we then fail to appreciate that corruption is necessary for the balanced maintenance of the whole. If organisms did not corrupt and die, this earth could not long survive. Paradoxically, death is necessary for life. Corruption, taken by itself, in isolation, is an ontological evil, but it is an ontological evil on which the good of the whole depends.

Moral evil, or sin, presents an entirely different case as far as God's will is concerned. God does not will moral evil in any way whatever. Earlier we observed that God does not will sin, but He wills the justice that serves to restore the order that was disturbed by sin. Once sin is subsumed within the larger and purifying atmosphere of justice, as it inevitably is, then a kind of comprehensive meaningfulness is established. Not that sin itself becomes meaningful—sin, as evil, remains forever intrinsically unintelligible—but its inherent meaninglessness is neutralized by reason of the relation it bears to God's providential plan, as specifically expressed in salvation history.

God's will, as we know, is perfectly one and undivided. But, in order to better understand the divine nature, we make any number of distinctions concerning it. And we also attribute to God , metaphorically not literally, certain states that are analogous to states that are part of our experience as human beings. We do this because the effects of God's action in our lives are comparable to the effects of certain human states with which we are familiar. For example, we speak of the anger of God. Now, God, as immutable, is quite incapable of the multiple kinds of changes that are involved in the passion of anger. We say that God is angry only by way of drawing attention to a correspondence that commonly occurs on the human level between anger and punishment, where anger is the cause of the punishment. So, by analogy, we metaphorically impute anger to God because the punishment that inevitably follows upon sin, is like the punishment which, on the human level, follows upon anger. To put it in different terms, when we say that God is angry with us because He punishes us for our sins, we are conveying the notion, through metaphorical language, that the punishment we suffer for our sins has a cause, and that cause is the justice of God.

We distinguish between what we call God's operational will and His permissive will. God's operational will is manifested when He brings something about directly. By His permissive will God brings things about indirectly, simply by not impeding the necessary and the free causes which He has established in His creation. As we said just above, God never directly wills evil. But the fact is, evil exists, and it can only exists because God permits it to exist. He permits it not because He wills the evil, but because He wills the larger context which is part of His whole providential plan, and to which even the evil, as we said above, is destined to be put to the service of the positive. And to repeat another point made earlier, God, while repudiating the manner in which a free agent employs his freedom, nonetheless wills the freedom of the free agent.

The only way God could have precluded moral evil from ever existing in the world would have been to make creatures who were not free, but if He were to have done that He would not have made creatures who are in His image and likeness. For all its baneful effects, the existence of moral evil in the world is proof positive of the existence of free will.

The Love of God

It is perfectly logical that the subject of love should compose part of a discussion of the divine will. We remind ourselves that the proper object, the end toward which the will is ordered, is the good, and the immediate and natural reaction on the part of the subject to a perceived good is love. This being the case, we could define the good as that which is loved. To love something is to want to be united with it. In human love, the degree of unity that it is possible to achieve between lover and beloved is always limited, with a concomitant limitation of the happiness that accompanies the union. But in God there is no distinction between the lover and the beloved, and hence there is no union that has to be brought about. There is perfect unity from all eternity. The loving God and the object of His love are one and the same.

In human love we distinguish between the love of concupiscence, or material love, and spiritual love. Material love is self-oriented. We want to possess the loved object for our own sakes. Spiritual love is always directed toward persons. Its chief characteristic is that it also puts the beloved first. We love the other person, not for any good that could accrue to us, but solely for the good of the other person, so we say that the essence of true love (i.e., charity) is to will the good for the other (*velle bonum alicui*). The heart of love, then, is not feeling but will, willing what is genuinely and permanently good for another person. In God there is of course no material love. He has no need to love anything for the sake of His own good, for that implies that something could somehow be added to His goodness, which is impossible, for He is goodness itself, the Supreme Good. God is at once, as we said, the source and the object of His love, so on that account we can simply assert that God is love.

In considering the knowledge and will of God, we saw that He both knows and wills things other than Himself. And though God most certainly wills and loves Himself—again, it would be a contradiction were He to do otherwise—His love is not limited to Himself. "God loves everything that exists," St. Thomas writes. "The reason for this is that everything that exists, just so far as it does exist, is good."[7] God loves Himself first and finally because He is goodness itself, but everything that exists as the result of His creative action is ontologically good in its essence, as coming from an all-good being, and for this reason He loves all things. And if pure, spiritual love is to will good for the other, then the love that God bears toward all things is maximally spiritual love, for He loves all things on account of the most foundational of all good, the good of being itself. Indeed, His love caused all beings to exist. And once He brought things into existence by His love, God, in His love, continues to infuse goodness into them, and to cause that goodness to increase.

The Justice of God

There are two additional attributes of God that St. Thomas includes in his treatment of the divine will: the justice of God and the mercy of God. God is just. What does that imply? The essential notion of justice can be expressed as follows: to give to another person what is due to him, in view of his intrinsic and inalienable dignity as a person. Philosophy has traditionally analyzed justice into three distinct kinds: distributive justice; commutative justice; legal or social justice. Distributive justice is the giving to members of a community, by those who have care of the community, what is due to them. Commutative justice is at play where members of a community render to one another what is due. This would be justice as practiced among peers or equals. Legal justice is the contribution to the common good of a community by the members of that community. Obeying the laws of a community would be an example of legal justice.

According to that analysis, the only kind of justice that could be said to apply to God would be distributive justice, for God, as the sovereign ruler of the universe, has the care of all things in His hands. But when we consider again the basic meaning of justice, could we rightly say that any kind of justice should apply to God? Justice is giving to another what is due to him, what is owed to him. But certainly God could not be said to owe anything to anyone, for to owe something to another person puts one in a subordinate position with respect to that person, and God is not subordinate to anyone or anything.

The solution to that problem is fairly simple. It is obviously true that God does not owe anything to anyone. In what, then, does His justice consist? Briefly, we could say that it consists in His being true to His own nature, particularly with respect to His status as Creator of all things. God, in creating a specific nature—human nature, say—ensures, in justice, that everything needed is provided to those who share that nature so as to enable them to attain the common end toward which their nature is ordered. Now, the common end of human nature is nothing less than God Himself. God, then, in justice, assures that human beings have everything they need in order to attain their proper end.

St. Thomas weaves together the justice of God and divine truth. Truth, for human beings, is the conformity of the intellect to things. For God, truth is the conformity of things to the divine intellect, the result of which latter conformity is the very existence of things. It is the divine intellect, under the aspect of justice, which established the regulatory laws by which all the things in the universe are properly ordered and governed. St. Thomas sum up: "Therefore the justice of God, which establishes the order in things in accordance with the design of His wisdom, which is simply His law, can properly be called truth." [8] The order and regularity that we see everywhere in creation is an effect of God's justice, and because all things exist because they are conformed to the divine intellect as to their measure, which conformity constitutes their ontological truth, we see reflected then, in the physical universe, at once the justice and truth of God.

The Mercy of God

To be merciful to someone, according to St. Thomas, is simply to bring him relief in his misery; it is the alleviation of a person's pain and sorrow. This is precisely what God does when, as we say, He exercises His mercy toward His creatures. But with respect to His rational creatures, those whom He created in His own image and likeness, and whose final end is the beatific vision, the specific meaning of God's mercy as applied to them is in the perfecting action of His grace upon them. He diminishes and dispels whatever defects they have, so that they might more easily attain their end. "Insofar, then, as God gives perfection to things," St. Thomas argues, "thus driving out imperfections, He is acting mercifully towards them." [9]

Not a few people seem to think that the justice and mercy of God are incompatible, that they cancel one another out, so that if God is just He abandons mercy, and if He is merciful He thereby disregards justice. Only a moment's reflection will show this view to be quite erroneous. It goes counter to everything that we have learned about the Divine nature. If in fact God's justice and His mercy were incompatible, what would become of God's simplicity, His unity, His immutability?

We have noted the fact that God is merciful in that He gives perfection to His creatures, and removes imperfection from them. All sin is inevitably accompanied by punishment, punishment being the response to sin of God's justice. Is punishment, as the response of God's justice, incompatible with His mercy? Clearly it is not, for, as it frequently happens—if we are cooperating with God's perfecting influences upon us—it is the punishment we incur by sin which turns out to be the merciful means by which God perfects us. Not only is there no incongruity between the divine mercy and the divine justice, but, as St. Thomas contends, the works of God's mercy are actually founded on the works of God's justice. God chastises those whom He loves, perfecting them through chastisement.

CHAPTER FOURTEEN

The Omnipotence of God

The Divine Power

Much emphasis has been given over the course of this study to the fact that there is no potency to be found in the divine nature. The potency which is being referred to when that claim is made, to be more precise about the matter, is passive potency. In Scholastic literature, the Latin word used to designate passive potency is *potentia*, and in that usage a good translation of the term would be "capacity," with the understanding that the capacity in question here is the capacity to be changed, to be acted upon, to be the recipient of the effects of an active principle. But the Latin word *potentia* also serves in the literature to designate active potency, in which case the best translation of the term would be "power." When the word "potency"is applied to the divine nature, it obviously can refer only to active potency, i.e., to the divine power.

Perhaps it would be well if we were to pause briefly at this point and refresh our memories with respect to the difference between active and passive potency. With regard to created being, both active and passive potency are to be thought of as categories of accidental being (in contrast to substantial being); specifically, they are the categories of action and passion. Active potency is the capacity of a substance to act as an efficient cause and to bring about change in another substance. It is a power to effect change. Passive potency is also a capacity, but in this case it is the capacity to receive rather than to give, the capacity to be reduced to act by something that is already in act.

It is precisely because passive potency involves change, is indeed the principal condition for change, that it can have no place in the divine nature. Besides the obvious fact that change is contradictory to God's immutability, there is the added consideration that change necessarily implies imperfection, for anything that changes is in a state of privation with respect to the terminus of the change. It is thus lacking in one way or another. St. Thomas provides us with a crisp summary of these matters: "Potency can be thought of in two ways, as passive, which is not at all to be found in God, and active, which can be said to be in God in a preeminent way." [1] The preeminent presence of active potency is omnipotence.

God is powerful. We say more: God is all-powerful, or omnipotent. We can better see how this is so, indeed how this must be so, if we consider the matter in terms of active potency, which would simply be a more technical way of describing God's power. On the natural level, a substance having an active potency is able to exercise that potency precisely to the extent that it is in act with respect to that potency. For example, someone would be able to act as an efficient teacher of Greek to the extent that he knows the Greek language and is skilled in the art of teaching. But when we consider the power of God, the first thing that we must be aware of is that His power is not, as it is for natural substances, an instance of accidental being, for of course there are no accidents in God. This means that power is not something that God *has*; power is what God *is,* which is to say that it is one and the same with the divine essence. The second consideration has to do with the fact that God is Pure Act. Now, if the efficacy of the power possessed by any being is directly related to the degree to which the being is in act with respect to that power, then a being that is Pure Act, which is to say a being completely devoid of passive potency, would be an all-powerful being, for there would be no limitations whatever to his power, In sum, then, because God is Pure Act, He is omnipotent.

St. Thomas, in developing the notion that God is all-powerful precisely because He is Pure Act, comments that, "it is most fitting that He is the principle of all action, and in no way of passivity in any form." [2] If there were passivity in God, this would mean that He could be acted upon by forces external to Himself, to which, as passive, He would be subject. And with that, of course, we would have a "God" who was not truly the supreme being. By saying that God is the principle of all action, St. Thomas is calling attention to two important points. First, God, as First Cause, is the efficient cause of all creation. Second, in any relation between a being *in actu,* where there is a transmission of action from one being to the other, the action in question is manifested in the recipient of the action, that is, the being which is *in potentia* with respect to the action. So, we say that in transitive action it is the receiving, not the giving, being that is perfected. But here we must recall a point made in the previous chapter, that the transitive action of God (the action that passes from God to creatures) is virtually transitive, and not formally or really transitive. The purpose of this refining distinction is to point out that while the effects of the divine action are like those of formally transitive actions, of which we have much experience in the natural world, there is no similarity with respect to the causes of those effects—God on the one hand, and natural substances on the other. The principal difference between the two is that God, in bringing about effects external to the divine substance, remains absolutely unchanging, whereas a natural substance is always changing in one way or another, even though the agent may not be changing with respect to a particular effect it is bringing about. For example, a teacher of Greek is not necessarily perfected in his knowledge of Greek, hence he is not changing in that respect by teaching Greek to others. But he is changing in other ways.

Another interesting distinction between active and passive potency that helps us better to understand the uniqueness of God's nature is the fact that passive potency is only intelligible in relation to active potency, whereas active potency is intelligible in itself. The very notion of passivity is only comprehensible in terms of the active, but the active— more precisely, something that is in act—can be understood without reference being made to anything beyond itself. The application of this distinction to the divine power, i.e., pure act, leads to the conclusion that this power need never to have manifested itself externally in order to be, what it eternally is, perfectly and completely intelligible. God's power would not be a whit less than what it forever is had He willed never to have created the universe. The universe might serve for us as a proof of God's omnipotence, but, taken in itself, that omnipotence did not need to be demonstrated in order to be what it is.

God's Power Is Infinite

In much that has been said thus far about God's power, it is pretty evident that the divine power is infinite, a fact clearly indicated by terms like "all-powerful" and "omnipotent." But now we want to be more explicit on that point, and there are few more efficient ways of making matters explicit than by putting the salient ideas pertaining to them in the form of an argument.

> The divine essence is infinite.
> The divine power is one with the divine essence.
> Therefore, the divine power is infinite.

We have already established the truth of the major premiss, that the divine essence is infinite. The truth of the minor premiss should be evident in terns of what we said just above, although we did not elaborate on the issue. One specific proof that can be advanced, to demonstrate that the divine power is one with the divine essence, has to do with the fact that the only other alternative to God's power being one with His essence—i.e., understanding God's power as being simply what He is—would be that the divine power is something that God possesses, as an accidental quality. But this alternative is quite unacceptable for, in God, there can be no accidents. The divine power, then, is one with the divine essence. The major and minor premises both being true, the conclusion follows necessarily: the divine power is infinite.

Once again, commonly used terms such as "omnipotent," "all-powerful," and "almighty," are strongly indicative of the infinite, unbounded quality of God's power. When St. Thomas discusses the omnipotence of God, the basic idea he develops is that God can do all things. Or, to state it negatively, we say that there is nothing that God cannot do; there is nothing that is beyond the scope of His power. Despite the solidity of such a truth, there always seems to be some philosophers who are willing to take exception to the claim that God is omnipotent. Invariably, however, the terms in which they have stated their objections show a profound lack of understanding of the divine nature on their part, with the result that in some cases the problems they pose turn out to be rather ludicrous. Below are three little "arguments" that serve as illustrations of the kind of reasoning that can be sanctioned by those who would deny God's omnipotence.

> God cannot change a man into an angel.
> Therefore, God is not omnipotent.

> God cannot make $5 + 5 = 13$.
> Therefore, God is not omnipotent.

> God cannot create another God.
> Therefore, God is not omnipotent.

It should be noted that the premises (the first statements) of the three discourses express things that a believer would immediately accept as true. It is undeniably the case that God cannot change a man into an angel, nor make $5 + 5 = 13$, nor create another God, but this does not at all argue against His omnipotence. We should be fully sensitive to the connotation of the verb "cannot" in this context. What is being stated in the premises of all these arguments are absolute or intrinsic impossibilities. There is an important distinction to be made between practical impossibility and absolute impossibility. Something is said to be practically impossible if its realization involves no inherent contradiction, but circumstances are such that it is not possible, here and now, with the resources which are available, to realize it. So, we say that something is theoretically possible, but it is not feasible. Practical impossibility applies only to created beings, and serves to accentuate our limited active potential. With God, there is no practical impossibility; if there is no inherent contradiction in a proposed action, God can do it. Something is said to be absolutely impossible if its realization would involve a contradiction, which simply means that there is no possibility at all that it could ever be realized. So, to say that God cannot do the intrinsically impossible does not in the least take away from His omnipotence. And it calls special attention to His wisdom. God cannot do the intrinsically impossible because God cannot contradict Himself; He cannot repudiate His own divine wisdom. A mathematical statement like $5 + 5 = 13$ is a falsehood, a reflection of non-being, an absurdity, and can have nothing to do with the source of all being and of all truth. It is precisely because God is the source of all truth that we are able to say that $5 + 5 = 10$, for this truth, like every other, is founded in the divine essence.

Rather than speak about what God cannot do, it would be more precise, St. Thomas suggests, to refer to what God *does* not do, for there can be no question of there being any kind of infringement of the divine power. God does not make $5 + 5 = 13$ because God does not traffic in absurdity. God can do "everything that is truly possible," [3] which is to say, everything that does not involve contradiction. Something is possible if it is inherently intelligible, if it does not represent an absurdity. God "cannot" make a square circle because a square circle is a contradiction in terms. God, who is Truth, and as such the source of intelligibility—of everything, to put it plainly, that "makes sense"— does not act contrary to His own essential nature.

God is omnipotent, then, His power is infinite, in the sense that He is able to effect anything that is intrinsically possible, anything that does not go counter to the very nature of things, a nature which He Himself has established. A seeming entity such as a square circle is in reality a "nothing," an empty name having no referent in the actual world of being. So, to play with words a bit, we could describe God's omnipotence by saying that God cannot do "nothing" because there is nothing to be done. "Therefore," St. Thomas sums up, "whatever does not involve contradiction, and would thus be included among those things we call 'possibles,' are what pertain to God's omnipotence." [4]

The Exercise of the Divine Power

One of the specific questions St. Thomas raises in his discussion of God's omnipotence is whether God could effectively undo the past. It should not surprise us to learn that his response to this question is negative, but the reasons he puts forward to support that response are worth taking note of. St. Thomas shapes his argument around the principle of contradiction. "Anything that in any way involves contradiction," he writes, "cannot fall under what we call the omnipotence of God." [5] The contradiction that would be involved in the supposition that God could make happen, retrospectively as it were, what in fact did not happen—which is what undoing the past would amount to—is precisely the same kind of contradiction that we would be dealing with if the setting were either in the present or in the future. Petronius cannot be both sitting and not sitting right now, and it would make no sense to say that God could arrange it to be otherwise, no more than it would make sense to say that God could so arrange things that tomorrow Susanna, at precisely 2 P.M., will be both walking and not walking. The same principle applies to the past. Yesterday at precisely 2 P.M. Chef Yorkshire was making pudding. It could not have been the case, then, that precisely at that time he was not making pudding. Again, it would make no sense to say that God could somehow negate the contradiction and make happen what in fact did not happen. Chef Yorkshire's not making pudding yesterday at 2 P.M. is a "nothing." God has nothing to do with nothing. For God supposedly to be able to do what involves contradiction would be for Him to go directly against His own divine wisdom. God is wisdom itself. To consider it as a serious possibility that God could change the past, apart from the inherent contradiction that would entail, would imply that what has already taken place as a result of His overall providential design was somehow lacking in wisdom, and now needs to be corrected. And there is also God's immutability to keep in mind. If, *per impossibile*, God would undo the past, we would have in that state of affairs something tantamount to a "change of mind" on God's part. We would have here, then, contradiction on top of contradiction.

Can God do what in actual fact He ends up not doing? The issue being suggested by that question may not be immediately obvious, so, to make it explicit, let us advert to the example employed by St. Thomas. He cites the events that took place in the Garden of Gethsemani when Our Lord was taken prisoner. Christ tells His disciples that He could ask His Father to send more than twelve legions of angels to rescue Him from His captors, but He does not do so. The question is, then: Could He have done what He did not do? The answer, in absolute terms, is Yes. In other words, what Christ refrained from doing was fully within His power to do; it involved no intrinsic impossibility. There would have been no contradiction involved in His having done what He chose not to do.

But there is an important way in which it makes perfectly good sense to say that God can only do what He actually does. In putting it in those terms we are not suggesting that there is any limitation to the divine power. Rather, the point being made is that the divine wisdom always prevails. Whatever God wills to do is the supremely wise

272 THE OMNIPOTENCE OF GOD

thing to do. That Our Lord chose not to request angelic assistance in the Garden of Gethsemani served to pave the way, so to speak, for the events that had to follow in order to bring about the redemption of the world. However, it is important to emphasize that when we say that God can only do what He actually does, we are not implying that He is somehow necessitated to do what He actually does. God's actions are always perfectly free.

Is God's Power Always Exercised to the Best Effect?

The German philosopher Gottfried Leibniz, whom we have encountered in earlier chapters of this book, argued that the world that God actually created was "the best of all possible worlds." The point behind his assertion would seem to have been that, absolutely speaking, this was the only world that God could have created. Such a point of view must be contested. God is in no way necessitated in His creative activity. What this means, specifically, is that this is not the only world that God could have created. Indeed, there is an infinite number of other worlds, in the infinite mind of God, that He could have created.

And yet there is an element of truth in Leibniz's point of view. While we can and should say that this is not the best of all possible worlds in the sense that it is the world that God *had* to create, we could rightly call it the best of all possible worlds in the sense that, because it is the world that God actually did create, it must be a world that is perfectly consonant with the divine wisdom, a world perfectly in accord with His providential designs. In sum, we can say that this is the best world because it is the one which God willed to create, but not because it is the only one He could have created.

Could God make something better than it is? The answer is No, *if* His doing so would involve changing the very nature of the being in question. For God to do something like that would be totally at variance with the dictates of divine wisdom. Every nature that God creates is good, precisely as He creates it. Of course, God can, through the action of His grace, make something better than it is in the sense that He perfects its nature. As we saw in the previous chapter, this perfecting influence of the divine action is what we mean by God's mercy. But changing the very nature of a being, making it something other than what it essentially is, would obviously not be making a particular being better. Such an operation would involve the annihilation of the proper nature of the being in question. The example St. Thomas uses to illustrate this line of reasoning goes something like this: God could not make a quartet better by adding another member to the ensemble, for by that addition it would cease to be a quartet and become a quintet. We would end up with, not an improved quartet, but something entirely other than a quartet. [6]

Creation

From our point of view, as creatures, nothing more emphatically proclaims the power of God than creation. God is the explanatory source of everything that exists. There is absolutely nothing that exists, from quarks to galaxies and beyond, that does not owe its existence to the creative action of God. St. Thomas quotes St. Paul to give dramatic stress to this fundamental truth: "From Him, and through Him, and in Him all things exist." [7]

All creatures are in possession of real being, but it is creaturely being they possess, which is to say, to use a more technical term, participated being. Participated being, or contingent being is, we remind ourselves, being that does not bear within itself the explanation for its own existence; it therefore owes its existence to another. St. Thomas states the case in precise terms: "What we have, then, is a situation in which every being other than God is a being whose essence does not entail existence, which is to say that all beings except God 'participate in being.' It is therefore necessary that with regard to all these beings which differ from one another according to the different ways they participate in being, and as such are more or less perfect, it is necessary, I say, that all these beings have a single, principal and most perfect cause." [8] When St. Thomas speaks of beings that are more or less perfect according to the different ways they participate in being, he is referring to the fact that some beings more perfectly imitate the divine essence than do others, according to how God created them to be. Rational beings, beings created in the image and likeness of God because of their possession of intellect and will, are more perfect than non-rational beings.

The ancient Greeks took it to be something like a truism that matter was eternal. According to their view of things, the physical universe in which we live, at least in terms of the material stuff out of which it was formed, had no beginning, nor would it have an end. The idea of creation, as we understand it, would have been quite foreign to all ancient peoples, a fact that is not contradicted by the various "creation narratives" which many cultures have passed down to us. Despite the name given to them, however, these are not creation narratives at all. They would be more accurately described as construction narratives, for in every case the divine fabricator starts with something. There is no bringing of being out of nothing. Two examples of these so-called creation narratives emerge from ancient Greece, in the form of the *Theogony*, by Hesiod, and the *Timaeus*, by Plato. In both cases, "in the beginning" there is chaos, which is to say, disorganized matter. In Plato's *Timaeus*, the demiurge (a primitive god of some sort) constructs the universe by using the materials at hand which are provided him by chaos. He makes an orderly system, a cosmos (the Greek word *kosmos* means "order"), but the material for this monumental project had been in existence from all eternity. In the beginning, then, there is chaos; there is something, not nothing.

Our understanding of creation precludes any preexisting matter, but might we not say that it would be consonant with Scholastic metaphysics to claim that when God created the world, while He did not begin with matter as we ordinarily understand it (what metaphysicians call secondary matter), He did begin with primary matter, which is to say, the principle of pure potentiality? According to this way of looking at creation, God would have created the multiple substantial forms that identify individual things and their natures, and then these substantial forms would have been received by the already existing primary matter. This would be, in fact, a quite erroneous interpretation of divine creation. Among other problems with this point of view that could be cited, it implies, in the pre-creation presence of primary matter, something which is over and apart from, and presumably independent of, God. Creation is thus turned into what might be called a joint venture, with God cooperatively working with primary matter. But God, when He creates, begins with literally nothing, not even a principle of pure potentiality. Primary matter, then, is not something which is antecedent to creation, but is itself a product of creation. God creates primary matter when He creates the world, as a principle intrinsic to secondary matter.

God's creation is *ex nihilo*, "from nothing"; that phrase reveals the very essence of what we mean by creation. We must take care not to think that the phrase "from nothing" refers to something that is somehow existing before creation, such as, for example, in the form of the chaos of the ancient Greeks, or in the form of primary matter. St. Thomas cautions us that we should not make "something" out of "nothing." "He who makes out of nothing," he pointedly observes, "does not make out of something." [9] What the phrase *ex nihilo* is intended to convey is the idea that before God's creative act there was no being, no thing existing, then, following upon that act, there was being. Creation might be imagined, albeit only very imperfectly, as the sequence of two pictures. The first picture is actually not a picture at all; imagine it as simply a blank. The second picture is teeming with being. The first "picture" is blank because it represents the situation before creation, when there was nothing. The second picture represents the situation at the moment of creation. There is no transition from the first picture to the second, but a replacement of one by the other. There is simply the first picture, then there is the second picture.

I used the phrase "before God's creative act" just above, but, to be really strict about the matter, that form of expression, which we cannot avoid, is inaccurate, for there was no "before" in relation to creation. "Before" is a temporal term, and time began with creation. When God creates a being He creates it in its totality, essence and existence together, and, if it is a material being, matter and form together.

In earlier pages of this work we made note of the fact that St. Thomas concurred with the Augustinian notion that what Plato referred to as the Ideas or Forms, and erroneously took to be independently existing eternal substances, were in fact eternal exemplars, or ideas, in the mind of God. In discussing creation, St. Thomas notes that the ideas in the divine intellect serve as the exemplary causes with regard to God's creative activity. To gain some understanding of what he means by that, think in terms of a human artist who is guided, in his "creative" activity, by the ideas he has in his mind. The artist seeks to realize those ideas in what he produces, so that the work of art is, as it were, his ideas made flesh. Now, because of the simplicity of God, St. Thomas is led to remark that, "God is the first exemplary cause of all things." [10] God Himself, the divine essence, is *the* exemplary cause. In another place he speaks in terms of multiple exemplary causes, or divine ideas. "In the divine wisdom," he writes, "there is to be found the generating models for all things, which we referred to above as *ideas*, that is to say, the exemplary forms in the divine mind." [11] The conflict here between one and many is only apparent. The claim that there are many ideas in the divine mind does not contradict the divine simplicity, once we see that the multiplicity enters the picture only as a means by which we attempt to grasp the operations of the divine nature. To be more precise, the multiplicity here is viewed from the point of view of the many things that God has actually created, understood as multiple imitations of the one, perfectly simple divine essence. The ideas in the divine intellect, therefore, are not many as they would be, for example, in the human intellect. Let us recall what we learned in this regard apropos of the divine intellect. In a human mind, many ideas mean many species (the mental images by which we grasp the nature of things), but in the divine intellect there is but a single species, which is the divine essence itself. So it is by a single species, a single "idea," which is again the divine essence itself, that God creates a multitude of things.

God, as the creator of all things, is the First Cause, the ultimate explanation for everything that exists. But He is also the final cause of creation. One of the ways we can explain God's creative act, by which He brings into existence beings other than Himself, is to speak of it as a diffusion of the divine goodness, to which reference was made in earlier pages. Creation can be regarded, then, as an over-flowing of the divine bounty, but an over-flowing, it is important to note, which takes place as a result of a free act of the divine will. The divine goodness is the "reason" for creation in the sense that it is both the source and the end of creation. God's goodness, which is to say simply God Himself, would of course not be an end that is somehow external to Himself. This being the case, we can say that God created for the sake of Himself, or, more precisely, for the sake of His goodness. But, we recall, the goodness in question here is supreme goodness, whose nature is to diffuse, to share, itself, so that, as St. Thomas puts it, God, in creating, "intends only to communicate His perfection, which is His goodness."[12] God created because He willed that other beings should know His goodness, which they do, on the most primitive level, simply by the fact that they exist.

We have already made clear that the correct understanding of creation turns on the phrase *ex nihilo*, "from nothing." Before God's creative act, the only being in existence was God Himself. In an earlier attempt to explain the nature of creation, we cited the erroneous view that God "created" by visiting a multitude of substantial forms upon an already existing primary matter, thus "informing" that matter. There is another erroneous view concerning creation that must be noted. It is closely associated with the philosophy of Neoplatonism, which dates to the third century A.D. According to Neoplatonic doctrine, all the physical things we see in the world came to be, ultimately, as the result of an "emanation," or flowing out, of the very being of God. The most important thing to note about this emanation of being from the divine substance is that it is not the result of an act of the divine will. It comes about by necessity.

It is easy to see that this idea of emanation has nothing to do with creation as properly understood. It is subject to many criticisms, but we will here cite but two items which have a special bearing on our discussion. First of all, the idea of emanation is diametrically opposed to the idea that God's creative action is totally free. God is not necessitated to create, not even by His very essence, nor, *a fortiori*, by anything external to Himself. Second, by the act of creation, God establishes in existence beings that are completely distinct from Himself. The Neoplatonic notion of emanation implies no real demarcation between divine being and created being, so that what supposedly flows forth in emanation can only be the divine essence itself, so that "creatures" are not really creatures, which is to say, beings really distinct from God. What we have, then, is divinity spread out, as it were, throughout the entire universe, with the inescapable result that the universe itself must be regarded as divine; the universe is God. This, of course, is pantheism. [13]

Creation is not to be confused with generation. In the case of the latter, where, for example, man generates man, we have a case of univocal causation, which means that the effect (children) is the same nature as the cause (parents). God of course does not create a being that is the same nature as Himself, for that would be as if God were creating another God, which is a metaphysical impossibility. We say, then, that God, as creator, is an equivocal cause of what He creates, which means that His creatures have natures which are totally other than His own.

Given the fact that God is immutable, it is evident that, in creating, God does not undergo any change. But may we say that creation itself represents a change? At first blush, it may seem that creation does indeed involve change, but if we attempt to explain how that might be so, we end up by saying that it is a change from non-being to being. However, there is no such thing. If we pause to review the Aristotelian analysis of change, we will recall that before any change can take place there must be a subject of the change, i.e., something that is able to undergo change. Change is a transition from one state of being to another, and it is just that fact that tells us why there can be no change in creation, for, in creation, there is no subject that is undergoing any kind of transition. In creation, the subject *begins* with the creative act. After that, it will of course undergo countless changes. But before the creative act, once again, there is simply nothing. We commonly use the term "creation" to describe human artistic activity, but in this usage the term can only be understood figuratively, not literally, for the human artist must always begin with matter of some form or another. The artist then works on that matter to give it a new form, according to the exemplary causes which are the ideas which guide his artistic activity. And, needless to say, change is an inextricable part of human artistry, for, among other things, what the artist does in producing a new form is to realize a passive potency in the matter he works with. And the artist himself undergoes any number of changes over the course of his artistic activity.

The act of creation establishes a relation of the deepest and most intimate kind between creature and Creator, a relation of utter dependency. A relation sets up a dependency, a dependency upon the term of the relation on the part of the subject of the relation. A woman can be called a wife only because she has a husband. She is the subject of the relation; her husband is the term of the relation. She, as a wife, is dependent on the term of the relation because the only rationale for her being identified as a wife is the fact that she has a husband. It would make no sense to call an unmarried woman a wife. It is because of this peculiar dependency that is set up by the very nature of a relation, a dependency of the subject upon the term of the relation, that we say that God cannot be the subject of a relation. If He were to be so, He would then be dependent upon the term of the relation. In other words, while creatures are related to God in a manner which makes them totally dependent upon God, God is not related to His creatures, for that would imply that He is dependent upon His creatures.

From time to time over the course of history there have been certain thinkers, and some of them rather formidable thinkers, who took the position that God delegates His creative powers to a number of His superior creatures, specifically, to angels. According to this point of view, God acts as the principal cause of the creative activity, and the delegated angels serve as instrumental causes. But this raises insuperable problems. In terms of what we know of instrumental causality, as we see it operative on the natural plane, the instrumental cause, besides receiving all its power and direction from the principal cause, always works on some definite material substance. But in this case we are talking about an instrumental cause that, albeit indirectly, supposedly brings being into existence out of nothing. But to create, to evoke being where there were no antecedents of any kind, is an act which only an omnipotent being can effect, an omnipotent being acting without any intermediary. Creation is "proper" to God, meaning that it belongs to Him and to no other being. One of the aspects of St. Thomas's ample argument against this position is his development of the principle that the more universal are the effects, the more universal must be the cause that produces those effects. He explains what he means by "more universal" effects. "But among all the effects we can consider, the most universal is being itself. Therefore, this is the proper effect that is fitting for only the first and most universal cause, which is God."[14] Indeed, what is more universal, in the sense of more foundational, than being itself? Putting St. Thomas's point in other terms, we can say that being, actual existence, is the most supreme of effects. Given this to be the case, only a supreme cause, the First Cause, can bring about such an effect.

We have been continuously referring to God as the one and only agent of creative activity. But in light of the revealed doctrine of the Holy Trinity, are we not perhaps better advised to be more precise in this matter, and rather than referring to God as the creator, should we not refer to one or another Person of the Trinity? No. St. Thomas maintains that, strictly speaking, it is the Blessed Trinity as such who creates. "To create," he writes, "is something which is proper to God in terms of His 'to be,' which is His very essence, which in turn is the community of the Three Persons. Therefore, to create is not peculiar to any Person, but is common to the Blessed Trinity as a whole." [15] If we are right then to attribute creation to the Blessed Trinity as such, we may argue, with St. Augustine, that there are to be found vestiges, or traces, of the Trinity within the created world, and especially in rational creatures. St. Thomas shows that he thinks along Augustinian lines in this respect, as is evident when he writes: "In rational creatures, therefore, who are possessed of intellect and will, there is to be found a representation of the Trinity in the form of images, because in them we can distinguish between the word, the idea, and the love which proceeds form both." [16] It is as if the Trinitarian God, in creating man, left the stamp of His Trinitarian nature upon him. St. Thomas's argument is a poignant one. The Trinity is reflected in our intellectual and volitional powers, those powers that mark us as having been created in the image and likeness of God. The words we speak are the images of our ideas, just as the Word is the image of the Father. And just as love follows upon what we know, by our willing those things that are represented by our words and ideas, and binding them together as it were, so the Holy Ghost proceeds from the Father and the Son as the Love of both.

Conservation

We tend to think of creation, particularly the creation of the universe, as something that happened "way back then." In a sense, it did, as viewed from our perspective, a perspective which is unavoidably framed by temporal considerations. Time is linear, and the creation of the world did happen a long time ago, indeed when time itself began. But we must remember that God is eternal. Creation did not happen a long time ago for God, because for God there is no such thing as time, long or short. Creation, for God, is happening in His eternal now. Looking at things from our point of view, we make a distinction between creation and conservation. We say that first God creates, then He conserves what He has created, maintaining in existence by the continuing influence of His power the beings that He had brought into existence. Such, then, is the basic idea behind conservation: that God keeps in existence what He initially put in existence. As a result of his own careful reflections on the relation between creation and conservation, St. Thomas comes to the conclusion that, "It should be said that the conservation of things in being is not a new action, but a continuation of that action that gives being." [17] With that observation in mind, we may rightly think of conservation as continuing, or extended, creation. Obviously, there would be no entrance into being for us without God's creative power, but it is equally obvious, or at least should be, that we could not remain in being without God's conserving power. It is God who sustains our existence every moment of our lives. This profound and thought-provoking truth, that "creatures are conserved in being by God," [18] is, St. Thomas teaches, something that we know by faith, but it is a truth that we can also come to know through natural reason.

In reflecting on this issue, St. Thomas notes that there are two ways that we can understand conservation, as a process that is carried out either directly or indirectly. Indirect conservation is manifested in those situations where something that is already in existence is preserved and protected so that it may remain in existence. So, what we know as a "conservationist" is someone who conserves in this manner; he seeks to preserve this or that aspect of the natural world, an endangered animal species, say, or a wetlands area in a given geographical locale. Someone who conserves something indirectly is not responsible for the very existence of that which he seeks to conserve. The conservationist did not bring a particular animal species into being; his intention is simply to prevent it from passing out of being.

Only God can exercise direct conservation. This is the kind of conservation by which a being is preserved in being in the absolute sense, from moment to moment, so that it does not lapse into nothingness. We can imagine a particular conservationist, of the kind described above, who could lose interest in trying to keep a particular endangered species in being, and ceases his efforts to do so. That does not mean that the endangered species in question is necessarily doomed. But should God withdraw his conserving influence from a being, the being would immediately cease to be. A fetching example that St. Thomas uses to illustrate direct conservation is an atmosphere, a given volume of air, that is illumined by the sun. So long as the sun shines, the atmosphere is illumined, but as soon as the sun's rays are withdrawn, the light is gone. The atmosphere, we might say, is alive with light as long as the sun shines, but it dies into darkness when the source of its life ceases to act upon the atmosphere. "Every creature is so dependent upon God that it could not remain in existence for a single moment,"

St. Thomas writes, quoting St. Gregory, "but would instantaneously lapse into nothingness unless the operations of the divine power were to preserve it in being." [19] In the *Summa Contra Gentiles* he expands upon this notion, bringing in the elementary distinction between essence and existence. "The existence of any created thing is explained neither by its nature nor by its essence—it is only in God that essence and existence are one. This being so, were the divine operation to cease [i.e., were God's conserving influence to be withdrawn], no created thing would be able to remain in existence." [20]

If we consider conservation from the point of view of causation, we say that the causation that is operative in God's conservation of His creation is causation with respect to being itself, so God's causative influence must be continuing if the being who is the recipient of that influence is to continue in being. This is to be contrasted with the type of causality which human beings are able to exercise, whereby we bring things into existence through our activity, but that activity does not have to continue in order that what has been brought into existence is to remain in existence. Take the example of a builder who builds a house. The causative action of the builder is necessary, otherwise no house will ever be brought into existence. But once the building process is completed and the house is finished, no further causative action on the part of the builder is necessary in order that the house might continue to exist. There are countless sturdy houses now doing excellent service for their inhabitants whose builders have long since departed from this life. With God it is quite different, for He creates; He does not construct. His causation brings into being in the absolute sense, but His causative influence does not cease with that. It is necessary that His causative action continue, so that what He brought into existence will remain in existence. God causes the very existence of things, and He causes the continuing existence of things.

There is an important distinction to be noted with regard to God's creative and conserving power. As we have seen, God and God alone can create, and without intermediaries. It is also true that, in the most fundamental sense, God and God alone can conserve a creature in being, for only His power is sufficient to prevent being from lapsing into non-being. But God wills to make use of secondary causes in effecting His conserving power. The dedicated conservationist is thus acting as a secondary cause in his conserving activities, although he may not be aware of the fact. A more poignant example of how creatures act as secondary causes in participating in God's conserving activity is to be found in the care and protection that parents bestow upon their children, particularly when they are very young and in an exceptionally vulnerable state.

Could God reduce a rational being to nothingness, simply by withdrawing from it His conserving influence? If by the question we mean, Is it within God's power to annihilate such a being, then the answer is Yes. And there is the additional consideration that, just as God is not necessitated to create, neither is He necessitated to conserve. On the other hand, just as it is His inextinguishable love that explains His will to create, so too it is His inextinguishable love that explains His will to conserve. Practically speaking, then, there is nothing to worry about. Annihilation is not a possibility because it is not something that God would ever will. There are any number of arguments that could be put forward to support this position. We could, for example, develop an argument that would employ God's immutability as a major premiss. We could also appeal to a point that was established earlier with respect to the divine will, to the effect that God, unlike human beings, does not negate any of His acts of will. His acts of will have the permanence of eternity itself. But it is specifically God's goodness that St. Thomas chooses to focus upon in arguing that God would not annihilate a creature originally destined to live with Him forever. God will never "forget" any one of His creatures, because of His infinite goodness. It was God's goodness that called us into being, and it is that goodness that keeps us in being—forever. "To reduce any existing being to nothing," St. Thomas observes, "simply does not square with the divine beneficence. Furthermore, nothing more emphatically demonstrates the divine goodness, and the divine power, than the conserving of things in being." [21] And he adds to that observation the thought that the power of God "is maximally displayed by His conserving things in being." [22]

A brief word on the subject of concurrence, which is closely related to conservation, which in turn, as we have seen, is closely related to creation, the latter two being so closely related, in fact, that one can consider them to be a single act, as looked at from different points of view. The basic difference between creation/conservation, on the one hand, and concurrence, on the other, is that the first has to do with God's causative action as effecting the very existence of a being, whereas concurrence is God's causative action as it enables an existing being to act. Recall the metaphysical distinction between first act and second act that was discussed earlier. First act is the act by which a thing exists; second act is that by which a thing behaves. In light of that distinction, we can say that creation/conservation relates to first act, and concurrence relates to second act. We could not exist without God's power; we could not act without God's power. God is the primary cause of our actions, meaning that He empowers us to act, but, as free agents, it is we who act, and it is we who are responsible for how we act.

CHAPTER FIFTEEN

The Providence of God

Providence: A Divine Operation with External Effects

All of the divine operations are, in the strictest sense, immanent operations, meaning that they have both their source and their absolute finality within the divine essence. But, as we saw earlier, in our discussion of the divine will, certain of the divine operations are said to be virtually transitive in that they result in effects that are external to the divine essence. And it is from the point of view of these effects that we refer to a divine operation as virtually transitive, for it is in that respect that a divine operation is like transitive action as we know it in the natural order. The act of creation would be the most prominent example of such an operation. Divine providence, the subject of this, the final chapter of our book, would be another example of a virtually transitive divine operation, for the effects of divine providence are very much external to the divine essence and are very much in evidence to us, everywhere present as they are in the world in which we live. The providence of God, regarded in the most general terms, can be described as the comprehensive manifestation of God's action as directed toward His creation.

The Definition of Providence

In order to arrive at a more precise definition of divine providence, we will begin with a little lesson in etymology. The Latin word *providentia*, from which is derived the English word "providence," means "foresight," or "foreknowledge." The Latin noun comes from the verb *providere*, which means "to see in the distance," or "to discern." With this background, perhaps we can better appreciate why it is that when we speak of a provident person we have in mind someone who is forward looking, someone who has the capacity to anticipate what is coming and then—this would be the crucial quality—is able to take appropriate action in order to be adequately prepared for what eventually comes to pass. The provident person is able to act in this fashion, St. Thomas adds, because (a) he makes good use of his memory, and (b) he is fully alert to present circumstances. Because he keeps freshly in mind how things have happened in the past, because he keenly sizes up what is going on right at the moment, the provident person is able to make very reliable judgments as to what will happen in the future. The ability to look ahead, we might then say, is based on the ability to look back, and to look around.

When we make reference to the providence of God we are, again speaking in general terms, calling attention to God's protective care for His creation. Let us recall the basic points already established concerning the divine nature. God, as Prime Mover, moves every individual thing that He has created toward its ultimate end, an end that it has in common with the whole of creation, and that end is God Himself. He does this for each individual creature considered separately, and He does it for all creatures taken together. Everything, without exception, is under God's providential care. God exercises His divine providence without any necessitation that arises from the divine nature. He simply acts, as St. Thomas puts it, from the divine intellect and from the divine will, which, as we know, are one with the divine essence. And it is just that divine knowing and willing directing of things to their proper ends which is the heart of what we call providence.

In our discussion of creation we saw that God is at once the Alpha and the Omega, the source and the end of all things. Specifically with respect to the fact that God is the end of all things—He is, ultimately, what the whole of creation is *for*—we may be permitted to say that it is then only logical that God should govern all things, for the purpose of that governance is to direct all things to their ultimate end. Because all things are ordered toward God, God takes care to ensure that the ordering process itself (i.e., God's providential governance) shall be fully realized and in no way frustrated.

The provident person, we said, is one who looks ahead, and who makes provisions for what he sees coming. With God there is of course no looking ahead, for there is no future with God. He subsists absolutely in the eternal now, and in that eternal now everything is always before His eyes. But the divine regard is not purely speculative; it is practical as well. God looks upon His creation protectively.

Divine Providence and Finality

We make a distinction between divine providence and divine governance; this is a logical distinction, one we rely upon in order better to understand the divine nature. By divine providence we refer to God's plan, as existing in the divine intellect, for the ordered direction of the whole of creation to its final end, which is God Himself. Divine providence is called immediate, which simply means that it is the plan as known by God without any mediation. Divine providence might be described as a feature of God's knowledge of Himself. By divine governance we refer to the execution, the actual working out in the created world, of God's providential plan. We say that divine governance is mediate because it is carried out through the mediation of creatures, which God makes use of in the process of governing. Another way divine providence and divine governance can be distinguished is to say that the first is in eternity, while the second is in time.

It is finality, or final causality, that fully reveals to us the natures of things. St. Thomas accordingly observes that things are not only good in themselves, but they are also good in terms of their being ordered toward their proper ends, but most especially are they good in terms of their being ordered toward their ultimate end, which is God Himself. The goodness of things resides in their finality, that for the sake of which they exist. And therein we have encapsulated the rationale, as it were, for divine providence. The plan for God's ordering of things toward their ends preexists in the divine intellect, and again, it is precisely that plan which we call divine providence, as St. Thomas makes plain: "Providence in the proper sense is just that plan for ordering things toward their end." [1] Providence, we may say, with the notion of finality particularly in mind, is God's plan for a comprehensive realization of finality.

We might compare the execution of divine providence to the way prudence functions in a human agent. Actually, the two are very closely bound up with one another. The provident person we described above is also an eminently prudent person. Now, when a human agent, through the exercise of prudence, orders things that are external to himself to their final ends, we can recognize a similarity between that process and the manner in which divine providence is exercised. With respect to divine providence, things are not ordered to anything external to the divine essence, but to the divine essence itself. On both the human level and the divine level we find an ordering toward ends; the difference is that, on the human level, the ends are external to the ordering agent, whereas on the divine level the ordering is, once again, always toward God Himself.

More than once St. Thomas discovers in the writings of the philosopher Boethius definitions of which he approves, and readily incorporates them into his own arguments. We saw that to be the case with regard to Boethius's definition of eternity, and it proves to be the case again with regard to the Roman philosopher's definition of providence. "Providence," Boethius wrote, "is the divine intellect itself, placed supremely over all things as their principle, and disposing all things."[2] We can immediately detect in that definition an implied allusion to the distinction between providence and governance, between the plan and the execution of the plan. It is God's knowledge, the divine intellect, which contains everything that is intended for the created world. Boethius aptly refers to the divine intellect as the principle of all things, meaning that the divine intellect is the originating source of all things, that from which all things proceed. In the second part of the definition, where he speaks of the divine intellect as disposing all things, reference is being made to execution, the actual ordering of all things to their ends.

Everything Is Contained Within the Embrace of
Divine Providence

Nothing in existence exists in any way, or operates as an existing thing, outside the domain of divine providence. The providential plan is absolute, comprehensive, unfailingly inclusive. There have been some thinkers, such as the ancient Greek philosophers Democritus (c. 460–c. 370 B.C.) and Epicurus (c. 341–270 B.C.), who, as St. Thomas notes, taught that the universe was brought about by chance. Now, needless to say, this is a point of view which is completely contrary to the notion of divine providence, for if divine providence means anything at all, it means that God is the source of everything that exists and that He exercises continuing care for His creation, ordering everything toward its proper end. Furthermore, given the fact that He who orders is omniscient and omnipotent, there is no possibility that this ordering process could be interrupted or frustrated by chance events. What God orders is always successfully ordered. Now, reflecting upon the phenomenon we call chance, we detect in it two salient aspects: the frustration of ends (which constitutes a disruption of order); ignorance on our part as to the cause of a chance event. To maintain that the universe came about by chance is to say that it had a cause that did not encompass within it an intended end. In other words, it was not the result of a specific plan preexisting in the divine intellect, a plan that was realized by a free act of the divine will. Other thinkers, St. Thomas notes, admitted that there was providence in the universe, but they claimed that it applied to spiritual substances only, not to material substances. We will return to this point presently.

In arguing against the notion that chance could in any way serve as the explanation for the governance of the universe, St. Thomas makes the common sense observation that all empirical evidence clearly demonstrates such an explanation to be egregiously wrong-headed. Chance can be identified as a surprising departure from the orderly (and therefore the predictable); chance is the exception to the rule. But what do we see as the dominant reality everywhere about us in the universe? It is not disorder, but order. To claim that chance governs things, then, would be like saying that exceptions to the rule somehow dominate the rule itself, that rare occurrences which are unpredictable trump what occurs on a regular basis and thus can be confidently predicted because of our knowledge of the laws of nature. St. Thomas gives special stress to the point that the prevailing order of the universe stands as an overwhelming repudiation of the claim that chance is the governing factor in that universe. Order is that which prevails. Chance is the direct antithesis of order. If chance is the governing factor, and is the direct antithesis to order, how is it able to give rise to order?

The very meaning of universe, of cosmos, is an ordered whole, the opposite of chaos, where chance does indeed dominate. The fact is, it is impossible that chance could govern an orderly universe, and, that being the case, it is incredible to suppose that it could ever bring an orderly universe into existence.

The erroneousness of the views propounded by Democritus and Epicurus should be obvious enough, that is, once we have a correct understanding of the nature of chance. To posit chance as an initiating cause is simply to posit a metaphysical impossibility; it is to do nothing else but commit oneself to contradiction.[3] However, the practice, dating to the ancient world, continues to this day. But the other view, which claims that divine providence is not universal and that it applies only to spiritual substances, is just as erroneous, for if, as it is claimed, the physical world does not fall under the protective care of divine providence, then the infiniteness and the omnipotence of God are called into question. The infinite and omnipotent God is not in the least bit limited in directing His creation toward its final end. Everything without exception comes under God's providence, St. Thomas reminds us, "not in some general way only, but specifically, with respect to each individual existing thing."[4] We might be reminded, in hearing that, of what we learned about the peculiar nature of the divine knowledge, to the effect that God knows things, not only as genera, or as species, but as individuals. St. Thomas's comment seems to anticipate a seriously defective understanding of divine providence which was to gain prominence in the eighteenth century, and was especially fostered by the Deists. A specious distinction was established by them between general providence and particular providence. They affirmed general providence, but rejected what they called particular providence as a fiction. General providence was the divine governance of nature as a whole, a governance which was manifested in the regularities of nature, the ordering and controlling effects produced by the physical laws. Particular providence was the supposed loving care which God extends to each and every one of His creatures. In denying particular providence, the Deists denied as well the efficacy of petitionary prayer. In all, there was a decidedly cold and impersonal quality to this view of providence. God was not a loving Father, but rather something like a master engineer who, after constructing the elaborate machine which is the universe and setting it in motion, then left it to continue on its own, Himself thereafter maintaining an attitude very much like indifference toward creation, especially towards those earthly creatures called human beings. The basic idea behind the distinction between general providence and particular providence was that God showed care (after a fashion) for the whole, but not for the parts that composed the whole. This theological theory thus contains at its heart a rather large inconsistency, for it is difficult to see how care for a whole does not necessarily include care for the parts of a whole.

If we recall the basic nature of contingent being, being, that is, which is completely dependent upon God for its very existence, and if we recall that every single created being can be nothing else but a contingent being, then it is immediately evident to us that God's providence must apply to every individual being. Contingent beings are beings that *are not* their existence; their nature is not "to be." Contingent beings participate in existence, as something which has been given to them through the creative act. And thus, "it is necessary that everything," St. Thomas writes, "to the extent that it participates in being, is, just to that extent, subject to divine providence."[5] Indeed, the subjection of contingent being to divine providence is foundational, just by reason of the fact that contingent being depends upon God for its very existence.

Can There Be Many Governors of the Universe?

We saw above that what principally distinguishes providence and governance is that the former is immediate and the latter is mediate. Providence is the divine plan for creation, and it is immediate in the sense that it is one with the divine intellect. God knows the plan simply by knowing Himself, and, needless to say, He is the origin of the plan. Providence is not external to God, as if it were something that He Himself were subject to. We call divine governance mediate because God, in executing the divine plan in time, makes use of secondary causes in doing so. Does the fact that God employs His creatures to assist Him in carrying out His providential plan mean that there is then more than one governor of the universe? It does not. There can be only a single governor of the universe, and that is of course God. If we consider the matter from the point of view of causality, as does St. Thomas, we say that although there are multiple instrumental causes (i.e., the many creatures whose actions contribute to the carrying out of the divine plan), there is but one primary cause. Approaching the matter from a different angle, and guided by an idea that is essential to governance—i.e., the ordering of things to their proper ends—then from this angle too we see that governance can only be effected by a single governor. The way St. Thomas develops this line of reasoning is particularly interesting. To order things toward their proper end simply means, for him, to order them to what is best for them. The goal of any ordering process, then, is the best. Now, the best, he argues, cannot be achieved by many governors; only a single governor can achieve what is best. It is almost as if he is saying that if a committee were to be put in charge of governing the universe, even a committee made up of the most elevated of spiritual beings, it would not be able to accomplish the task. But if we think of "the best" in more concrete terms, we realize that it is nothing else than the ultimate final end of all creatures, which is God Himself. The best, then, is quintessentially "one," and therefore only the quintessentially "one" can achieve it. To put it in plainer terms, only God can properly order all things to God.

So, then, God's governance is one, as reflecting the perfect unity that is God. Granting that, it is no contradiction to go on to say that there are multiple expressions of God's singular governance, in the form of the various specific means by which He leads all things back to Himself as to their final end. St. Thomas cites as a specific instance of the divine governance the fact that God preserves creatures in the good they already possess, such as would be the case when He preserves a soul in a state of sanctifying grace. His governance would also be exemplified in those instances where God moves a soul to seek higher degrees of perfection. Yet another example cited by St. Thomas is reflected in those situations in which the moral goodness of one person has a salutary effect on the behavior of another person. He is referring to the common experience of good example, and it is an engaging thought that he sees this as an instance of divine providence at work in the world. The good example of one person might be the occasion for another person's abandoning a life of vice, or, less radically, of bidding goodbye to moral mediocrity and making a serious commitment to the pursuit of perfection. This last example clearly reveals the mediate quality of divine providence, whereby God uses His creatures to fulfill His divine plan.

The diverse ways by which God governs His creatures can be said to be a fitting response by God to the diversity which is actually to be found among those creatures, a diversity which is there, of course, because of God's creative action. The diversity to be found among creatures can be said to represent , in however imperfect and oblique a manner, the infinite richness of the divine essence itself. God governs by a single art, as St. Thomas expresses it, but that single art is sufficient for meeting the needs of all the diverse beings which are to be found in the universe and which are the recipients of that divine art. [6]

Mediated Divine Governance

We must now consider more closely the mediated quality of divine governance. To repeat, we describe the divine governance as mediated because God exercises it through the mediation of His creatures. God is both the cause and the governor of everything that exists. Things exist only because they were created by God, and nothing is able to remain in existence without divine governance. But when we reflect upon the fact that God exercises His divine governance mediately, do we not discover in that fact something which could be said to diminish the divine sovereignty and omnipotence? And are we even to think that the reason God exercises His governance mediately is because He simply has no choice but to do so, the governance of the universe being a task that is too huge for Him, and which He can therefore accomplish only with the cooperation of His creatures?

Clearly, questions of that sort reflect a woefully inadequate way of viewing this matter. In responding to the mode of thinking represented by those questions, St. Thomas pursues two lines of reasoning. He begins by reminding us that the whole idea of governance is to lead the governed to perfection. Recall the point alluded to above, to the effect that the end of governance is the best. How is the best to be achieved, in practical terms? For St. Thomas, one very specific practical expedient that can be taken by a governor in order to perfect the governed is to communicate his own perfection to the governed. And this is precisely what God does with respect to His creatures, but in more cases than not He does this indirectly, through the mediation of creatures. But does not this indirect method of communication detract from the intrinsic efficacy of that which is being communicated? Not at all. A gallon of milk could be gotten to your house by being brought directly there by a dairy farmer, or the milk could arrive at your doorstep indirectly, through the mediation of various wholesalers and retailers. Should the milk come to you indirectly, it is no less milk, it is no less nourishing, no less perfective of your physical person.

It is noteworthy that St. Thomas argues that God's providential care for the world is expressed in a special way by reason of the fact that He chooses to exercise that care mediately. He uses an arresting example to illustrate this point. A good teacher teaches others, he says, not simply so that his pupils might become learned, but so that they might one day become teachers themselves and in their turn bring learning to others. God is as it were the Master Teacher, who makes use of a whole array of assistant teachers, His creatures, through whose actions the wisdom of the Master Teacher is communicated. And it is precisely because creatures cooperate in the execution of the providential plan that they themselves come to have a keener understanding of and appreciation for the beauty of that plan. It is because all of us, in one way or another, act as the instruments of God's governance of the world, that we become more vividly aware of how we are all caught up in and carried along by the providential care of God. Parents who conscientiously show loving care for their children are especially sensitive to the poignant truth that we are all children of God.

St. Thomas makes another comment on this question, almost in passing, which is worth pausing over. Let us suppose that things were different from what they actually are, and that God were to govern the world immediately, without any assistance from creatures. St. Thomas maintains that God's direct, immediate governance of the universe would actually detract from the causal perfection of things. How is that so? Given such a state of affairs, God would be the one and only real cause in the universe. Now, to be sure, God, as Creator, is the First Cause of all that exists, but as Creator He brought into existence creatures that are themselves real causes (secondary causes in relation to the First Cause) because they are the originating sources of their actions, and as real causal agents they are imitative of the divine essence in a special way. As secondary causes they are dependent on the First Cause for their ability to operate causally, but if they are creatures who are endowed with intellect and will, then for that reason they are closer, in being, to the divine essence, and can thus imitate His causality more perfectly.

Rational creatures exercise causality as free agents; they are not only conscious of the fact that they are cooperating with God's providential plan, but they can actively will to do so, and for that reason they are endowed by God with a special dignity. But now, if it were the case, as we are supposing, that God is the one and only true cause in the universe (i.e., if He governed the universe immediately, not mediately), then there would be no secondary causes of any kind, there would be no truly free acts on the part of creatures, and the special dignity with which creatures have in fact been endowed would be non-existent.

In sum, then, the fact that God exercises the governance of the world mediately (1) takes nothing at all away from the divine sovereignty and omnipotence, and (2) adds considerably to the dignity of His creatures, especially those who have been created in His image and likeness. After all, it is God Himself who has willed that things should be as they are, and His wisdom is unfailing. We have in the fact that God governs the world mediately a special expression of His love. The divine love, as we saw, is naturally diffusive; it flows out with unchecked liberality from the divine essence, so that all creatures might be bathed in it. Indeed, it is divine love that explains why those creatures are there in the first place. God's willingness to share with His creatures the governance of the world is a specific manifestation of His willingness to share His love with them.

Does Anything Operate Outside the Bounds of Divine Providence?

There have always been philosophers, both ancient and modern, who persist in the vain effort to create a coherent cosmology which is founded upon chance. But, as I hope has been made clear earlier, this is to pursue an impossible dream, a dream dreamed by those who seem willing to take any expedient to try to exclude God from His universe. But now we must look a little further into this matter. Chance occurrences, which are to be sure real occurrences, might lead the unwary or the lax of mind to believe that there are certain things that somehow manage to operate outside the governing influence of divine providence. This is not the case, however, nor could it ever be the case. An expected effect may on occasion fail to follow upon a particular cause with which it is regularly associated, and an altogether unexpected effect eventuate, and in that scenario we have an instance of that peculiar kind of lawlessness to which we give the name chance. Another feature of this peculiar kind of lawlessness, and a most important one, is that it is always limited. As we said, chance is the exception, not the rule. If it were the rule, it would thereby cease to be chance. Another important remark to be made about chance, from an epistemological point of view, is that it is the label of choice as a cover for our ignorance. Nothing whatever happens in this universe that has not been caused to happen, very much including what we call chance events. To say, "X happened by chance," does not mean that X does not have a cause. What the statement means is, "I do not know the cause of X."

If chance is what we appeal to in an effort to cover our ignorance, it stands to reason that were there an intelligent being in whom there was no ignorance whatsoever, an intelligent being who was omniscient, then for such a being there would be no such thing as chance. Now, there is of course such a being, God Himself. Because of our immense ignorance concerning the whole range of physical laws and how they interrelate with one another, we must perforce of necessity often designate this, that, or the other event as a chance event. We are face to face with a real effect, but we have no idea of how that effect came about; we are ignorant of its cause or causes. But God has perfect and complete knowledge of the universe which He Himself has created, and therefore He knows, down to the last minute detail, the explanation for all that happens in the universe, for things which are for us quite inexplicable.

But let us suppose, just for the sake of argument, that it were possible for something to take place beyond the governing influence of God's providence. What could we say happened in such a case? St. Thomas gives a pointed answer to that question: Nothing happened, because nothing could happen. "If something were to be totally outside the province of divine governance," he writes, "it would be totally non-existent."[7] Nothing, absolutely nothing, happens outside the governing influence of divine providence.

It would be foolish to suppose, then, that anything could ever resist divine providence. If you were to imagine that happening it would be like imagining a physical body that succeeds in resisting the influence of gravity. Simply by reason of being brought into existence, a creature is, by that very creative act, settled within the embrace of divine providence. In the light of what was established earlier apropos of free will, we can say now, apropos of divine providence, that we as rational creatures who are possessed of free will, invariably fulfill the larger designs of divine providence, even when, in specific instances, we may be going against the will of God. We are always, in whatever we do, in a most fundamental and permanent way, oriented toward our absolute final end, who is God. When, on the face of this earth, we deliberately turn our backs on the sun and try to flee from it, we are running infallibly toward the sun. This is the point behind St. Thomas's observation that, "even sinners intend something that is good." [8] In our moral choices we cannot do other than choose what we perceive as good, though in some cases the good we choose is only apparent, not real. We choose a false good over a true good, one that will not be genuinely perfective of us. But we always choose what we choose "under the aspect of good" (*sub specie boni*), and in doing so, even in spite of ourselves, we are fulfilling God's providential plan, for He created us as creatures who are good and who have a natural, ineradicable orientation to the good. We were made for the good.

We will conclude these reflections on the divine governance by citing two summary observations of St. Thomas. Considerable stress has been given to the point that the divine governance is simply the execution, the working out in time and over time, of God's providential plan. St. Thomas provides us with a sharply focused insight into that divine governance when he describes it as, "nothing else than simply the imposition of order on things." [9] One cannot help but think, in reading that, of St. Augustine's definition of peace as "the tranquility of order." The governing providence of God, because it brings order, simultaneously brings peace. But what is the purpose of order? St. Thomas explains: "To rule and govern providentially is nothing else than, through intelligence, to move things toward their proper ends." [10] Things can only be said to be ordered if they are ordered *toward* something, a specific end. God orders all things in His providential governance because He is drawing them toward their ultimate end, the very reason for their being, the very source of their being—Himself.

Divine Providence and the Existence of Evil

Here and there in the preceding chapters of this book we have had occasion to discuss the dismal subject of evil. We must return to that subject once again, within the context of our discussion of divine providence, and in doing so we will be following a long-standing custom in the discipline of natural theology. What is the reason for treating the subject of evil alongside the subject of divine providence? The reason for doing so quickly becomes clear if we address our subject under the more elaborate tile of "the problem of evil." Why has evil traditionally been regarded as a problem in relation to divine providence? The precise nature of the problem can be expressed in the following terms. If we are correct in understanding God's providence as His loving care for His creation, whereby He leads all things to the ends for which He has created them, then does not the presence of evil in the world—ontological or physical evil, and most especially moral evil—stand in blatant contradiction to the very notion of providence? Does not evil represent, in effect, a clear and continuing undermining of any supposed beneficent plan for the universe? These are hard questions, and St. Thomas, who was never one to evade hard questions, faces them squarely.

As is typical of St. Thomas in dealing with a problem of this sort, he takes it to be very important that we make sure right at the outset that we are clear concerning basic issues. In other words, in this case, before we launch into an effort to reconcile the existence of evil with divine providence, we must first make sure we know precisely what we are talking about when we talk about evil. For if we forge ahead without a sound understanding of the nature of evil, our investigation will inevitably end in confusion. Furthermore, and on a more positive note, if we have a right understanding of the nature of evil, then much of the difficulties which otherwise would have figured large for us, concerning the relation of evil to divine providence, will very likely solve themselves.

St. Thomas begins his examination of the nature of evil by focusing attention on its causes. If we call to mind the brilliant Augustinian definition of evil as "the privation of good" (*privatio boni*), it should not at all surprise us to hear the Angelic Doctor, thinking in the most elementary of terms, present us with the paradoxical assertion that only good can be the cause of evil. How is this so? Evil, we remind ourselves, is not a "something"; it is a lack of a something. The Zoroastrians and the Manichaeans, who posited a positive principle of evil, were literally attempting to make something out of nothing, that is, to give substantial existence to the absence of existence. When we say that good is the primitive cause of evil we are only calling attention to the fact that evil as such is a non-entity, and therefore it can only be identified in terms of the being (which is intrinsically good simply as a being) which it infects. Regarding evil from the point of view of causality, then, we can boldly assert that it is impossible for evil, just as such, to be a cause, for a cause has to be a something, and evil is a lack of something. Privation taken in itself cannot be a cause; a being that is beset by the privation can be. Only being can function as a cause, and all being is good; therefore, good is the cause of evil in the sense that there must first be being, before there can be a lack of being. These, then, are the general principles St. Thomas is working with, which he sums up as follows: "It is not possible for anything to be a cause unless it is good. This is so because nothing can be a cause unless it actually exists, and whatever actually exists is, just for that fact, good." [11]

Evil is defined as a privation of good. What is the exact nature of the good that is lacking here? It is what we may call a proper good, a good, that is, which properly belongs to a particular being in question, given the nature of that being. So, we have evil manifesting itself when we have an actually existing being, which as such is intrinsically good, missing something which it should have in terms of the kind of being it is. This leads us to the distinction between a simple lack of being, and that peculiar kind of lack of being which we identify as evil. A simple lack of being in a being is called a negation, an example of which would be the lack of sight in a tree. It is undeniably true that trees lack the power of sight, but we do not call that lack an evil, for it does not belong to the nature of a tree to be possessed of sight. However, a blind horse would be an instance of evil, specifically ontological or physical evil, because the power of sight is proper to the nature of a horse. A horse is supposed to be able to see; therefore, a horse lacking the power of vision lacks something which, by nature, it should not lack. And hence the evil.

So, then, good can be said to be the cause of evil, in the rudimentary sense that unless there is being (good in itself) there can be no lack in being. It is not possible to have a privation unless there is first a subject for the privation. Another, a more technical way we can express the causative relation good bears toward evil, is to say that good is the indirect (*per accidens*, in the vocabulary of St. Thomas), not the direct (*per se*), cause of evil. In pursing his causal analysis of evil, St. Thomas then expands his investigation to take into account the full array of causes. In our discussion thus far, in which we have identified good as the cause of evil, the specific type of cause we are dealing with is the material cause. Good is the material cause of evil in that it, so to speak, provides the material, the real being, that then can suffer a privation of one sort or another. But, to repeat, good is the material cause of evil only indirectly. But there are three other causes besides the material cause, and they are the formal cause, the final cause, and the efficient cause. How do these three causes relate to evil? To be more specific, can evil be said to have a formal cause, a final cause, and an efficient cause?

Does evil have a formal cause? No, we can immediately eliminate that possibility. The formal cause is that principle that determines a thing to be precisely what it is. It establishes it as being, in terms of its proper nature. To put it plainly, the formal cause is that which makes something something. With that in mind, it should be clear that evil cannot have a formal cause, for evil is not something; it is not an entity. Only real being is formally determined; that is what makes it real being.

Does evil have a final cause? Again in this case, the answer is No. The final cause is "that for the sake of which" any action is undertaken; it is the end, the purpose of the action, and as such it actually defines the action as an action, that is, as intelligible motion. Only being can serve as a end. But evil, having no being as such, cannot serve as a final cause. We cannot have "nothing" as a purpose toward which we are striving. This can be made clearer if we think in terms of moral evil, the evil for which free agents are responsible. As we noted above, we always make our choices as free agents "under the aspect of good." What this means, in practical terms, is that we never choose evil as evil. It is always being, never non-being, that we establish as the end toward which our actions are directed. And it is for that reason that evil cannot be said to have a final cause.

That leaves us with the efficient cause. We have already said that there is a material cause of evil, but only indirectly (*per accidens*); the same can now be said of an efficient cause of evil. The efficient cause is that which brings something about as the result of its transitive action. In the case of moral evil, the efficient cause would be the rational agent, the human being who actually does evil. The free agent, even when he does what is objectively evil, acts in terms of what he perceives to be good. So, the rational agent is indeed the efficient cause of evil—it is his action that actually brings about the evil—but he is the efficient cause only indirectly, and that is because he does not directly intend the evil. What are we to say of ontological or physical evil? That surely has a cause, but in that case the cause is not a free agent. However, it seems that even in the case of ontological evil we can speak of the efficient cause as operating only indirectly and not directly, and that is because all purely physical causes are directed in their causality toward being, rather than non-being, and in that sense they are "intending" the good.

An additional word on the material cause of evil. It is easy enough to identify the rational agent as the efficient, indirect cause of moral evil. But would we be justified, in the case of moral evil, in identifying the agent as the material cause as well? It would seem so, in that the agent would be the subject in which the privation (the evil) is to be found. Here again, the agent would be the material cause only indirectly, for the agent, the rational being, is, just as such, good.

Our first response, then, in attempting to reconcile the fact of divine providence with the fact of evil, is to establish evil in its proper context, and that context, quite emphatically, is the good. Evil can only exist because of the good, and the good (i.e., being) can exist only because of God. It is good—which is to say, simply, being—that is foundational, that is absolutely elementary. It is a grave mistake, then, a mistake which we are too often inclined to make, to begin the discussion of evil with evil itself, for by doing so we begin, not with being, not with what *is,* but with a lack of being, with what *is not*. The great strength of St. Thomas's whole approach to the question of the relation of divine providence to evil is that he begins by getting us properly oriented, faced in the right direction so to speak, toward being and not toward non-being. He concentrates our attention on actual existence. Evil is essentially a parasitic phenomenon, as the philosopher Jacques Maritain liked to repeat; it feeds on being, and it can only be understood, insofar as it can be understood at all, in and through being. We can understand negation—and evil is the supreme negation—only through affirmation, the supreme affirmation which is being.

If it could in any way be demonstrated that God, as the Supreme Good, is the direct cause (*causa per se*, in St. Thomas's Latin) of evil, then indeed we would have an insurmountable problem on our hands, in any attempt to reconcile the existence of evil with the providence of God. But no such demonstration is possible. Not that attempts at such a demonstration have not been made. There is a classic atheistic argument that purports to provide such a demonstration. Needless to say, it fails to do so, for the impossible has a way of eluding all attempts to achieve it. But because of the notoriety this argument has gained, and because a critique of it would be germane to our concerns as students of natural theology, it is fitting that we give some consideration to the argument in this context.

An Atheistic Argument Against Divine Providence

The argument, which is of ancient vintage, is still made use of today, and in fact usually figures as a key item in that standard set of arguments on which the atheist regularly depends as he carries on his relentless war against theism. The argument turns around two of the attributes of God which we discussed previously, the goodness of God and the omnipotence of God. In the account of the argument I give below I make a deliberate attempt to be as rhetorically forceful as possible, so you might be able better to appreciate how it is that many people have found the argument to be persuasive—for all the wrong reasons, however. We should remind ourselves here of a very simple truth about argument, which is too often overlooked, and it is this: an argument can be persuasive, it can convince people to believe certain things and commit themselves to certain things, and yet be quite fallacious. The persuasive quality of an argument and the truth of an argument, although by no means mutually exclusive, do not necessarily go together. That is why there is no substitute for sound logic in analyzing an argument. As you read what follows, imagine that it is the atheist himself who is speaking, and that he is addressing you personally.

You believers claim that God is both all-good and all-powerful, and that he is providentially guiding the destinies of the world and of men. I want to inform you that that is just so much mushy sentimentality. But, more to the point, those dual claims that you make about your God are flatly contradictory.

Let me explain. If God is all-good, then he is not all-powerful, for consider this: You obviously admit to the existence of evil in the world. How could you do otherwise? We are surrounded by it. The world is drenched in evil. Now, if God, as you say, is all-good, if, as you say, he is showing a continuous providential concern for the world, surely he would not tolerate the existence of evil in the world. He would surely do all in his power to destroy that evil. But evil exists. The only thing we can reasonably conclude, then, granting that God is in fact all-good, is that he is not all-powerful. So, your God is beneficent, but impotent. We can assume that he would like to do something about the evil in the world, but he cannot. He is helpless in the face of it, like the rest of us. He is not able to act providentially.

You don't particularly like that conclusion? Well, all right, let's try the other possibility. Let us grant that God is in fact all-powerful. But even with that we are still living in a world that is beset by evil on every side. What are we to make of this? If, as we are granting, God is all-powerful, that means he could do something about evil in the world. Indeed, as all-powerful, he could wipe it out with a wave of his almighty hand. But he doesn't do so. The only thing we can conclude from this is that he is perfectly indifferent to the existence of evil in the world. And anyone who is indifferent to evil cannot be good, much less all-good. God, therefore, though all-powerful, is not all-good. God simply doesn't care about the evil in the world. There is nothing very providential about that.

So, my believing friend, you are left with these alternatives: Either your God is all-good, but not all-powerful, or he is all-powerful, but not all-good. Neither alternative is particularly attractive, but unfortunately you have no other choices. A God lacking either omnipotence or goodness would not seem to be much of a God.

Response to the Atheist's Argument

Perhaps you will agree that the argument, as presented, carries with it a certain amount of rhetorical force. From a purely practical point of view, that is its strength, for, even though untrue, it has been shown to have the power to persuade. But why, because it is appealing to reason? Superficially it may seem to be doing so, but in fact it is directed principally at the emotions. And emotion has the ability to swamp reason. Now, the absolute worst way to respond to an argument that is riding on emotion is to try to meet it on its own terms, that is, by responding emotionally to it. There is only one thing that can deflate emotion that is put to the service of falsehood, and that is reason. What a reasoned response to the argument shows us is that, for all its verve and superficial glitter, it is essentially irrational, and it is irrational because it roundly violates some of the most basic principles of sound reasoning. The argument rests upon illogic; it floats upon fallacy.

Before I show how this is so, by pointing out the argument's specific violations of sound reasoning, I want first to make some general observations about a principal point of emotive emphasis in the argument. Notice the great play that the atheist gives to evil. This is, incidentally, typical. The appeal to the existence of evil in the world is a favorite ploy of the atheist, and that is because he believes that the existence of evil is one of the strong "proofs" against the existence of God. In his on-going argument with God, the atheist returns to evil again and again. And this fact tells us a great deal, I believe, about the psychology of atheism. The atheist would seem to have something like a fixation with regard to evil; he would seem to be fairly obsessed by it. Now, I would like to suggest that there is a certain logical inevitability to this state of affairs. At any rate, there is a remarkable consistency being displayed in the focused emphasis the atheist gives to evil. Let us remind ourselves of the essential nature of evil. It is negation, lack, absence, void. The atheist's whole position, his entire world view, is founded upon the most seminal and consequential negation a human being is capable of making—the denial of God, the denial of the being without whom the atheist would not be. Once a person surrenders to that negation, his whole life becomes oriented toward negation, toward non-being. He becomes enveloped in an atmosphere of negation; he takes it in with his every breath. He is totally sensitized to it, completely tuned to it. What the atheist sees first and foremost everywhere he looks is not what is there, but what is not there. He becomes as it were blind to being, and that is why Being Itself becomes for him the central problem of his life.

As for the logical problems attending the above argument, they are many, but I wish to concentrate here on only two of them, both very important. Whatever rhetorical force the argument commands depends directly on its commission of two very elementary logical fallacies, the *non sequitur* fallacy, and the false dilemma fallacy. The first is the more basic of the two. We have already called attention to the emphasis the atheist gives to the existence of evil. That emphasis does very important duty in the discourse, for the existence of evil performs the function of being the contents of an argumentative premiss. What we discover, in the argument taken as a whole, are two minor arguments whose special force consists precisely in the fact that they are implied rather than stated explicitly. But now we are going to chase them out of the shadows and expose them to the full light of day. The two minor arguments, stated explicitly, are as follows:

> There is evil in the world.
> Therefore, God is not all-powerful.
>
> There is evil in the world.
> Therefore, God is not all-good.

Now, what we have in those two little argument are two textbook examples of the *non sequitur* fallacy. The atheist wants us to accept the conclusion of each of these arguments on the basis of the premiss of each, but the conclusions are unacceptable. Why is that, because the premisses are false? No, the premisses are quite true, and any theist would readily concede their truth. The conclusions are false simply because they do not follow from the premisses, and what that means, more precisely, is that the premisses offer no logical support for the conclusions. There is simply nothing whatsoever in the truth that there is evil in the world that would force our intellects to conclude, so as to avoid irrationality, that God is not all-powerful, or that God is not all-good. Because there is no logical bond between premises and conclusions in these arguments, they prove nothing. And in fact, although they take on the trappings of arguments (e.g., by the employment of the logical indicator "therefore") they are in fact not really arguments at all. What we have here is a pair of juxtaposed statements with no intrinsic logical relation between them.

Now let us turn our attention to the final paragraph in the discourse. That is the heart of the argument, and it represents a rather bold instance of the fallacy of the false dilemma. What is the nature of this fallacy? We must first acquaint ourselves with the vocabulary that describes it. The word "dilemma" comes form the Greek, and it means two propositions, or two possibilities. There are real dilemmas in the world, that is to say, there are situations in which we have two options and two options only. But a *false* dilemma is a fallacy precisely because it makes the claim that there are only two options in a given situation or context, when in fact there are more than two. A person who commits the false dilemma fallacy, then, is one who attempts to persuade his audience to accept a distorted view of reality. In effect, he wants to curb their freedom by attempting to convince them that they must act on the basis of falsified data, telling them that there are only two possibilities open to them when in fact there are more than two, a fact which it is the whole purpose of the fallacy to hide. In sum, the false dilemma fallacy tries to fabricate a purely fictional either/or situation.

Notice what the atheist is attempting to do in this argument. He is presenting us with what he wants us to believe are the only possibilities available to us: (1) If we maintain that God is all-good, then we must admit that He is not all-powerful; or, on the other hand, (2) if we maintain that God is all-powerful, then we must admit that He is not all-good. That is a false dilemma, and we should not allow ourselves to be drawn into it. As a matter of cold logical fact, the two possibilities that the atheist presents to us are not the only two available to us. There is a third possibility, significantly more important than the two presented to us for, unlike them, it happens to be true. The atheist wants to cow us into accepting a fictional either/or situation, but reality is not as narrow and suffocating as the atheist wants us to believe it. So then, it is not a matter of either/or. In other words, the third possibility that the atheist is trying to distract us from, the truth of the matter, is this: God is both all-good and all-powerful. And there is nothing at all in the atheist's argument that proves otherwise.

Let us look more closely at what the argument is attempting to constrain us to accept. The only force we should submit to in argument is the force of reason, but there is no such force at work in this discourse. The only basis on which I should be willing to admit that God is not all-powerful, on the one hand, or that He is not all-good, on the other, is that the two terms, all-good and all-powerful, are mutually exclusive, and therefore, if I accept one I must, in order to avoid irrationality, reject the other. But in point of fact there is nothing at all mutually exclusive about complete goodness and complete power. There is no contradiction involved in conjoining the two. Therefore, not only is there no reason why I should opt for one to the exclusion of the other, it would actually be irrational for me to do so, for there would be no logical basis for such a choice.

The atheist's argument rests on the sheer *supposition* that the goodness of God and the omnipotence of God are mutually exclusive, that their presence in a single being would constitute a contradiction. He wants us to believe that it is of the very nature of goodness to preclude omnipotence, and vice versa. Does he say this in so many words in his argument, or even strongly intimate it? No, he does not. He would not dare do so, for if he were even to suggest that goodness and omnipotence were mutually exclusive, we would immediately be aware of the fallacious reasoning on which the argument is being built, and that is because we know for a fact that the two are not mutually exclusive.

A final observation. One has to be especially alert to notice a major unstated assumption upon which rests much of the weight of the atheist's argument. The assumption is that God does nothing about the evil that exists in the world. What could the atheist offer us to justify such an assumption? Nothing at all. The implicit argument behind the assumption is as follows: There is evil in the world; therefore, God does nothing about it. And here we have another *non sequitur*. The existence of evil does not prove divine inactivity with respect to evil.

Divine Providence and the Good

To repeat an important point made above, any attempt to show that God is responsible for the existence of evil in the world must fail. And the reason for that has to do with the very nature of being. "God is not the author of evil," St. Augustine writes, "because He is not the source of any tendency whatever toward non-being." [12] Being itself, and as itself, is good. God, the source of all being, has to do only with what is good.

Any evil that represents a defect in an action, St. Thomas argues, is traceable to a defect in the agent who is the source of that action. If a musician blows a series of sour notes on a clarinet that is in perfect condition as an instrument, the defect is in the musician, not in the clarinet. But with respect to that supreme agent who is God, the First Cause, there can be no defect whatever. Well, then, to return now to the question with which we began, How do we explain the defects that are to be found in creatures, and how do we reconcile them with divine providence? First of all, we state clearly and unequivocally, that God, as the all-perfect Creator and First Cause of the universe, cannot be the direct cause of those defects. But God can be considered to be their indirect cause in the elementary sense that He created the beings in which those defects are to be found. To put it differently, God is not the cause of the defects, but He is the cause of the cause of the defects. The most heinous kind of evil, we might even say the only real evil, is moral evil, because that is the conscious turning away from God on the part of creatures who are free to do otherwise. Now, God could have created a universe completely free of moral evil, but He could only have done that by creating beings that were deprived of free will.

If God had never created Lucifer, then it follows with flawless logic that Lucifer would then never have rebelled against God. But the point is that God did not create Lucifer so that he might one day rebel against Him; He created Lucifer so that Lucifer might enjoy the luminescent vision of his Creator forever. In other words, God created Lucifer for one purpose only, that Lucifer might love Him, in return for the love that brought Lucifer into existence. But there was only one way that God could have created a Lucifer who could love Him, and that is by creating him as a being possessed of free will, for love without freedom is impossible. God gives free will to creatures so that they might exercise that freedom in order to attain happiness, supreme happiness, which is nothing else than God Himself. But a creature who is truly free has the real option of choosing that which will negate his own happiness. That is the great paradox, the great irony, of freedom. It is a metaphysical impossibility to have creatures who are truly free and who are not capable of choosing evil rather than good, non-being rather than being. God chose to create beings possessed of free will because He wanted beings that would imitate as closely as possible His own divine essence, in their ability to love.

It would be naively superficial to pretend that it is an easy task for our severely limited intellects to reconcile God's loving providence with the existence of evil in the world. But if we take care to keep certain very basic facts in mind, we will be able to see the inherent rationality in an overall scheme the particulars of which we cannot comprehend. God's providential governance of the world means that He directs all things toward their ultimate end, which is to say, their ultimate good. The good is what God wills for His creatures, and He wills that good even when—perhaps we should say especially when—those creatures, endowed with free will through the goodness of God, exercise that free will in a way that counteracts the good that God wills for them.

In the final analysis, and following the reasoning of St. Thomas as he considers the subject of evil from the point of view of causality, we can say that the goodness of anything is not determined by how it is affected by particular causes, but rather in terms of (a) its own proper identity, and (b) in terms of how it relates to the order of the universe taken as a whole. There is a single overriding cause (*causa communis*) which governs all particular causes in the universe. There is one primary principle of being. On the level of particular causes, we witness many contrary and conflicting movements; these are the explanations for the evil in the world. But there is a way in which all those particular causes, in their activity, are subsumed within the governing influence of the primary principle of being. In other words, God's providential plan for the universe, despite all apparent evidence to the contrary, will one day, surely and fully, be realized. It is, as a matter of fact, being realized right now. Our philosophy does not clearly see this, but our faith does. With St. Paul we can confidently assert that all thing, *all* things, work together unto good.

Notes

Introduction

1. "Everything treated in theology [*sacra doctrina*] relates to God, those things pertaining directly to God Himself, or those things as they relate to God as their first cause and final end." (*S.T.,* I, q. 1, a. 7.)

2. In the encyclical *Aeterni Patris* (1879), Pope Leo XIII wrote: "A perpetual and varied service is further required of philosophy, in order that sacred theology may receive and assume the nature, form, and genius of a true science." (Boston: Pauline Books & Media, no date, p. 7.)

3. *Summa Theologiae*, I, q. 2, a. 3.

Chapter One

1. *Summa Theologiae*, I, q. 2, a. 1, ad 1.

2. Ibid., ad 2.

3. Ibid., ad 3.

4. The arguments given in this section are a restatement of those which St. Thomas develops in the main body of his response to the question, "Whether the existence of God is self-evident." (See *S. T.*, I, q. 2, a. 1.)

5. There is much dense meaning compacted in that Latin phrase, *homo capax Dei*. The essential idea it is attempting to convey is that man is by his very nature potentially "in tune" with God for the simple reason that God is the source, the explanation, for man's very existence. Man is "capable of" God because he comes from God.

6. Moral virtue is the perfection, or realization, of a potential. The potential is given us as part of our nature, but we must realize that potential through our free acts. Cf. *S. T.*, I-II, q. 55 passim, but especially a. 1.

7. Jacques Maritain. *Approaches to God* (trans. Peter O'Reilly). New York: Harper & Brothers Publishers, 1954, p. 8.

8. John F. McCormick, S. J. *Scholastic Metaphysics, Part II, Natural Theology*. Chicago: Loyola University Press, 1931, 1959, p. 18.

9. Søren Kierkegaard. *Philosophical Fragments: Johannes Climacus. Kierkegaard's Writings, VII* (trans. Howard V. Hong and Edna H. Hong). Princeton, New Jersey: Princeton University Press, 1985, p. 39.

10. Ibid., p. 46.

Chapter Two

1. *Summa Theologiae*, I, q. 1, a. 1.

2. Ibid., q. 2, a. 2, ad 1.

3. The text, translated by G. M. A. Grube, reads as follows: "Do you realize what a debater's argument you are bringing up, that a man cannot search either for what he knows or for what he does not know? He cannot search for what he knows—since he knows it, there is no need to search—nor for what he does not know, for he does not know what to look for." (80e) See *Plato: Complete Works*, ed. John M. Cooper. Indianapolis: Hackett Publishing Company, 1997, p. 880.

4. The fallacy of the false dilemma attempts to distort reality by claiming that we have only two choices before us, A or B, when in fact there are other options besides A or B.

5. This is the description provided by Father Jesus Azagra, O. P. and Father Mateo Febrer, O. P. in their Introduction to Book I of St. Thomas's *Summa Contra Gentiles*. (Madrid: Biblioteca de Autores Cristianos, 1952, Vol. I), p. 51.

6. *Summa Theologiae*, I, q. 2, a. 2, ad 2.

7. Ibid., ad 3.

8. One marvels at the confidence of certain philosophers who will assert as a matter of incontestable fact that Kant has definitively shown that the existence of God cannot be demonstrated. And one wonders, Have they ever read Kant on this subject, or are they simply passing on, unexamined, a professorial opinion they learned in graduate school?

9. Kant writes: "All objects of any experience possible to us [i.e., sense experience, experience of the objective order] are nothing but appearances, that is, mere representations, which, in the manner in which they are represented, as extended beings, or as a series of alterations, have no independent existence outside our thoughts." (Immanuel Kant. *Critique of Pure Reason* (trans. Norman Kemp Smith). New York: St. Martin's Press, 1965, p. 439.) He also writes: "The thing in itself [*die Sache selbst*, in the original German] is indeed given, but we can have no insight into its nature." (Ibid., p. 514) And he writes of "things of which, as they are in themselves, we have not yet the least knowledge." (Ibid., p. 484) In light of all this, Kant can claim that "the world does not exist in itself" (Ibid., p. 448), the strong implication being that it exists only in our minds.

10. Kant refers to "philosophers, whose task is to examine concepts...." (*Critique of Pure Reason*, p. 451). The emphasis here is totally misplaced. The task of the philosopher does indeed involve the examination of concepts, but only secondarily. The principal concern of the philosopher is not concepts, but the things to which the concepts refer. *Non conceptus, sed res!* ("Not concepts, but things!") should be the motto of every philosopher.

11. The classical epistemological principle being referred to here is expressed in Latin as follows: *Nihil est in intellectu quod non prius fuerit in sensu.* "There is nothing in the intellect that was not first in the senses." In other words, all our intellectual knowledge, that knowledge which is represented by ideas, is based upon sense knowledge, the knowledge that is represented by sense images. The ideas in our mind have their ultimate source in things in the world.

12. Kant writes: "For how can experience ever be adequate to an idea? The peculiar nature of the latter consists just in the fact that no experience can ever be equal to it." (*Critique of Pure Reason*, p. 518) Kant's question is answered by saying that experience can be adequate to an idea because the idea derives from experience, and has no other source but experience. There is never anything like perfect mathematical equality between experience and idea, of course, but there is a real, completely reliable correspondence between the two. Kant could ask the above question because he looked upon ideas as having their source in the mind itself, not in the world outside the mind. Given this epistemological point of view, ideas, rather than informing us about the state of the world, inform us about the state of our mind.

13. One of the paradoxical aspects of Kant's gratuitous claim that we cannot know "the thing in itself" is that he is constantly informing us of various features of that whose true nature, supposedly, we can know nothing. It is as if Kant's agnosticism comes accompanied with a penetrating gnostic power which is lacking to the agnosticism by which the rest of humanity is beset. If in fact we cannot know the thing in itself, then that very phrase, "the thing in itself," is impermissible in responsible philosophical usage, for if we know nothing of the essence or nature of things, what could it mean to refer to something as "in itself"? How do we know it has the peculiar quality of being possessed of an intrinsic identity which, seemingly, is complete in itself, and separates it off from things other than itself?

It was not due to mere oversight on Kant's part that he failed to provide any demonstration for his contention that we do not know the essences or the natures of things. He did not provide any such demonstration because there is none available. The proof positive that we do know the essences or natures of things is to be found in language, specifically in the fact that we attach different words to things. If in fact we did not know things in themselves, then no discrimination at all would be possible for us with regard to the external world. All our experience would be completely homogeneous, in the sense that no one thing in our experience would be distinguishable from any other thing, and indeed the very idea of "thing" would be quite foreign to us. But this, obviously, is not how it happens. We make clear and confident distinctions among chairs, and tables, and chipmunks, and we do this, not because we are born with the ideas of these things, and then, after clothing them with words of our choice apply those words to our experience, but because there are real chairs, tables, and chipmunks in the world and we really know them as such, and, knowing them, i.e., having the right ideas about them, we give them their proper names.

14. *Critique of Pure Reason,* p. 393.

15. Ibid., p. 446.

16. Actually, Kant wants us to draw from this exercise not only the conclusion that one metaphysical argument is just as good, or bad, as another, but the much stronger conclusion that no metaphysical argument can be productive of truth. He writes: "we are obliged to denounce both the opposed dialectical assertions as false." (Ibid., p. 463). The assertions are "dialectical" in the sense that they apply only to the realm of ideas and not to the objective order of things.

17. Ibid., p. 440.

18. Ibid., p. 476.

19. Ibid., p. 464.

20. Ibid., p. 498.

21. Kant's analysis of the ontological argument is to be found in the edition of his *Critique of Pure Reason* that I have been citing, pp. 500–507. The final paragraph of that analysis is worth quoting here: "The attempt to establish the existence of a supreme being by means of the famous ontological argument of Descartes [the argument did not originate with Descartes, but he provided an influential version of it] is therefore so much labour and effort lost; we can no more extend our stock of [theoretical] insight by mere ideas, than a merchant can better his position by adding a few noughts to his cash account." (Ibid., p. 507)

22. Ibid., p. 508.

23. An interesting question concerning Kant's treatment of the physico-theological argument: Did he, in showing a qualified approval of the argument, end by conceding too much, and thereby undermine his whole anti-metaphysical point of view? He writes: "The utmost, therefore, that the argument can prove is an *architect* of the world who is always very much hampered by the adaptibility of the material in which he works, not a *creator* of the world to whose idea everything is subject." (*Critique*, p. 522, emphasis his) The principal aim of Kant's argument has been to show that metaphysical reasoning cannot establish anything, one way or another, concerning the nature

of existence in a realm that transcends our experience. But to admit, as Kant seems to be doing here, that the physico-theological argument can be allowed to demonstrate the existence of an "architect of the world," is to admit that metaphysics can do what it supposedly is not able to do, for surely any being that deserves the formidable title of "architect of the world" is a being that would transcend our experience in a rather dramatic fashion.

24. I will mention just one of these difficulties, and not necessarily the most prominent of them. During the course of his treatment of what he calls the cosmological argument, Kant makes the observation that "whatever it may be that exists, nothing prevents me from thinking of its non-existence." (Ibid., p. 515) This assertion can be understood in two ways, but the way in which Kant wants it to be understood is unclear, and that is in good part because of what I believe to be a confusion on his part concerning the important distinction between absolute necessity and relative necessity, a point I mentioned in the text of this chapter. I can think of anything that actually exists as non-existing in the perfectly acceptable sense that I recognize a particular existent as a contingent being. The being actually exists now, but there is no intrinsic necessity to its existing, now or at any time (i.e., existence is not of the very essence of the being), and I know this to be a fact because at one time the being did not exist, and at some time in the future the being will not exist. But there is another way in which I could not think of the non-existence of any actually existing being without falling into contradiction, and that is if I were to suppose that, *per impossibile*, the being could both exist and not exist at the same time and in the same respect.

25. It seems reasonable to conclude that if Kant did not offer us particularly impressive versions of the arguments from contingency (his "cosmological argument") and the argument from finality (his "physico-theological argument") it was not because he was deliberately attempting to take an unfair advantage by doing so, but simply because he was presenting the arguments in the only versions he was familiar with, and, as it happened, those versions leave much to be desired. To the best of my knowledge, Kant was not familiar with St. Thomas's Five Ways. Had he known them, one wonders if he would perhaps have been tempted to think in entirely different terms concerning metaphysics in general and natural theology in particular.

Chapter Three

1. Jacques Maritain. *Approaches to God* (trans. Peter O'Reilly). New York: Harper & Brothers, 1954, p. 12.

2. Ibid., p. 13.

3. Referring to Book X of Plato's *Laws*, Professor Taylor writes: "Plato appears at once as the creator of natural theology and the first thinker to

propose that false theological belief—as opposed to insults to an established worship—should be treated as a crime against the State and repressed by the civil magistrate." (A. E. Taylor. *Plato: The Man and His Work.* Mineola, New York: Dover Publications, Inc., 2001, p. 489.)

4. Plato, *Laws*, 894c, 4–6. The translation of the *Laws* I am citing here is found in *Plato: Complete Works* (Indianapolis, 1997), pp. 1318–1616. See Bibliography for complete citation.

5. Ibid., 894d, 2–3.

6. Ibid., 894d, 9.

7. Ibid., 895a, 2–3.

8. Ibid., 895b, 4.

9. Ibid., 899b, 4–7.

10. Ibid., 891e, 4.

11. The key chapters for the argument to be found in Book XII of the *Metaphysics* are 6 and 7 (1071b, 3–1073a, 13). The English translations from which I quote in the text are from *The Basic Works of Aristotle,* Richard McKeon, ed., New York, 1941.

12. Aristotle, *Physics*, 259a, 12–14.

13. Ibid., 267b, 26.

14. Aristotle, *Metaphysics,* 1072b, 28–30.

15. St. Augustine's proof for the existence of God composes Book II of *The Free Choice of the Will*. The translation of this work which I use in the text is found in *Readings in Medieval Philosophy*, Andrew B. Schroedinger, ed. New York: Oxford University Press, 1996, p. 22. It is interesting to note that in the passage from which the quoted statement is taken St. Augustine, while admitting that the knowledge we have of God's existence through natural reason is inferior to that which we have through faith, seems to suggest, as indicated by his use of the phrase "as yet," that he believed that our natural knowledge of God is subject to improvement.

16. Ibid., p. 10.

17. Ibid., p. 13.

18. Ibid., p. 22.

19. See *Summa Theologiae*, I, q. 2, a. 1, ad 2.

20. St. Anselm. *Basic Writings* (trans. S. N. Deane). La Salle, Illinois: Open Court Publishing Company, 1962, pp. 7–8. The argument composes Chapter II of the *Proslogium*. St. Thomas, in his *Summa Contra Gentiles*, provides us with his own succinct version of the ontological argument, and it reads as follows. "By the name of God we understand something than which a greater cannot be thought. This notion is formed by the intellect by one who hears and understands the name of God. As a result, God must exist already at least in the intellect. But he cannot exist solely in the intellect, since that which exists both in the intellect and in reality is greater than that

which exists in the intellect alone. Now, as the very definition of the name points out, nothing can be greater than God. Consequently, the proposition that God exists is self-evident, as being evident from the very meaning of the name of God." (*Summa Contra Gentiles*, Book I, Chapter 10, Section 1.) The translation of the above passage is my own. See Bibliography for the citation of Anton C. Pegis's very fine translation of the entire *Summa Contra Gentiles*.

    21. *Summa Theologiae*, I, q. 3, a. 1.

    22. *Summa Contra Gentiles,* Book I, Chapter 11.

Chapter Four

    1. *Summa Theologiae,* I, q. 1, a. 1.

    2. One might wonder, once the *terminus ad quem* has been reached and the apple is completely red, and therefore in act with respect to red, if we could then say that now it is in privation with respect to green? No. A thing that changes can be said to be in privation with respect to a particular state only if it is capable, in the natural order of things, of reaching that state. Because red apples do not, under ordinary circumstances, naturally become green apples, we would not say that a red apple is in privation with respect to greenness. Greenness is not a privation in red apples, but we could call it a simple negation. The kind of change that takes place in the ripening of apples is in one direction only. In a different kind of change, where there can be a reversal of direction, such as in a pendulum swinging back and forth, then there can be a reciprocal exchange of privation. For example, in the case of a swinging pendulum, when the pendulum is in the extreme left position, it is in privation with respect to the extreme right position, and then, when it reaches the extreme right position, it is in privation with respect to the extreme left position.

    3. It might appear that an apple could be both red and green at the same time with no contradiction involved. For example, what about the case of an apple that is in the process of ripening and therefore displays both red and green coloring? In such a case, one would have neither a green apple, nor a red apple, but a green and red apple. By green apple we mean one with no trace of red in it; and a red apple would be one with no trace of green in it. With that understanding of the relevant terms, we see how it would be a contradiction for any apple to be both green and red at the same time.

    4. If we look more closely at the internal elements that explain bodily movements, we discover there as well a distinction between mover and moved, at least in a qualified sense. The will is the direct cause of bodily movement, but the will always acts according to the knowledge which is provided to it by the intellect. The will can thus be said to be moved by the intellect in the

sense that it is illumined by it, but not in the sense that the will is strictly determined to act in a certain way by the intellect.

5. The other three first principles are: the principle of identity, the principle of contradiction, and the principle of excluded middle. A full account of these principles may be found in my *Metaphysics* (Elmhurst & S. Abington Township, Pennsylvania: The Priestly Fraternity of St. Peter, 2004, 2019), Chapter II.

6. Ibid., Chapter XIII and Chapter XIV.

7. The original Latin reads: *Causae autem dicuntur ex quibus res dependent vel esse vel fieri.* For greater clarity, I have altered, in my translation, the number of the noun and the voice of the verb in the first part of the definition.

8. *Summa Theologiae,* I, q. 104, a. 1.

9. St. Thomas Aquinas. *Commentary on Aristotle's Physics,* Book Two, Lecture 6.

10. Perhaps one of the reasons we are inclined to think that an infinite series of accidentally subordinated causes is possible is that we are influenced by the potential infinity which obtains in mathematics. A series of whole numbers, for example, can be extended indefinitely, but only in one direction, in the direction of continual increase. Going in the opposite direction, you must eventually arrive at one, and there is no going further, for it is one, and not any fraction of one, which is the source of all number. Moving from any multiple of one back toward one could be considered comparable to moving back along a series of accidentally related causes. You must eventually reach "one," i.e., the original cause, otherwise you are left without any explanation for the series itself.

Chapter Five

1. *Summa Theologiae*, I, q. 2, a. 3.

2. For Aristotle, "first act" is first in the sense that it posits, establishes, existence. The first act of every entity is its substantial form, that which determines it to be what it is. "Second act" is the sum total of all the accidental forms of a given entity. The characteristic behavior of a particular organism would be an example of second act. Obviously, second act is totally dependent on first act, for unless an organism actually exists, it could not behave in any way.

3. *Summa Theologiae*, I, q. 2, a. 3.

4. God and God alone can bring something into existence in the absolute, unqualified sense, in the totality of its being, and this is what we have in mind when we refer to God as the Creator. Creation takes place when God establishes a being in existence, gives it its being, and, antecedent to that act, there was nothing. All human "creators" are so only analogously, as faintly imitating the creative activity of God. Artists can make being, but they must always start with being. They give new shape to what is already established in existence.

5. The Latin for the phrase is: *quod aliquid sit causa efficiens sui ipsius."* (*Summa Theologiae*, I, q. 2, a. 3.)

6. Ibid.

7. Once again in this case readers are made immediately aware that a *quia* argument is being presented to them. The argument begins with "things in the world," i.e., effects. The task before us is to discover the cause of those effects.

8. Father Henri Renard writes: "On the other hand, by the expression *necessary being having a cause for its necessity*, St. Thomas designates a being whose essence, because fully actuated by a distinct 'to be,' has no capacity, no potency, to cease to exist. Such is a spiritual form; such also, as thought medieval philosophers, were the celestial bodies. These beings are necessary, that is, incorruptible. Nevertheless, since the 'to be' is really distinct from essence, they are not absolutely necessary beings in the order of existence, but their necessity depends upon the active potency of an extrinsic agent." (Henri Renard, S. J. *The Philosophy of God.* Milwaukee: The Bruce Publishing Company, 1951, p. 38.)

Chapter Six

1. *Summa Theologiae,* I, q. 2, a. 3.

2. An added difficulty in judging the comparative worth of something like a musical performance is that there may be sincere differences of opinion among genuine experts as to the quality of the performance. And, in a way, it could not be otherwise, for the judgment in question does not concern a matter of fact (i.e., whether or not a musical performance actually took place), concerning which there could not be any disagreement among those who have the pertinent knowledge available to them, but rather the judgment has to do with the evaluation of the fact (i.e., the quality of the performance), concerning which, it would seem, disagreements are unavoidable.

3. The question that has to be asked is this: Does the concept of a hottest object involve a contradiction? It would seem not. It is altogether possible that there is in the universe, right now, a physical object—a star, say—that has a temperature that is higher than the temperature of any other existing object. The possibility of the existence of such an object, and the possibility of its existence ever being empirically verified, are separate questions, but there is nothing inherently irrational in the supposition that such an object does exist. Of course, there is always the possibility that there could be more than one object with the same "hottest" temperature. It is precisely because of this second possibility that we should not suppose that, in the argument, St. Thomas is talking simply about accidental maximums. You could have two beings that maximally display the same quality—i.e., two physical objects with the same maximally elevated temperature, but you could not have two

entities that were maximum in being, that is, in terms of their substantial realities. The entity that is maximum in being is, by definition, unique.

4. Aristotle, *Metaphysics,* 993b, 27-28.

5. St. Thomas Aquinas. *Commentary on Aristotle's Metaphysics* (trans. John P. Rowan). Notre Dame, Indiana: Dumb Ox Books, 1995, p. 112, sect. 294.

6. *Summa Theologiae*, I, q. 2, a. 3.

7. Immanuel Kant. *Critique of Pure Reason* (New York, 1965), p. 520.

8. We speak rather freely at times of "animal intelligence." There is no particular harm in using this phrase, so long as we are clear about its limitations, what it can mean, and what it cannot mean. Reference to animal intelligence can correctly refer to the fact that animals act for the sake of an end, and the higher animals do so consciously. But the phrase would be incorrectly employed if it was intended to mean that animals possess intellects, and that they are therefore aware of ends precisely as ends. Animals act intelligently, but they do not know that they act intelligently; therefore, as is the case with plants and of inanimate things, the source of their intelligent behavior is external to them. The intelligence in question here is to be explained, ultimately, in terms of God's creative activity.

Chapter Seven

1. Not all arguments that are carried on within the area of philosophical discourse are honest arguments. Not all criticisms of arguments are honest criticisms. These truisms are best explained, on the most basic level, simply by pointing to the human condition, and specifically to man's fallen state. Man's intellect is capacious and powerful, assuming at times in certain individuals prodigious proportions, but it must carry on its labors in a realm of permanent twilight. What is an honest argument? It is one that makes no compromises with respect to the truth. Honest criticism, for its part, responds to an argument as presented, to the argument itself and not to what is extraneous to it. A dishonest critic often approaches an argument with his own special agenda in mind, and his engagement with the argument is but the occasion for furthering that agenda. For example, some philosophers attacking St. Thomas's arguments are not particularly concerned with responding carefully and conscientiously to the specifics of his reasoning, and that is because they actually have larger targets in mind: Catholicism, religion in general, or, simply, theism.

2. It can be argued that the discovery of first causes is not the proper province of empirical science just as such. Empirical science is principally concerned with how things stand with the material world, here and now, and though we can assume that the things now existing and operating in the material world have a history to them, and ultimate origins, the empirical scientist need not necessarily concern himself with either the history or the ultimate

origins of things. The task of the philosopher is quite different in this respect, however. He must be especially concerned with the ultimate origins of things.

3. Isaac Asimov. *Understanding Physics, Vol. I, Motion, Sound, and Heat.* New York: Barnes & Noble, 1993, p. 24.

4. "The visible stars," he wrote, "are bodies for which the law of inertia certainly holds to a high degree of approximation." (Albert Einstein. *Relativity: The Special and the General Theory.* New York: Crown Publishers, Inc., 1961, p. 11.)

5. *Understanding Physics,* p. 25.

6. Einstein never uses the phrase, "whatever is moved is moved by another," but that is incidental, for the operative idea of the principle is to be found everywhere in his writings.

7. The example is as follows: "I am standing in front of a gas range. Standing alongside of each other on the range are two pans so much alike that one may be mistaken for the other. Both are half full of water. I notice that steam is being emitted continuously from the one pan, but not from the other. I am surprised by this, even if I have never seen a gas range or a pan before. But if I now notice a luminous something of bluish colour under the first pan but not under the second, I cease to be astonished, even if I have never before seen a gas flame. For I can only say that this bluish something will cause the emission of the steam, or at least *possibly* it may do so. If, however, I notice the bluish something in neither case, and if I observe that the one continuously emits steam whilst the other does not, then I shall remain astonished and dissatisfied until I have discovered some circumstance to which I can attribute the difference behavior of the two pans." (*Relativity: The Special and the General Theory,* p. 72.)

8. Einstein provides us with a vivid illustration of the Newtonian idea of space and time in the following passage: "The idea of an independent existence of space and time can be expressed drastically in this way: If matter were to disappear, space and time alone would remain behind (as a kind of stage for physical happening)." (*Relativity,* p. 144.)

9. Ibid., p. 9.

10. "In the general theory of relativity," Einstein writes, "the doctrine of space and time, or kinematics, no longer figures as a fundamental independent of the rest of physics. The geometrical behavior of bodies and the motion of clocks rather depend on gravitational fields, which in their turn are produced by matter." (From his essay, "What Is the Theory of Relativity?" in his book, *Essays in Science.* New York: Philosophical Library, 1934, p. 58.)

11. This is a point that one has to be careful not to exaggerate, for the thought of Einstein, as a natural philosopher, is not without its ambivalence. There was to be sure a decidedly realist bent to his thinking, as reflected in bold, unequivocal statements such as the following: "The belief in an external

world independent of the perceiving subject is the basis of all natural science." (*Essays in Science,* p. 40.) But his admiration for the thought of Kant is a tell-tale indication of a weakness he had for philosophical idealism. (The respect he had for Leibniz might also be mentioned in this regard.) And when he makes statements such as, "It seems that the human mind has first to construct forms independently before we can find them in things" (*Essays in Science,* p. 27), we have strong hints of an idealist point of view. But Albert Einstein is by no means alone among modern empirical scientists, especially theoretical physicists, who show a marked penchant for philosophical idealism. The principal cause of the significant presence (one could almost say prevalence) of philosophical idealism among modern scientists is, I believe, the abiding influence of Immanuel Kant.

12. Werner Heisenberg. *Physics and Philosophy: The Revolution in Modern Science.* Amherst, New York: Prometheus Books, 1999, p. 71.

13. Ibid., p. 119.

14. Stanley L. Jaki. *Is There a Universe? The Forwood Lectures for 1992.* New York: Wethersfield Institute, 1993, p. 48. Interestingly, and apropos of the observation by him quoted in the text, Father Jaki believes that the principle of indeterminancy is better described as the principle of imprecision.

15. Anthony Kenny. *The Five Ways: St. Thomas Aquinas' Proofs of God's Existence.* Notre Dame, Indiana: University of Notre Dame Press, 1980, p.3.

16. Ibid., p. 71.

17. Ibid., p. 95.

18. Ibid., p. 1.

19. The account of Dr. Adler's position that I provide in the text is based on the presentation found in his book, *How to Think About God.* (New York: Macmillan Publishing Company, 1980.) The heart of his argument is to be found in Chapters 12 and 13.

20. George H. Smith. *Atheism: The Case Against God.* Los Angeles: Nash Publishing, 1974, p. 236.

21. Ibid., p. 251.

22. Ibid.

23. Ibid., p. 238.

Chapter Eight

1. When philosophers and historians of philosophy use the term "modern philosophy" they are speaking of a philosophical movement that began in the seventeenth century and continues to dominate Western culture to this day. René Descartes is usually acknowledged to be the father of modern philosophy. So large and varied and complex a phenomenon such as is modern philosophy cannot be summed up in a few words, but, looking at the phenomenon from

a Scholastic point of view, modern philosophy can be said to represent, for the most part—all honorable exceptions appreciatively acknowledged—a tragic down-turning in the history of philosophy. With modern philosophy, philosophical thought departed from the main stream of common sense reasoning, as the result, among other things, of its succumbing to an irrational skepticism regarding the foundational reliability of sense knowledge. In effect, modern philosophy represents a loss of faith in the objective order of things, and a lapse into disoriented subjectivism.

2. It was just on this point that another French philosopher, Blaise Pascal (1623–1662), a younger contemporary of Descartes, accused his compatriot of effectively using God as a *deus ex machina* in the effort to prop up his rickety philosophy. "I cannot forgive Descartes," Pascal wrote in his *Pensées*. "In all his philosophy he would have been quite willing to dispense with God. But he had to make Him give a fillip to set the world in motion; beyond this, he had no further need of God." (*Thoughts*, #77, in *The European Philosophers from Descartes to Nietzsche,* Monroe C. Beardsley, ed. New York: The Modern Library, 1992, p. 105.) For Pascal, Descartes' "God" was a quintessential example of what he called the "God of the philosophers," a "God" not to be confused with the true God, the God of Abraham, Isaac, and Jacob.

3. Elizabeth S. Haldane and G. R. T. Ross, ed. and trans. *The Philosophical Works of Descartes. Volume I.* Cambridge: Cambridge University Press, 1977, p. 158.

4. Ibid., p. 162,

5. Ibid., p. 165.

6. Ibid., p. 166. "In some way I have in me the notion of the infinite earlier than the finite—to wit, the notion of God before that of myself."

7. Ibid., p. 167.

8. Ibid., p. 170. " And consequently the only alternative is that it [i.e., the idea of God] is innate in me, just as the idea of myself is innate in me."

9. Ibid., pp. 170-71.

10. G. W. Leibniz. *Theodicy.* Chicago: Open Court, 1985, p. 123. Elsewhere in the *Theodicy* Leibniz writes: "But since reason is a gift of God, even as faith is, contention between them would cause God to contend against God." (p. 96)

11. The French *philosophe* Voltaire expressed scoffing dismissal of the principal thesis of Leibniz's *Theodicy* in his novella *Candide*, a book which enjoyed wide popularity in its own day, and continues to find readers today, at least among academics. Many intellectuals have seemingly been quite persuaded by the argument of *Candide*, intellectuals for most of whom, I do not think it reckless to suggest, Leibniz is but a name and the *Theodicy* a completely closed book. But by any fair comparison between the two works, *Candide* comes across as an exercise in sophomoric meandering, and the

Theodicy as the carefully wrought disquisition of a formidable intellect.

12. See section XXIII of Leibniz's *Discourse on Metaphysics* (Beardsley, *The European Philosophers from Descartes to Nietzsche*, pp. 273–74), and his *Monadology*, section 45 (Ibid., p. 294.)

13. Leibniz, *Discourse on Metaphysics*, section XIX, which is entitled, "*The utility of final cause in Physics*" (in *The European Philosophers*), pp. 269–270.

14. Leibniz, *Theodicy*, p. 279.

15. Ibid., p. 148.

16. Ibid., p. 332.

17. William Paley, D.D. *Natural Theology: Or, Evidences of the Existence and Attributes of the Deity Collected from the Appearances of Nature* (with illustrations by James Paxton). New York: Sheldon & Company, 1854, p. 10.

18. Ibid.

19. Ibid., p. 246.

20. Ibid., p. 292.

21. Ibid., p. 212.

22. The atheistic evolutionist Richard Dawkins, in his book, *The Blind Watchmaker* (New York: W. W. Norton & Company, 1978) offered an explanation for the genesis of the eye which was guided by orthodox evolutionary principles. According to this account, the eye came about by a series of mere chance mutations over a very long period of time. In effect, it is the product of a plethora of accidents. And there was most definitely no purpose in the coming into being of what has to be recognized, by any disinterested observer, as an eminently purposeful organ. I cannot recall off hand if Professor Dawkins makes any reference to William Paley in his book. But I would invite the reader to do a little experiment in comparative literary criticism. Read Professor Dawkins' account of the genesis of the eye in *The Blind Watchmaker*, then read Dr. Paley's treatment of the eye in *Natural Theology,* then judge for yourself which argument you find the more convincing. My own judgment is that Dr. Paley takes the prize. He deals in facts, for which he offers a coherent and cogent explanation. Professor Dawkins, for his part, embarks upon a veritable spree of conjecture, conjecture which, so it seems to me, is driven in no small part by wishful thinking.

23. *Natural Theology,* pp. 233–34.

24. Ibid., p. 42.

25. Ibid., p. 38.

26. Ibid., p. 106. See also p. 158, where Paley discusses the proboscis of the elephant, and p. 242, where, addressing what might rightly be described as Darwinism gradualism, he pointedly observes "that the hypothesis remains destitute of evidence." The argument that Paley makes here uncannily anticipates the line of reasoning that was eventually to be developed by

Professor Michael J. Behe in his book, *Darwin's Black Box* (New York: Simon and Schuster, 1996), in which he tellingly argues that a multitude of mechanisms in nature, which manifest what he describes as instances of "irreducible complexity," cannot be explained in terms of principles that are central to Darwinian evolutionary theory.

27. C. S. Lewis. *Miracles: A Preliminary Study.* New York: The Macmillan Company, 1947, pp. 40–41.

28. Ibid., p. 42.

29. Ibid., p. 44.

30. Ibid., p. 10.

31. Ibid., p. 45.

32. Jacques Maritain. *Approaches to God.* New York: Harper & Brothers Publishers, 1954, p. 72.

33. Ibid., p. 82.

34. Ibid., p. 77.

35. Ibid.

36. Ibid.

37. One wonders if Dr. Adler was ever aware that there was a potential problem in this point of view, but a problem that might prove to have interesting consequences in that it could open up a new productive line of reasoning. Let us grant Dr. Adler's contention that all the things in the universe are only superficially contingent. That means that all the things in the universe are dependent upon other superficially contingent beings, and they, in turn, upon others. Does not this confront us with the problem of infinite regress? And would not the impossibility of infinite regress provide us with the possibility of arguing for the existence of a necessary being, even if we were to begin with the assumption that the only things existing in the universe are superficially contingent things?

38. This, I think, is a debatable point. Dr. Adler seems to be saying that if we assume that X has a beginning (be X a universe or anything else) then if we also assume that what had a beginning also (and necessarily) had a cause of its beginning, then we are thinking fallaciously, specifically by begging the question. But this does not at all appear to be the case. If the effect that is now before us is something that we are attempting to understand, and if in that attempt we assume that the thing had a beginning, and if that assumption is a reasonable one, then we are not begging the question by adding yet another assumption: that the existence of something that has a beginning necessarily implies something that caused that beginning. To address the specific question at issue, by assuming that the universe had a beginning we are not, by that assumption, assuming that God exists. We are simply assuming that what has a beginning must have a cause for its beginning. Having made that assumption, we then set out to discover what

that cause is. One does not beg the question by assuming that a problem one is attempting to solve has *a* solution; one begs the question only by assuming at the outset, before even examining the problem, that one has *the* solution to the problem.

39. The fallacy of composition admits of varying interpretations, and it would seem that the way that Dr. Adler is applying the fallacy here is open to question. There are, to be sure, certain things that can properly be said of the parts of a whole that cannot be said of the whole as such. For example (the one Dr. Adler uses), because all human beings (members of the whole) have a mother, we cannot conclude that the human race (the whole) has a mother (unless, that is, we want to give due honor to mother Eve). What is motherhood? It indicates a relation, and a relation may obtain among the parts of a whole, though it cannot be appropriately applied to the whole itself (i.e., by relating the whole to something else, according to the same relational foundation). But if we are concerned with intrinsic, essential aspects of the parts of a whole, those aspects may be legitimately predicated of the whole itself. For example, if we know that each and every human being is rational, then it is not improper to speak of the human race, the sum total of human beings, a concrete reality (we are not speaking of an abstraction here, i.e., "humanity,") as being rational. Now, Dr. Adler, for the sake of argument, has admitted the assumption that all the things in the universe are radically contingent. But what is radical contingency? It is an intrinsic, essential aspect of each and every part of the whole which is the universe. Just as we can predicate "rational" of the human race, then, we can in like manner predicate "radically contingent" of the universe as a whole. This would not constitute a commission of the fallacy of composition.

40. While one readily accepts the contention that we live in a possible (i.e., non-necessary) universe, it is doubtful that Dr. Adler has offered the strongest kind of support for that contention. He writes: "We can infer it [i.e., a possible universe] from the fact that the arrangement and disarray—the order and disorder—of the present cosmos might have been otherwise, might have been different from what it is." (*How to Think About God*, pp. 143–44.) The disarray and disorder of the universe are anything but facts. They can be interpreted as no more than indications of the radical limitations of our knowledge of the universe. To someone who is witnessing a game the rules of which he is completely ignorant, the activities of the players may appear to him as disordered. But there is no disorder on the field; there is in fact perfect order, an order established and maintained by the rules of the game. The limitations are not to be found on the field, then, but in the mind of the spectator. Relatedly, Dr. Adler also cites chance as an index of a possible universe. But, strictly speaking, there is no chance in the universe. An appeal to chance is simply our favorite way of announcing our ignorance of what is

going on in the physical world. In addition, Dr. Adler cites the possibility of other universes as a reason for regarding this one as possible. That would seem to be a rather uncertain position, for here one is using conjecture as proof, as well as, so it would seem, engaging in circular reasoning: the possibility of other universes proves that this universe is possible.

41. *How to Think About God*, p. 150.

42. Ibid.

Chapter Nine

1. John Henry Cardinal Newman. *An Essay in Aid of A Grammar of Assent.* Notre Dame; London: University of Notre Dame Press, 1979, p. 97.

2. Ibid., p. 99.

3. Ibid., p. 101.

4. Ibid.

5. Ibid., p. 106.

6. Sigmund Freud. *New Introductory Lectures on Psychoanalysis* (trans.. James Strachey). New York: W. W. Norton & Company, Inc., 1965, p. 61.

7. There are several passages in the *Theodicy* like the following: "But it will be said evils are great and many in number in comparison to the good: that is erroneous. It is only want of attention that diminishes our good, and this attention must be given to us through some admixture of evils." (*Theodicy.* Chicago: Open Court, 1985, p. 130.)

Chapter Ten

1. St. Thomas Aquinas. *De Trinitate*, q. 6, a 3. Quoted in Maurice R. Holloway, S. J. *An Introduction to Natural Theology*. New York: Appleton-Century-Crofts, Inc., 1959, p. 162, n. 2.

2. The telling Latin phrase St. Thomas uses to describe the Beatific Visioin is *visio divinae essentiae*, "the vision of the divine essence."

3. St. Thomas Aquinas, *De Veritate,* q. 10, a. 12, ad 7.

4. Ibid.

5. The terms "essence" and "nature," as applied to God, mean virtually the same thing, and with that understanding in mind I use them more or less interchangeably in the text. They both refer to *what* God is, the divine *quidditas* as it were.

6. The conventional manner of expressing the principle in Latin is: *Quiduid recipitur secundum modum recipientis recipitur.* I would alter that conventional expression slightly, to give greater accentuation to the line of explication that I develop in the text, thus: *Quidquid recipitur secundum modum essendi recipientis recipitur.* "Whatever is received, is received according to

the very mode of being of the recipient." The basic idea here is that we come to know things only in terms of the kind of beings we are.

7. The principle is commonly expressed in Latin as follows: *Nihil est in intellectu quod non prius fuerit in sensu.* "There is nothing in the intellect which was not first in the senses." See note #10 for Chapter Two.

8. St. Thomas brings a nice focus to the various ideas discussed in the text in the following passage: "The human understanding cannot go so far by its own natural powers as to grasp [God's] substance, since under the conditions of the present life the knowledge of our understanding commences with sense; and therefore objects beyond sense cannot be grasped by them through the senses." (*Summa Contra Gentiles*, Book I, Chapter 3.)

9. *Summa Contra Gentiles,* Book I, Chapter 14.

10. *De Potentia*, q. 7, a. 5, ad 2.

11. *Summa Theologiae,* I, q. 13, a. 1.

12. The Jesuit philosopher Fr. Maurice Holloway gives a pointed summary of these ideas. "Now God is the being he is because he *is* his own act of existing, and creatures are the beings they are because they *have* (more or less perfectly) their acts of existing. It is clear, therefore, that between creatures and God there is some proportionality, because just as the creature is the being it is because of its relation to its act of existing, so God is the being he is because of his identity with his act of existing." (*An Introduction to Natural Theology,* pp. 226–27.)

13. The English translation is that of the epigraph which introduces Chapter 6 of Father Maurice Holloway's *An Introduction to Natural Theology,* p. 194. Father Holloway cites the chapter and verse of the passage (*Exodus*, 3: 13–14), but he does not indicate what translation he is using. Perhaps it is his own. In any event, the translation brings out with special forcefulness the fact that God's very nature is "to be."

14. I am indebted to Fr. Maurice Holloway for the ideas I developed in this section. See *An Introduction to Natural Theology,* pp. 224–27.

15. *De Veritate,* q. 10, a. 12, ad 7.

Chapter Eleven

1. The passage is from St. Paul's First Letter to the Corinthians, Chapter XIII, Verse 12. The Latin of the *Vulgate Bible* reads: *Vidimus nunc per speculum in aenigmate; tunc auten facie ad faciem.* "We see now as through a mirror, darkly, but then, face to face." The word *aenigmate* could be appropriately translated "indirectly."

2. *Summa Theologiae,* I, q. 3, a. 2, ad 3.

3. Ibid., a. 4. St. Thomas's Latin reads: *Non erit primum ens: quod absurdum est dicere.*

4. Ibid., a. 7.

5. Ibid., q. 4, a. 1.

6. Ibid., a. 2.

7. Ibid., ad 1.

8. Ibid., a. 3.

9. Professor Donald Williams, on the subject of mathematical infinity, writes: "The prevalent opinion in the philosophy of physics and even of mathematics is that there is no literally infinite collections, and that 'infinity' appears in mathematical expressions only as a convenient symbolic short-cut between one finite quantity and another." Donald Williams. *The Ground of Induction.* Cambridge: Harvard University Press, 1947, p. 157.

10. *Summa Theologiae*, I, q. 8, a. 1. The original Latin reads: *sicut agens adest ei in quod agit.*

11. Ibid.

12. Ibid., ad 2.

13, Ibid., a. 2.

14. Ibid., ad 3.

15. Ibid., a. 3, ad 3.

16. Ibid., a. 3.

17. Ibid., a. 4.

18. The definition, in the original Latin, reads: *Aeternitas est interminabilis vitae tota simul et perfecta possessio.* It comes from Boethius's most famous work, *The Consolation of Philosophy (De Consolatione Philosophiae).*

19. Ibid., q. 10, a. 1.

20. Ibid.

21. Ibid., a. 2, ad 1.

22. Ibid., ad 3. The Latin reads: *Aeternitas non est aliud quam ipse Deus.*

23. Ibid., a. 5. The Jesuit philosopher Fr. Henri Renard gives a short but precise explication of aeviternity in his book, *The Philosophy of God* (Milwaukee: The Bruce Publishing Company, 1951), pp. 99–101.

24. Ibid., q. 11, a. 1.

25. Ibid., a. 3.

Chapter Twelve

1. *Summa Theologiae,* I, q. 14, a.1.

2. I do not think I took undue liberties with St. Thomas's Latin: *Et sic seipsum per seipsum intelligit.* (Ibid., a. 2.)

3. Ibid., a. 5.

4, Ibid., a. 6.

5. Ibid. The Latin reads as follows: *"Unde manifestum est quod Deus cognoscit omnes res propia cognitione...."*

6. The English word "intuition" is derived from the Latin verb *intuere*, which means "to look at."

7. *Summa Theologiae*, I, q. 14, a. 8.

8. Ibid., a. 9.

9. Ibid., a. 10.

10. Though pronounced differently, the Latin word St. Thomas uses, from which of course the English word comes, is exactly the same as the English: *idea.*

11. See Henri Renard, S. J. *The Philosophy of God.* Milwaukee: The Bruce Publishing Company, 1951, p. 138ff.

12. *Summa Theologiae*, I, q. 15, a. 1.

13. Ibid., a. 2.

14. Ibid., q. 16, a. 5.

15. The elementary metaphysical principle involved here has its classical Latin expression in the statement, *Omne agens agit propter finem,* "Every agent acts for the sake of an end." If all ends were now to disappear, the whole universe would instantly grind to a halt.

16. The Gospel according to St. John, Chapter 14, Verse 6.

17. Ibid., q. 18, a. 3.

Chapter Thirteen

1. *Summa Theologiae,* I, q. 19, a. 1. The original Latin, which I fleshed out a bit in my translation, reads as follows: *Et sicut suum intelligere est suum esse, ita suum velle.*

2. Ibid., ad. 3.

3. Ibid., a. 5.

4. Ibid., a. 7.

5. Ibid. St. Thomas's Latin reads: *Potest enim aliquis, eadem volunate immobiliter permanente, velle quod nunc fiat hoc, and post fiat contrarium.*

6. Ibid., a. 8.

7. Ibid., q. 20, a. 2.

8. Ibid., q. 21, a. 2.

9. Ibid., a. 3.

Chapter Fourteen

1. *Summa Theologiae,* I, q. 25, a.1.

2. Ibid.

3. Ibid., a. 3. St. Thomas writes: *Deus dicatur omnipotens, quia potest omnia possibilia absolute.* "God is said to be omnipotent, because He is able

to do whatever is intrinsically possible." That is, God is able to do anything that does not involve contradiction.

4. Ibid.

5. Ibid., a. 4.

6. Ibid., a. 6. St. Thomas's exact statement reads as follows: *Sicut etiam non potest facere quaternarium majorem: quia, si esset major, jam non esset quaternarius, sed alius numerus.* "In like manner, it would not be possible to make a set of four (a quaternary) larger, because, if it were larger, it would no longer be a set of four, but a different set."

7. Epistle to the Romans, 11:36.

8. Ibid., q. 44, a. 1.

9. Ibid., q. 45, a. 1, ad 3.

10. Ibid., q. 44, a. 3.

11. Ibid.

12. Ibid., a. 4.

13. It should be noted that St. Thomas, in discussing creation, uses the Latin word *emanatio*, but he does not at all mean by that term what a Neoplatonist would have in mind in speaking of "emanation." In his *Latin-English Dictionary of St. Thomas Aquinas*, Professor Deferrari describes *emanatio* as "a general term for something proceeding from a principle." (Boston: St. Paul Editions, 1986, p. 339.) St. Thomas makes it clear that he uses *emanatio* as a synonym for *creatio* when he says, "and so this emanation we designate by the name 'creation'." (*S.T.*, I, q. 45, a. 1.)

14. *Summa Theologiae,* I, q. 45, a. 5.

15. Ibid., a. 6.

16. Ibid., a. 7.

17. Ibid., q. 104, a. 1, ad 4.

18. Ibid., q. 104, a. 1.

19. Ibid.

20. *Summa Contra Gentiles*, Book III, Chapter 65.

21. *Summa Theologiae,* I, q. 104, a. 4.

22. Ibid., ad 1.

Chapter Fifteen

1. *Summa Theologiae,* I, q. 22, a. 1.

2. Ibid.

3. For an explanation of the metaphysical impossibility of a chance event acting as an initiating, or first, cause, see my *Metaphysics*, pp. 271–72.

4. *Summa Theologiae,* I, q.22, a. 2. *Necesse est dicere omnia divinae providentiae subjacere, non in universali tantum, sed etiam in singulari.*

"It must be said that everything is subject to divine providence, not only in terms of creation taken as a whole, but in terms of each individual as well."

5. Ibid.

6. Ibid., q. 103, a. 5, ad 2. *Sic igitur secundum unam artem Dei gubernantis, res diversmode gubernatus, secundum earum diversitatem.* "And so it is that by a single art exercised by God the Governor, things are governed diversely so as to correspond with their diversity."

7. Ibid., a. 7, ad 1.

8. Ibid., a. 8, ad 1.

9. *Summa Contra Gentiles*, Book III, Chapter 64.

10. Ibid.

11. *Summa Theologiae*, I, q. 49, a. 1.

12. This is quoted by St. Thomas in the *Summa Theologiae,* I, q. 49, a. 2.

Bibliography

Adler, Mortimer J. *How to Think About God*. New York: Macmillan Publishing Company, 1980.

Anderson, James F. *Natural Theology: The Metaphysics of God*. Milwaukee: The Bruce Publishing Company, 1962.

Aquinas, St. Thomas. *Summa Contra Gentiles,* 5 Volumes (in English, trans. Anton G. Pegis, F.R.S.C.). Notre Dame, Indiana: University of Notre Dame Press, 1975.

_____. *Summa Theologica,* 5 Volumes (in English, trans. Fathers of the English Dominican Province). Westminster, Maryland: Christian Classics, 1981.

Aristotle. *Metaphysics*. (Richard McKeon, ed. *The Basic Works of Aristotle*. New York: Random House, 1941.)

_____. *Physics*. (Richard McKeon, ed. *The Basic Works of Aristotle*. New York: Random House, 1941.)

Baisnée, Jules A., S.S. *Readings in Natural Theology*. Westminster, Maryland: The Newman Press, 1964.

Beardsley, Monroe C. *The European Philosophers from Descartes to Nietzsche*. New York: The Modern Library, 1992.

Bittle, Celestine N., O.F.M., Cap. *God and His Creatures: Theodicy*. Milwaukee: The Bruce Publishing Company, 1953.

Boedder, Bernard, S.J. *Natural Theology*. London: Longmans, Green and Co., 1921.

Borne, Etienne. *Atheism*. (trans. S. J. Testor). New York: Hawthorne Books, 1961.

Donceel, J. F., S. J. *Natural Theology*. New York: Sheed and Ward, 1962.

Feser, Edward. *Neo-Scholastic Essays*. South Bend, Indiana: St. Augustine's Press, 2015.

_____. *Five Proofs for the Existence of God*. San Francisco: Ignatius Press, 2017.

Glenn, Rt. Rev. Msgr Paul J. *Theodicy: A Class Manual in the Philosophy of the Deity*. St. Louis: B. Herder Book Co., 1949.

Gornall, Thomas, S. J. *A Philosophy of God: The Elements of Thomistic Natural Theology*. New York: Sheed and Ward, 1962.

Haldane, Elizabeth S. and G. R. T. Ross, ed. and trans. *The Philosophical Works of Descartes, Volume I*. Cambridge: Cambridge University Press, 1977 (1st ed., 1941).

Hartshorne, Charles. *Anselm's Discovery: A Re-examination of the Ontological Proof for God's Existence*. La Salle, Illinois: Open Court Publishing Company, 1965.

Holloway, Maurice R., S. J. *An Introduction to Natural Theology*. New York: Appleton–Century–Crofts, Inc., 1959.

Joyce, George Hayward, S. J. *Principles of Natural Theology*. London: Longmans, Green and Co., 1924.

Kant, Immanuel. *Critique of Pure Reason* (trans. Norman Kemp Smith). New York: St. Martin's Press, 1965.

_____. *Lectures on Philosophical Theology* (trans. Allen W. Ward and Gertrude M. Clark). Ithica: Cornell University Press, 1978.

Kenny, Anthony. *The Five Ways: St. Thomas Aquinas' Proofs of God's Existence*. Notre Dame, Indiana: University of Notre Dame Press, 1980 (1st publ., 1969).

Kierkegaard, Søren. *Philosophical Fragments: Johannes Climacus. Kierkegaard's Writings, VII* (trans. Howard v. Hong and Edna H. Hong). Princeton, New Jersey: Princeton University Press, 1985.

Leibniz, G. W. *Theodicy* (trans. E. M. Huggard). Chicago, Illinois: Open Court, 1985.

Lewis, C. S. *Miracles: A Preliminary Study.* New York: The Macmillan Company, 1947.

Maritain, Jacques. *Approaches to God.* New York: Harper & Brothers Publishers, 1964.

Mazzei, Alfred M. *Does God Exist?* (trans. Daisy Corinne Fornacca, Ph.D.). New York: Society of St. Paul, 1956.

McCormick, John F., S. J. *Scholastic Metaphysics, Part II, Natural Theology.* Chicago: Loyola University Press, 1959.

McInerny, D. Q. *Philosophy of Nature.* Elmhurst Township, Pennsylvania: The Priestly Fraternity of St. Peter, 2001, 2014.

_____. *Metaphysics.* Elmhurst, Pennsylvania: The Priestly Fraternity of St. Peter, 2004, 2019.

McInerny, Ralph. *Being and Predication*, Ch. 16, "On Behalf of Natural Theology." Washington, D.C.: The Catholic University of America Press, 1986.

_____. *Characters in Search of Their Author:* The Gifford Lectures, Glasgow, 1999-2000. Notre Dame, Indiana: University of Notre Dame Press, 2001.

_____. *Praeambula Fidei: Thomism and the God of the Philosophers.* Washington, D.C.: The Catholic University of America Press, 2006.

Miceli, Vincent, S. J. *The Gods of Atheism.* Harrison, New York: Roman Catholic Books, 1971.

Newman, John Henry Cardinal. *An Essay in Aid of A Grammar of Assent.* Notre Dame; London: University of Notre Dame Press, 1979.

Paley, William. *Natural Theology: Or, Evidences of the Existence and Attributes of the Deity Collected from the Appearances of Nature* (illustrated by James Paxton). New York: Sheldon & Company, 1854.

Plato, *Laws*. (In *Plato, Complete Works*, ed. John M. Cooper and D. S. Hutchinson. Indianapolis: Hackett Publishing Company, 1997.)

Renard, Henri, S. J. *The Philosophy of God*. Milwaukee: The Bruce Publishing Company, 1951.

Schroedinger, Andrew B., ed. *Readings in Medieval Philosophy*. New York: Oxford University Press, 1996.

Sheen, Fulton J., M.A., Ph.D. *God and Intelligence in Modern Philosophy*. London: Longmans, Green and Co., 1930.

Smith, Gerard, S. J. *Natural Theology: Metaphysics II*. New York: The Macmillan Company, 1951.

Suarez, Francisco. *The Metaphysical Demonstrations of the Existence of God. Metaphysical Disputations 28–29* (trans. John P. Doyle). South Bend, Indiana: St. Augustine's Press, 2004.

Tresmontant, Claude. *Toward the Knowledge of God* (trans. Robert J. Olsen). Baltimore: Helicon Press, 1961.

Index